Heresy in the University

Heresy
in the University

The *Black Athena* Controversy and the Responsibilities of American Intellectuals

Jacques Berlinerblau

Rutgers University Press
New Brunswick, New Jersey, and London

Library of Congress Cataloging-in-Publication Data

Berlinerblau, Jacques.
   Heresy in the University : the *Black Athena* controversy and the
responsibilities of American intellectuals / Jacques Berlinerblau.
     p. cm.
   Includes bibliographical references and index.
   ISBN 0-8135-2587-X (cloth: alk. paper). — ISBN 0-8135-2588-8 (pbk. :
alk. paper)
   1. Bernal, Martin. Black Athena.   2. Greece—Civilization—
Egyptian influences.   3. Greece—Civilization—Phoenician
influences.   4. Greece—historiography.   5. Learning and
scholarship—United States.   6. Afrocentrism—United States.
7. United States—Intellectual life—20th century.   I. Title.
DF78.B3983B47   1999
949.5—dc21   98-8499
                                                              CIP

British Cataloging-in-Publication data for this book is available from the British
Library

Manufactured in the United States of America

Then came Herodotus, who spoke of "the great deeds of the Greeks *and* the barbarians." All of science comes from this spirit, even modern science, and the science of history too. If someone is not capable of this impartiality because he pretends to love his people so much that he pays flattering homage to them all the time—well, then there's nothing to be done. I do not believe that people like that are patriots.

Hannah Arendt, "'What Remains? The Language Remains':
A Conversation with Günter Gaus"

To Laurette and Rubin Berlinerblau

Contents

Acknowledgments

I began this project in the summer of 1995, confidently and erroneously expecting that it would be completed within eighteen months. Three years later, I recognize how senselessly sanguine that estimate actually was; at least a decade would be required to explore the *Black Athena* Controversy thoroughly. Be that as it may, a certain instinct for professional survival and a certain contractual obligation dictated that I bring this endeavor to an abrupt conclusion. My healthy generalist appetite now sated, it would seem prudent to retreat to what C. Wright Mills called the "lazy safety of specialization."

Critique aimed at everyone and in all directions is the ethic which animates the present work. I reserve the right, however, to bracket this ethic in my acknowldgements. Brooklyn College, where I taught for nearly five years, felt like home. The students who live with their parents and/or children, the avuncular humanists and Marxists, the location in New York's—if not the world's—most relevant borough, summated to provide a university environment unlike any I have ever encountered. In particular, I would like to express my gratitude to Dr. Sara Regeur, Dr. Robert Viscusi, Dr. Jacqueline DeWeever, Dr. George Cunningham, Dr. Joanne Bernstein, and Dean Kathy Gover for the infinite kindnesses they extended to me.

The vertiginous transition to my new institution, Hofstra University, has been rendered easy and pleasant by my new colleagues in Calkins Hall. Dr. Helene Waysek, Dr. Neil Donahue, and Dr. George Greaney cannot be thanked enough for their warmth and support. Dr. Sondra Farganis of the New School for Social Research is a constant source of encouragement and counterintuitive wisdom. Throughout the years I have benefited immeasurably from occasional conversations with Dr. Craig Calhoun of New York University, Dr. Mustafa Emirbayer of the New School, Dr. David Sperling of Hebrew Union College, and Dr. Michael Walzer of the Institute for Advanced Study.

I would like to praise Dr. Martin Bernal, central protagonist of the forthcoming drama. He has answered every query; he has spent hours listening to my criticisms of him; he has kindly consented to read a few of the chapters in the present text. Considering the contents of these chapters, I can only explain his tolerance of me as an indication of his own commitment to the values of scholarship. I identified a similar commitment in the person of Dr. Molly Myerowitz Levine of Howard University. Professor Levine graciously forwarded to me a pound of remote materials which I otherwise would never have had time to track down. Unparalleled master of the *Black Athena* bibliography that she is, Dr. Levine made me aware of a variety of contributions whose existence was completely unknown to me.

Leslie Mitchner, editor of Rutgers University Press, is the ultimate author of this enterprise. Ms. Mitchner provided the original idea, the objective, and even the occasional pep talk, all while respecting my right to editorialize as I saw fit. She and her colorful staff have mastered the difficult art of being considerate, helpful, and humane while shaking down an author in arrears. Ms. Diane Grobman performed a truly heroic act of copy editing a chaotic text.

I do not expect to make many friends writing this volume, so let me hold on to the ones that I have now. Claudia Schaler's love and intelligence made the writing of this text possible. I wish to thank Jimmy Eisenberg, Blanca Benavides (whose bibliographical skills were of great help to me), Beth Godley, Natalie Indrimi, Dr. Sabine Loucif, Dr. Paul Albert Ferrara, and Camala Projansky. Not to be forgotten are my nephews, Marc and Jeremy, and their parents Michael and Michele. Ippolita Spadavecchia is to be lauded for introducing every imaginable beautiful thing into my life for nearly a decade.

This book is, once again, dedicated to my parents Laurette and Rubin Berlinerblau, humanists from, and of, the Old World. There would be no book, no languages, or happiness without them.

Jacques Berlinerblau
April 12, 1998
Brooklyn, New York

Heresy in the University

Introduction

Epistemological

Canyons

The Anomic Academy

Nevertheless, there are many reasons why it is all but impossible for a serious writer of fiction to engage his craft as such in a political cause, no matter how worthy, without violating his very special integrity as an artist in some serious way. All of these reasons are complicated and some may seem downright questionable, but perhaps none is more important than the fact that, as well-meaning as he may be, the truly serious novelist has what almost amounts to an ambivalence toward the human predicament. Alarming as such ambivalence may seem, it is really fundamental to his open-minded search for the essential truth of human experience.

—Albert Murray, *The Omni-Americans: Some Alternatives to the Folklore of White Supremacy*

"Unriddle the Mysteries of Human Nature!"

More than a decade has elapsed since Professor Martin Bernal of Cornell University published the first installment of a projected multivolume study. The classicist Edith Hall observes that his undertaking "has excited more controversy than almost any other book dealing with Greco-Roman antiquity to have been published in the second half of the twentieth century." Historian Mario Liverani refers to it as "the most discussed book on the ancient history of the eastern Mediterranean world since the Bible." "Whether we like it or not," writes V. Y. Mudimbe of Duke University, "Bernal's enterprise will profoundly mark the next century's perception of the origins of Greek civilization and the role of ancient Egypt." In 1993, reflecting on the spectacular controversy that his volumes had elicited, a weary Bernal quipped: "With the exception of *of,* I have been criticized for every word in my title, *Black Athena: The Afroasiatic Roots of Classical Civilization.*"[1]

The passing of time has done little to quell the controversy. In 1996 classicist Mary Lefkowitz of Wellesley College, contributed not one, but two, book-length additions to an already expansive bibliography on *Black Athena.* Her

Not Out of Africa: How Afrocentrism Became an Excuse to Teach Myth as History rendered a decidedly negative verdict on Bernal's project as well as on those of his alleged Afrocentrist colleagues. *Black Athena Revisited*, edited by Lefkowitz and Guy MacLean Rogers, was no less dismissive. This 522-page collection of twenty-one essays, written by nineteen scholars representing seven different disciplines, is a sort of "encyclopedic compendium" of every major criticism that has been hurled at *Black Athena*. It was also in 1996 that *Lingua Franca*, a magazine with the singular power to consecrate a scholarly debate as relevant, devoted a lengthy article to Bernal's hypothesis and the fulminations which it inspired. It thus bestowed upon the text the status of a discursive landmark—an authentic field of battle in the American culture wars.[2]

That a work of scholarship would stimulate intense academic interest is by no means unusual. As Kafka once declared (albeit while contemplating an entirely different problematic), "After all, it's happened before." What has rarely happened before, however, is for a work of scholarship to arouse such great interest in the nonacademic sphere of American culture. Mass-circulation weeklies are generally impervious to the charms of lengthy scholarly tomes. Be that as it may, *Newsweek* magazine—in the way American mass media have of decorticating complex topics—splashed the question "Was Cleopatra Black?" on the cover of its September 23, 1991, issue. Readers of the accompanying article were treated to a glossy picture of the Cornell professor seated with a bust of the cinnamon-colored Egyptian queen Nefertiti.[3]

This was not the only time that *Black Athena* would venture into the nonacademic, or civilian, sphere. The author and his many critics have been featured in two separate documentaries. Bernal has made numerous appearances on television and radio talk shows. A recent "chat" on the Internet between Bernal and Lefkowitz (sponsored by the latter's publisher) generated a few thousand rather unceremonious responses. And through it all, the nonscholarly print media—auctioneers of the culture wars—have relayed the proceedings to a lay public eager to learn about events occurring on dystopic American campuses.[4]

All of this has occurred in spite of the fact that Bernal's *Black Athena* cannot be described as a pleasure of text. Historian Gerda Lerner makes the following remark about the second volume, released in 1991: "The book is badly organized, tediously repetitive, and overloaded with technical detail. It is not a book for the general reader and a lay public, which makes for another contradiction: Bernal attacks the Academy and the Classics establishment, but he makes little effort to appeal to lay audiences or the uninitiated with lucid, comprehensible prose."[5] While this remark is somewhat heavy-handed, it is not without substance. The layperson who wishes to read *Black Athena*'s two published volumes will need to traipse through nearly 1,000 pages of text, more than 3,000 footnotes, and 120 pages of bibliography. While certain chapters—especially a few in the first volume—make for compelling reading, most are simply impenetrable to all but a few assorted academic specialists.

Yet by all indications (*pace* Lerner, myself, many others) Bernal's style—

a bewildering hybrid of serious scholarship and searing polemic—*has* enticed nonacademic opinion makers and cultivated laypersons. From outraged conservative journalists to outraged undergraduate radicals, the text has been widely discussed and passionately debated. As of today, the series—not counting sales in England or from the French, German, Spanish, and Italian translations—has sold nearly 70,000 copies, a preternatural occurrence, an eclipse in the microuniverse of academic publishing. "Unriddle the mysteries of human nature!" as Kafka might say.[6]

City of Contentious Discourses

These considerations lead us to pose the following questions: What is it about *Black Athena* which has kindled the passions of so many scholars in so many different disciplines? And, why did this particular densely worded, minutiae-laden academic text excite interest outside of the university? In order to answer these questions we should familiarize ourselves with the rudiments of Bernal's argument. Insofar as I will spend the next few hundred pages rehearsing his hypotheses in some detail, I will here permit myself the luxury of oversimplification.

Speaking very broadly, *Black Athena* advances two interrelated theories, each of which draws upon a different academic discipline. Martin Bernal's historical argument—I repeat that I am speaking in broad terms—claims that the ancient Egyptians and Phoenicians exerted massive cultural influence upon inchoate ancient Greek civilization. It is held that this process began (at least) as early as the eighteenth century B.C.E. and continued, albeit unevenly, down through the Classical (ca. 480–323 B.C.E.) and Hellenistic (323–ca. 30 B.C.E.) periods. The ancient Greeks themselves, demonstrates Bernal, freely acknowledged their enormous respect, intellectual debts, and even ties of kinship to the older, more sophisticated civilizations of the East.

Permit me to introduce an Ellisonian theme into this synopsis. That Americans do not know who they are—and perhaps do not even care to know—is an idea that recurs in Ralph Ellison's fiction and essays. *Black Athena* makes a similar claim about those who have traditionally extolled the virtues of Western civilization. The ancient Greece which they revere and posit as the Occident's foundational culture is construed as ethnically and culturally "white" and European. But Bernal's early ancient Greece, to borrow a phrase from Ellison's colleague, Albert Murray, is *"incontestably Mulatto."*[7] Bernal observes:

> I argue that there is need for a radical reassessment of the image of Ancient Greece and that we should turn from one of a civilization which sprang—like Athena from the head of Zeus—virgin and fully formed, to one in which Greece grew up at the intersection of Europe, Africa and Asia as a thoroughly mixed and eclectic culture. *The greatness and extraordinary brilliance of Greek civilization in antiquity was not the result*

of isolation and cultural purity but of frequent contact with and stim-
ulus from the many surrounding peoples on the already heterogenous
natives of the Aegean.[8]

Sociology, or more precisely the sociology of knowledge, provides the
basis for a second theoretical initiative. The author of *Black Athena* contends that the belief in Egyptian and Phoenician influence on ancient Greece
had been a commonplace from Classical antiquity until the nineteenth century C.E. This idea's two-and-a-half-millennia legacy was abruptly interrupted
less than two centuries ago. Modern European scholars, he contends, became
the first among the chroniclers of history to cast doubts upon the relatively
banal notion of *ex Oriente Lux* (Light from the East). Eventually, they would
come to establish a body of scholarship which maintained that the purported
Egyptian and/or Phoenician contributions to ancient Greece were either irrelevant or nonexistent.

What accounted for this sudden historiographical shift, this *coupure*, this
unprecedented endeavor to detach ancient Greece from its Eastern moorings?
The author's answer to this question has been widely, one might even say conveniently, misrepresented. In journalistic accounts, *Black Athena* alleges
that racism and anti-Semitism are responsible for the denial of what Bernal
called "Afroasiatic" (i.e., Egyptian and Phoenician) influences. In other words,
white Christian intellectuals would not accept that persons of African descent
(equated with ancient Egyptians, according to Bernal) and Jews (equated with
ancient Phoenicians, according to Bernal) had played a decisive role in the formation of ancient Greece—"the first universal civilization . . . the cultural
ancestor of the Europeans." It is certainly true that Occidental chauvinism
figures prominently in Bernal's sociological explanation of the aforementioned
shift. But in my fourth chapter it will be demonstrated that racism and anti-
Semitism are but two variables in a much more detailed, more thought-
provoking, and less marketable hypothesis.[9]

With this brief sketch now drawn we are prepared to address the questions posed above. To a certain degree, *Black Athena*'s appeal across the disciplines can be explained by the Weberian megalomania which has gripped
its author. Like Max Weber, Bernal has arrogated the right to discuss any and
all cultural and historical phenomena (it should be noted that the great
German sociologist wrote in a far less specialized age). The narrative Bernal
recounts spans the ages from the fourth millennium B.C.E. to the present day.
Along the way, he trespasses across all disciplinary boundaries, he digresses
eruditely, he surveys vast expanses of scholarly literature, and he occasionally recounts what might be labeled scholarly human-interest stories.

Bernal's rather disarming lack of modesty as well as his sheer intellectual audacity have done much to turn his text into a monument of interdisciplinarity. Nearly any scholar in the humanities and any historian can
browse the index of *Black Athena* and find a name or subject which he or she
knows well or perhaps even wrote a dissertation about. Some did more than
browse the index: the lament of the exasperated specialist, fastidiously chron-

icling Bernal's many errors, has emerged as a veritable genre in the literature of the *Black Athena* Controversy.

But the multidisciplinary scope of this work cannot be adduced as the sole explanation for its ability to attract widespread scholarly attention. Nor can it account for its tremendous impact *outside* of the university. In order to make sense of the interest garnered by *Black Athena* it must be situated within the context of the PC debates of the 1980s, which eventually escalated into the culture wars of the 1990s. Whatever one may think of Bernal's theories, it is indisputable that the issues he raises—or the issues that have been read into his work—are singularly relevant to those which currently preoccupy American intellectuals. From racism to racism in the academy to Afrocentrism to Eurocentrism to multiculturalism to Orientalism to "Western civilization" to Western imperialism to identity politics—Bernal and his critics have canvassed many avenues of inquiry in our city of contentious discourses.[10]

The Realignment

The "popularity" of *Black Athena* may thus be attributed to its ability to address, with vigor and intelligence, the aforementioned docket of explosive issues. Bernal's positions on these matters can usually be understood as attempts to rebut and/or provoke a renascent intellectual and political conservatism. It is not widely known that Bernal's archnemesis was none other than Allan Bloom, author of *The Closing of the American Mind.* Also published in 1987, Bloom's is one of the few recent academic texts which created even more sustained controversy than *Black Athena.* In a rarely cited interview with Walter Cohen, Bernal discloses:

> In volume one, I didn't bring out the influence of Allan Bloom on my work. Coming into Telluride, a scholarship house at Cornell, where his influence and the whole Straussian cult of Greece were still felt strongly, made me realize the reactionary potential of the Romantic interpretation of Greece. I had been brought up in Cambridge, where the classicists were stuffy liberals, but not harmful in any sense. But here, though this was the mid-seventies, I suddenly saw a potential for the extreme right-wing intellectual movement that didn't actually take power until the 1980's.[11]

The endeavor to antagonize Bloom did much to turn *Black Athena* into a primer on how to antagonize America's intellectual conservatives. The basic instructions might be described as follows: posit multicultural origins for ancient Greek civilization; question the originality of Greek innovations in science, mathematics, philosophy, and politics; depict the modern university as congenitally Eurocentric; cast aspersions on the moral character of great Enlightenment thinkers; reject the notion of "objective," apolitical scholarship.[12]

Not surprisingly, many conservative commentators were rankled by the ideological torque of these provocative theories. *Black Athena* receives dishonorable mention in Dinesh D'Souza's *Illiberal Education: The Politics of Race and Sex on Campus,* as it does in reviews published in the *New Criterion,* the *National Review,* and the National Association of Scholars' *Academic Questions.* A contributor to the latter journal, historian of science L. Pearce Williams, terminated his eleven-paragraph review: "I closed *Black Athena* and relegated it to the trash heap of politically and racially inspired garbage."[13]

But the conservative reaction to Bernal's text is less interesting—and far less significant for future intellectual historians—than that of their old adversaries. After all, an "establishment" liberal such as Arthur Schlesinger, Jr., somehow managed almost to replicate D'Souza's critique of *Black Athena.* The *New York Review of Books* published three rather unflattering appraisals of the two published volumes. In 1997 a scholar writing in the *Times Literary Supplement* confidently eulogized *Black Athena.* In the preface to his second volume Bernal charged that the *New York Times* had intentionally ignored his work. "I suspect," he declared, "that there is a fundamental discomfort with the ideas that a respectable academic discipline could have racist roots and that racism has permeated liberal thought as well as that of obvious bigots."[14]

By my rough estimate, negative scholarly reviews of *Black Athena* have outweighed positive or moderate ones by a margin of approximately seven to three. It might be inferred that this ratio testifies to the inherent implausibility of Bernal's hypotheses. After all, an ideologically disparate collection of academicians concur that Bernal's theories are simply untenable. Yet the existence of this scholarly consensus must be qualified by one telling fact. What is significant—note this—is that the majority of Bernal's defenders have emanated from the radical tier of the academic world.[15]

In this manner the divisions which have emerged in the *Black Athena* Controversy replicate a larger realignment within American intellectual culture. In recent years, the old (and internally heterogenous) districts of conservative, liberal, and radical have been gerrymandered. There is some validity, I believe, to Roger Kimball's observation that in the culture wars "the real battle is not between radicals and conservatives but between radicals and what we might call old-style liberals." A similar point is made by Neil Smelser who observes that within the academy "the contemporary political situation has torpedoed those comfortable political alliances and fashioned a new, unfamiliar political quilt." Admittedly, it is difficult to speak with any precision on the subject of the political affiliations of scholars. Be that as it may, I believe that in general terms this division of conservative/liberal versus radical has heuristic validity.[16]

A few examples should suffice to demonstrate this point. At the end of an article entitled "The Value of the Canon," Irving Howe poses a rather remarkable question to himself: "*What you have been saying is pretty much the same as what conservatives say. Doesn't that make you feel uncomfortable?*" Or, perhaps one thinks of Daphne Patai and Noretta Koertge's *Professing Feminism: Cautionary Tales from the Strange World of Women's*

Studies. In their chapter entitled "From Dogma to Dialogue: The Importance of Liberal Values" they write:

> Even the most radical politicos among feminists, those most likely to sneer at every mention of the L-word, grow outraged when they feel their point of view is not being given a fair hearing. For all these reasons, feminism in the academy should abandon its simplistic and debased notion of the "political," its grandiose claims, its know-it-all strictures, and its radical rhetorical flourishes and return to professional practices consistent with the principles of liberal education.[17]

As a final example, let me cite Nathan Glazer's discussion of *A Curriculum of Inclusion*—the infamous 1989 report solicited by the New York State commissioner of education, which has been accused of an anti-European bias. Glazer notes that "most of the signers of the statement attacking" this controversial document "were well-known liberals."[18]

The radicals (or progressives), for their part, have been quick to portray their liberal compeers as the Reagan Democrats of the culture wars. Liberal pluralism, in these accounts, is seen as nothing but the status quo adorned with a little multicolored bunting. Henry Giroux, who advocates "insurgent multiculturalism," speaks of "quaint liberalism." In his riveting essay on the Salman Rushdie affair, anthropologist Talal Asad writes, "Violence becomes a serious object of liberal concern only when something that they really value seems to be threatened." Stanley Fish, ever eager to profane another liberal sacrament, dubs his colleagues "boutique multiculturalists."[19]

We must also recognize that in recent decades the political demography of the university Left has changed radically, so to speak. In his *Twilight of Common Dreams: Why America Is Wracked by Culture Wars*, Todd Gitlin argued that for the radical wing of the academic Left the campus had become a "Surrogate World." Politically, their candidates and issues had been decisively rejected by the American electorate. Control of the university emerged as what Gitlin calls a "consolation prize." Accordingly, the political demise of the radical Left has been, paradoxically, accompanied by its intellectual recrudescence. As Nancy Fraser observed in 1989: "We are seeing the emergence of a vital academic left counterculture. One consequence is a veritable explosion of new theoretical paradigms for political and cultural critique, paradigms ranging from variants of Western Marxism, Foucauldian new historicism, and the theory of participatory democracy, to deconstruction, postmodernism, and the many varieties of feminist theory."[20]

Conservative commentators have also noted a preponderance of "tenured radicals" in institutions of higher education. While greatly exaggerated, their claims do possess some merit. Contemporary American universities—not only the elite, opinion-influencing institutions but the so-called second-tier schools as well—feature an astonishing variety of leftist scholars whose ideas cannot be easily characterized as mainstream, liberal, liberal pluralist, and so on.[21]

What the alarmist conservatives (and a growing number of liberals) fail to recognize, however, is that these progressive schools have often enough produced work of exceptionally high intellectual quality. Further, in many cases, the radicals are every bit as scholarly as their detractors to the right (if not more so); they are steeped in the canonical, theoretical, and methodological traditions of their disciplines (which they seek to subvert); they publish regularly in refereed academic journals, attend conferences, train graduate students, master bibliographies, learn languages, and engage in nearly all the routine revolutions of scholarly life.

Epistemological Canyons: Gazing into the Abyss

It is among this thriving Left counterculture—composed of many loosely related and occasionally mutually antagonistic schools of thought— that *Black Athena* has found its most receptive audience. And it was precisely this corpus of scholarship which was ignored in Lefkowitz and Rogers's *Black Athena Revisited.*

The editors' rather undialogical approach reflects broader trends within contemporary intellectual culture. At present, the topography of the American professorate is cratered by a series of epistemological canyons. Those on the countercultural Left often predicate their research on assumptions which are incommensurable with those of their mainstream colleagues (and vice versa). Where exactly is the common ground between those who see scholarship as an objective search for truth and those who deny the existence of objectivity and speak of "truth"? ("Truth" and truth have been the first casualties of the culture wars.) How do we further a dialogue between a cohort that regards modern Europe as congenitally destructive and another that fetes its accomplishments as among the redeeming graces of humanity? If and when the gap is this wide, ignoring one's adversaries—as did Lefkowitz and Rogers— emerges as the most pragmatic alternative.

Of course, I do not wish to say that all current intellectual conflicts are cast in such Manichaean terms. Nor do I argue that dissensus is such a bad thing to have within the university. My point is this: Over the last decade some American scholars have left the confines of their discipline—and their academic prose—to address a wider public on a variety of issues pertaining to the common good. This migration (or pilgrimage perhaps) into the public sphere has exposed some fundamental differences of position on issues of tremendous relevance to the lives of all Americans—issues such as education, race relations, class differences, gender inequality, sexual preference, and child rearing.

Those scholars who engage in these public dialogues—and I include myself—are beholden to certain protocols, lest we compromise the "special integrity" of *our* craft. Respect for one's adversaries, critique of one's own camp, critical distance, and that "ambivalence" which Albert Murray ranked among the novelists' most precious characteristics—these are the moral obligations of scholarship and public intellectuality. That these obligations are ideals and thus not necessarily attainable by many human beings is an observation which animates my concluding discussion of intellectual responsibility.

The editors of *Black Athena Revisited* did an admirable job of collecting mainstream—and thus highly critical—evaluations of Bernal's text, yet the contributors made little effort to discuss opinions emanating from the other side of the divide, the radical tier. Indeed, in some instances these did not even appear in Lefkowitz and Rogers's lengthy bibliography. This erasure of the adversary did much to convince credulous journalists and scholars that a definitive academic consensus had been reached. Reading through the glowing reviews of *Black Athena Revisited* and *Not Out of Africa* one repeatedly encounters the implicit or explicit assumption that the decade-long altercation was now over—that the assembled spectators should proceed peacefully to their homes. Or, to paraphrase one reviewer, *Black Athena* was dead.[22]

After reading Lefkowitz's twin projects, a French commentator, Sophie Basch, could not understand why *Black Athena* was even translated into her language. An Israeli scholar in the Hebrew-language *Ha-aretz* declared, "It is left to us only to congratulate [Lefkowitz] for her bravery in publishing this type of book in the atmosphere that prevails today at so many American universities." Writing in the *New York Review of Books*, Jasper Griffin remarked, "From the standpoint of scholarly inquiry and academic discussion as we know it, there can, I think, be no doubt that all the positive assertions of [Bernal's] two large volumes have been refuted."[23]

Although I strongly disagree with Griffin's statement, I do recognize that Lefkowitz and her colleagues advanced some insightful, penetrating, and occasionally devastating criticisms of *Black Athena.* For I am not arguing that a more balanced assessment of Bernal's text would result in its triumphant vindication. Bernal has made many mistakes. Some of these he has frankly acknowledged—a courtesy which many of his critics seem unwilling to recognize or emulate.

But a more dialogical approach to the issue would have done much to advance the cause of nonpartisan scholarship which Lefkowitz and other opponents of the radical tier repeatedly identify as their primary concern. A more dialogical approach would have permitted readers to gaze into the abyss—that empty, menacing space which represents the locus of fundamental disagreements within the political and intellectual field of a given society. "What an abyss of uncertainty," as Proust would say. This is, undoubtedly, a spiritually and psychologically wrenching experience. Yet gazing at what is unsightly is constitutive of the intellectual endeavor. Had the editors of *Black Athena Revisted* included other perspectives in their volume, nonacademicians would have been able to ponder not only the size of the gulf, not only the uncertainty, but the sheer complexity of the questions which Martin Bernal raises.

The Radical Tier and *Black Athena*

With these considerations borne in mind, I would like to acquaint readers briefly with those scholars who rendered sympathetic readings of *Black*

Athena. In most cases Bernal's supporters made their remarks in passing. With few exceptions, only his detractors have devoted comprehensive studies to his work. These efforts have resulted in a thoroughly justified rhetorical victory for those who argue that the text is of little scholarly value.

Black Athena's emphasis on the composite nature of ancient Greek civilization is consonant with various multicultural projects. Proponents of what I call *external multiculturalism* seek to apprise school chancellors and university administrators of the accomplishments of cultures which lie outside the ambit of the Occident. Bernal's view, by contrast, may be labeled *internal multiculturalism.* He argues that Western civilization, when judiciously assessed, will show itself to be the by-product of diversity. Those who wish to dispute the notion of a pure, monocultural Western tradition can make good use of these findings. Sandra Harding, who excerpted a chapter of *Black Athena* in her collection *The "Racial" Economy of Science: Toward a Democratic Future,* employs the text as a means of pointing to the Occident's debt to "early non-Western scientific traditions."[24]

In his *All-American Skin Game; or, The Decoy of Race,* the inimitable Stanley Crouch explained the rise of ethnic studies departments as follows: "*So what college campuses do is, they say, 'Well, how much money will it cost us to keep the black students' feet off the president's desk this year?'*" Martin Bernal certainly finds more intellectual and moral justification for programs in African-American studies. In accentuating the African contribution to ancient Greece, Bernal participates in what Charles Taylor (who is not a radical) has called "the politics of recognition." That educators consistently withhold recognition of Egyptian influence on Greece is construed as a "form of oppression." Bernal articulates the tacit assumption of the monocultural view of Greece as follows: "You blacks are inherently uncivilized, and if you want any civilization you must become like us whites." *Black Athena,* conversely, sets out formally to recognize "Egypt as an African civilization with a central role in the formation of Greece."[25]

Bernal, then, is not merely praising Afroasiatic civilizations in and of themselves—a standard tactic of "boutique multiculturalism." Rather, he is aggressively (re-)inserting Africans and Semites into the genealogy of Western civilization by contending that they have played a formative role in the genesis and burgeoning of the Hellenic. This initiative has gained the attention of multicultural educators and has inserted this text into acrimonious debates about elementary and high school curricula.[26]

Approaches which deny the multicultural origins of ancient Greece, contends Bernal, run counter to glaringly obvious historical facts. For one, this monocultural perspective betrays the actual testimony of the ancients. Samir Amin paraphrases Bernal's argument: "Not only did [the Greeks] recognize what they had learned from the Egyptians and the Phoenicians, but they also did not see themselves as the 'anti-Orient' which Eurocentrism portrays them as being." Further, the denial of a mulatto Greek civilization, claims Bernal, contradicts a historical tradition which extends from the Persian

Wars, through the Patristic period, through the Renaissance, through the first century of the Enlightenment.[27]

In his first volume, pointedly subtitled *The Fabrication of Ancient Greece, 1785–1985*, Bernal sets out to explain this unprecedented paradigm shift. His analysis draws heavily upon Edward Said's *Orientalism*—a text that could serve as the theoretical preface to *Black Athena*. While there are differences in their approaches, the impact of Said's writing on Bernal's thought is considerable. As Amin notes, many of the "architects" of Orientalism discussed by Said figure prominently in Bernal's narrative. To borrow a phrase from Aijaz Ahmad, both concentrate on "European humanism's complicity in the history of European colonialism." One finds *Black Athena* approvingly cited in Said's recent work, as it is in the writings of other so-called postcolonial theorists.[28]

These approaches bear affinities to projects which seek to deconstruct and/or destabilize the narrative of Western civilization. Silvia Federici sums up Bernal's thesis as follows: "'Western Civilization' was produced in surprisingly recent times and for preeminently political reasons, which tells us more about the intentions of the elites that have promoted it than about Hellas and Ptah." Not coincidentally, one finds *Black Athena* footnoted or appreciatively cited in a variety of literary journals where the imbricated theoretical perspectives discussed in this section are commonplace.[29]

Another striking feature of *Black Athena* consists of what one commentator called its "full-scale assault" on the discipline of classics. Even prior to Bernal's screed, scholars of Greco-Roman antiquity were undergoing what Martha Malamud calls "spasmodic bursts of self-examination." As with all of the disciplines clustered around the study of antiquity, classics has been attempting to bring itself more in line with twentieth-century intellectual developments—many of which emanate from the "radical tier." Consequently, Bernal found allies among seditious classicists who were in the midst of their own reformist or revolutionary projects. Nancy Sorkin Rabinowitz, coeditor of *Feminist Theory and the Classics* remarks, "As Bernal's analysis in *Black Athena* makes clear, classics as a modern discipline developed on the basis of racist paradigms." Shelley Haley writes, "Martin Bernal shows the impact of Black slavery, racial science, and Romanticism upon the reading of ancient evidence."[30]

This brings us to the Afrocentrists, the most controversial of Bernal's nonmainstream supporters. This school is somewhat different from the aforementioned countercultural Left. To begin with, Afrocentrists have not achieved the same acceptance within the university as, for example, postcolonial scholars or deconstructionists. While there are exceptions, this has much to do with the frequently less than rigorous nature of the scholarship which they produce. Moreover, aside from a general animus toward Eurocentrism, Afrocentrists share few theoretical or methodological affinities with the radical schools of thought discussed above.[31]

For reasons which will be explored in my eighth chapter, *Black Athena* has become inextricably bound with Afrocentrism. Here is Dinesh D'Souza in *Illiberal Education:*

> All over the country, there is a new black scholarship, which seeks to establish the greatness of Africa based on an appropriation of the achievements of Egyptian civilization which is held to have taught the ancient Greeks and Romans most of what they knew. This amazingly popular notion is promoted by speakers on the lecture circuit, on talk shows, and in books and pamphlets circulated among black organizations; it is now virtually part of the conventional wisdom among blacks on the American campus. . . . The most prominent work of the genre is Cornell Professor Martin Bernal's *Black Athena: The Afroasiatic Roots of Civilization.*[32]

The charge that the author of *Black Athena* is an Afrocentrist has been repeatedly made and repeatedly denied. It will be argued that both Bernal and his detractors have succeeded in completely confusing this question. Afrocentrists, as we shall see, retain a far better understanding of the relation between their approaches and the work in question. For now, I will call attention to the existence of an oddly symbiotic relation. Bernal's alleged association with Afrocentrism did much to put a copy of *Black Athena* in the hands of every culture warrior in America. Conversely, that a white Ivy League professor would seem to endorse these ideas did much to bring the previously peripheral claims of Afrocentrists into the epicenter of American intellectual debate.

With its lengthy discussions of racism, *Black Athena* successfully tapped into one of the main intellectual and political concerns of the contemporary United States. Interestingly, the author's arguments about anti-Semitism have been almost completely ignored. The silence on this issue strikes me as significant, and an examination (and critique) of Bernal's "Semitic hypothesis" and his ambiguous relation with Jewish-American intellectuals will serve as the subject of my final chapter.

Also ignored by radicals and conservatives alike has been this text's attack on the academy. *Black Athena* may be read as Martin Bernal's systematic effort to deforest the verdant ideology of the modern research university. His work points to the moral and intellectual failure of precisely that institution which has been entrusted to safeguard Occidental civilization from its more deleterious tendencies. If its defenders view it as a bastion of open inquiry, a rare arena in which might does not make right, a forum in which dissenting voices are protected, tolerated, and even occasionally exalted, then nearly every morpheme of Bernal's text screams the contrary. The very structure of the university, argues Bernal, militates against impartial inquiry, the judicious assessment of heterodox claims, and intellectual innovation.

The indictment of the university extends to the norms of scholarly behavior as well. The most radical aspect of Bernal's work consists of the manner in which he challenges—by personal example—the contemporary understanding of what constitutes scholarship. It is this component of *Black Athena*—remarked upon by few, vicariously experienced by many—which will rank it as one of the most subversive academic works of the late twentieth century. These concerns will be addressed at length in Chapter 6.

Enter the Heretic

To this point, I have enumerated *a few* of Martin Bernal's heresies. These ranged from a philippic delivered to the classics establishment to a thoroughgoing revision of the ancient record. Yet to be discussed is the astonishing fact that the author of *Black Athena*, while an insider to the academic world, is an outsider to those disciplines which he both employs and/or excoriates. By training Martin Bernal is a Sinologist. He is not a classicist, Semitist, Egyptologist, Mediterranean archaeologist, or intellectual historian. And he is certainly not a sociologist, even though he often describes his project as a study in the sociology of knowledge.

For those who are wondering how it came to be that a metic to all of these disciplines could write about them so vigorously—and win an American Book Award in the process—I submit the following biographical sketch. Martin Gardiner Bernal was born in London in 1937, the son of the writer Margaret Gardiner and the renowned—or infamous—Communist scientist, John Desmond Bernal. The latter will be discussed momentarily. Martin Bernal's mother immersed her son in her circle of intellectuals and artists. Her salon included cultural lights such as the poets W. H. Auden and Dylan Thomas, the writer E. M. Forster, and the painter Ben Nicholson, among others. These people, according to Bernal, were "always around the house." Bernal's grandfather, Sir Alan Gardiner, was one of the seminal figures in the history of academic Egyptology.[33]

Between 1947 and 1954 Martin Bernal attended the Dartington Hall school in London, an institution often considered to be a seedbed for cultured radicals. He served in the Royal Air Force for two years prior to matriculating at King's College, Cambridge, in 1957. After doing graduate work at Harvard and Berkeley he received his doctorate in Oriental studies from Cambridge. From 1966 to 1972 he lectured on modern Chinese history at this institution and at the University of London. Thereafter, he crossed the ocean and accepted a tenured position in Cornell University's Department of Government.[34]

For the first fifteen years of his academic career (1961–1976) Bernal wrote extensively, and more or less exclusively, on modern China, Vietnam, and the history of socialism in the Far East. Throughout this period he contributed frequently to a more youthful incarnation of the *New York Review of Books*. No reader of those essays and reviews could fail to recognize the author's radical leanings. Bernal showed himself to be an enthusiastic—though not entirely uncritical—supporter of Mao, a fairly uncritical admirer of the Vietnamese resistance, and an unyielding critic of American military involvement in Southeast Asia. Here he is in 1972: "Trapped by their bureaucratic minds, American officials are always looking for nerve centers or key points which they believe can be found and destroyed, causing all Vietnamese resistance to collapse. They are unable to face the reality that for the Vietnamese nothing is indispensable except the people itself. Only genocide can defeat them."[35]

In addition to his politically oriented contributions, Bernal frequently wrote for scholarly fora. The culmination of these efforts was the monograph *Chinese Socialism to 1907*. Published in 1976, this text received positive reviews in academic journals, elicited few fireworks, and established Bernal as a respected figure in his field. Following the release of that work—which was originally intended to be three volumes—Bernal took the unusual step of completely changing the trajectory of his scholarly research.[36]

As the 1980s approached, the *Chinese Socialism* trilogy was abandoned. In the preface to *Black Athena* the author reveals that he experienced "a midlife crisis" in 1975. The end of the Maoist era and the Vietnam War were precipitating causes. These events coincided with a personal search for his distant Jewish roots. (Apparently, those Bernals who settled in Ireland in the seventeenth century were Sephardic Jews.) The interest in ancestry led Bernal to study ancient Hebrew, which led him to another northwest Semitic language, Phoenician. From there he became interested in the contacts between speakers of the latter and the ancient Greeks. The possibility of Egyptian influence in the Bronze Age Aegean became his next object of scrutiny. Bernal's critics had their own reading of his biographical narrative. Guy MacLean Rogers refers to *Black Athena* as "a massive, fundamentally misguided projection upon the second millennium B.C.E. of Martin Bernal's personal struggle to establish an identity during the later twentieth century."[37]

During the period from 1975 to 1986 Bernal would undertake the mammoth task of training himself in all of the aforementioned languages. He describes the professional aspects of this situation: "The Government Department at Cornell was very tolerant about how I spent my time. I had tenure; they couldn't do much about it." And the rest is revisionist history. Or, as Bernal would say, a return to the traditional view held by the ancient Greeks.[38]

Prior to the publication in the U.K. of the first volume of *Black Athena* in 1986 (the U.S. version was released in 1987), Bernal had submitted a few article-length sketches of his hypothesis. In 1990 his *Cadmean Letters: The Transmission of the Alphabet to the Aegean and Further West before 1400 B.C.* was released by a small academic press specializing in Near Eastern antiquity. This complex, relatively serene study of Greek and Semitic epigraphy was mostly overlooked. Not overlooked, however, was the long-anticipated second volume of *Black Athena* (1991), which was subtitled *The Archaeological and Documentary Evidence*. It was here that Bernal left the realm of nineteenth- and twentieth-century intellectual history and began to confront the ancient historians on their own highly specialized turf. And it was also here that reviews of his undertaking became increasingly negative. The reaction was led by a phalanx of classicists and Egyptologists who seemingly lost patience with this *"enfant terrible* thumbing his nose at his elders."[39]

Needless to say, this is as unorthodox a biography as one is wont to find in contemporary academe. Few scholars change from a discipline to various disciplines in the middle of their careers. Even fewer have the temerity to expose the fruits of such labor to the desiccating glances of scholarly observation. And hardly any would use the opportunity to challenge the fundamental assumptions of their new host discipline(s).

If Bernal had any model or genetic precursor for these unconventional actions, it would have to have been his father, John Desmond Bernal (1901–1971). In 1991 Bernal would say, "Since I started working on *Black Athena* . . . my father's style has taken over: bold, synthetic, wide-ranging." The entry in *A Dictionary of Marxist Thought* describes the father as "arguably, the most eminent of the 'red scientists' of the 1930's." Over the objections of military intelligence officers, Lord Mountbatten enlisted John Desmond Bernal on a variety of top-secret wartime projects, most notably the tactical planning of the Normandy invasion. Conservative critics of Bernal the younger were more likely to point out that his father was an ardent supporter of Stalin and a proponent of Lysenkoism.[40]

The dedication in the first volume of *Black Athena* reads as follows: "To the memory of my father, John Desmond Bernal, who taught me that things fit together, interestingly." By neither training nor temperament am I suited to engage in a work of intellectual biography. At present I will only mention three broad similarities between father and son. First, it seems safe to say that the two Bernals are exceptionally brilliant individuals. Second, by intellectual disposition both were inclined toward what we may call "big picturism." They share an ability to synthesize research from a wide variety of intellectual fields. As such, their scholarly writings evince a mischievous disdain for traditional disciplinary boundaries. As Robert Young notes of Bernal Senior: "His imagination was perhaps too restless for him to focus long and deeply enough on a particular problem to lead to the highest scientific achievements as conventionally conceived."[41]

Most important, both Bernals agitated from within the establishment, one as a scientist at Cambridge and president of influential international scientific organizations, the other as a tenured Ivy League professor. That both Bernals were insiders is of no mean significance. Throughout the sociological sections of this work, I will argue that it is this peculiar structural position that the heretic occupies which accounts for his or her subversive power. The heretic is an insider; the heretic is one of us.[42]

The Heretic in the Anomic Academy

As the reader may have already gleaned, I intend to charge Martin Bernal, possessor of an impeccable intellectual pedigree, with the crime of academic heresy. From a sociological perspective an accusation of intellectual deviance does not necessarily bear any dishonor. As Emile Durkheim observed a century ago: "Socrates was a criminal. . . . However, his crime, namely, the independence of his thought, rendered a service not only to humanity but to his country."[43]

The word *hairesis* can be traced to classical Greek sources, where it refers to "a belief *chosen* by an individual or sect." By the time of Saint Paul, the term often connotes dissenting views within the emerging Christian community. In one epistle (Titus 3:9–10) Paul speaks of heresy as something associated with "foolish questions . . . contentions and strivings about the law." As Edward Peters observes, in Paul's letters *hairesis* had the sense of "discordant," though not necessarily "theologically deviant," beliefs. It is only in the later writings of the Church Fathers, Peters demonstrates, that the word begins to signify "specific doctrines" that run "counter to Christian truth." It is within this context that the opinions of the heretic come to be associated with spiritual and social danger.[44]

It is an orthodoxy, of course, which experiences these dangers most acutely. In *A Letter concerning Toleration* John Locke made the ingenious observation that "every one is Orthodox to himself." True—but as I have noted elsewhere, within most societies only one religious group (or coalition of groups) retains the requisite capital, the means of physical coercion, the instruments of propaganda to become an orthodoxy in word and deed. This means that *heresy* is a relative and relational term. A heresy is a heresy only because an orthodoxy says so.[45]

But are the old dialogical partners heresy/orthodoxy still relevant today? Admittedly, it is not easy to transpose these concepts into the key of modernity or postmodernity. The word *heretic* originally meant "to choose," and many are now free to choose as never before. In modernity, writes Peter Berger, *"picking and choosing becomes an imperative."* As for the old orthodoxies, they have either disappeared or gone into hiding. In this society at least, a central, omnipotent orthodoxy, flush with its own sense of destructive power, no longer exists. This must be reckoned as a structural precondition for the postmodern moment. "Power is everywhere," declared Michel Foucault. And perhaps this explains why he was so enthralled by the words of the French poet René Char: "Développez votre étrangeté légitime"—"cultivate your legitimate strangeness." Needless to say this is not a project one undertakes—or even imagines—in an age of orthodoxies and inquisitions.[46]

Whereas the history of religion offers many examples of omnipotent orthodoxies, the contemporary university does not. In accord with the times, the academy is rapidly becoming an anomic institution. For better or for worse, today's university is a locus of theoretical and methodological dissensus. So when I speak of academic heresy, I recognize that it is distinct from the types of religious heresy encountered in premodern and early modern societies. We no longer burn heretics; we occasionally tenure them.

Bearing this in mind, I cautiously suggest that Martin Bernal has trespassed upon the increasingly constricted grounds of an aging and evaporating academic orthodoxy. To begin with, there are his transgressions against an already contested intellectual status quo. Bernal, and many others in the radical tier, are challenging a congeries of historical and epistemological beliefs which have assumed the status of givens. As with all heretics, be they premodern, modern, or postmodern, the author of *Black Athena* plays an epistemological zero-sum game. That is to say, if he is right then much of what most everyone else believes is wrong. As he declared in the introduction to his first volume, if his theory is correct it will be necessary *"to rethink the fundamental bases of 'Western Civilization.'"* I repeat, Bernal is not the only college professor to play the zero-sum game. There is no such thing as a heresy of one.[47]

Yet the author's transgressions against academic *orthopraxy* are even more jarring. Bernal's practices qua scholar over the preceding decade were unorthodox in the extreme. His big-picturism, his conscious politicizing of the historical record, his solicitation of lay audiences, and the strident tone of his text are blatant transgressions of normal scholarly comportment. I will argue in my sixth chapter that underneath the controversy surrounding *Black Athena*, and underneath the culture wars in general, there lies a conflict about the very definition of what scholarship is and about the moral responsibilities of the scholar.

The Inquisitor/The Inquisition: *Je Chante pour Moi-Même*

Prior to closing this chapter, and in accord with the spirit of the times, something must be said about the inquisitor. As the sociologist Pierre Bourdieu has noted again and again, self-reflexivity "is the necessary prerequisite of any rigorous sociological practice." Problematically, when scholars go into their self-reflexive mode—and it seems like everybody is doing it these days—they tend to lapse into "narcissism," "self-fascination," "self-pleasuring," and other behaviors which suggest that the human ego is a very delicate apparatus indeed. I regret to say it, but self-reflexivity, as currently practiced, often amounts to little more than oh-so-many variations on Carmen's theme, "Je chante pour moi-même."[48]

So I sing.

The sociologist Bennett Berger has suggested a sensible ground rule for maintaining the integrity of self-reflexive "admissions." The responsible researcher must provide his or her audience with "all the evidence one can muster to *distrust* the ideas one is about to convey." The reasons which might render the present study untrustworthy could fill a separate monograph (or even a tragic opera). Considerations of space and time restrict me to identifing four. First, there is the issue of scholarly credentials. While the scope of *Black Athena* is multidisciplinary, many of its individual arguments are often rendered in remarkable detail. Accordingly, it has become something of a tradition among those who have discussed Bernal's work to confess to their inability to judge it in its entirety. As John Baines remarks, "His work is also so wide-ranging and touches on so many disciplines and categories of evidence that few have the competence to evaluate more than individual elements in it." Classicist Molly Myerowitz Levine suggests that it would take "a committee to review Bernal properly."[49]

I too must confess. Although trained and credentialed in two distinct scholarly disciplines, I am unable to assess expertly the vast majority of *Black Athena*'s initiatives. As a student of northwest Semitic antiquity and its attendant languages, I am ill-equipped to evaluate Bernal's philological claims pertaining to Greek and Egyptian. At best, I can bring my own "feel" for the ancient Near East to bear on his theories pertaining to the Bronze and Early Iron Age Mediterranean. My second field, the sociology of religion, is also at some distance from the material investigated by Bernal. As noted above, the author labeled *Black Athena* a study in the sociology of knowledge. Insofar as sociology is one of the few academic disciplines that has had almost nothing to say about *Black Athena*, it will be necessary to advance a sociological reading of this text. But I warn the reader in advance: beware of sociologists of religion who masquerade as sociologists of knowledge.

In deference to Berger's edict, however, I think I could do better, or worse as the case may be. The reader should distrust this work, because its author greatly esteems heretics and professes solidarity with them (that is, those who conform to his definition of how they should behave). The reader might also distrust this study because I have already publicly defended Bernal and chided his detractors—perhaps excessively—on the pages of a well-known magazine of opinion. One might also be suspicious of my ideas because I was, for a brief period, a student of Cyrus Gordon—one of the biggest influences on Bernal's historical work. And there are, I assure you, many other reasons to distrust me. A certain generosity of the spirit impels me to leave these reasons for others to discern.[50]

And now to the inquisition. The first goal of this work is to apprise readers of *Black Athena*'s major theories. As noted earlier, these are numerous, complex, and often extremely difficult to understand. For these reasons, I will be obliged to pare down his hypotheses so as to render them comprehensible to both academic and lay readers. This will necessitate that I too—for the first time in my short career—indulge my Weberian megalomania. What will be forwarded in these pages, then, is a general sketch of the *Black Athena* hypothesis. Much will be left out as I hop, skip, and jump from one area of academic inquiry (which I am not trained in) to another (which I am also not trained in). For this transgression, I too fully deserve to hear "the lament of the exasperated specialist."

As regards those aspects of Bernal's hypothesis which I do scrutinize, I will often provide genealogical ambiance. It must be stressed that the author is not simply inventing and improvising arguments as he goes along. On the contrary, for nearly every proposal he makes he has found an ally (or allies) in the scholarly literature. The author builds his case(s) on research which has been forgotten, ignored, defeated, or perhaps only half digested by the present generation of scholars, all while embracing more orthodox positions which fit his argument. *Black Athena* is a very creative work, but it is at the same time a rather impressive synthesis and renovation of existing scholarship.[51]

Whereas much energy will be devoted to making Bernal clear to his readers, equal efforts will be exerted to making Bernal clear to himself. I recognize that this claim is unconscionably arrogant. Nevertheless, I will demonstrate, especially in my analysis of his sociology of knowledge, that Bernal sometimes tends to ignore glaring contradictions in his arguments, to understate or misrecognize his own often ingenious ideas, and to fail to see the implications of some of his bold theoretical initiatives.

I also wish to inform readers of the basic criticisms made of the text in question. Since its release in 1986, well over a hundred reviews and articles have been written about *Black Athena*. In many instances, the author published responses to his critics. The result is an immense bibliography. And those who are familiar with it may quite justifiably feel that they are listening to academic dueling banjos of the most cacophonous and antagonistic sort. This rather sizable body of material, including videotaped conferences, movies, and Internet discussions, constitutes what I will call the Controversy. Whenever possible, I will attempt to adjudicate among the competing views that have been expressed over the years. It goes without saying that I will advance my own criticisms of both Bernal and his critics.

Aside from advancing a theory of academic heresy, this study will concentrate on what might be called the rhetorical dimensions of the Controversy. As I have argued above, in form and content, the debate over *Black Athena* mirrors larger disputes within contemporary American intellectual culture. I will call attention to the manner in which scholars speak to one another, the manner in which epistemological fissures prevent them from speaking to one another, the rhetorical strategies which they employ, the discursive fouls they commit, and so on.

This line of analysis will permit me to address issues of intellectual responsibility, particularly among the professorate. The questions that interest me can be stated as follows: What are the moral obligations of the scholar? What are our (we scholars, that is) responsibilities to one other and to a general reading audience? What has the *Black Athena* Controversy revealed about the university's capacity to accommodate dissenting voices?

The present text will be divided into three sections. The first will concentrate on Bernal's reconstruction of ancient history. In the second, I will turn to his ignored sociology of knowledge. In the final section I will set his text within the context of the culture wars by focusing on Afrocentrism, the

Egyptian phenotype, and the blacks-and-Jews debate. My hope in writing this book is that it will facilitate future discussions of the very important issues raised by Professor Bernal. I confess that I am generally sympathetic to *Black Athena*'s basic theories. And it is precisely for this reason that I have a responsibility to be extremely critical of them. The eradication of one's biases, I will argue, is an impossible task. Yet it is the belief that this can be done which stands as both the heroism and the pathos of the scholar.

Part One

The Historical

Argument

There is, in archaeological science, an illusion so singularly tenacious that it needs to be debunked more than once in order to get rid of it. Put simply, we may call it, *the Oriental illusion.*
—Salomon Reinach, "Le Mirage Oriental"

These were the two greatest swings of the East Mediterranean pendulum. Chronologically, the swings from East to West preceded those from West to East. Long before Hellenism imposed itself over the ancient civilizations of the East, Semitism had exercised no less an impact upon the young civilization of Greece. Hellenism became the epilogue of the Oriental civilizations, but Semitism was the prologue of Greek civilization.
—Michael Astour, *Hellenosemitica: An Ethnic and Cultural Study in West Semitic Impact on Mycenaean Greece*

The deeper [Plato and Isokrates] went towards the true Hellenic roots of Greece, the closer they came to Egypt.
—Martin Bernal, *Black Athena* 1

1

The Ancient

Model

Hard Moderns versus Idiosyncratic Ancient

According to this model, the ancestors of the Greeks had lived around the Aegean in idyllic simplicity until the Phoenicians and rulers from Egypt arrived and acquired territories, built cities, and founded dynasties. The strangers also introduced many of the arts of civilization, notably, irrigation, various types of armaments, writing, and religion.
—Martin Bernal, "Race, Class, and Gender in the Formation of the Aryan Model of Greek Origins"

In unguarded moments of pride we may even be tempted to tell Thucydides that we know more about Athenian tribute lists than he ever did.
—Arnaldo Momigliano, "The Place of Herodotus in the History of Historiography"

The question which animates the historical sections of the first volume of *Black Athena* may be phrased as follows: How have students of history, from Classical antiquity to the present day, explained the origins of Greek civilization? In Martin Bernal's estimation this problematic has been approached through four theoretical frameworks. The earliest is labeled the Ancient Model. In the nineteenth century, according to Bernal, there developed the Broad Aryan Model and its offshoot, the Extreme Aryan Model. The Ultra-Europeanist Model comes into being in the latter half of the twentieth century.

The endeavor to reduce and divide 2,500 years of historical speculation into four schools of thought leaves Bernal susceptible to the accusation of slapdash big-picturism. Ostensibly, this tidy scheme does injustice to the com-

Table 1.
Martin Bernal's Five Models of Greek Origins

	Ancient Model	Revised Ancient Model	Broad Aryan Model	Extreme Aryan Model	Ultra-Europeanist Model
Time	ca. 500 B.C.E–1820/1830 C.E.	1986–?	1830/1840/1850–1925/1945–present	1890–1900 and 1920–1930	1970–Present
Founders and/or Intellectual Precursors	Herodotus, Aeschylus, Isokrates, Plato, Aristotle, etc.	V. Bérard, C. Gordon, M. Astour, M. Bernal	K. O. Müller founders of Indo-European, B. Niebuhr, C. Thirlwall, G. Grote, G. Curtius, E. Curtius	K.O. Müller founders of Indo-European, B. Niebuhr, S. Reinach, J. Beloch, R. Carpenter	K. O. Müller, C. Renfrew, V. Georgiev
Means of Explaining Origins of Greek Civilization	nd	modified diffusion (via Egyptians and West Semites)	diffusion (via Aryans)	diffusion (via Aryans)	"Isolationism"
Composition of Greek Language	nd	50% Indo-European 25% West Semitic 20–25% Egyptian*	50% Indo-European 50% Pelasgian or Pre-Hellene	50% Indo-European 50% Pelasgian or Pre-Hellene	Indo-European
Language of the Pelasgians	Not Greek	Indo-Hittite	Pre-Hellenic, not Indo-European	Pre-Hellenic, not Indo-European	nd
"Race" or Ethnicity of Pelasgians	nd	southern Anatolian	Caucasian	Caucasian	nd
Indo-European Invasion of Aegean?	no	yes, ca. 2300 B.C.E	yes, ca. 2300 B.C.E	yes, ca. 2300 B.C.E	no

Egyptian Colonization of Greece?	yes	yes	no	no	no
Phoenician colonization of Greece?	yes	yes	possibly	no	no
Accuracy of Greek Documents	nd	accurate	inaccurate (*Interpretatio Graeca*)	inaccurate (*Interpretatio Graeca*)	nd
Hyksos arrival in Aegean	1600–1500 (Parian Marble)	1730 B.C.E	no arrival	no arrival	no arrival
Time of transmission of West Semitic Alphabet to Aegean	1600–1500 (Parian Marble)	ca. 1800–1300	9th–8th century	9th–8th century	nd
Conquests of Sesóstris	Thrace, Scythia, India, Anatolia	Anatolia, Levant (Sesóstris= Senwosret I)	no conquests	no conquests	nd

nd = no data

*In 1997 Bernal suddenly offered a new breakdown. Now 15% of Greek was seen as having Semitic origins and 20% as having Egyptian origins (Responses to *Black Athena*," 88–89).

plex reality it aspires to represent. Yet for whatever it is worth—and I believe it is worth something—the author of *Black Athena* is fully cognizant that there are drawbacks to his broad schematizing. "By 'model,'" explains Bernal, "I mean a reduced and simplified representation, and I am acutely aware that creating models inevitably distorts the complex contours of the past." He then proceeds to state that models, despite all of their flaws, "are essential for organized thought." Only rarely does the author of *Black Athena* stumble into academic minefields. As with most heretics, he commits his crimes in cold blood.[1]

The Ancient Model is the theoretical foundation and intellectual inspiration for a fifth approach, invented by Martin Bernal and called the Revised Ancient Model. Thus, the pages of *Black Athena* feature a modular competition; the five models (Ancient, Revised Ancient, Broad Aryan, Extreme Aryan, Ultra-Europeanist) are set against one another in order to see which one accounts most convincingly for the evidence which we have at our disposal. That the competition is rigged, that it is tilted toward the "stunning" triumph of Bernal's Revised Ancient Model, is an accusation which I shall address in the following chapter. At present, I shall rehearse the basic themes and criticisms of the Ancient Model.

A Doubly Refracted Paradigm

On the first page of *Black Athena* Bernal succinctly states the rudiments of the Ancient Model as follows: "The 'Ancient Model' was the conventional view among Greeks in the Classical [ca. 480–ca. 323 B.C.E.] and Hellenistic [ca. 323–ca. 30 B.C.E.] ages. According to it, Greek culture had arisen as the result of colonization, around 1500 BC, by Egyptians and Phoenicians who had civilized the native inhabitants. Furthermore, Greeks had continued to borrow heavily from Near Eastern cultures."[2] This model is said to be ancient insofar as the ancient Greeks themselves, during Classical and Hellenistic times, were beholden to this particular understanding ("conventional view") of their historical origins.

The reader should note that the evidence which Bernal uses to erect the Ancient Model is mostly based on documents composed between the fifth and first centuries B.C.E. When Herodotus, Plato, and Aristotle, among others, discussed what Bernal labels the Ancient Model, they were reflecting on events that had occurred in their own hoary antiquity—more than a thousand years before they wrote. The Ancient Model, then, is a doubly refracted paradigm. It is Martin Bernal's reconstruction of the distant past based on how those in the distant past reconstructed their own distant past.

As I see it, there are four overlapping sets of assumptions which comprise the Ancient Model. The first are *assumptions of Eastern colonization.* Here the ancients maintained that parts of mainland Greece and the Aegean in general were, a long time ago, settled by Egyptians and Phoenicians. The second may be labeled *assumptions of kinship.* These pertain to statements which indicate that the Greeks thought that they were in some way related to these Easterners. *Intellectual assumptions* refers to the belief that something of great cultural value (e.g., philosophy, the alphabet, mathematics) was imparted to them by these Afroasiatic civilizations. Last, and to use an inelegant phrase, *assumptions of Oriental greatness* alludes to the opinion that Egypt, and to a lesser extent Phoenicia, were the source of ideas and institutions which were worthy of the Greek's admiration.[3]

Let us start by discussing the colonization narratives. Central to the Ancient Model are a variety of ambiguous and conflicting accounts concerning the original inhabitants of the ancient Aegean and their interactions with settlers from the East. Some of these indicate that upon arriving in this region, the Egyptians were to encounter a group referred to as the Pelasgians, or *Pelasgoi.* While the ancient reports concerning their ethnic identity and language are scarce and contradictory, a few Greek sources implied that the Pelasgians comprised the indigenous population of mainland Greece. These natives, alleges *Black Athena,* were thought to have been "converted to become something more Greek by the invading Egyptians." In Bernal's view, writers in the Classical and Hellenistic periods viewed the arrival of the Egyptians as the event which decisively stimulated the genesis of Greek civilization.[4]

Let us now turn from the colonized Pelasgians to their colonizers. In examining Greek myth and drama Bernal identifies a series of traditions which center around two legendary figures: Kadmos (generally associated with Phoenicia) and Danaos (often associated with Egypt). In the opening scenes of Aeschylus's *Suppliants,* for example, we encounter the fifty daughters of Danaos who have just arrived in Argos. This region (located in the northeast Peloponnese) is the homeland of their ancestor, Io. The fifty virgins are fleeing from Egypt and the sons of their uncle (Aigyptos). Or, in the words of the young women, "To Argos, bound to us by ancient ties of blood, / Driven by loathing of unholy rape in Egypt?" Here we receive a vague indication that the Greeks construed their historical experiences as somehow bound with those of the Egyptians. The reference to "blood" also hints at some sort of kinship between Egyptians and Greeks.[5]

Other ancient writers associated the Danaan settlement of Greece with the arrival of a group known as the Hyksos. According to Hekataios of Abdera, for example, the Hyksos had been expelled from Egypt, and the displaced members broke off into two groups. One settled in Canaan, and it is claimed that these are the Israelites who in the Book of Exodus fled Pharaoh through parted waters. The second group, the Danaans, washed ashore in Greece. As we shall see in Chapter 2 below, the notion of colonizing Hyksos is the centerpiece of Bernal's Revised Ancient Model.[6]

Kadmos, our second colonizer, is seen as "a mythical founder figure" of Thebes.[7] In Euripides's (ca. 485–406 B.C.E.) *Phoenician Women,* ill-fated Jokasta, mother/ex-wife of Oedipus, opens the tragedy by claiming:

Sun, flaring in your flames, what a harmful ray
you hurled at Thebes that day when Kadmos quit
seaswept Phoenicia, and came to this country.[8]

According to the chorus, Kadmos's homeland was in Tyre on the coast of modern-day Lebanon. Here again, we receive a literary report of contact between an Afroasiatic civilization and mainland Greece. Momentarily we will look at another important tradition involving Kadmos.[9]

Bernal goes on to cite rather unambiguous statements from the renowned orator Isokrates (436–338 B.C.E.) and the philosopher Plato (427–347 B.C.E.) to the effect that Eastern colonizations of Greece took place. The latter goes so far as to suggest that bonds of kinship exist between his own state and that of the Egyptians. In the Platonic dialogue *Timaeus,* a reference is made to the existence of a family relation between the district of Sais in the western Egyptian Delta and Athens.[10]

Assumptions of cultural influence, argues Bernal, can be seen in Aristotle's (384–322 B.C.E.) writings where he attributes the development of the mathematical arts to Egyptian priests. Most of the Greek thinkers discussed so far, as well as others, were also quick to point to the tremendous respect they had for the ancient Egyptians. Bernal calls attention to Isokrates's flattering portrait of Egypt in his *Busiris.* He also cites Greek reports that revered figures such as Pythagoras (ca. 580–ca. 500 B.C.E.), Plato, Eudoxos (ca. 400–ca. 350 B.C.E.), and the pre-Homeric figure Orpheus had acquired their ideas from the Egyptians. As further proof of the great esteem which the Greeks had for this culture, the author notes that Alexander the Great (356–323 B.C.E.) was not only buried in Egypt, but, while alive, proclaimed himself the son of the Egyptian god, Ammon. The impact of Egyptian religion on ancient Greece and Rome is seen as also proving this admiration for an Afroasiatic civilization. In 1995 Bernal writes, "After the third century B.C.—outside the offical state cults—Oriental and Egyptian religion flourished around the Mediterranean and in Roman Europe."[11]

Herodotus and Sesōstris

The fifth-century historian Herodotus (ca. 490–ca. 425 B.C.E.) once remarked in his work *Histories* that Egypt was the gift of the Nile. In many ways, *Black Athena*'s Ancient Model is the gift of Herodotus's *Histories.*[12]

Bernal wishes to show that as far as the "father of history" was concerned, Phoenician and Egyptian culture had profoundly influenced the development of ancient Greece. The following quote from Herodotus, which Bernal cites frequently, merits repetition here: "How it happened that Egyptians came to the Peloponnese, and what they did to make themselves kings in that part of Greece, has been chronicled by other writers; I will add nothing, therefore, but proceed to mention some points which no one else has yet touched upon." What I find most striking about this passage is Herodotus's belief that the colonization stories are well known within the world in which he lives; no defense of these tales is seen as necessary since their validity is not contested.[13]

One of Bernal's more important lines of evidence—and the foundation of the Semitic component of his hypothesis (see Chapters 2 and 9 below)—also comes from Herodotus. The latter reports that the alphabet was transmitted to the Greeks by the Phoenicians. Herodotus writes, "The Phoenicians who came with Cadmus [or Kadmos] . . . introduced into Greece, after their settlement in the country, a number of accomplishments, of which the most important was writing, an art till then, I think, unknown to the Greeks."[14]

Herodotus also speaks of an Egyptian king named Sesōstris who engaged in military campaigns in Europe and Asia. Upon returning from these expeditions Sesōstris stopped at the river Phasis in Colchis (a region located on the eastern shores of the Black Sea, south of the Caucasus Mountains) and left behind an undisclosed number of soldiers. Herodotus states that their descendants, who he claims to have viewed with his own eyes, have "black skins" and are "woolly-haired." The inference which Bernal drew from this—an inference which would lead to some of the more spectacular exchanges in the Controversy (see Chapter 8 below)—was that these Egyptian soldiers, and hence their leader as well, were "black."[15]

Before rounding out this brief sketch of the Ancient Model, I would like to call attention to a point which Bernal repeatedly stresses. That the aforementioned Greek authors would frequently mention their kinship, colonial past, cultural debts, and admiration vis-à-vis Phoenicians and Egyptians is rather remarkable. In reference to Plato and Isokrates, Bernal observes, "Thus, despite their ambivalence if not hostility to the ideas, the two leading intellectual figures of the early 4th century BC were forced to admit the critical importance of foreign colonization, and massive later cultural borrowing from Egypt and the Levant, in the formation of the Hellenic civilization they both loved so passionately."[16]

The point which Bernal makes here is compelling. Even the unequivocal ethnocentrism of the ancient Greeks could not keep them from persistently mentioning an obvious, and somewhat humbling, fact. These writers freely acknowledged foreign influence, even though such an admission was antithetical to the "Panhellenic, anti-'barbarian' passions of the time."[17]

The Critique of the Ancient Model: Source Criticism

One of the most oft encountered objections to Bernal's Ancient Model, and his historical methodology in general, centers around the manner in which he interprets ancient texts. It has been repeatedly charged that the author of *Black Athena* reads these documents literally, uncritically, and selectively. Egyptologist John Baines speaks of Bernal's "overconfident use of sources," and goes on to note, "He gives [Greek myths and legends] credence to an extent hardly found in other modern writing on such subjects." Emily

Vermeule criticizes Bernal's "endearingly childlike faith in the absolute historical value of Greek myths."[18]

Charges of this nature have been made most frequently in regard to Bernal's treatment of Herodotus. "I am thus afraid," writes V. Y. Mudimbe, "that Bernal is not sufficiently critical of Herodotus's pronouncements." Mary Lefkowitz refers to his "eager credulity about Herodotus." In a delicious turn of phrase, classicist Stanley Burstein speaks of the author's "Herodotean fundamentalism." Burstein continues, "The problem is that [Bernal] treats Herodotus solely as a reporter of Egyptian traditions while Herodotus' text strongly suggests that his share in the creation of his narrative was much greater than that."[19]

An adjunct accusation is that Bernal pays little attention to the complex political, intellectual, philosophical, aesthetic, and religious contexts of the Greek documents that he uses to erect the Ancient Model. As classicist Tamara Green remarks:

> Too often, Professor Bernal has removed the production of his literary texts from their social setting. Contemporary events gave meaning to the past as sharply as any overall view of the universe, and the perception of the present defined the interpretation of the past. Any analysis of the Greeks' interpretation of their own past demands an examination not only of the actual events themselves (as far as they can be determined), but of their changing views of religion, philosophy, politics, etc.[20]

The common denominator which runs throughout the preceding observations is that Martin Bernal does not conduct his inquiry as would a modern historian, that he is not sufficiently versed in the methods, theories, and intellectual orientations which are constitutive of the *scholarly* study of ancient history. As an example, we might point to Bernal's attitude toward "source criticism"—an attitude which Michael Poliakoff described as "skeptical, if not contemptuous."[21]

"Source criticism" is an imprecise term which can be applied to a multitude of distinct theoretical and methodological approaches to the study of ancient texts. These can range from biblical scholars debating what source or document a given passage in the Hebrew Bible stems from (in its simplest form J, E, D, P), to an inquiry as to the documents upon which an ancient historian reconstructed a particular event, to an attempt to identify the precise political context in which Flavius Josephus composed *Against Apion*. If I understand Poliakoff correctly he is using "source criticism" in its general sense, encompassing the many different critical methods which modern historians apply to ancient texts.[22]

At the risk of generalizing, I would say that source-critical approaches are predicated on the assumption that ancient texts are, for a number of differing reasons, inherently untrustworthy. Their lack of reliability is often attributed to the inadequacies of their authors. Moses I. Finley observes that ancient historians "failed to develop techniques of source criticism" and retained an incredible "capacity to believe" and "invent." In *Did the Greeks Believe in Their Myths? An Essay on the Constitutive Imagination,* Paul Veyne would remark that "history then and history now are alike in name only." Veyne argues that the ancient historians did not use sources and documents, merely reproduced what they had heard, were not skeptical; in short, they were the very opposite of their exacting modern counterparts.[23]

I would call attention to another potential difference between ancient and modern historians. In *The Flight from Ambiguity: Essays in Social and Cultural Theory,* sociologist Donald Levine argued that from the seventeenth century onward an increasing disdain for imprecision and equivocality is witnessed in European social thought. The systematic removal of ambiguity, in "all departments of life" as Weber would say, became a sort of Western imperative. Levine's research among the Amhara of Ethiopia led him to the recognition that some cultures routinely employ, even cultivate, ambiguity, in conversations, art, social practices, and so forth. Levine makes the fruitful observation that while Enlightenment thinkers attempted to eradicate the equivocal, the very roots of their classical traditions are filled with ambiguity. "The Jews," he writes, "created a book [i.e., the Hebrew Bible] whose sparse detail has been a standing invitation for evocative interpretations."[24]

Extrapolating from these remarks, I would suggest that while the modern historian manifests an aversion to ambiguity, the literati of the ancient civilizations they study may often have intentionally employed ambiguity in their writing of history. For example: did Jephthah really mean to sacrifice his daughter in the eleventh chapter of the Book of Judges? The possibilities are so maddeningly numerous that one might be led to believe that the biblical authors deliberately obfuscated the issue.[25]

The modern study of ancient history is characterized by, to adopt a phrase from Paul Ricoeur, a "hermeneutic of suspicion." Trust is a courtesy which the professional historian rarely extends to an ancient author. It follows that skepticism is the requisite psychological orientation for the academician who studies the ancient world. This orientation has stimulated a variety of methodological imperatives: the contents of an ancient document are never to be read at face value; the political motivations of its author(s) are to be called into question; the text must be scrutinized for information which its original writers did not realize they yielded to posterity; internal contradictions are to be exposed; external data from other texts or archaeological findings must be brought into play in order to corroborate or debunk the original account; ambiguities are to be clarified. For the professional scholar of antiquity, then, the text has to be worked over, so to speak. It cannot stand on its own as a witness to the past. It relinquishes its insights unwillingly, only after the application of exegetical and theoretical methods.[26]

It is the practice of academic source criticism (in the broad sense) with its "hermeneutic of suspicion" toward the ancients, its intolerance of ambiguity, which Martin Bernal seems to reject. In the conclusion to the present chapter, I will identify the argument which predisposes the author to adopt this dissenting position. Prior to doing so, I would like to advance my own critique of the Ancient Model.

The Critique of the Ancient Model: Reification

In *Black Athena* only one ancient critic of the Ancient Model is mentioned. Bernal refers to Plutarch's (ca. 46–ca. 120 C.E.) essay "On the Malice of Herodotus," written in the early second century C.E. as "the closest to what one might call an attack on the Ancient Model." In a brief submission, classicist Pamela Gordon suggested that Bernal may have overestimated the unanimity of this model in antiquity. "Implicit dissent from the Ancient Model," she writes, "is evident in many other ancient sources." Diogenes Laertius, for example, writing in the third century C.E., was opposed to the notion that Easterners had contributed anything of value to Greek culture.[27] Gordon concludes by noting that these protestations of the Ancient Model actually confirm Bernal's hypothesis: "Although ancient sources are less unanimous than Bernal implies, the fact that Diogenes Laertius' denial of foreign influence is framed as an attack on previous writers *supports Bernal's claim that the Greeks generally believed that they owed cultural debts to Egypt and the East.*"[28] But I would like to challenge Bernal's—and to a far, far lesser extent Gordon's—suggestion that something called the Ancient Model actually existed in the periods discussed above. What Bernal labels a model was, I will argue, a series of vague, unquestioned assumptions sprinkled throughout the writings of a few of the most eminent minds of the Classical and Hellenistic periods.

Let us first look at the manner in which Bernal characterizes the Ancient Model in Greek thought. In a 1995 contribution he alleges that this approach "was fully articulated in the fifth century B.C., but there is strong evidence to suggest that it had existed much earlier." Elsewhere he states, "By the fifth century B.C., most Greeks perceived their history in a framework that can usefully be called the 'ancient model.'" And with even more certainty: "This historical scheme was used by most Greek writers concerned with understanding their distant past, omitted by one or two, but denied by none."[29]

Phrases on the order of "fully articulated," "most Greeks perceived their history," and "denied by none" are unwarranted. Do we know what "most" Greeks actually believed? Can it be said that by the fifth century B.C.E. the Ancient Model was "fully articulated"? Neither Herodotus nor Aeschylus nor anyone else set out to prove Eastern influence on ancient Greece. None of the ancient writers discussed by Bernal proffered any systematic treatment of the assumptions collected in his Ancient Model. In fact, no one Greek author ever adumbrated *all* of the tenets of the model. For this framework is a composite. It is based on strands of testimony scattered throughout the written record of Classical and Hellenistic antiquity and eventually collated by Martin Bernal. The Ancient Model qua model did not exist until the publication of *Black Athena* in 1986.

We should not be surprised, then, to learn that this view had no self-professed proponents or opponents at the time of its earliest appearance. The Ancient Model was not consciously debated in the manner that early Christians, for example, argued about the merits and demerits of circumcision. I would suggest that this is so because there is no need to defend a proposition which is uncontested—or, perhaps, not of cardinal significance. This absence of dialogue makes it even more difficult to accept that we are dealing with a "model." Bernal himself stipulates that models are typically in "competition" with one another. But where in Classical antiquity is the antithesis to the Ancient Model?[30]

Now, it is true that Plutarch and Diogenes Laertius challenged the belief in Eastern influence on Greece. They did so, however, more than six hundred years after Bernal claims the Ancient Model took hold. Even here, as Gordon noted above, the dissent is mostly "implicit." Further, these writers are not arguing against the Ancient Model as described in the first volume of *Black Athena.* Why? Because there was no such thing as an Ancient Model in ancient times. Diogenes Laertius attacks the idea that putatively Greek achievements may be attributed to Babylonians, Assyrians, Indians, Celts, Gauls, Thracians, Libyans, Egyptians, and Phoenicians. Bernal's Ancient Model has nothing to say about the majority of these peoples. Plutarch's essay on Herodotus deals with a variety of issues, most having little to do with the four assumptions which comprise the framework discussed above.[31]

To those who would respond that to distinguish between an "assumption" and a "model" amounts to quibbling, I would counter that the distinction is of some significance. To imply that Greeks "perceived their history" within this framework is to ascribe to the Ancient Model a discursive solidity which it did not possess. Reading *Black Athena* one is led to believe that for the Greeks the Ancient Model comprised a coherent set of historical principles predicated on intensive observation, debate, and sustained discussion. Moreover, the reader receives the impression that it was a central theme in Greek thought, a view which "most Greeks" accepted. But a few references in the writings of highly educated, literate individuals cannot be taken as accurate indexes of what most members of a society actually believed. As Sturt Manning observes: "Herodotus is just one view (which happens to have been preserved), and there will have been many others. . . . There was no one Ancient Model."[32]

This does not mean that the Ancient Model is wrong. On the contrary, Bernal has certainly identified the existence of a presupposition which surfaces, albeit somewhat nebulously, in the thought of various ancient authorities. In so doing, he provides us with an extremely useful heuristic for future scholarly research. My only concern is that the author reifies *his* model: what is a useful theoretical construction for Martin Bernal was not necessarily a discursive reality for all ancient Greeks.

Conclusion: Exegetical Skepticism and *Sola Scriptura*

Professional scholars of antiquity, as we have seen, place far less trust in ancient texts than does Martin Bernal. Conversely, Martin Bernal places far more trust in ancient texts than he does in professional scholars of antiquity. Or, as classicist Lawrence A. Tritle phrased it, "In [Bernal's] view—or so it appears—what an ancient author states can only mean what he says, whereas modern authors with their hidden agendas, usually racist or anti-Semitic (or both), never mean what they say." Tritle's clever remark descries one of Bernal's more astonishing "outrages." By rejecting—or at least ignoring—source critical methods and remaining rather faithful to the words of Herodotus, the author of *Black Athena* challenges what is, perhaps, the ultimate conceit of the modern age: the belief that we have transcended the ancients.[33]

It should be recalled that this conviction is born of relatively recent times. As Eric Hobsbawm has observed, it was only three hundred years ago that there had "been a serious debate about whether the moderns could ever surpass the achievement of the ancients." In her study *Ancients against Moderns: Culture Wars and the Making of a Fin de Siècle* Joan DeJean chronicles the acrimonious disputes which took place in France in the waning years of the seventeenth century. It was here that the shocking suggestion was made that those who lived in the time of Louis XIV had achieved literary superiority over the ancients. As Charles Perrault, one of the primary instigators of the *Querelle des Anciens et des Modernes,* wrote in 1687: "Antiquity was always venerable, but I never believed it was worthy of adoration."[34]

With the advent of the Enlightenment the long-held belief in the categorical preeminence of the ancients would gradually disappear. As Joyce Appleby, Lynn Hunt, and Margaret Jacob argue in *Telling the Truth about History:* "Beginning with the new dictionaries and encyclopedias, enlightened literary criticism, the hermeneutical art, subjected myths and stories to rigorous scrutiny. Ruled out of court were the Biblical stories and the fables of the ancients."[35] In the field of academic history the victory of the moderns has been almost total. Aside from a tiny minority of theologians in the field of biblical studies, few scholars today would read an ancient document at face value. Even fewer still would compose paeans to the historians of yore. And almost none would counsel their graduate students to use Thucydides or the P(riestly) source of the Hebrew Bible as a paragon for their doctoral research.

Nor would Martin Bernal. Be that as it may, he does not share the standard misgivings regarding the ancient sources and their authors which so characterize modern scholarly research. In fact, it is modern scholarly research itself which emerges as the most persistent object of Bernal's hermeneutic of suspicion. The author devotes considerable efforts to chronicling the rise of the Ancient Model, its intellectual reign across nearly two and a half millennia, and its sudden—and Bernal believes unjustified—overthrow in the nineteenth century. In explaining its collapse he points to the emergence of a new ethos which gripped nineteenth-century historians of antiquity. Bernal refers to it as *Besserwissen*, or "knowing better." Equipped with new tools of historical analysis, and a new ideology of "progress" (see Chapter 4 below) these scholars surmised that their capacity to establish historical truth was far greater than that of the ancients, regardless of the latter's greater temporal proximity to the events which they described.[36]

Source criticism was the highest methodological expression of the *Besserwissen* ethos. It is the development of this method which Bernal holds partly accountable for the fall of the Ancient Model. "Using 'source criticism,'" he writes, "the scholar could dismiss the quantity or wide spread of ancient attestation and focus on the one 'good' source that suited his purpose." Historians were now self-licensed, contends Bernal, to delete any ancient testimony which indicated an African or Semitic influence on a "white," "European" Greece. In so doing, they were flush with a sense of their own objectivity—a quality which the ancients purportedly lacked.[37]

The rise of source criticism (and the fall of the Ancient Model) came to fruition in the person of the nineteenth-century German scholar Karl Otfried Müller. Bernal argues that Müller placed "the onus of proof on those who accepted the massive ancient testimony rather than on those who challenged it." Bernal's dismissal of the methodology he imputes to Müller helps us to understand the gulf which separates his results from those of most professional historians. The author of *Black Athena* starts from an entirely inverse premise. As far as he is concerned, the burden of proof lies on the scholar who wishes to disprove a claim made by an ancient writer; the ancient text is presumed innocent until proven guilty. Throughout *Black Athena* Bernal points to "kernels of historical truth" and "nuggets of historicity" in ancient myth. He repeatedly concludes that a Classical source relinquishes plausible information. He often affirms that some ancient author offers us a "working hypothesis" for further scrutiny. "Herodotus may have been lying or mistaken," he avers, "but one should hesitate a long time before dismissing him."[38]

There are three possible readings of Bernal's radically different approach to source criticism and modern historical methods in general. The first, a somewhat caricatural image drawn by his most vehement detractors, suggests that he reads ancient texts without a particle of suspicion. In this view, Martin Bernal emerges as the Martin Luther of the classics discipline—urging *sola scriptura* and charging that the institution of source criticism serves ungodly ends. The second reading is that Bernal is a thoroughgoing relativist. As David Lowenthal observes, "Any distance—in time, in space, in culture, in point of view—widens the gulf between the narrator and the audience." In other words, since there is no privileged, objective vantage point from which to reconstruct history, then why accept that source critical methods are an automatic improvement upon Herodotus's method?[39]

The third reading—which I prefer—is that Bernal does not accept that the modern age has achieved moral or intellectual supremacy over previous epochs. He will not elevate modern historians too far beyond ancient historians because the former are, after all, as human as the latter. Irrational hatred of the other is a characteristic of the species—and it is precisely this attribute, he argues, which displayed itself in abundance in the thought of nineteenth- and twentieth-century European scholars. "Most of the founders of the Aryan Model," he charges, "were much less 'objective' than the ancient Greeks."[40]

Bernal's critique could thus be seen as concentrated more on those who use source-critical methods than on source criticism itself. In this reading, *Black Athena* can be construed as a call for greater introspection: let the historian gaze into the hand mirror of self-reflexivity. In so doing, he or she should acknowledge that the deployment of this or that method is not a guarantee of historical objectivity. This is an unobjectionable and unheretical sentiment. One thinks of the words of the great scholar of historiography, Arnaldo Momigliano: "Self-examination is a necessary step not only to personal redemption, but also to objective historical research."[41]

With this generous reading now rendered I would like to note that Bernal has offered no viable alternative or corrective to the approaches which he believes are responsible for the fall of the Ancient Model. Nor does he distinguish among better or worse types of exegetical and hermeneutic approaches, leaving us with the impression that he believes all are equally corrupt. His methodological credo seems to be *The Ancients could very well be telling us the truth.* While this is plausible, it is incumbent upon the author to advance a method which might help us to determine how scholars might go about distinguishing truthful accounts from untruthful ones. As Egyptologist John D. Ray asked, "Where are the final criteria to lie?" To this point, Bernal has neglected to articulate such criteria, and this leaves him vulnerable to Mary Lefkowitz's charge of "eager credulity" toward the ancient sources.[42]

Conversely, any reader of Bernal's thick volumes recognizes that his attitude toward contemporary historians is anything but credulous. It is a peculiarity of *Black Athena* that its author subjects modern historians to the types of criticism which they usually apply to the ancients. Bernal questions their motives in writing ancient history. He ponders the impact of their religious and political beliefs on their intellectual production. He exposes their discursive machinations and delineates the errors they make. This is undoubtedly warranted; but academic criticism is an omnidirectional enterprise. Bernal's undertaking would have benefited immeasurably had he applied his formidable powers of critique to the ancient authors as well.

Being an inquisitor who likes to play devil's advocate, however, I would note that Bernal's wholly idiosyncratic methodology poses a variety of troubling questions to "Hard Moderns" such as myself and others. In the third chapter of *Not Out of Africa* Mary Lefkowitz reviews the texts which Bernal used in order to build his Ancient and Revised Ancient Models. "The idea that Greek religion and philosophy has Egyptian origins," she asserts, "may appear at first sight to be more plausible, because it derives, at least in part, from the writings of ancient Greek historians." These words are the prelude to what could be read as a veritable manifesto of the Hard Modern position—the approach which characterizes how most professional scholars go about studying ancient history.[43]

Lefkowitz advances an unyieldingly critical appraisal of the writings of Herodotus, Diodorus, Plato, Strabo, and the Church Fathers on the subject of Egypt. These figures cannot be counted on to offer us objective accounts due to their "respect for the antiquity of Egyptian religion and civilization, and a desire somehow to be connected with it." This admiration inclined them to overemphasize their dependency on, and contacts with, the land of the Pyramids. But the presence of a pro-Egyptian bias in Greek thought is not the only drawback which Lefkowitz discovers. In true Hard Modern fashion she enumerates the failings of the ancients qua historical researchers. The Greeks were not sufficiently skeptical or critical of their informants and sources. They did not speak Egyptian, nor did they draw upon Egyptian archives. They misunderstood the very Egyptian phenomena they studied. Their linguistic surmises were predicated on simplistic and erroneous assumptions. They looked at Egypt "through cultural blinkers," producing an image that was "astigmatic and deeply Hellenized."[44] Again and again Lefkowitz pounds the point home—how poorly the Greeks performed when compared to us: "Unlike modern anthropologists, who approach new cultures so far as possible with an open mind, and with the aid of a developed set of methodologies, Herodotus tended to construe whatever he saw by analogy with Greek practice, as if it were impossible for him to comprehend it any other way."[45]

Lest there exist any remaining question as to the reliability of the ancients, Lefkowitz proceeds to pulverize the final link in the chain of historical transmission. Not only were the Greeks unreliable, but so were their Egyptian informants. Jewish and Christian Egyptians supplied the gullible Greeks with self-aggrandizing information as "a way of asserting the importance of their culture, especially in a time when they had little or no political powers."[46]

In my own work on the Hebrew Bible I have argued, with no less passion, that we simply cannot believe what this text reports. Accordingly, I concur with her objections, and I find Lefkowitz's overarching skepticism justified. Yet in her haste to skewer Bernal, Lefkowitz avoids considering the drawbacks or implications of her—I should say "our"—position. At one point in *Not Out of Africa* she speaks of the "important," "generally accurate," and "useful information" which Herodotus makes apropos of the Nile, Egyptian monuments, and individual pharaohs. The problem is that Lefkowitz never pauses to tell us why she considers these particular observations to be "generally accurate." Further, she and other critics of Bernal often evince their own "eager credulity" toward ancient texts, especially when it permits them to criticize Bernal. Lefkowitz, for instance, is not averse to citing and accepting Herodotus's testimony if it helps her to refute *Black Athena*'s historical claims.[47]

And here we arrive at the paradox of the modern study of ancient history; the very documents whose accuracy and integrity we everywhere subject to withering skepticism are often the best sources of information we have about the ancient world. Like a vassal prince who sits at the king's table, the exegete is at once disdainful and dependent. The categorical rejection of an ancient document as a source of historical information is a luxury which we simply cannot afford. The challenge of studying ancient history consists of figuring out a way to extract accurate data from a corpus—a very small corpus—of maddeningly problematic texts.

While quick to criticize the verisimilitude of his sources—and often rightly so—Bernal's critics have neglected to confront any of the hard questions which his heresy has posed to Hard Moderns. How do we go about wresting useful information from ancient sources which we acknowledge are deeply flawed? In what instances can we concede that the ancients are in a better position to illuminate historical truth than the moderns? Are there any instances in which ancient writers offer us veridical information? If so, what are the criteria we invoke to come to such a conclusion?

2

The Revised

Ancient Model

The Heretic's Cocktail

This model accepts, on the one hand, that Egyptians and Phoenicians settled in and had a massive influence on Ancient Greece. On the other hand, it takes into account the undoubted fact that Greek is fundamentally an Indo-European language.

—Martin Bernal, *Black Athena, 2*

Renfrew clearly feels a need to establish a fundamental and *echt* Greece unaffected from the outside or at least from the south east. . . . I believe that such purity is illusory and that there have been contacts between Greece and the Near East since the Neolithic. These have been more or less intense at different periods and at certain times the cultural drift was from the Aegean to Egypt and the Levant. In general, however, for the period 3400–400 BC, the principal flow of influence was from the Near East to the Aegean.

—Martin Bernal, "Phoenician Politics and Egyptian Justice in Ancient Greece"

Martin Bernal views his Revised Ancient Model as a corrective to the biased Aryanist renderings of history. Some commentators have neglected to report that he sees his preferred paradigm as a considerable improvement on the Ancient Model as well. As much as the author might value the testimony of the ancients, as much as he is skeptical of contemporary historical research, he is no intellectual Luddite. As we shall see, the Revised Ancient Model is steeped in the methods, theories, and, most importantly, the bibliographies of modern scholarship. Moreover, it borrows consciously from the very Aryan Models which are dubbed racist and anti-Semitic on every other page of *Black Athena*. Unlike other campus radicals, Martin Bernal has no moral qualms about using the master's tools to dismantle the master's house.

Martin Bernal's Extended Seminar

In the initial installment of *Black Athena* (1986/1987), Bernal expressed his desire to demonstrate the *"competitive plausibility"* of the Revised Ancient Model. The explicit goal of the first volume, then, is not to prove that the Aryan Models are wrong. Rather, it is to show that they provide a "less plausible" means of accounting for the historical evidence and a less useful "framework for future research" than the Revised Ancient Model. In the conclusion to Chapter 3 below we will have an opportunity to discuss the notion of "competitive plausibility" at some length.[1]

For now, we should bear in mind that the publication of volume 2 in 1991 marked—in Bernal's eyes at least—a significant change in approach. The author was now far less reluctant to champion his paradigm unreservedly: "I have given up the *mask* of impartiality between the two models [Revised Ancient versus Aryan]. . . . Now, instead of judging their competitive heuristic utility in a 'neutral' way, *I shall try to show how much more completely and convincingly the Revised Ancient Model can describe and explain the development and nature of Ancient Greek civilization than can the Aryan model.*"[2]

Yet few scholars would accept that Bernal wore the mask of impartiality in volume 1, only to shed it, reluctantly, in obedient deference to the facts by volume 2. Timothy Reiss, writing in the *Canadian Review of Comparative Literature,* observes: "*Black Athena 1* was emphatically not a measured comparison of the forms of knowledge. It was not intended to be. Bernal's provocation was quite deliberate." Molly Myerowitz Levine refers to it as "unabashedly one-sided" and "passionately argued." And Martha Malamud remarks, "Aware that he will be taken to task both for his ideas and for his status as an interloper in the field of Hellenic studies, Bernal comes out with his guns blazing." I am in accord with these opinions. Bernal seemed as intent on endorsing the Revised Ancient Model and discrediting the Aryan Models in 1986 as he was in 1991.[3]

Polemical consistency notwithstanding, there are in fact substantive differences between the two volumes. In volume 1, the author speaks predominantly as a risk-taking sociologist of knowledge and intellectual historian, thrashing the academic establishment and its intellectual status quo. Five years later, a disciplinary metamorphosis occurs. He now speaks as a heretical historian/archaeologist/philologist, thrashing the academic establishment and its intellectual status quo. The second installment also offers the first comprehensive exposition of the Revised Ancient Model. In presenting it, Bernal would shift some of his attention—and derision—away from the Aryan Model onto a new paradigmatic culprit: the Ultra-Europeanist Model. He would also reassess various components of the historical reconstruction outlined in the introductory chapter of his 1986 volume.[4]

But it is the quality of presentation which provides the most glaring contrast between the volumes. A recurring criticism of volume 2 concerns its lack of coherence and internal organization. Emily Vermeule complains that "confusion is the cost of reading it." Classicist Ann Michelini felt as if she were "in the presence of a brilliant mind filled with diverse information but lacking a braking mechanism." Once again, I agree. Bernal's credo seems to be *Information (about the ancient world) wants to be free.* The author pummels his readers with excessive details and minutiae. He digresses bewilderingly. He spends pages on tangential issues which could have been dealt with appropriately in the span of a footnote. He often neglects to address some of the most fundamental questions raised by his hypothesis.[5]

There is also a seminarlike quality to the second volume. At points, especially in his etymological analyses, Bernal appears to be floating theories before his audience. As Michelini points out, he has a penchant for hesitant locutions on the order of "It is just possible" or "It seems quite plausible that," and so on. Of course, there is nothing wrong with a little conjecture, particularly in the study of ancient history. Yet insofar as dozens, sometimes hundreds, of hypotheses are mentioned per chapter, the second volume bears resemblance to a work in progress. In an age when the scholar is a sober, prudent specialist, there is nothing quite like *Black Athena* and its author, a congenital intellectual gambler.[6]

But gambling occasionally has its rewards, especially for those who know how to play the house. Bernal's cheery war cry of "*Je m'en fiche*" in the face of scholarly convention permits him to break with traditions of dubious value. Most contemporary studies in ancient history are hyperspecialized, occasionally to the point of absurdity. *Black Athena*, by contrast, offers readers a "grand theory"—as C. Wright Mills might say—of the Bronze Age Mediterranean. Working within this macrohistorical framework it succeeds in raising new questions, reinvigorating old ones, and identifying interrelations which provide leads for future research. Stanley Burstein's remark that Bernal "has succeeded in putting the question of the origin of Greek civilization back on the historical agenda for the first time in decades" illustrates just one example of this text's positive contribution. In spite of the burdens it presents to readers, *Black Athena* is creative and thought-provoking scholarship.[7]

It is my goal in this chapter to present a general exposition of the Revised Ancient Model as best I understand it. Considerations of space will lead me to do considerable violence to the complexity of the original. Innumerable details of the author's historical reconstruction will be omitted from the forthcoming analysis. And in spite of these omissions the present chapter is, like the second volume itself, long, tedious, and difficult.

The Intimate Mediterranean: The Gordon-Astour School

In the introduction it was noted that Bernal's work must be understood as a synthesis of previously existing scholarship. Perhaps no body of research has had so much influence on *Black Athena* as that of the Semitists Cyrus Gordon and Michael Astour. Bernal freely acknowledges that he is "standing on the shoulders" of these controversial philologists. The correspondences are so clear that one may conceivably view the author as a disciple of a Gordon-Astour "school." Its foundational texts were Astour's *Hellenosemitica: An Ethnic and Cultural Study in West Semitic Impact on Mycenaean Greece* (1965), Gordon's *Common Background of Greek and Hebrew Civilizations* (1962) and *Ugarit and Minoan Crete: The Bearing of Their Texts on the Origins of Western Culture* (1966), as well as numerous articles published throughout the 1950s and 1960s. These two scholars were themselves influenced by earlier and contemporary proponents of *ex Oriente Lux*, such as Robert Brown, Victor Bérard, T.B.L. Webster, Hans G. Güterbok, Gabriel Germain, Chester Starr, and John Pairman Brown, to name but a few.[8]

Gordon and Astour each attempted to Orientalize the cultural genealogy of the Occident. Nuzi, Ebla, Crete, Cyprus, Tyre, Ugarit, Israel, Babylon, and the Egyptian Delta—these are seen as the formative loci of the Western narrative. Periclean Athens is but a late chapter. In their conception, the genesis of the West occurred not in the middle of the first millennium, but in the Bronze Age, the first half of the second millennium in particular. The concept, indeed the very phrase, "Western civilization" is as much an obsession for Gordon as it is for Bernal. In 1966 Gordon writes, "Ugarit was in contact with the forerunners of the classical Greeks and Hebrews, who were destined to found Western civilization by their combined and parallel achievements." In a 1968 contribution he would even Semitize the Latin half of the Greco-Roman legacy by observing that the Phoenicians were "in Italy at the dawn of Roman history." In contrast to the dominant "isolationist" conception of the Aegean, these scholars found cosmopolitanism, "ethnic integration," and internationalism within the ancient Near East.[9]

An extremely positive evaluation of ancient Phoenician (and to a much lesser extent, Egyptian) civilizations stands as one of the more noticeable tenets of their approach. Bernal, like Gordon and Astour, repeatedly affirms that for most of the Bronze Age (ca. 3200–1200 B.C.E.), and even prior, these Afroasiatics were more culturally and militarily advanced than their neighbors in the Aegean. (Though Bernal does place much more emphasis on the Egyptian side of the equation than Gordon and Astour would.) Insofar as the pinnacle of Greek civilization is traditionally dated to the fifth century B.C.E., this assumption of Eastern superiority in hoary antiquity is not altogether controversial.[10]

More controversial, however, is their understanding of the impact which these Eastern cultures had on the Aegean in hoary antiquity. A phrase which one repeatedly encounters in *Black Athena* is "massively influenced," as in, "Taken together, the cultic, mythical, toponymic and archaeological evidence strongly suggests that Boiotia and other regions of Greece were massively influenced by Egypt and the Levant during the Bronze Age." This can be compared to Astour's notion of a "revolutionizing wave of Near Eastern influence" on Crete.[11]

In order to accept this idea of massive Oriental influence we must assume that Afroasiatics had the means and the desire to infiltrate the Aegean world in the Bronze Age. Bernal adamantly supports this position. As with his predecessors, his ancient Mediterranean is intimate and concatenated. Its cardinal points are linked by trade networks whose grooves have been inscribed by thousands of years of economic activity. Whereas other scholars envision the Mediterranean in terms of cultural seclusion, these writers see mobility and interaction. In one telling passage Bernal remarks that "contacts between Egypt and the Aegean [in the third millennium] can be seen in many ways as local traffic."[12] In this intimate and fluid Mediterranean the predominant flow of armies, commodities, and ideas in antiquity was from East to West. In Bernal's scheme—and I find this approach very attractive—these infiltrations came not all at once, but at different points in history, resulting in a layering process (see below). The notion of the Aegean's prolonged, albeit uneven, soaking in the oils of various Egyptian and West Semitic (eventually by the second millennium, Phoenician) cultures strikes me as a good example of Bernal's willingness to theorize the historical process in all of its awesome complexity.[13]

A rather large degree of trust in the accuracy of ancient texts is another hallmark of the school. Source criticism, as we have seen, is not Bernal's forte. In 1962 Gordon made an argument which Bernal would replicate a quarter of a century later: "Herodotus . . . knew about the early Phoenician penetration of what is now Greek territory. But many modern scholars still choose to discount his testimony and instead follow current schools of thought. . . . The Phoenicians were influential throughout the East Mediterranean early in the second millennium B.C."[14] As with Bernal and Gordon, Michael Astour would read ancient myths and find "kernels of truth" and "genuine traditions."[15]

The Gordon-Astour school did not carry the day. The once vaunted name of Gordon, in particular, has in some quarters come to be associated with crankiness. This is mostly attributable to his theories regarding interrelations between the hemispheres in works such as *Before Columbus: Links between the Old World and Ancient America* and *Riddles in History* and the infamous controversy sparked by his championing the authenticity of "The Canaanite Text from Brazil." The reviews of Astour's *Hellenosemitica* were also generally dismissive, if not hostile. Not surprisingly, both scholars lived in a state of high tension with what they perceived to be the academic status quo. With varying degrees of candor, each charged that the massive influence of Semitic civilizations on those of the Aegean had been unjustly ignored by their colleagues. In *Hellenosemitica* Astour would rather cryptically allude to "undeniable partiality" and "old prejudices" against admitting any Semitic influence upon Greece. Gordon would presage Bernal's sociology of knowledge by alleging that the idea of genuine architectural relations between Canaan and Minoan Crete has "disturbed some writers who want to keep Minoan civilization free of Asiatic—and particularly Semitic—'contamination.'"[16]

Modified Diffusionism

The aforementioned assumptions of interaction, massive East-to-West influence, extensive trade contacts, colonizations, and so on, bear much in common with a theoretical approach to pre- and ancient history known as *diffusionism.* Colin Renfrew offers the following definition: "The so-called diffusionist view held that nearly all the significant advances in prehistoric European culture, and especially in technology, were brought about by influences, by the diffusion of culture, from the Near East." Renfrew is actually one of the leading figures in the turn away from diffusionist (or migrationist) approaches to Aegean prehistory. The distinguished Cambridge prehistorian's sophisticated antidiffusionist methods and theories have carried the day; up until very recently this approach has occupied a central place in anthropological, archaeological, and linguistic approaches to prehistory.[17]

It is Colin Renfrew, in fact, who surfaces as the master villain of the second volume of *Black Athena.* I would note that the villain sneaks up on us, so to speak. In the first installment Bernal spent most of his time concentrating on the Aryan Model and its architects. By 1991, however, Renfrew suddenly emerges as Bernal's full-blown dialectical partner. The latter characterizes the former's approach as "Isolationist" or "Ultra-Europeanist." According to Bernal this model maintains that "there has been no culturally significant settlement of Greece from the outside since the beginning of the Neolithic period."[18]

Renfrew is critical of the type of diffusionist perspectives which characterize the work of the Gordon-Astour school, among others.[19] Note the absence of interaction, massive East-to-West influence, extensive trade contacts, colonizations, and so on, in the following quote from Renfrew's *Before Civilization: The Radiocarbon Revolution and Prehistoric Europe:*

> It cannot be doubted that there were indeed contacts between Crete and both the Levant and Egypt from about 3000 B.C., but a critical examination makes it doubtful whether they were of any great consequence to the society. *I believe, indeed, that this first European civilization was very much a European development, and that most of its features can be traced back, not to the admittedly earlier civilizations of the Near East, but to antecedents on home ground, and to processes at work in the Aegean over the preceding thousand years.*[20]

Renfrew's zeal to see European prehistory "as the result of local processes, in essentially European terms," has made him an object of Martin Bernal's "sociology of knowledge."[21]

As opposed to the extreme diffusionism described and criticized by Renfrew, Bernal identifies himself as a "modified diffusionist." Once again, Bernal is basing himself on the work of earlier scholars, in this case the once influential theories of V. Gordon Childe and Oscar Montelius. As a modified diffusionist Bernal believes that "cultural change can take place as the result either of outside influences or of internal developments, *or most commonly from a complex interplay of both.*" Be that as it may, the differences between Renfrew's "model of autochthonous origins" and Bernal's Revised Ancient Model could not be more pronounced. Bernal's Mediterranean is far more spatially compressed, far more interactive, far more Orientalized, far more hybrid, and, as we shall see below, far more "multicultural" than Renfrew and others would accept.[22]

The questions that Bernal asks himself are ones that Renfrew would find irrelevant and misguided: In what precise manner did Oriental cultural diffusion occur in this intimate Mediterranean? Was this massive Afroasiatic influence achieved through military invasion, colonization, suzerainty, a "sphere of influence" (i.e., direct diffusion)? Or, in a more roundabout manner, through trading networks and diplomatic ties (i.e., indirect diffusion)? We are witnessing one of those discursive fissures mentioned in my introduction: the Renfrew school works from the premise that cultural diffusion cannot explain the origins and subsequent development of Aegean civilizations. This same premise, conversely, is the very basis of Bernal's Revised Ancient Model.

The Third and Fourth Millennia/A Compromise Model

Its diffusionist foundations now enunciated, we may turn to an examination of the basic tenets of the Revised Ancient Model. This analysis might be best pursued by drawing comparisons between the claims of the two Ancient Models. Both agree that colonizers from the East infiltrated the Aegean. Both maintain that the invaders encountered a population of Pelasgians (i.e., the indigenous population of mainland Greece according to Classical sources). The paradigms offer somewhat different answers as to the linguistic identity of this group. Herodotus (representing the Ancient view) maintained that the people in question were non–Greek speaking. In the Revised Model, these Pelasgians are held to be southern Anatolian speakers of an Indo-Hittite language who settled mainland Crete and Greece in the seventh millennium.[23]

The Revised Model, then, posits Indo-Hittite speakers in the Aegean. When did contacts between these Aegean-dwelling Pelasgian Indo-Hittites and Afroasiatics begin? Bernal adduces evidence which points to encounters in the fourth and third millennia, though he insinuates that this process may have begun much earlier. In the first four chapters of volume 2, Bernal states his evidence in favor of Afroasiatic influence on the Aegean in the fourth and third millennia. He believes that in this period there might have been Egyptian and West Semitic colonizations. (Note that the northwest Semitic Phoenicians arrive on the historical scene only in the second millennium.) He is certain, however, that there were diplomatic and trade contacts between the two regions at this time.

Pursuing Astour and Gordon's lead, Bernal concentrates on the island of Crete, arguing seductively that in this period it "received massive cultural influences from the Near East in general and Egypt in particular." Crete in this scheme is cast as a crossroads of Anatolia, the Greek mainland, and the Egyptian and Levantine coasts. Bernal refers to it as a meeting point of "many different East Mediterranean cultures." Centrally located as such, Crete often functioned as a "transmitter" and "filter" of these Afroasiatic cultures to Mainland Greece.[24]

In attempting to prove Afroasiatic impact on Crete, the author advances a wide variety of arguments, only a few of which I shall now mention. Following Keith Branigan, Saul Weinberg, and others, he points to correspondences between pottery and pottery production techniques in third-millennium Crete and Palestine. Similar Levantine affinities are found with Cretan burial customs. Elsewhere, Bernal argues that the Cretan Linear A word *yane* (wine) can be equated with the Semitic forms for wine such as Hebrew *yayîn* and Akkadian *inu*. All this leads to the conclusion that "early Minoan culture was permeated by Near Eastern and Egyptian influences."[25]

Bernal brings the same model of massive influence to his study of mainland Greece in the third millennium. Basing himself on an article in Greek by Theodore Spyropoulos, "Egyptian Colonization of Boiotia," Bernal points to the existence of "a pyramid" in Thebes. He proceeds to sift through ancient legends which suggest that Kadmos the Phoenician (in the second millennium) recolonized this city. Again following Spyropoulos and others, the author suggests that the massive drainage projects undertaken in Boiotia were stimulated by Egyptian techniques in hydraulic engineering.[26]

As with Astour, Bernal is fond of using place names (toponyms) as means of establishing Eastern presence in the Aegean. In looking at toponyms such as Boiotia and Arkadia, Bernal floats a variety of etymological theories which connect these with Egyptian and Semitic words. After a lengthy and complicated discussion he remarks: "What can be made of these various etymologies? The fact that so many of them appear to originate from Egyptian and West Semitic *would seem to suggest the presence of Egyptian and West Semitic speakers when the names were given.*"[27]

So far we have seen Bernal posit an Egyptian and West Semitic presence in the Aegean in the fourth and third millennia. It is at this point that the Revised Ancient Model takes an unexpected turn. For the Pelasgians of the Aegean are held not only to have been massively influenced by Afroasiatics, but, eventually, by Indo-Europeans as well. The latter are seen as having repeatedly infiltrated Greece from the north in the middle of the third millennium.[28] This intricate argument is summarized in Table 2.

Surprisingly, Bernal is borrowing a basic premise from the Aryan Model. This approach made much of hearty, white, chariot-riding Indo-Europeans sweeping down on Greece (and other regions of the world) from the north in the twenty-third century B.C.E. or thereabouts (see Chapter 3 below). It is this concession to orthodox scholarship which would lead the author eventually to refer to his revised version as "a compromise model."[29]

Sesōstris(Re-)Visited

The author's Revised Ancient Model also agrees with most of the Ancient Model's reports on Sesōstris. As the reader will recall, the latter appears

TABLE 2.

The Pelasgians, Their Invaders, and the Subsequent Development of Greek Language and Culture (according to Bernal)

7000–6000: Indo-Hittite speakers from southern Anatolia arrive in Aegean (Greeks of the Classical period would later identify them as "Pelasgians")

7000–4000: Probable contacts between the Indo-Hittite "Pelasgians" and various entering Afroasiatic cultures

4000–3000: Increased likelihood of contact between Afroasiatics and "Pelasgians" (most likely indirect diffusion, but possibly direct diffusion)

ca. 2500: Indo-European speakers invade from the north and settle the Aegean

1750–1570: Hyksos invasion and colonization of Aegean. Possible period of alphabetic transmission via Phoenicians

1470–1200: Massive trade between Mycenaen Greece and the Middle East under the auspices of a Pax Aegyptiaca. Possible period of alphabetic transmission via Phoenicians

---

in the writing of Herodotus and others as a conquering Egyptian monarch who dispatched a garrison of possibly black soldiers to the Colchis.

Bernal devotes the entire fifth and sixth chapters of volume 2—nearly ninety pages—to an analysis of Sesōstris, his son, and their epic movements. Why would the author lavish so much attention upon an issue which, as we are about to see, is peripheral to *Black Athena*'s central argument? First, he will use the Sesōstris evidence as a means of strengthening his claims regarding Egyptian imperial activities in the Levant and the Aegean. The author wishes to challenge the Aryan Model's assumption that the Egyptians were always "'stay-at-home' conservative people"—not the type of civilization which might be inclined to venture out into the Aegean.[30]

Second, he uses these chapters as a means of proving that the ancient sources he so frequently cites are often reliable and trustworthy. Modern historians, Bernal charges, have generally viewed the Sesōstris tales as "the most absurd set of stories told by Herodotus and Hellenistic Greek writers." If Herodotus's account of Sesōstris could be corroborated by recent findings, then a vindication of ancient historiography—and *Black Athena*'s methodological program—would be achieved.[31]

The analysis of Sesōstris focuses on three lines of evidence: (1) the Mit Rahina Inscription, (2) the Tôd Treasure, and (3) the archaeological data of destruction levels from Anatolia in the early second millennium. The recently discovered Mit Rahina Inscription sheds light on the land and sea expeditions of two kings of the Egyptian Middle Kingdom. These monarchs, Senwosret I and his son Amenemhe II, are held to have ruled between 1959 and 1882 B.C.E. According to one school of thought, the Senwosret I mentioned in the inscription is none other than the fabled Sesōstris of Herodotus and other Classical writers. If this were the case, the recently discovered Mit Rahina Inscription would indicate that the Egyptians were anything but "stay-at-home" types. In Bernal's reading of the inscription, there is evidence that these monarchs campaigned in Syrio-Palestine, Anatolia, and Cyprus.[32]

The Tôd Treasure consists of a variety of metal objects discovered in a sanctuary of the God Mont built in Tôd, not far from Luxor in Egypt. The artifacts discovered were found in caskets inscribed with the name of Senwosret's son. It is reasonable to assume that these objects may tell us something about these two kings and their times. Since silver objects were found in the treasure and since these could come only from silver-producing regions such as Anatolia, the Caucasus, and the Balkans, Bernal posits an Egyptian presence in these regions.[33]

Last, let us turn to the Anatolian destruction levels. When an archaeologist speaks of "destruction levels" it means that the site which is examined shows clear signs of having been destroyed at a certain point in time. Thus, when Bernal comes across scholarly literature which discusses concomitant destruction levels in Anatolia, Thrace, Scythia, and the western Caucasus around the beginning of the second millennium, he raises the possibility that Sesōstris(= Senwosret) and his son were the culprits. In light of the three lines of evidence discussed above Bernal claims that these monarchs can be feasibly situated in the vicinity of Colchis. The Revised Ancient Model also accepts as plausible the aforementioned legends of "black" Egyptian soldiers permanently stationed in the Colchis (see Chapter 8 below).[34]

Next—and here his argument is practically impossible to follow—he examines the legend of Jason and the Golden Fleece (some of which takes place around Colchis). Some versions of the Jason epic, he demonstrates, refer to the Colchians as dark skinned. This is taken as an indication that the originators of this story knew of a "black/Egyptian" community (= Senwosret's troops). After offering a few alternate theories, an attempt is made to equate the name Colchis with a somewhat similar Egyptian place name which referred to Upper Nubia. The implication here is that the Colchis of the Black Sea region may have been named by Egyptian conquerors after a comparable place in their homeland.[35]

Shifting his attention to Senwosret's son, Amenemḥe II, Bernal notes that his family was from the south of Egypt, and hence of Nubian (read "black") origin. Bernal attempts to equate Amenemḥe II with Memnōn, a figure who appears in (Asiatic) Ionian legends. In a series of incredibly difficult passages, the author argues that the mythical king of Ethiopia (Memnōn = Amenemḥe II) was cast as a "Black prince with a large army marching through Western Anatolia." This would account for soldiers which Herodotus would label "dark-skinned" and "wooly-haired." Bernal then points to the stories of the fabled Memnōn which arose in northwest Anatolia, precisely where he believes Amenemḥe campaigned. Finally, it is noted that to the north of Colchis one can still find a "black" population today. Bernal speculates that the members of this contemporary community are descendants of the troops dispatched by these adventurous Egyptian kings. This provocative claim will be examined in greater detail in my eighth chapter.[36]

Yet throughout these confusing chapters Bernal does not claim that Senwosret and Amenemḥe penetrated mainland Greece. It is for these reasons that I have labeled the entire Sesōstris exposition as "peripheral." This argument, with its emphasis on trustworthy Greek writers and peripatetic Egyptians, is used to lay the groundwork for the centerpiece of *Black Athena*.[37]

Heretical Operations: The Second Millennium

It is only after 275 pages of the second volume that we arrive at the nucleus of Bernal's argument: Afroasiatic/Aegean contacts occurring in the second millennium, particularly between the eighteenth and thirteenth centuries B.C.E. It is only within this period that the author will unhesitatingly posit the existence of actual Egyptian colonizations of, and suzerainty over, mainland Greece, the Cyclades, and Crete.[38] The years 1750–1570 are seen as especially important in his analysis: "The formative period of Greek culture must be pushed back . . . to the 18th and 17th centuries BC, in Hyksos times—the age portrayed in the Thera murals. It is most likely that *it was in this earlier period that the amalgam of local Indo-European with Egyptian and Levantine influences that we call Greek civilization was first and lastingly formed.*"[39] This passage calls attention to the two central initiatives of the second volume: the redating of the massive volcanic explosion on the island of Thera and the Hyksos invasion of the Aegean. In confronting these topics Bernal will do nothing less than attempt a hostile takeover of the reigning academic status quo.

One of Bernal's most daring acts consists of the challenge he poses to the standard chronologies used by historians of the Late Bronze Age (ca. 1700–1200 B.C.E.) Mediterranean. This means that he redates historical events which a community of scholars have already dated to their satisfaction. Tinkering with dates is dangerous business, for scholars, often unquestioningly accept these chronologies and base their research on the dates they provide. Subsequent generations of researchers predicate their findings on those who have unquestioningly accepted the reigning system, and so on. Accordingly, when a heretic correctly redates these events, an academic domino effect occurs whereby one theory collapses only to discredit a subsequent theory, and so on. As far as antiquity studies go, an attack on a chronology is an unparalleled act of aggression.

One of Bernal's chronological heresies centers around the dating of the famous explosion on the island of Thera. Most scholars of antiquity have fixed the date at 1450 or 1500 B.C.E.—an assumption which had stood for nearly half a century. Bernal, braced by research from the hard sciences as well as a small group of dissenting archaeologists, argues persuasively that this event actually occurred in 1628 B.C.E. In recent years consensus has begun to tilt toward the higher dating proposed by Bernal and others.[40] The author was not one to miss the heretical implications of his hypothesis: "The 1500 and 1450 dates were embedded in a whole chronological fabric. This fabric was, in fact, the most effective means of defending the orthodoxy. With the establishment of the higher date, we have to reconsider the chronology of the Late Bronze Age, not merely in the Aegean but throughout the East Mediterranean basin."[41]

The redating of the Thera explosion provides a foundation for the Hyksos hypothesis—an initiative which exemplifies all that is invigorating and exasperating about *Black Athena.* In proposing this audacious scheme the author advances an extraordinarily innovative reconstruction of events occurring in the eighteenth century B.C.E. He offers his readers a theory so broad in scope that it can account for a sequence of seemingly unrelated happenings transpiring across three continents. Unfortunately, those who wish to understand *Black Athena*'s historical reconstruction must essentially reconstruct it on their own insofar as it is very difficult to understand.

According to the third-century B.C.E. historian Manetho, the Hyksos who invaded Egypt hailed "from the regions of the East" and were "invaders of obscure race."[42] The neighboring Syrio-Palestinians were far too familiar to the Egyptians to have been referred to as "obscure." This would seem to rule out a West Semitic origin for these invaders. Conversely, an Egyptian text, roughly contemporary with the expulsion of the Hyksos from Egypt in the early sixteenth century, explains their origins differently. In "The War against the Hyksos" King Ka-mose claims: "I went north because I was strong (enough) to attack the Asiatics through the command of Amon, the just of counsels. My valiant army was in front of me like a blast of fire."[43] The term *Asiatics* in Egyptian literature is often used to refer to those West Semites who frequently infiltrated Egypt via the Sinai. So who exactly were the Hyksos? The obscure Easterners of Manetho or the local Semites of Ka-mose? Bernal's answer to this question combines a little Manetho, a little Ka-mose, and a little modern scholarship.

According to *Black Athena* the Hyksos were a mixed multitude, so to speak. The author begins by turning to the writings of various nineteenth- and early-twentieth-century historians, such as Eduard Meyer, who drew an association between the Hyksos and the Hurrians. The latter, also known as the Mitanni, resided in northern Mesopotamia and eastern Syria but spoke neither an Afroasiatic nor an Indo-European language. The Hurrians/Mitanni, apparently, were at some point conquered by Indo-Aryan speakers who left two distinct marks on the vanquished: the names of Aryan deities who the Mitanni regularly invoked and military technology centered around the horse and chariot.[44]

Bernal's Hyksos, however, are not your garden-variety Aryan (or Aryanized) invaders. And this is were things get very complex. The Hyksos, as conceived in *Black Athena*, are not pure-blooded white northerners—as they are envisioned in earlier theories—but a sort of ethnic composite. Beginning in the eighteenth century the aforementioned Aryanized Hurrians march south from their original homeland, which Bernal describes as being in the vicinity of Kurdistan "covering Eastern Anatolia, Northern Syria and Mesopotamia and possibly the Southern Caucasus." As the core group proceeds southward they come across the (West) Semitic cultures of Syrio-Palestine. The result of this encounter is that the northern invaders (i.e., the Aryanized Hurrians) become "Semitized." By the time they reach (and colonize) the Egyptian Delta in the 1740s or 1730s, the Hyksos are a mixture of Indo-Aryan, Hurrian, and Syrio-Palestinian elements and are "overwhelmingly Semitic-speaking."[45]

Bernal is not unaware of the fact that by positing the Indo-Aryan/Hurrians as the drivetrain of the Hyksos he is again flirting with some of the more disquieting aspects of the Aryan Model. For here we have (nominally) Aryan northerners, armed with their superior chariots and horses, rapidly and efficiently bearing down on the sluggish southerners (the Levantines and Egyptians). Nazi images of a master race were predicated on such theories. While acknowledging the implications of his hypothesis the author refuses to flinch, noting that "one should clearly distinguish between what one likes and what is likely."[46]

After penetrating the Egyptian Delta some of the Hyksos were to settle down, whereas others would immediately take to the sea. In the following passage Bernal reconstructs the Hyksos' southward movement through the Levant and Egypt and their ensuing journey north to Crete, the Cyclades, and mainland Greece:

> Just as the greatest "Hyksos" influence on Egypt was the introduction of neigbouring Palestinian culture, it would seem likely that in the Aegean the greatest influence of a "Hyksos invasion" would come from Crete. Thus, while the Egyptian Hyksos would seem to have been Indo-Aryan-Hurrian-Semitic and those in Crete would be Indo-Aryan-Hurrian-Semitic-Egyptian, those in the Cyclades and Mainland Greece would have been Indo-Aryan-Hurrian-Semitic-Egyptian-Cretan.[47]

One aspect of the Hyksos invasion which Bernal stresses is the incredible speed with which they infiltrated the Aegean. Within no more than ten years after overrunning Egypt a group of Hyksos invades Crete, around 1730. There they established themselves as rulers, perhaps as "some kind of confederation of Hyksos princes at times under the hegemony of the Egyptian Hyksos pharaoh." In support of his theory the author concentrates on archaeological finds on Crete from the MM III period (1730–1675 B.C.E.). He attributes the destruction and quick rebuilding of three Cretan palaces at the beginning of this period to the arrival of the Hyksos. Bernal also calls attention to the sudden appearance in Cretan artwork of the sphinx and the griffin—two symbols which he sees as official emblems of the Hyksos.[48]

Bernal sees the somewhat uncivilized Hyksos as having been eventually swallowed by the older and more sophisticated Minoan traditions which they encountered on Crete. Accordingly, the cultural impact of the former on the latter was minimal. This was not the case, however, for mainland Greece, where "the indigenous culture was at a rather low ebb." Thus, when the Hyksos arrived on the mainland they imparted both their own culture and that of the Cretans. In this manner, Minoan forms are transmitted throughout the Aegean via the Hyksos. According to this scheme much of what is generally

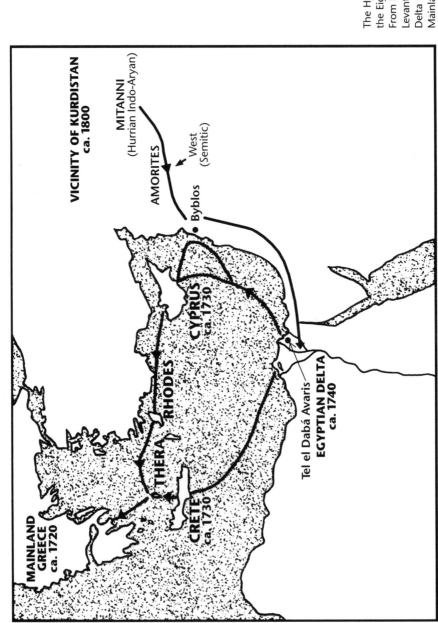

The Hyksos Migration in the Eighteenth Century: From Kurdistan to the Levant to the Egyptian Delta to Crete to Mainland Greece

VICINITY OF KURDISTAN
ca. 1800

MITANNI
(Hurrian Indo-Aryan)

AMORITES

West
(Semitic)

Byblos

CYPRUS
ca. 1730

RHODES

THERA

CRETE
ca. 1730

Tel el Dabá Avaris
EGYPTIAN DELTA
ca. 1740

MAINLAND
GREECE
ca. 1720

considered to be Mycenaean culture in pottery, the arts, architecture, and so forth, is actually a survival of "Hyksos international style."[49]

In attempting to prove that the Hyksos were on mainland Greece, Bernal resurrects a more or less forgotten theory of the Cambridge classicist Frank Stubbings. In his article in *The Cambridge Ancient History* Stubbings analyzed the remains of the famed shaft graves found in Mycenae. An exhaustive analysis of the origins of the burial goods suggested to him that "the possibility of conquest by invaders from Egypt and the Levant deserves serious attention, not least because it is supported by Greek traditions."[50]

As subsequent research was to show, these shaft graves do not solely demonstrate Egyptian (= Hyksos) influence. A variety of other influences (Aegean, eastern Anatolian, Syrio-Palestinian) are also present. The Egyptian, Aegean, and Syrio-Palestinian influences can be accounted for, but how can those from eastern Anatolia be explained within the framework of the Revised Ancient Model? As noted earlier, *Black Athena* assumes that the original core of the Hyksos came from Anatolia and the Caucasus. As such, the transmission of sub-Caucasian culture to mainland Greece came with the Hyksos who first went through the Levant, Egypt, Crete, and the Cyclades.[51] In positing their impact on Mycenaean culture, Bernal writes:

> After a time, the "barbaric" Hyksos warriors of the Shaft Graves were succeeded by more cultivated rulers and traders. For over a century between *c.* 1720 and *c.* 1570 BC there was a cosmopolitan mercantile "Hyksos world"—represented by the Theran frescoes—which included Egypt, parts of the Levant, Crete, the Cyclades and the richer areas of Mainland Greece. Thus, in many ways, what is known today as "Mycenaean" material culture could usefully be seen as "Hyksos" or at least the "Hyksos of the non-Cretan Aegean."[52]

The Alphabet

The aforementioned Hyksos invasion of the mainland was to have a major impact on the development of the Greek language. "In the long run," writes the author, "their chief function was to introduce Egyptian and West Semitic culture and language, which in the succeeding centuries mixed with the native Indo-European-speaking population."[53] This then is the decisive moment in Greek history. Bernal declares: "The period, . . . *c.* 1700–1500 BC, was the one in which Greek as a language and the 'Greek' cultural or national identity were formed and that, during much of this period, considerable areas of Greece were dominated by Semitic- and Egyptian-speaking dynasts and that these high-status cultures and languages had a critical impact on the formation of both Greek and Greece."[54] For Bernal, it was during this same period that the West Semitic alphabet was most likely transmitted to the Aegean by the invading Hyksos princes. The centrality of this issue to the *Black Athena* project is not often recognized. We should recall, however, that the author devoted an entire separate monograph to precisely this question. In *Cadmean Letters: The Transmission of the Alphabet to the Aegean and Further West before 1400 b.c.* (1990), Bernal argued with impressive erudition against yet another orthodox position. The indefatigable heretic challenged traditional "Aryanist" schemes which posit the eighth, ninth, or eleventh centuries B.C.E. as the period in which the West Semitic alphabet was conveyed to the Aegean. Bernal makes the rather radical claim that this process actually occurred as early as the eighteenth century and no later than the fourteenth century.[55]

As usual, the impetus for this hypothesis comes from ancient Greek sources. The author builds upon Herodotus's remark that the alphabet was introduced to Greece by Kadmos the Phoenician. Sorting through a large variety of Greek traditions (as well as the modern scholarship of Michael Astour) Bernal concludes that kernels of historical truth are preserved in these accounts. In his reading, these legends retain an accurate memory of alphabet-bearing West Semites who penetrated and colonized the Aegean world during the Hyksos invasion.[56] In pondering the precise moment of alphabetic reception, Bernal conjectures: "This could be linked to the Egyptian expansion of the Middle Kingdom during the twentieth to eighteenth centuries *but is much more likely to have been during the Egyptian–West Semitic conquests by the Hyksos and their subsequent settlements in and around the Aegean in the eighteenth and seventeenth centuries.*"[57] Although there is little space to mention it here, I would add that Bernal also manages to equate the Hyksos with the Israelites. He argues that the eventual expulsion of the Egyptian wing of the Hyksos from Egypt in the sixteenth century is bound up with the tales recounted in the biblical Book of Exodus. Not surprisingly, this view is attested in the ancient sources as well.[58]

The Critique

As we have seen, the second volume of *Black Athena* makes hundreds of detailed philological and archaeological surmises. With only a few exceptions, these were to elicit a large, rapid, and overwhelmingly negative response from professional ancient historians.

Since the publication of the second volume critics have repeatedly focused on the philological shortcomings of Bernal's enterprise. Some insinuated, or explicitly stated, that the amateur language enthusiast was in over his head. Emily Vermeule writes that "many of Bernal's linguistic claims are no more than assertive guesses." Egyptologist James Weinstein speaks of "factual errors, misstatements, citations of outdated and inappropriate sources, flimsy toponymic identifications and a host of methodological difficulties." In a scathing piece in *Black Athena Revisited*, linguists Jay Jasanoff and Alan Nussbaum of Cornell University charged that their colleague "repeatedly advances etymologies that rely on superficially suggestive but demonstrably secondary phonetic resemblances between Greek and Egyptian or Semitic words." The authors conclude their essay by parsing *Black Athena* with other works of "crank linguistic literature." A similar theme was on the mind of the Dutch scholar Arno Egberts: "As long as [Bernal] persists in distorting the plain linguistic facts, I am prone to regard him as the very crank he is anxiously professing not to be."[59]

Others questioned the soundness of Bernal's philological methodology. Classicist Lawrence A. Tritle charges that Bernal works from "the least satisfactory level of linguistic analysis." For when he wishes to demonstrate similarities between Afroasiatic and Aegean languages he usually focuses on toponyms, mythical elements, trade items, weaponry, and so on. Yet these correspondences may be the result of mere casual contact between geographically distant cultures. If Bernal (and Gordon and Astour by association) wants to prove massive influence or Afroasiatic colonization, Tritle continues, he would need to identify correspondences in the phonological and grammatical structure of Egyptian/Phoenician and Greek, for only these types of similarities would be indicative of intensive and extensive Egyptian, West Semitic, and Phoenician presence in the Aegean.[60] As one Egyptologist writes: "Had the Hyksos indeed established a dynasty in Greece, Semitic and Egypto-Coptic would have been heavily imposed on Greek, in phonetic structure and even in grammar. Evidence of this level of influence is lacking, and hence Bernal's thesis of Hyksos colonization of Greece remains unproven."[61]

In a 1989 piece Bernal would describe the Greek language and culture as "an Afroasiatic superstrate on an Indo-European base." Perhaps, then, he could respond to these charges by claiming that insofar as Greek is an Indo-European language then its grammatical structure, not surprisingly, should evince little in the way of Afroasiatic influence. My problem here is that Bernal seems to be negating an earlier, and I think attractive, component of his hypothesis—namely, massive Afroasiatic influence occurring between the seventh and third millennia prior to the arrival of the Indo-Europeans. In other words, if Egyptian and West Semitic influence was so extensive and commonplace from the Neolithic to the Late Bronze Age, then why should we not observe Afroasiatic presence in the grammatical base of ancient Greek?[62]

Bernal's specific etymological conjectures were also challenged, none more so than the one that informs the title of his book. In his first volume, Bernal derived the name of the Greek goddess Athena from that of the Egyptian goddess Ḥt Nt. Jasanoff and Nussbaum argue that this suggestion "perfectly illustrates the deficiencies of his method." Mary Lefkowitz concludes "the semantic fit is not so close as Bernal suggests." With less rancor, Egyptologist John D. Ray finds this suggestion, among others, "very hard to accept." It is safe to say that this has been the most popular verdict regarding Bernal's efforts to derive Greek words from Egyptian and Semitic etyma.[63]

Objections to the hypothesis have also been raised on archaeological grounds. In his long and sober article *"Black Athena*: An Egyptological Review," Frank Yurco deems it unlikely that Senwosret I (= Sesōstris) marched triumphantly through Anatolia. The Aegean-based silver found in the Tôd Treasure, suggests Yurco, could just as well have been an "import from Greece, worked in Syria and then paid to Egypt as tribute." This stands in opposition to Bernal's view of this metal as some form of Aegean tribute to an Egyptian suzerain.[64]

Egyptologist David O'Connor doubts that the Mit Rahina Inscription can be read as proof of substantial Egyptian military activities in Asia Minor. In his reading of the text, it reports mostly peaceful expeditions and "only one serious raid." Tritle contends that the inscription is fragmentary and unclear, and that Bernal has failed to convey this fact to his readers. Others have alleged that hard archaeological evidence for massive Egyptian influence in the Aegean is lacking.[65]

The Hyksos hypothesis has also not fared well. Ann Michelini referred to it as "a very strange jumble." Frank Yurco sees it as "particularly contradictory." John Coleman points out that Egyptian and Near Eastern records in the Bronze Age "make no mention of a conquest of Greece, either by the Hyksos or by any other people."[66] James Weinstein reacts to the theory thus: "This is all nonsense. No Hyksos royal names have been found in 18th- or very early 17th-century B.C. deposits in Egypt or anywhere else. There is no evidence for the Hyksos being in control of Syria or for being what Bernal describes as a 'multinational corporation.'"[67]

Another frequently voiced objection centers around the overwhelmingly East-to-West trajectory of Bernal's hypothesis. The author, it is claimed, has underestimated cultural flow in the opposite direction. Mary Lefkowitz suggests that any invasion in the Hyksos period "went from Greece to Egypt, rather than in the other direction." Guy MacLean Rogers asserts, "The cultural road to early Greece apparently was not a one-way street; rather there were many two-lane highways of cultural exchange, connecting many different Near Eastern cultures not only with the early Greeks but also with each other."[68]

Many of the aforementioned scholars have accused Bernal of "strawmanship." Here it is alleged that contemporary historians *have* recognized the importance of Egyptian and Levantine culture in the Aegean. Edith Hall asserts that the theory of Middle Eastern influence on Greece in the Bronze Age "is a less controversial contention than Bernal's plangent tone suggests he would like it to be." Stanley Burstein shows that since the 1970s "scholarly views concerning relations between Greece and Egypt have changed significantly." Gleaves Whitney surveys college textbooks on the ancient Near East and finds a patently respectful attitude. "Since at least the early 1950s," he writes, "the best 'Western civ' textbooks have credited Greece's neighbors generously with contributing to the rise of Hellenic culture." Indeed, the list of contemporaries of the Gordon-Astour school discussed above as well as the work of contemporary researchers suggest that Bernal is not alone.[69]

Of course the scholarly literature which Hall, Burstein, Whitney, and others cite does not speak of Hyksos colonization, "Cadmean letters," or "massive Afroasiatic influence." And as we have just seen, *Black Athena*'s critics have almost categorically dismissed these suggestions. Interestingly, many of these same scholars who reject direct diffusion—and argue that Bernal is obsessed with the idea of colonization—are open to his claims of indirect diffusion and casual contacts between these regions in the Late Bronze Age. Frank Yurco, for example, doubts Bernal's theories of Hyksos invasions, though he views the idea of trade relations and diplomatic contacts as "in essence reasonable."[70]

I would speculate that if any sort of common ground will emerge in *Black Athena*'s second decade, it will be on the role of Afroasiatic trade influences, particularly in the final frame of the Bronze Age, where Bernal speaks of a *Pax Aegyptiaca*.[71]

Conclusion: From the Root to the Petal

In Chapter 4 below we shall see that one of the basic assumptions which informs *Black Athena* is that when historians reconstruct the past they are profoundly affected—be it consciously or unconsciously—by the political and intellectual climate of their own times. Given Bernal's acute awareness of this rather banal sociological truism, it is somewhat surprising that he fails to recognize the congeniality of his own hypothesis with the current multicultural *Zeitgeist*. Everywhere in *Black Athena* there is mixture: cultural hybridity, diversity, cosmopolitanism, interaction between disparate peoples yielding newer and more exquisite fruits of civilization.

Conversely, his analysis permits little space for monoculturalism. For Bernal the idea of a pure, unadulterated Greek protoculture is a chimera. In a contribution to the 1989 special issue of *Arethusa* Bernal makes an assertion very much in the spirit of the current academic age: "The notion of *purity* is, in fact, my essential enemy. Purity is always a mirage even in the most isolated societies, but to try to impose purity on a peninsula and archipelago in the middle of the East Mediterranean is particularly absurd."[72]

Nowhere is this disdain for the monocultural approach more evident than in the Hyksos hypothesis. For as they advance the Hyksos adopt and assimilate new peoples and thus new cultural forms, such as language, military technology, architectural styles, and artistic techniques. What we have, then, is a kind of militant multicultural juggernaut—heterogenous to the core, open to influences from other cultures, spreading these around the map, mutating into an even more complex cultural mosaic as they come into contact with (and overrun) other societies.[73]

Bernal's analysis of the Greek language serves as yet another example of his multicultural *Weltanschauung*. It is only through the mixture of various tongues that the Greek language is formed. A very simplified recipe for Bernal's heretical cocktail may be served as follows:

Pelasgian Indo-Hittite[74]+
WEST SEMITIC and EGYPTIAN (7000–2000 B.C.E.) +
INDO-EUROPEAN (2500 B.C.E.) +
EGYPTIAN (via Hyksos) +
WEST SEMITIC (via Hyksos)[75] =

the GREEK LANGUAGE

In a 1990 interview Bernal remarks: "I'm not trying to challenge the centrality of Greece to the European tradition, but I do challenge the nature of Greece itself. Greek culture is so exciting because it represents a mix of the native Balkan-Indo-European-speaking population with Egyptian and western Semitic populations. The linguistic and cultural mix was extraordinarily productive in cultural terms."[76]

Hence the Greece he renders us, the western Civilization he envisions, is anything but pure. Instead, ancient Greece is viewed as heterogenous from its very genesis, saturated by cultural innovations of African and Near Eastern provenance. As noted in our second epigraph, this process is seen as beginning in the fourth millennium (perhaps earlier) and culminating three thousand years later. It is certainly not a coincidence that the temporal parameters discussed in the epigraph extend to the fifth century B.C.E.—Classical Greece. Once again, *Black Athena* is emitting what Molly Myerowitz Levine referred to as its "high-voltage ideological charge." For it is has become a commonplace of Western intellectual thought that the Classical period was among the most glorious of Greek—if not human—history. The author is claiming that this Golden Age cannot be viewed as a consequence of some unique, unadulterated Greek genius. Rather "the greatness that was Greece" was the result of a long, slow process of borrowing from older, more advanced Afroasiatic civilizations.[77]

Now, when Martin Bernal says that to accept the Revised Ancient Model is "*to rethink the fundamental bases of 'Western Civilization'*" (emphasis in original), we must take him literally and figuratively. Figuratively, he is saying that the Western intellectual tradition, whose origins are placed in Classical Greece, owes a debt to the achievements of the Afroasiatic East. Yet the literal dimensions of this claim are even more jarring. From the very moment of its conception, Greek culture and language are inextricably bound with those of Semitic and African civilizations. Bernal's Revised Ancient Model, then, contends that the delicate flower which we refer to as Classical Greece is a hybrid from its seed to its stem to its petals.[78]

3

The Aryan

Models

The preceding analysis of the tradition regarding the alleged Phoenician colonization over the Aegean Sea has hopefully made clear that it completely lacks a historical foundation, and that it rests on the basis of nothing more than late and transparent combinations of myths and place names.

—Julius Beloch, "Die Phoeniker am aegaeischen Meer"

And so it is with our own past. It is a labour in vain to attempt to recapture it: all the efforts of our intellect must prove futile. The past is hidden somewhere outside the realm, beyond the reach of intellect, in some material object (in the sensation which that material object will give us) of which we have no inkling. And it depends on chance whether or not we come upon this object before we ourselves must die.

—Marcel Proust, *Swann's Way*

The Revised Ancient Model, as we have just seen, evokes soothing multicultural themes. The Hyksos are construed as—to borrow a line from Nabokov—"a salad of racial genes." The Greeks are cast as intellectual disciples of Afroasiatic mentors. The cosmopolitanism and internationalism of the ancient Near East are repeatedly stressed. The sublime civilizations of antiquity are understood as by-products of human cultural diversity.

The Aryan Models, by contrast, summon the considerably less soothing and less multicultural specter of modern race-thinking. Proponents of the Aryan Models spoke in terms of "racial purity," "unadulterated blood," "African and Semitic inferiority," "the superiority of the German people," the "negative characteristics" of other "races," and so on. Born in the nineteenth century, the Aryan Models are the intellectual hellspawn of a monocultural age.

It would be overstating the case, however, to view Bernal's Revised Ancient and Aryan Models as irreconcilable opposites. We have already seen—and we shall see again—that the competing paradigms share basic theoretical assumptions. Be that as it may, the author expresses little enthusiasm for the Aryan versions. In *Black Athena* it is claimed that these were "conceived in what we should now call sin and error." Elsewhere, it is asserted that the Aryan Model is "untenable," "bankrupt," "extraordinarily inefficient," "an aberration," and "unable to cope." Not surprisingly, Bernal predicts that his Revised Ancient Model will soon dethrone its Aryan counterpart.[1]

In what follows I would like to review Bernal's reconstruction of what he has called the Broad Aryan Model (which he usually refers to as simply the Aryan Model) and the Extreme Aryan Model. I will identify those assumptions which are found in both Aryan paradigms. Once their common ground has been explored, I will proceed to survey the distinct theoretical territory inhabited by each of these approaches. Prior to doing so, however, I shall briefly review some of the basic tenets of the Indo-European language hypothesis as it emerged in the late eighteenth and early nineteenth century. This short detour will make it easier for the reader to understand *Black Athena*'s substantive claims.

"The World Is Not the Same World"

In his *Archaeology and Language: The Puzzle of Indo-European Origins,* Colin Renfrew recounts eloquently the tale of "a quite extraordinary discovery." In 1786 Sir William Jones, an English supreme court judge stationed in India, noticed that there existed an abundance of similarities between disparate and seemingly unrelated languages. Jones had realized that definite resemblances could be detected in the grammatical structure of Sanskrit (the classical language of ancient India), Latin, ancient Greek, Gothic, Celtic, and Persian. In positing a connection between Sanskrit and ancient Greek Jones, the father of modern Indology, was to proclaim: "Pythagoras and Plato derived their sublime theories from the same fountain with the sages of India."[2]

In 1813 another Englishman, Thomas Young, would invent the term *Indo-European* (although some scholars would eventually employ *Indo-Germanic, Caucasian,* and *Aryan,* among other usages). In this category he and others placed the aforementioned languages along with many of those spoken in nineteenth-century Europe. What is important to recall, then, is that these researchers established a link not only between Sanskrit and Greek, but between these ancient tongues and the languages of European modernity. For it was soon established that contemporary German, French, Italian, and English, among others, were younger members of this linguistic grouping.[3]

The first generation of Indo-European researchers were confronted with a basic question, a question which Renfrew refers to as "one of the most notable and enduring problems in the prehistory of the Old World." Stated succinctly: How could the astonishing resemblances between these geographically dispersed languages be accounted for? One plausible solution—but not the one which Renfrew favors—was predicated on the metaphor of the family tree. In this conceptualization, a language is seen as possessing corre-spondences to other languages within its family. Contemporary French, Spanish, and Portuguese, for example, are seen as branches, or relatives, who share a series of common ancestors (e.g., Latin, Italic).[4]

The oldest common ancestor within a given language family is known as the *protolanguage*. Modern linguists, it must be stressed, have never heard or read the words of any protolanguage. It is an entirely theoretical language, one reconstructed from common words found in its descendants. *Proto-Indo-European*, for example, is often seen as the prehistoric progenitor of the languages mentioned above. The vocabulary of this language is conjectured on the basis of similarities identified in its offspring (e.g., Latin, Old Persian, Sanskrit, Greek).

Many early Indo-European researchers maintained that the Proto-Indo-Europeans comprised a linguistically homogenous group sharing a common territory. Scholars differed as to where this original *Heimat* (homeland) was situated. The favorite candidates were Central Asia or the southern Russian steppe in the vicinity of the Caucasus Mountains. At various points in his-tory, according to one widely accepted hypothesis, groups of these Proto-Indo-European speakers departed from the homeland. The various waves of migrations led some to Iran, India, and Greece, to name but a few destinations. (Notice that in each of the preceding cases the Indo-European invaders bear down upon these regions from the north.) And now we may better understand the family-tree approach to the great Indo-European question. In time, each of these splinter groups, isolated from the homeland, was to develop its own language—one related to, albeit distinct from, Proto-Indo-European. Thus, the existence of similarities between languages spoken in such far-flung regions was attributed to their shared relation to a common ancestor.[5]

The impact which these findings had on all departments of nineteenth-century thought cannot be overemphasized. One commentator remarked, "Not in a merely scientific or literary point of view, but in one strictly practical, the world is not the same world as it was when men had not yet dreamed of the kindred between Sanscrit, Greek, and English." Or, as Maurice Olender writes in *The Languages of Paradise: Race, Religion, and Philology in the Nineteenth Century*: "The discovery of Indo-European caused a furor that extended well beyond the discipline of comparative philology. All the human sciences, from history to mythology, and soon to include 'racial science,' were affected by the discovery of a tongue that was known not only as Indo-European but also as Aryan."[6]

The Aryan Models: Common Assumptions

I have already had occasion to note that many of the theoretical struc-tures and analytical frameworks found in *Black Athena* are consciously bor-rowed from earlier scholarly work. Bernal's examination of the rise of the Indo-European language hypothesis and its relation to various ideological impulses of the nineteenth century is no exception. This line of inquiry has been explored in such well-known studies as Léon Poliakov's *Aryan Myth* and *History of Anti-Semitism,* vol. 3, and Edward Said's *Orientalism,* to name but a few.

As I see it, Bernal makes three original contributions to this conversation. First, he places the rapid ascent of Indo-European theory and racial science within the context of a sudden and unprecedented collapse of the Ancient Model. Arguing as a historian of ideas, the author posited the existence of a belief in the Semitic and African antecedents of Greek civilization. He further claimed that this Ancient Model was a commonplace for nearly 2,500 years. Having constructed this framework, Bernal is able to portray the rise of the Indo-European hypothesis not just as a new idea, but as a new idea whose emergence roughly coincided with the categorical negation of an old idea (the Ancient Model).

His second contribution consists in advancing a compelling ideological reading of theories which focused on the "Pre-Hellenes." We shall examine this initiative momentarily. The third is to subsume the Indo-European language hypothesis under the more general rubric of his Aryan Model. As such, the former emerges as the major, albeit not the only, intellectual foundation of the latter. It is, of course, not coincidental that Bernal employs this sinister nomenclature: "I call the new model 'Aryan' rather than 'Indo-European' because, as used in the nineteenth and twentieth centuries, the word 'Aryan' does not merely convey 'Indo-European.' It also connotes a belief in the desirability of northern purity."[7] With this said, we may now proceed with our sketch of those assumptions shared by both Aryan Models.

The Aryan Models are seen by Bernal as a radical rupture in human thought. If we were to conceive of Western civilization as a railroad line upon whose tracks various conceptions of the world have traveled, we could only be impressed by the tremendous distance covered by the Ancient Model. The first station would be the Classical period, where we find this view assumed across the writings of Aeschylus, Herodotus, Euripides, Plato, and Isokrates, among others. Its journey continues, in relatively unaltered form, through the rise of Christianity, the so-called Dark Ages, the Middle Ages, and the Renaissance. It rolls along through the incipient decades of the Enlightenment. Finally, between 1830 and 1860 the Ancient Model is bumped from the tracks by the steely new Aryan Model and is consigned to the stockyard of abandoned Western thought.[8]

According to *Black Athena* there developed in the first decades of the nineteenth century a radically new conception of ancient history. It was, in large part, inspired by the vertigo-inducing linguistic breakthrough discussed above. The Aryan Model's first assumption is that waves of Indo-European invaders arrived at mainland Greece from the north around 2300 B.C.E. This northern invasion is seen as the decisive event in the linguistic history of Western civilization, for the invaders would impart their Indo-European language—not Egyptian and Phoenician as suggested by the Ancient Model—upon the indigenes. In this manner ancient Greek could be configured as a distinguished and early member of the Indo-European language family.[9]

By the 1830s the Indo-European hypothesis was to undergo its racialist turn. Scholars now held that the original speakers of this language were members of the Aryan "race." In terms of phenotype, its members were construed as blue-eyed, blond-haired, and "white." As Olender observes, researchers often "ascribed to the groups they called Aryan (or Indo-German or Indo-European) characteristics they attributed to the Greeks." In the extremely racist climate of the time, argues Bernal, the belief emerged that these Aryans were superior to all other "races"—a distinction which they had repeatedly earned by victoriously sweeping down upon feeble southerners with horses and iron chariots.[10]

In a review of *Black Athena,* Constantine Giannaris calls attention to the self-serving and tautological nature of this nineteenth-century belief in Aryan supremacy: "The unquestioned superiority of this *Heimat,* this civilization, this language, in comparison with the surrounding civilizations of the Eastern Mediterranean, obviously explained the subsequent superiority of Western European countries, the rapid development of their industrial resources and, hence, their moral right to conquer the rest of the world." We might say that it is at this point in Western intellectual history that the theory of an Indo-European/Aryan language family mutates into the theory of an Indo-European/Aryan racial dynasty—an ageless monarchy whose present and future rule is legitimated by virtue of glorious conquests in the distant past.[11]

The Pre-Hellenes: "Racially Pure, Linguistically Mixed"

Thus, Aryanists held that mainland Greece was invaded by Indo-Europeans in the middle Bronze Age. Who did these Aryans encounter when they arrived? There are two answers to this question within Bernal's somewhat confusing scheme: the Pelasgians and/or the aboriginal "Pre-Hellenes."

It will be recalled that in the Ancient Model the native inhabitants of mainland Greece were referred to as Pelasgians. Bernal's revised paradigm held that these Pelasgians were Indo-Hittite speakers whose language was eventually massively influenced by Egyptian and West Semitic. In the Aryan Models, by contrast, the native inhabitants of Greece are not held to be Indo-European-speaking. As such, they were linguistically distinct from their conquerors. In the nineteenth century Aryanists viewed the indigenes as Pelasgians. By the second decade of the twentieth century they would begin to refer to this group as the "Pre-Hellenes."[12]

Yet Bernal stresses that according to the Aryan Model, the Pelasgians, or Pre-Hellenes, and the invading Aryans were construed as being of similar "racial stock." The author cites Ernst Curtius, writing in 1857, who viewed the Pelasgians as "inferior Aryans." If Bernal is correct, the racist implications of this scheme cannot be exaggerated. The Hellenic Aryans who invaded Greece in successive waves encountered other "white" peoples on the mainland (the

Pelasgians or Pre-Hellenes); one "white" population is superimposed upon another, and ancient Greek prehistory (and blood) is rid of Semitic and Egyptian (read, non-white) elements.[13] In an interview with Michael Eric Dyson, Bernal elaborates on his analysis of the Pre-Hellene hypothesis:

> The Aryan Model . . . maintains that Greece was inhabited by "soft" but civilized people who were conquered from the north by people speaking an Indo-European language called Aryan. It also maintains that Greek civilization is a result of all that mixture, especially the conquest by the Europeans over the local population, who were white, not Egyptian or Semitic. So you have a linguistic mixture in that they're Indo-European speakers and something else. But no racial mixture. So the Greeks are racially pure and linguistically mixed.[14]

The Reliability of the Ancient Sources

The nineteenth-century architects of the Aryan Model, contends Bernal, were confronted with two rather formidable obstacles. First, as discussed in Chapter 1 above, the ancient Greeks themselves seemed convinced of Egyptian and Phoenician influence on their civilizations. There were, after all, a not inconsiderable number of documents in which this view was chronicled in some detail. And herein lies the second problem: the same did not hold true as regards the purported Aryan invasion. Bernal demonstrates that at the time of the inception of the Aryan Model (1830–1860), there was no ancient textual documentation or archaeological evidence which attested to the types of northern, Indo-European migrations envisioned by the Aryanists. Nor did such evidence exist as regards the Pre-Hellenes in the early twentieth century. This resulted in what Bernal dubbed the "appeal to oblivion": in the absence of any hard evidence, researchers had to "fabricate" facts in order to buttress their scheme.[15]

It was in response to this state of affairs that another major thrust of the Aryan Models was to develop. The ancient Greek sources were indicted and convicted on the charge of historical inaccuracy. According to *Black Athena,* the key figure in developing this accusation—and in fact immuring the Ancient Model until its recent rescue by one Martin Bernal—was Karl Otfried Müller. In his writings the brilliant nineteenth-century philologist—who Bernal views as "probably anti-Semitic"—called into question the reliability of those ancient works which discussed Egyptian influence on ancient Greece. Salomon Reinach once referred to him as the "avowed enemy of the hypothesis of Oriental influences." It was Müller's hypothesis that actual contacts between Egyptians and Greeks were "late." In other words, the really significant encounters between these societies occurred between the fifth and first centuries B.C.E., not between the eighteenth and fifteenth centuries B.C.E. Müller reasoned that writers living in the Classical and Hellenistic periods were in no position to offer valid data pertaining to events occurring a thousand years in their past. Hopefully, the reader can see the correspondence between this position and what I labeled earlier the Hard Modern approach.[16]

The ravages of time, apparently, did not equally impair the accuracy of nineteenth-century European philologians. For although they stood nearly 3,500 years away from these same events, it was their belief that their new paradigms of knowledge (i.e., the Indo-European language hypothesis) and tools of historical inquiry (e.g., comparative linguistics, source criticism) rendered their conception of antiquity more scientific and hence more valid. Bernal employs the German word *Besserwissen*, or "knowing better," as a means of describing the attitude of superiority which characterized the writings of these modern historians. From their perspective they had surpassed their ancient colleagues: Aeschylus rendered obsolete by the Aryan hypothesis, Plato's testimony invalidated by the discovery of Proto-Indo-European.[17]

Such an approach laid the groundwork for a convenient refutation of the Ancient Model. Scholars working within the Aryan paradigms began to speak of *interpretatio Graeca:* the erroneous belief of the ancients that their civilization had been heavily influenced by the Egyptians and southwest Asians. As the Africanist Basil Davidson observes, Aryan scholars were "obliged to shove whatever the ancient Greeks had thought and written about African origins right under their academic carpet, and lose it there." This task, Bernal believes, was accomplished with great efficiency. Between 1820 and 1860 C.E. the long-lived Ancient Model had been discredited by professional scholars of antiquity.[18]

There is, of course, a poignant irony in this development. The very Greeks who are credited with having produced the most sublime civilization of antiquity are simultaneously held to have been shoddy historians suffering from some sort of collective Orientomaniacal delusion. Bernal maintains that for Aryanists the Greeks "were superior in every aspect of their culture except their writing of ancient history and their understanding of Greece's relationships with other cultures."[19]

The Two Models: The Broad and Extreme

To this point I have articulated six basic historical tenets of Bernal's reconstructed Aryan Model: (1) mainland Greece was invaded from the north by successive waves of Indo-European speakers; (2) these Indo-Europeans were members of a (superior) "white," "Caucasian," or Aryan "race"; (3) they encountered a non-Indo-European-speaking population (the Pre-Hellenes, or Pelasgians) on mainland Greece; (4) the indigenes, while speaking a different language, were nevertheless the same "race" as the northern invaders; (5) the superimposition of this Indo-European Hellenic language on top of that of the non-Indo-European-speaking Pelasgians/Pre-Hellenes results in what we have come to recognize as ancient Greek; and, (6) the ancient Greeks themselves misconstrued their own ethnic origins and intellectual roots insofar as they attributed them to Oriental civilizations.

Both Aryan Models share these beliefs. There are, however, a few differences between the versions. The (Broad) Aryan Model, which blossomed in the 1840s and 1850s, denies the validity of ancient legends of Egyptian colonization. Accordingly, references to colonizing Egyptians (e.g., the story of the Danaans, legends of Hyksos invasions, etc.; see Chapter 2 above) are parsed under the rubric of *interpretatio Graeca*. Herodotus, with his tales of extensive Oriental influence, is thoroughly discounted, as are like-minded ancient authors. In a similar vein, all modern archaeological finds of Egyptian artifacts in the Aegean region are ignored or explained away as insignificant coincidences.[20]

Proponents of the Broad Aryan Model, says Bernal, do not completely reject the notion of Afroasiatic influence on Greek culture, for while Egyptian influence is denied, the possibility of *Phoenician* colonization and cultural penetration in the Aegean is left open. Be that as it may, Phoenician contributions (e.g., the transmission of the alphabet to the Greeks) and colonizations (e.g., the legends of Kadmos) are often seen as questionable and/or inconsequential. The author maintains that the Broad Aryan Model survived until 1925–1935, with a recrudescence occurring in the 1960s and 1970s. Accordingly, we are presently living under the hegemony of the Broad Aryan Model.[21]

The rise of the Extreme Aryan Model is correlated with the ascendancy of European anti-Semitism in the nineteenth and twentieth centuries. Bernal argues that in the 1890s and between 1920 and 1930 (when it temporarily replaced the Broad Aryan Model) the Extreme Model enjoyed its greatest popularity. (By 1985 this paradigm had lost ground and a general return to the Broad version is witnessed.) The Extreme Model may be construed as a more thoroughly Eurocentric and anti-Semitic version of the Broad Aryan Model. Its early proponents, men like Julius Beloch, Rhys Carpenter, and Salomon Reinach (who was Jewish), denied not only Egyptian influence on the Aegean, but Phoenician influence as well. All Afroasiatic traces were thus expunged from Greek prehistory. Bernal writes, "Thus, by the Second World War, it had been firmly established that Greece had not significantly borrowed culturally or linguistically from Egypt and Phoenicia and that the legends of colonization were charming absurdities, as were the stories of Greek wise men having studied in Egypt."[22]

Although it has not garnered much attention in the Controversy, *Black Athena* sporadically makes reference to a fifth paradigm, referred to as the Ultra-Europeanist Model. The Broad and Extreme Aryan Models as well as the Revised Ancient Model all share a basic "diffusionist" assumption. As we saw in the previous chapter, in this view Greek language and culture developed through the interaction of distinct human societies. In the Ancient Models, the external stimulus on the Aegean comes from the Afroasiatic south and southeast. In the Aryan versions, from the Indo-European north.[23]

The Ultra-Europeanist Model is predicated on an *isolationist*, as opposed to a diffusionist, assumption. The metaphor of the migrating, subdividing language family, so resourcefully employed by nineteenth- and twentieth-century students of Indo-European, is rejected. Instead, such scholars as Renfrew and V. I. Georgiev speak of "a model of autochthonous origin." Here it is suggested that cultures may develop in relative isolation. As such, internal "processes"—not invasions, migrations, and trade—are seen as the primary determinants and stimulants of linguistic evolution. In Renfrew's estimation, the Greek language developed in Greece from a population of earlier Indo-European speakers who had been there since the Neolithic.[24]

In this scheme ancient Greek is not held to be a hybrid; neither Aryan nor Afroasiatic invasions are seen as having played a significant role in the development of Greek language and culture. The term *Ultra-Europeanist* thus refers to the tendency of proponents of this model to see the evolution of ancient Greek (as well as other European languages) as a relatively independent process—one which borrowed little from non-European cultures.[25]

The Pleasure of Recognition

To this point, I have scrutinized those historical arguments which Bernal believes derailed the Ancient Model. In so doing, I have essayed to unpack the following claim made on the second page of *Black Athena*: "According to the Aryan Model, there had been an invasion from the north—unreported in ancient tradition—which had overwhelmed the local 'Aegean' or 'Pre-Hellenic' culture. Greek civilization is seen as the result of the mixture of the Indo-European-speaking Hellenes and their indigenous subjects."[26] It must be restressed that the type of mixture posited in Aryanist readings is linguistic, not racial. "The Pre-Hellenic Aegean populations," Bernal points out, "were sometimes seen as marginally European, and always as Caucasian; in this way, even the natives were untainted by African and Semitic 'blood.'" It might be said that upon encountering one another the invading Aryans and the vanquished Pre-Hellenes experienced the pleasure of recognition; both groups are held to have been "white" Europeans.[27]

Given Bernal's disdain for the ideological ramifications of these views, it is somewhat surprising to learn that he agrees with a few of the Aryan Model's basic claims. This approach is consistent with his belief that the racist character of a theory does not necessarily undermine its factual legitimacy. While he rejects the Pre-Hellenic hypothesis as well as assumptions of Caucasian/Aryan superiority, he nevertheless accepts the major tenet of the Aryan Model. In volume 2 he writes, "Greek is essentially Indo-European and hence . . . at some stage there must have been one or more invasions or infiltrations from the north." The author's (and hence the Revised Ancient Model's) disagreement with the Aryan versions is one of degree.[28]

In order to understand this difference we must begin by noting that a good deal of the ancient Greek vocabulary which we possess cannot be conclusively related to Indo-European. As philologian Gary Rendsburg notes, words such as *Athēnai* (Athena), *sophia* (wisdom), *nektar* have never been convincingly connected to words or roots in the conjectured Indo-European protolanguage. In Bernal's estimation, these three examples are not mere exceptions to the rule. Philologists who work within the Aryan paradigm, he claims, have been able to relate only half of the ancient Greek lexicon to Indo-European etymologies. This is perhaps the most important single statistic advanced in *Black Athena*, for this leads Bernal to speculate as to where the other half of the Greek vocabulary might have come from. As a means of engaging this issue he would state the following methodological rule of thumb: "I maintain that in cases where there is no plausible Indo-European etymology for a Greek word, it is permissible to look for loans to neighboring languages, especially those like Egyptian and West Semitic for which there is strong archaeological, documentary and traditional evidence of close contact with Greece."[29]

In discussing the composition of the Greek lexicon Bernal proffers a provocative recalculation: ancient Greek is 40 to 50 percent Indo-European (i.e., the percentage which has been conclusively connected to Indo-European by previous researchers), nearly 25 percent Semitic, and 20 to 25 percent Egyptian. This opinion stands in sharp contrast to that of "Aryanist" scholars. They typically viewed the non-Indo-European half of ancient Greek as emanating from a "Pre-Hellenic" substratum.[30]

The Critique: Libel and Credibility

The critique of Bernal's Aryan Model has been somewhat less voluminous, though no less vociferous, than the critique of his Revised Ancient Model. With varying degrees of rancor, scholars have questioned the accuracy of his depictions of eighteenth- and nineteenth-century writers. It is frequently charged that the author of *Black Athena* has misread, misrepresented, and oversimplified the work of those he has accused of supporting the Aryan Model. The following remark of the intellectual historians Suzanne Marchand and Anthony Grafton epitomizes this line of critique: "Bernal simply has not done enough work to deserve respect or attention as a historian of European thought about the ancient world."

In many instances, his detractors explicitly question his scholarly credibility. Others stop just short of accusing him of libeling his subjects. Rhetorical indulgences aside, I would observe that this critique is, quite often, convincing. Let it be noted unequivocally: Bernal has made many, many mistakes. An honest accounting of these errors will be necessary if he wishes to maintain the integrity of his Aryan hypothesis.[31]

As we shall see in the following chapter, during the half decade of the Controversy most scholars of antiquity, even the hostile ones, accepted Bernal's assertion that their disciplinary ancestors were in some way racist and anti-Semitic. With the publication of *Black Athena Revisited* in 1996, however, a more skeptical evaluation of this claim was advanced. Writers in this volume generally limited their focus to one or perhaps two of the many dozens of figures Bernal had either explicitly or implicitly classed as intellectual

Aryanists. Whereas Bernal the generalist painted in broad strokes, these specialists concentrated on the specific details of his canvas. This scrutiny uncovered notable deficiencies in the author's scholarly technique. In his article "The Tyranny of Germany over Greece?" Robert Norton examines *Black Athena*'s treatment of Johann Gottfried Herder. Here is Bernal on the legendary scholar in the first volume:

> Herder himself stayed within the universalist bounds of the Enlightenment, maintaining that all peoples, not merely Germans, should be encouraged to discover and develop their own genii. Nevertheless, the concern with history and local particularity, and the disdain for rationality or "pure reason" apparent in his views and those of other late-18th- and early-19th-century German thinkers including Kant, Fichte, Hegel and the Schlegels, provided a firm basis for the chauvinism and racism of the following two centuries.[32]

Norton, in a revision of an essay delivered to a scholarly panel sponsored by the International Herder Society, takes exception to the suggestion that Herder's writings are in some way responsible for subsequent chauvinism and racism. He proceeds to make a variety of observations all unified by the theme that a thorough and responsible scholar, one who was truly familiar with Herder's work, would never make the types of claims found in *Black Athena*. Bernal's discussions of Herder, he charges, "rest virtually exclusively on secondary sources." Even more damaging, it is shown that Bernal cited an allegedly anti-African excerpt from Herder without actually having read it. When Norton tracks down the quote in question, it becomes clear that Herder's passage could not possibly be interpreted as chauvinistic.[33]

Norton acknowledges that Herder evinced some racist tendencies in one of his "youthful essays." Yet this must be counterbalanced by the fact that the more mature Herder, far from being an Egyptophobe, "has nothing but the highest praise for the Egyptians." He adduces evidence which proves that Herder warned his colleagues against the ethnocentrism inherent in their works. (Herder, in this reading, even seems to adumbrate a version of the Ancient Model.)[34]

What Norton does for Herder, Guy MacLean Rogers does for George Henry Grote. In his essay "Multiculturalism and the Foundations of Western Civilization," Rogers argues that Bernal has inaccurately labeled the British classicist a racist, anti-Semite, and Romantic. The argument which Rogers forwards is persuasive; my own examination of *Black Athena*'s treatment of Grote reveals that nearly every criticism Bernal makes of him focuses on the latter's positivism and uncritical admiration for Greece. It is only at one point in his text that Bernal labels Grote a racist. In commenting on Barthold Niebuhr, Connop Thirlwall, George Grote, and Ernst Curtius he writes, "There is also no doubt that all were racist and that all were Romantics with a passionate love for their images of Greece."[35]

But where in *Black Athena* did Bernal substantiate his claim that Grote was a racist? The answer is, Nowhere—and unfounded accusations such as this one justifiably infuriate Bernal's critics. The problem is compounded when we consider that Grote may have been no rank anti-Semite. As Rogers points out, Grote, who held various positions in the University of London, was committed "to higher education for Jews, dissidents and Nonconformists." Rogers ushers the reader to the following conclusion: If Bernal could be so wrong about Grote, how can we trust that similar errors were not made in his discussions of dozens of other scholars?[36]

Josine Blok's critique in the *Journal of the History of Ideas* is of especial interest insofar as she has mastered the bibliography of Karl Otfried Müller, the very individual Bernal accused of destroying the Ancient Model. As with the scholars mentioned above, Blok points to a variety of simplifications, erroneous readings, absences, and errata in Bernal's scattershot analysis of the storied Classical scholar. She observes that Bernal discussed "only four of Müller's several hundred publications" and relied extensively on the secondary literature. This lack of familiarity, predictably, leads Bernal to commit a variety of errors. It emerges from her discussion that Müller was neither a simple Eurocentrist nor pronouncedly anti-Semitic.[37]

Last, I would add that Bernal commits identical errors in his brief discussions of Max Weber. In a 1989 contribution on the nature of Phoenician slave society, the author refers to the German sociologist as being "true to the Extreme Aryanism of his time." Why is Weber depicted in this manner? Because (1) he believed that slave society emerged in Greece, not Phoenicia, and (2) he included no chapter on the Phoenicians in his *Agrarian Sociology of Ancient Civilizations* (published posthumuously in 1924).[38]

By now the reader knows what is coming. To begin with, Weber's study does feature chapters on ancient Mesopotamia, Egypt, and Israel. By Bernal's criteria, how does that signal conformity to the Extreme Aryan Model? Further, the same Weber accused of walking lockstep with the Extreme Aryanism of his day is none other than the scholar who tirelessly campaigned to find a university post for his Jewish colleague Georg Simmel, the same Weber who in his "Science as a Vocation" lamented that a Jew trying to find a job in the German academy had no chance, or as he wrote, "lasciate ogni speranza." While not without ambiguity, Weber's relation to anti-Semites in Germany was extremely antagonistic, as Wolfgang Mommsen has shown. As for racism or race-thinking, we could look at Weber's jeremiad served up to the racist and anti-Semite, Dr. Alfred Ploetz.[39] Among other observations indicating an unusually forward-looking perspective on these issues for the year 1910, we have this biting remark: "I feel myself to be a cross section of several races or ethnic nationalities, and I believe there are very many in this group who would be in a similar position. I am partly French, partly German, and as French surely somehow Celtically infected. Which of these races then . . . flowers in me? Which race must flower in me if social circumstances in Germany are to flower?"[40] Anyone looking for further evidence on this issue should consult Ernst Moritz Manasse's 1947 article, "Max Weber on Race."

It leaves little doubt that aside from an essay Weber wrote at the age of six-teen, his views on race were well ahead of his Extreme Aryanist times.[41]

All of this seriously impugns Bernal's reliability. I do not doubt that he has identified authentic instances of chauvinism among nineteenth- and twentieth-century scholars, but R. A. McNeal is correct in charging that "Bernal is far too careless in his use of the term racism." It is thus understandable that some commentators simply refuse to trust Bernal. It is the author's respon-sibility to acknowledge and amend these errors and refine his arguments. It is also the author's responsibility to stop using a rhetorical formula which he has made excessive use of over the years. He often responds to a specialist's challenge with an answer like, "Sure I'm wrong, *but . . .*" Although his admissions of error are not infrequent, I cannot think of any major compo-nent of his original hypothesis which he has actually abandoned.[42] In order to foster a more constructive dialogue with his critics, Bernal needs to aban-don, categorically and unequivocally, the many erroneous claims made in his work.

Conclusion: Competitive Plausibility; or, Proof as Ruse

With the historical unit of our inquiry drawing to a close, we are now familiar with each of *Black Athena's* five major models of Greek origins (Ancient, Revised Ancient, Broad Aryan, Extreme Aryan, and Ultra-Europeanist). As noted in Chapter 1 above, Bernal originally averred that the Ancient Models were more "competitively plausible" than the others. In Chapter 2 it was demonstrated that the majority of historians balked at this claim. "Competitive, but not very plausible," quipped Egyptologist James Muhly. Other critics have challenged the concept of competitive plausibil-ity itself. Robert Pounder professes that "undergraduate term papers are failed everyday for indulging in 'competitive plausibility.'" It is my belief, how-ever, that the notion of competitive plausibility ranks as one of *Black Athena's* most timely theoretical contributions to the study of the ancient world. Even though the author seems to abandon this initiative in his second volume, or perhaps betray its rhetorical code of honor, I feel obliged to explain and defend it here.[43]

Martin Bernal opposes any type of historical research which presumes that an absolute, definitive understanding of events occurring in deep antiquity can be achieved. In order to gain perspective on this idea, we must ponder the sheer massiveness of the void which confronts us. We reconstruct proto-Indo-European even though we have never heard or read any of its original words; we speak of Pelasgians in spite of the fact that we have no documentation from the second millennium as to their existence; we write dissertations about the date of the Thera explosion in the absence of any contemporaneous account of its occurrence.

In my own research on pre-Exilic ancient Israelite religion, I have called attention to the glaring scarcity of data concerning women, nonprivileged strata, and heterodox elements. As regards Early Iron Age Palestine—nowhere near as undocumented as Bronze Age Greece—we are fairly ignorant of the social and religious lives of groups which account for far more than half of its population. (And what little information we do possess can rarely be said to be trustworthy.) The existence of this void prompts Bernal (and me and others) to affirm—reasonably, I think—that few theories about the ancient world may be proven true or false. Certainty may almost never be achieved. The job of the ancient historian, as Bernal notes, is to propose "the least bad historical narrative." I think of a remark from David Lowenthal's *Past Is a Foreign Country*: "The most detailed historical narrative incorporates only a minute fraction of even the relevant past; the sheer pastness of the past precludes its total reconstruction."[44]

But this is not, Bernal contends, the humble ethos which has guided most researchers. He deplores the rise of what he calls the "scientific historians" of the nineteenth and twentieth centuries. They, it is alleged, viewed the writing of history as a process akin to scientific investigation. In their view a given theory could be proven over and against a weaker one. For Bernal, this positivist approach functioned as a veiled mechanism for defending the status quo. With their preferred theories set in place, establishment historians could simply vitiate any opposing theory by saddling it with the burden of proof.[45] In this understanding proof is a ruse, a means of silencing dissenting voices: "Proof or certainty is difficult enough to achieve, even in the experimental sciences or documented history. In the fields with which this work is concerned it is out of the question: all one can hope to find is more or less plausibility. . . Debates in these areas should not be judged on the basis of proof, but merely on *competitive plausibility*."[46]

Bernal repeatedly challenges the positivist use of "the argument from silence." Aryanist historians, he alleges, discount an opposing claim unless direct, unambiguous archaeological or documentary proof for it can be identified. Thus, even a theory which is predicated on good circumstantial evidence will be rejected by these scholars, if it challenges their beliefs. The author counters that given the inevitable gaps in the archaeological and literary record the absence of evidence pertaining to a good theory does not rule it out. (Bernal himself, unfortunately, occasionally uses the argument from silence.)[47]

Is Bernal espousing a hard methodological relativism? Is he asserting that any historical interpretation is as good as the next, in light of the impossibility of achieving certainty? As opposed to some of his critics, I do not believe this to be the case. Witness the following remarks: "Advocacy of competitive plausibility *is not the same as urging complete relativity or that 'anything goes.'* Although evidence itself is to some extent subjective and often allows or even encourages several different interpretations, it provides limits."[48]

Although not wholly relativistic, Bernal's scheme is not entirely unproblematic. First, he has not convinced me that the majority of ancient historians have been, or are, rank historical positivists. Most, I would venture, are acutely aware that certainty is impossible to achieve. Yet I would concede that many are reluctant to dwell on this unpleasant issue in print. Second, Bernal does not seem to apply the notion of competitive plausibility with any consistency. By 1991, as we saw in Chapter 2 above, he was ready to maintain that the Revised Ancient Model was not only competitively plausible, but a better historical framework than the Aryan Models. As Molly Myerowitz Levine pointed out, "Bernal himself seems now to have moved at least in principle from his earlier posture of competitive plausibility, with its implications of neutrality, to a more conventional scholarly mode of argumentation." In so doing, he seems to betray his critique of certainty in ancient historical research. Adding to the confusion, Bernal continued to invoke the idea of competitive plausibility in his second volume as well as subsequent publications in the 1990s. I would also observe that Bernal's ardent zeal for his Model (throughout the entire Controversy), and contempt for others, does not seem consistent with the sober, dispassionate affect of one who truly believes that theories are merely more or less plausible than one another.[49]

But the most glaring drawback in his exposition of competitive plausibility is one that we have seen before. The author has again neglected to articulate a program for the implementation of his ideas. How exactly do we distinguish plausible theories from implausible ones? Bernal offers no answers to this vexing question, much in the way he neglects to identify any method for gauging the credibility of ancient sources (see Chapter 1 above).

Others have raised adjunct concerns. John Coleman writes, "A case that is implausible but that cannot be ruled out as impossible, as so often happens with archaeology, is not a strong one." Echoing the sentiment is Guy MacLean Rogers: "What may have happened in the past is certainly not the same thing as what probably happened, as best we can reconstruct it, based upon a careful, thorough, contextualized evaluation of *all* the evidence."[50]

Yet the same critique of Bernal can be directed at these scholars, a state of affairs which demonstrates how utterly problematic research in ancient history can be. Where and how, exactly, do they draw the line between the implausible and the impossible? The possible and probable? Will the "thorough, contextualized, evaluation of *all* the evidence," recommended by Rogers yield insight as to which contemporary historical interpretation is probable? I think the answer is no because in most cases *all* the evidence we currently possess is equivalent to but a particle of the evidence that we would need to achieve verisimilitude. The answer is no because our awesome lack of knowledge about the ancient world imprisons us within a discourse of plausibilities, not probabilities. In what must be the most flippant contribution to the Controversy, Sturt Manning sums up the difficulties which confront the ancient historian: "It seems a depressing reality unless one simply chooses to ignore it."[51]

The professional study of ancient history thus requires an etiquette of humility: We ought apologize to our readers for a sparse and often inaccurate historical record; we should qualify our statements endlessly; we are obliged to speak about our preferred hypotheses with considerable understatement; we must repeatedly acknowledge our helplessness in the face of wracking gaps in the historical record. Such an etiquette was distressingly absent in various broadsides aimed at *Black Athena,* nowhere more so than in the writings of Mary Lefkowitz. When she resolves that "the results of [Bernal's] research still cannot be taken as *positive proof* of an Egyptian presence in Greece," she misses the entire point of Bernal's argument—namely, that the unreasonable demand for "positive proof" is a defensive mechanism which annihilates discourse and congeals orthodox positions.[52]

To her credit, Lefkowitz's *Not Out of Africa* was written in clear, coherent English, accessible to the layperson. Unfortunately, the specialist refuses to apprise her general reading public of the great degree of uncertainty involved in her craft. She leaves readers with the impression that there are facts about the ancient world which we (the historians) know; issues that are no longer problematic; truths that have been proven beyond a shadow of a doubt. In lamenting the burdens of having to devote time to refuting Afrocentrists, she notes, "To respond to the kinds of allegations that are now being made requires us in effect to start from the beginning, to explain the nature of the ancient evidence, and to discuss what has long been known and established as if it were now subject to serious question." Elsewhere she writes, "The basic outlines of chronology in the Mediterranean are well known, and all the texts under discussion are readily available in translation in all university libraries."[53]

This notion of "established" facts and translations strikes me as being of the most marginal utility for the study of ancient history. My experience as a student of biblical literature suggests that "established" data have an extremely unpredictable shelf life. How many times has an "established" translation of a biblical verse—one inscribed in the prayer books of hundreds of millions of faithful worshipers—been rendered completely problematic by the discovery of a new corpus of documents or archaeological objects? (Of course, the prayer books are rarely revised even as biblical scholars overturn the most recent retranslations in our profane laboratories of exegesis.) Lefkowitz herself, I would note, is not averse to challenging established translations of Herodotus when it permits her to refute Bernal.[54]

It is understandable, however, if Lefkowitz and other ancient historians feel somewhat manipulated by the heretic's rhetoric. Bernal's concept of competitive plausibility is the solvent of academic orthodoxy—a perfect vehicle for his hostile takeover of the status quo. It demands that accepted theories, monopolies if you will, be forced to compete with others. It makes openness to dissenting voices the foremost responsibility of the historian. It relegates all prevailing assumptions to the status of temporary solutions, to be employed until something more plausible comes along. Once again, Bernal has made a virtue out of necessity. This should not, however, diminish the importance of the issues he forces us to confront.

Part Two

The
Sociological
Argument

Expectations of colleagues and superiors within his department exert pressure upon the junior incumbent to play by the rules of the academic game. These rules require, among other things, intellectual discipline, the observance of fixed standards of scholarship, attention to the contributions of senior men, and, above all, respect for the boundaries of the various specialized fields. Those who attempt to create *ab ovo* are likely to be considered "unreliable" "outsiders" to be mistrusted. Such an emphasis discourages potential generalizers, and young scholars may well feel that safety lies in involvement with narrow problems rather than with broad questions.

—Lewis Coser, *Men of Ideas: A Sociologist's View*

Orthodoxy, straight, or rather *straightened* opinion, which aims, without ever entirely succeeding, at restoring the primal state of innocence of doxa, exists only in the objective relationship which opposes it to heterodoxy, that is, by reference to the choice—*hairesis*, heresy—made possible by the existence of *competing possibilities* and to the explicit critique of the sum total of the alternatives not chosen that the established order implies. It is defined as a system of euphemisms, of acceptable ways of thinking and speaking the natural and social world, which rejects heretical remarks as blasphemies.

—Pierre Bourdieu, *Outline of a Theory of Practice*

4

Atmospheric

Determinism

After the defence of Christianity and the idea of "progress," racism was, I believe, the third major force behind the overthrow of the Ancient Model; the fourth was Romanticism.

—Martin Bernal, *Black Athena*

The rise of the extreme Aryan Model was clearly related to the triumph of European Imperialism and the emergence of modern racial anti-Semitism. Consciously or unconsciously, almost every educated European of the late nineteenth and early twentieth centuries saw Greece as the quintessence of Europe and the Aryan race, and the Phoenicians were seen as resembling their Semitic kinsmen, the Jews.

—Martin Bernal, *Cadmean Letters: The Transmission of the Alphabet to the Aegean and Further West before 1400 b.c.*

Whither Sociology?

To what does Martin Bernal attribute the mercurial rise of the Aryan Model and the swift, unprecedented collapse of its ancient counterpart? (From now on, I shall refer to these two developments simply as the "paradigm shift"). The next three chapters examine *Black Athena*'s sociological response to this question—a response that is at once provocative, schematically flawed, conducive to the generation of intriguing secondary hypotheses, an act of academic heresy, conveniently misrepresented, and—remarkably enough—not one of the more hotly debated aspects of the *Black Athena* Controversy.

The lack of attention to this issue may be blamed, in part, on professional sociologists. In the decade since the publication of Bernal's first volume only one sociological journal—and an obscure one at that—has discussed *Black Athena*. Conversely, nearly every other discipline in the humanities and social sciences has had its encounter (or collision) with this controversial text—as have postmodernists, antipostmodernists, scholars of gender, postcolonial theorists, Afrocentrists, and a battalion of culture warriors. The silence of the sociologists is doubly perplexing when we take into consideration that Bernal repeatedly and proudly labeled his analysis "a sociology of knowledge."[1]

Perhaps this silence might be explained in terms of certain dysfunctions within the culture of sociology. As Craig Calhoun has noted, there is a tendency for workers in this discipline to ignore historical research. Lewis Coser speaks of "the unhappy divorce between sociology and history." Bennett Berger remarks that sociologists, "save for the relatively few exceptions at the top, [are] neither very cultivated nor broadly and humanistically educated." Yet there might be other reasons which account for their absence in the Controversy. Bernal's sociology of knowledge does not resemble the type of scholarship produced by authentic practitioners of the craft. Unlike his research on antiquity and intellectual history, his discussions of sociology do not draw upon the relevant scholarly literature. He almost never cites any sociologists or social theorists in his bibliography. In fact, his entire sociology of knowledge is predicated solely upon one work: Thomas Kuhn's somewhat dated classic *The Structure of Scientific Revolutions*.[2]

Bernal the ancient historian bases his argument on the published research of innumerable scholars. Bernal the sociologist (of knowledge), on the other hand, relies mostly on intuition. And even though his intuition is sometimes quite good, his theories are stated with far less depth and precision than would be desirable. What emerges is an analysis that is not so much explicitly stated and theoretically framed as it is insinuated and improvised. This, as we shall see time and again, renders his hypothesis problematic in the extreme.

Be that as it may, I am of the opinion that his work has redeeming sociological value. The author's "sociological imagination" is impressive. As Perry Anderson phrased it, Bernal has a "remarkable flair for the sociology—perhaps one should say politics—of knowledge." Although never formally trained in this discipline, Bernal manages to raise truly interesting questions about knowledge production and radical innovation. Moreover, his research offers us an abundance of empirical data pertaining to nineteenth- and twentieth-century European intellectual history. This may be used by any sociologist who wishes to explore the interpenetration of ideology (however one wishes to define it) and scholarship.[3]

In the present chapter I will try to identify the basic theoretical assumptions of the author's sociology of knowledge. In Chapter 5 I will criticize them. My sixth chapter will concentrate on Bernal's analysis of the research university. To the best of my knowledge, this represents the first effort to reconstruct and critique *Black Athena* systematically through the optic of any sociological tradition. Unlike my analysis of his historical argument, I do not have the luxury of a preexisting body of research which interrogates the text, interprets the material, establishes critical frameworks, and so on. I can only hope that my exposition is plausible and that it stimulates sociologists and social theorists more experienced than I to advance the discussion.

Is Martin Bernal a Marxist?

As one reads through the reviews, responses, and ripostes which comprise the Controversy, certain claims about *Black Athena* are repeatedly encountered. Some are true. Some are false. Some are both.

It is often alleged that Bernal is a conspiracy theorist (not true), reinventing the wheel (often true), a radical (true!), a racist (false, as far as I can tell), a Eurocentrist (probably untrue, but see below and Chapter 7), an Afrocentrist (true and false; see Chapter 7 again), and a Marxist. The last claim is most germane to our present inquiry. H. M. Currie writes, "I seem to detect in the tone of Bernal's discourse on the alleged contamination of the interpretive tradition more than a touch of the Marxist conspiracy theory of history." David Gress remarks: "What, precisely, is Bernal's ideology? Behind his fashionable anti-Western façade lurks a very traditional Marxism. After all, Bernal dedicates his work to his father, the well-known scientist and Communist fellow traveller John Desmond Bernal."[4]

At first glance, this claim seems improbable. As Edith Hall observes, there is "not a shred of dialectical materialism" in *Black Athena*. Bernal never ventures down those avenues of inquiry traditionally visited by Marxist historians. One thinks of classic works like G.E.M. de Ste. Croix's *Class Struggle in the Ancient Greek World* or Norman Gottwald's *Tribes of Yahweh*, both standard Marxist readings of antiquity. Unlike these authors, Bernal says nothing about class, class conflict, private property, the Asiatic mode of production, and so on. In fact, Karl Marx is branded as an adherent to the dreaded Aryan Model in volume 1. And then there is Martin Bernal himself in 1991 saying, "I am not a Marxist like my father, though I do belong to the Left." So the issue is resolved: Gress is wrong; Bernal is not a Marxist.[5]

Yet if this neat resolution is correct, then we must wonder why the author proclaimed himself a "loose Marxist" in a 1989 contribution. We have seen that prior to researching *Black Athena* in the late 1970s, Bernal wrote *Chinese Socialism to 1907*. This work explored the reception of neo-Marxist ideas in China at the turn of the century. There is also, of course, the influence of his father, the storied "red scientist." More importantly, both Marx and Bernal employ—or can be accused of employing—deterministic models of knowledge production. As Bernal notes: "In some vague way, I feel that the material base—if not always determinant—is always important in the development of society."[6]

A theory that is deterministic claims that "all events and changes in nature, society, and thought are determined by causes and are governed by definite laws." Critics of Marx and his intellectual progeny have often accused them of "economic" determinism. They charge that historical materialists attempt to explain every aspect of human social existence (e.g., art, philosophy, sexual behavior, monumental architecture) by reference to the prevailing mode of production. As Raymond Williams observes in *Marxism and Literature*,

"According to its opponents, Marxism is a necessarily reductive and determinist kind of theory: no cultural activity is allowed to be real and significant in itself, but is always reduced to a direct or indirect expression of some preceding and controlling economic content, or of a political content determined by an economic position or situation."[7]

It is not difficult to apply economic determinism to the fields of literature, art, scholarship, and so forth. Literary critic Terry Eagleton demonstrates that a crudely deterministic or "vulgar Marxist" approach endeavors to explain literature as *"nothing but* ideology." For example, this view would lead one to construe fictional works produced in western Europe in the nineteenth century as solely, irreducibly, the expression of the dominant ideology of burgeoning capitalism. An essential corollary to this view might be labeled the "unidirectionality of causation." This means that while the forces and relations of production influence the type of literature that is produced, the opposite never holds true. Since such "cultural activity" can never be autonomous, it can have no tangible effect on any aspect of the materialist foundation of a society.[8]

Both Williams and Eagleton make the important observation that Marx's (and Marxist) thought is far more supple than critics allege. They point to Friedrich Engels's famous letter to Ernst Bloch in which he disputed the charge of determinism in Marx's writing. The great Antonio Gramsci contested this charge as well: "The claim, presented as an essential postulate of historical materialism, that every fluctuation of politics and ideology can be presented and expounded as an immediate expression of the structure [i.e., the base], must be contested in theory as primitive infantilism, and combatted in practice with the authentic testimony of Marx."[9]

We need not pursue this debate any further. For now the reader should simply grasp the concept of deterministic models of knowledge production. Here, human intellectual production is not attributed to a person's unique, inspired genius. A scholar, for instance, is not seen as an autonomous locus of creativity. Instead, his or her thought is seen as wholly conditioned by some outside force which acts *through* them. It must be stressed that there are different types of determinism. One could argue, as a number of Marxists do, that the economy is the master variable that determines one's intellectual production. Or, one could invoke other variables, such as gender, biology, and so on.

External Factors

As the reader has probably gathered by now, Martin Bernal maintains that the Ancient Model was not inferior to the Aryan Model. Its interpretive framework did not account for the data, the author insists, in a less plausible manner. Its rejection by the majority of nineteenth- and twentieth-century academicians is thus not attributable to its lack of explanatory power.

So why did this paradigm collapse in the first decades of the nineteenth century? The fall of the Ancient Model is explained as a result of what Bernal calls *external factors*. The rise of the Aryan Model is seen as due to *internal factors*. And with this we encounter one of *Black Athena*'s most convoluted initiatives. Only rarely does Bernal explain what he means by these terms. When he does, the results are confusing and contradictory.[10]

For now, let us begin our discussion of external factors (internal factors will be discussed in the next chapter) with the following passage: "A clear distinction has to be made between the fall of the Ancient Model, which can be explained only in externalist terms—that is, through social and political pressures—and the rise of the Aryan one, which had a considerable internalist component—that is to say, developments within scholarship itself played an important role in the evolution of the new model."[11]

In the passage just cited Bernal equated "externalist reasons" with "social and political pressures." In an exchange with Egyptologist John Coleman, Bernal achieves somewhat greater clarity: "I am convinced that the Ancient Model was abandoned for 'externalist' (non-scholarly or ideological) reasons and not because of any advances within the scholarly fields concerned." In 1995 he stated that external factors "are those forces and concerns throughout society as a whole that have an impact on the scholar and his or her work." Elsewhere in *Black Athena* he describes "externalist reasons" as being part of "the overall intellectual atmosphere."[12]

This metaphor of "intellectual atmosphere," or what he sometimes refers to as "*Zeitgeist*" is frequently employed by Bernal. In the following passage the author explores two distinct meanings of the phrase "in the air":

> In one sense, the phrase implies something that people are scenting for the first time—the emergence of new notions. This applied at the time to democracy and the extension of the franchise, etc. These ideas were "in the air." Therefore, they were an area of fierce intellectual and political contention. There is, however, another sense in which we use "in the air." *This sense implies something that pervades everything so much that one is no longer aware of it. I think that after the 1830s, racism was so much "in the air" in Northern Europe that people hardly noticed it, and it is only with historical retrospect that we can identify it.*[13]

According to the author, there are world views, ideas, widespread intellectual beliefs, and the like, which hover throughout and saturate the intellectual atmosphere of a society. In the nineteenth and early twentieth centuries the European "air," he contends, was permeated with ideas about African and Jewish inferiority, European superiority, the desirability of cultural purity, the unparalleled greatness of ancient Greece, and so on.[14]

And here we arrive at the first basic premise of Bernalian sociology: Scholarly work is determined by external factors such as "ideology," "social and political pressures," and "the overall intellectual atmosphere." Throughout *Black Athena* Bernal establishes a causal link between these external factors and academic research. In other words, the conclusions which academicians reach are an effect of "non-scholarly" influences prevalent in the culture at large. This process may be diagrammed as follows:

ATMOSPHERIC DETERMINISM
(1) Overall Atmosphere (= external factors)
conditions/determines
(2) Scholars and their research
which results in
(3) The creation/maintenance/overthrow of paradigms

Since no one likes to be called a determinist these days, I must be precise in documenting this charge. Bernal's determinism may be clearly identified in, literally, hundreds of remarks scattered throughout *Black Athena* and his writings in the Controversy. For example: "German Romanticism was the mainspring of the Aryan Model and 'Classics' as we know it today."[15] Or: "The Industrial Revolution and the triumph of European expansion throughout the world in the eighteenth and nineteenth centuries was an extraordinarily heady experience for Europeans. This deeply affected their historical views, leading them to project back from this period of utter European superiority into the past."[16] Or again: "I am convinced that historians and linguists were substantially affected by the intense racism and anti-Semitism of the nineteenth and early twentieth centuries." Notice that in each case Bernal begins with an event, aesthetic position, or ideological belief (i.e., external factor found in the atmosphere, or the *Zeitgeist*) and proceeds to suggest that this affected scholars and their intellectual output. For Martin Bernal, apparently, the realm of thought is not autonomous, but externally determined.[17]

Later on, I will also show that Bernal's determinism differs considerably from the "vulgar Marxist" variety. Further, I will point to nuances and advances in Bernal's thought. For now, however, I will affirm that Martin Bernal is a determinist. Whether he is a Marxist and a Marxist determinist will be discussed in Chapter 5 below.

Variables

Now to repeat our first question: To what does Martin Bernal attribute the mercurial rise of the Aryan Model and the swift, unprecedented collapse of its ancient counterpart? In what follows we will examine those external factors which the author believes stimulated the paradigm shift. Each external factor should be seen as an independent variable. These caused a change in a dependent variable, that is, the status of the Ancient and Aryan Models in nineteenth-century thought.

Race-thinking/Racism

Within the conceptual scheme adumbrated in *Black Athena,* European race-thinking is repeatedly identified as one of the most important reasons for the fall of the Ancient Model. In volume 2, Bernal states, "The great anomaly that brought down the Ancient Model was the contradiction between its tenet that Greece had been civilized by Egyptians and Phoenicians and the *Weltanschauung* of the 19th century, in which races were seen as primary determinants of history and their hierarchical descent white > brown > black was axiomatic."[18]

Essential to Bernal's analysis is an understanding of the African slave trade's effect on European thought. The association between skin color and human intellectual and moral inferiority is, historically speaking, of rather recent vintage. In *Before Color Prejudice: The Ancient View of Blacks*, classicist Frank M. Snowden, Jr., makes a convincing case for the absence of this equation in antiquity: "The ancient world did not make color the focus of irrational sentiments or the basis for uncritical evaluation. . . Nothing comparable to the virulent color prejudice of modern times existed in the ancient world. . . . The ancients did not fall into the error of biological racism; black skin color was not a sign of inferiority."[19]

Basil Davidson reaches a similar conclusion as regards early modern Europe. Arguing that the association between skin color and inferiority was not prevalent before the sixteenth century, Davidson remarks that this "central myth of European expansion . . . first took place on the deck of a slaving ship."[20]

Bernal views the rise of racist doctrines between the seventeenth and nineteenth centuries as the intellectual excrescence of the expansionist activities of the European powers. He would seem to agree with Hannah Arendt's claim that "racism is the main ideological weapon of imperialistic politics." Race-thinking, then, was that ideology which legitimated the inhumane enslavement of Africans, the fiscally lucrative and morally bankrupt colonization of the Americas, and the annihilation of indigenous Native American populations.[21]

The Ancient Model (i.e., dependent variable) collapses, in part, because scholars of antiquity were beholden to the racist world view of their time. This widespread view (i.e., an external factor, independent variable) pervaded the research agendas of those who studied the ancient Near East in the nineteenth century. In light of these ideologies of race, emendations of the historical record were now necessary. There was the bothersome fact that ancient Egypt was in Africa and that most modern inhabitants of this country were not "white." This unacceptable state of affairs required a scholarly corrective:

> If it had been scientifically "proved" that Blacks were biologically incapable of civilization, how could one explain Ancient Egypt—which was inconveniently placed on the African continent? There were two, or rather, three solutions. The first was to deny that the Ancient Egyptians were black; the second was to deny that the ancient Egyptians had created a "true" civilization; the third was to make doubly sure by denying both. The last has been preferred by most 19th- and 20th-century historians.[22]

Conversely, Bernal draws a correlation between the recent decrease of racist thinking and the decline of the Aryan Models. In the period following World War II, he argues, there was a general drop in racism and this accounts for the retrenchment of the Extreme and Broad Aryan Models. The reader should take note of the "cause and effect model" again employed by Bernal: a decrease in racism in the culture at large results in a less-biased research agenda and hence a more congenial environment for the acceptance of Bernal's Revised Ancient Model.[23]

Anti-Semitism

Bernal's treatment of anti-Semitism is intimately linked with his analysis of racism, for it is a racial, as opposed to a religious, anti-Semitism which he regards as partly responsible for the collapse of the Ancient Model. Léon Poliakov discusses this new kind of anti-Semitism which emerged during the Enlightenment:

> As for the Jew, the new turn of mind had the effect of depicting him as bad "in himself" because he was biologically what he was, and no transcendental agent, God or Devil, had the power to change whatever it was that he was. The progress made by biology and the discovery of the genetic laws only confirmed this view. The Jew's responsibility became total and inexorable; the harmfulness inherent in his race and blood was derived from a scientific "necessity."[24]

While racism against Africans led scholars to deny Egyptian influence, racialist anti-Semitic doctrines, Bernal contends, resulted in a skeptical attitude toward the possibility of Phoenician impact on ancient Greece. The ancient Phoenicians were a Semitic-speaking people who once inhabited regions of the Levant, North Africa, and Mediterranean Europe. By the early nineteenth century philologians were well aware that Phoenician was closely related to another northwest Semitic language, biblical Hebrew. Bernal believes that the former were perceived as belonging to the same racial stock as the Jews, perhaps the most despised minority group in nineteenth- and twentieth-century Europe. (In Chapter 9, I contest his association between Phoenicians and Jews.) Thus, the "social and political pressures" of anti-Semitism had pervaded the arteries of university research; the consequence was to downplay the significant accomplishments of ancient Semites.[25]

As noted in Chapter 3 above, the success of the Extreme Aryan Model is correlated with outbursts of European anti-Semitism. As such, the periods 1890–1900 and 1920–1939 were especially important moments for a theory that denied Phoenician impact on ancient Greece. With a lessening of anti-Semitic sentiment and the subsequent opening of the gates of academe to Jewish scholars in the aftermath of World War II, the Extreme Aryan Model withers.[26]

Progress

In *Black Athena* it is argued that conceptions of "progress," a formidable presence in eighteenth- and nineteenth-century social thought, contributed to the paradigm shift. A detailed exposition of the theories and theorists associated with the progressive movement is beyond the purview of the present work. For now, I would like to articulate briefly those themes which are germane to an understanding of the author's treatment of this issue.[27]

"Progress," as Antonio Gramsci aptly phrased it, "is an ideology." In *Critique and Crisis: Enlightenment and the Pathogenesis of Modern Society*, Reinhart Koselleck offers an insight into some tenets of progressive ideology:

> The eighteenth century witnessed the unfolding of bourgeois society, which saw itself as the new world, laying intellectual claim to the whole world and simultaneously denying the old. It grew out of the territories of the European states and, in dissolving this link, developed a progressive philosophy in line with the process. The subject of that philosophy was all mankind, to be unified from its European centre and led peacefully towards a better future.[28]

It was an axiom of progressive thought that the European powers retained the ability—if not the moral imperative—to lead non-Europeans out of a supposed state of cultural inferiority. To quote anthropologist Talal Asad, "Old universes must be subverted and a new universe created" in order to fulfill "the European wish to make the world in its own image."[29]

"Progress," observes Frank Manuel, "was a capacity inherent in the growth of rational intelligence." Foremost among the rudiments of progressive philosophy was the conviction that such growth could be achieved through the development and deployment of modern science. Readers of the marquis de Condorcet, Henri Saint-Simon, Auguste Comte, and Karl Marx, to name but a few, are undoubtedly familiar with the almost religious faith which these theorists placed in the emancipatory potential of modern science.[30]

How did this conception of progress impact upon the Ancient and Aryan Models? For one thing, the architects of the latter viewed themselves as true men of science. The claims of the Ancient Model were viewed as incommensurable with the scientific truths which the new moderns had discovered. Bernal writes, "To these German and British scholars, the stories of Egyptian colonization and civilizing of Greece violated 'racial science' as monstrously as the legends of sirens and centaurs broke the canons of natural science."[31]

Bernal also argues that progressive thought was beholden to the idea that "later is better." As such, scholars of antiquity were quick to downgrade the Egyptians, whose pinnacle occurred well before that of the Greeks. The latter now represented a progressive improvement upon the former, merely by dint of having achieved their cultural splendor at a later date. Bernal writes, "Egypt represented an earlier, lower and strangely dead stage of human evolution which had been raised by the European genius of Hellas to a qualitatively higher and more vital level."[32]

As noted above, the idea of progress was inextricably bound with a belief in European supremacy. Since Europe itself was held to be the "progressive" continent, contends the author, its foremost thinkers could not countenance the belief that the arts of civilization could have been imparted to their ancestors (i.e., the ancient Greeks) by those of retrograde Africans and Asiatics.[33]

Romanticism

It has been forcefully argued that Romantic thought has had a deleterious effect on non-European peoples and cultures, if not humanity in general. Many of the malefactors discussed in Edward Said's *Orientalism* are seminal figures in the development of Romantic thought. Hannah Arendt suggests that race-thinking in Germany was attributable to "political Romanticism." Gavin Langmuir, in *History, Religion, and Antisemitism*, notes, "Xenophobic hostility was aggravated by the reaction to the eighteenth-century emphasis on reason known as Romanticism."[34]

One of the axioms of Romantic thought, according to Bernal, was the belief that unadulterated races or cultures actually existed and that this state of purity was wholly desirable. This sentiment was coupled with the conviction that "'racial' and cultural purity is beneficial to cultural development." Throughout *Black Athena* it is argued that views such as these provided yet another truss for the racist infrastructure of nineteenth-century social thought.[35]

In the *Journal of Mediterranean Archaeology* Bernal calls attention to one more aspect of Romanticism which was relevant to the paradigm shift. This would consist of the belief that "fundamental cultural diffusion can only occur from light-skinned to dark-skinned 'races' or among peoples of similar appearance, speaking related languages." These assumptions may be detected in the Aryan Models. As we saw in Chapter 2 above, any notion of dark-skinned Afroasiatics imparting their culture to light-skinned ancient Greeks was categorically rejected by the Extreme version. Instead, it was held that Caucasian Aryans were responsible for influencing the cultural development of their racial kinsmen, the "Pre-Hellenes."[36]

Aside from stimulating racist thought, the Romantics evinced a well-known infatuation with Sanskrit and ancient India. The net result of "romantic linguistics" was (1) to turn scholarly attention away from the Middle East and Africa, and (2) to predispose researchers toward finding connections with their Aryan, Indo-European "cousins" in India. Last, the Romantics evinced a preference for small, free states as opposed to large bureaucratized empires. Greece was construed as a case of the former, Egypt as an exemplar of the latter.[37]

Christianity

In the second chapter of volume 1 Bernal demonstrates that the Church Fathers had accepted the Ancient Model's tenet that "the Greeks had learnt most of their philosophy from the Egyptians." In early Christianity, at least, there was no pronounced antagonism to the Ancient Model. Until the late seventeenth century, says Bernal, Christian thinkers generally accepted most of its basic premises.[38]

Shortly thereafter, things were to change drastically. Within intellectual circles an intense debate was to develop regarding the comparative merits of Christianity and ancient Egyptian religion. In response to the claims of late-eighteenth-century scholars like Charles François Dupuis that Egypt was the fount of all religion, Christian thinkers retaliated by belittling ancient Egypt. This was achieved by calling attention to the heathen and magical proclivities of its religion.[39]

The rivalry was also exacerbated by tensions between mainstream Christianity and heretical sects such as the Freemasons, Rosicrucians, and Hermeticists. All three were notoriously fond of Egyptian culture and religion. Last, Bernal notes that the defense of Christianity against Egypt meshed with the "progressive" movement. It was now held that Christianity had come later and was thus "better" than Egyptian religion. All of these currents conditioned the research of scholars of antiquity, the overwhelming majority of whom belonged to mainstream Christian denominations.[40]

Eurocentrism

Bernal's claim that "the political purpose of *Black Athena*," was "to lessen European cultural arrogance" has functioned as the preeminent sound bite of the Controversy. In a recent study, Samir Amin argues that Eurocentrism may be construed, in part, as "one dimension of the culture and ideology of the modern capitalist world." Another major component of Eurocentric thought, Amin observes, is the belief that imitation of the Western model by all peoples is the only solution to the challenges of our time." It was this presumption of Western superiority which was to condition the opinions of scholars of antiquity. By the nineteenth century, it is alleged, it had become unthinkable that Africans and Asians were, *or could ever have been,* more culturally advanced than Europeans. Propelled by this logic, researchers systematically expunged any record of European (i.e., ancient Greek) cultural subservience from the historical record. This was achieved by denying the Ancient Model's views about the superiority of Egyptian and Phoenician culture.[41]

Imperialism

Although Bernal did not explicitly discuss it in the first volume, one does not have to read between the lines in order to find him accusing European imperialism of contributing to the paradigm shift. This observation is confirmed by the following remark made by Bernal in a 1987 contribution: "There is little doubt that the change from the Ancient to the Aryan model was related to increasing European self-consciousness and confidence deriving from successful expansion into other continents."[42]

European imperialism, as Charles Tilly notes, began in earnest in the fifteenth century with the Portuguese penetration of North Africa. In *The Age of Empire, 1875–1914* Eric Hobsbawm proffers the following survey of the eventual development of the European imperialist project: "Between 1876 and 1915 about one-quarter of the Globe's land surface was distributed or redistributed as colonies among a half-dozen states. Britain increased its territories by some 4 million square miles, France by some 3.5 millions, Germany acquired more than 1 million, Belgium and Italy just under 1 million each."[43]

In the name of legitimating European imperial ventures in the Middle East and North Africa, argues Bernal, it was imperative that scholars of antiquity demonstrate the past inferiority of the presently colonized peoples. It became necessary to deny that Afroasiatics had ever engaged in any imperialistic activity of their own, since only Europeans were capable of such lofty undertakings. The ancient Greeks were thus seen as spry colonizers, the Egyptians as sedentary "stay-at-home" types. As Peter Allen observes, "They reconstructed the past in the image of the colonial present, which involved, among other things, suppressing evidence of Asiatic and African (especially Egyptian) influence on Greek culture." Furthermore, if the *mission civilisatrice* was to be successful, it would be important to neutralize any suggestion that those who were to be civilized (i.e., Africans and Asians) ever had a civilization worth speaking of.[44]

By 1994 Bernal would make passing reference to the notion of "hegemony." It has often struck me that his hypothesis can be read through a Gramscian filter. Following the Italian political philosopher we could see the pervasiveness of the Aryan Model as a victory of capitalist hegemony. In various European countries, a hegemonic or "leading group" had successfully controlled the consent-generating institutions of civil society, such as primary schools, churches, the media, and universities. The task of their intellectual cadres was to cast Africans and Semites as eternally uncultured barbarians, desperately in need of European "assistance." In this way they manufactured consent for costly and potentially unpopular imperialist endeavors.[45]

Philhellenism

Another major stimulant of the paradigm shift was the development of an intense philhellenic streak in European intellectual culture. This adoration of ancient Greece was fueled by many sources. Among the most prominent were (1) the rediscovery of Classical sources in the Renaissance, (2) the discovery of the Indo-European language family and the place of ancient Greek and the modern European languages within it, (3) the Greek War of Independence of 1821, and (4) the particularly German perception that there existed a special relation between themselves and the Greeks.[46]

The philhellenism of the day had two basic consequences for the Ancient and Aryan Models. Scholars who studied the Greeks, as Bernal demonstrates, were incapable of maintaining any sort of critical distance from their subject matter. The ancient Greeks were seen as "semi-divine," bearers of some type of extraordinary virtue. Ostensibly, this resulted in highly biased opinions among scholars of antiquity. Bernal writes of nineteenth-century attitudes,

"All normal laws and analogies are suspended when it comes to the Ancient Greeks and . . . it is inappropriate—if not improper—to judge them as one would other peoples."[47]

Second, these sentiments were to engender the belief that the ancient Greeks were the paramount civilization of antiquity. A corollary of this assumption was the view that Afroasiatic civilizations could in no way have surpassed, or even influenced, those of the Greeks.

Positivism

In volume 1 Bernal sporadically refers to a few other variables which contributed to the paradigm shift. In a few instances he calls attention to the role of positivism. In his introduction the author alleges that the archaeological components of the Aryan Models were "set up by men who were crudely positivist and racist." In the same chapter it is suggested that the insistence on "proof" inherent to the positivist method was to set the ship of antiquity studies in a disastrous direction. In an effort to discredit the accounts of Afroasiatic influence found in the Ancient Model, Aryanists demanded incontrovertible proof from proponents of the Ancient version. Bernal counters, as we know now, that the study of ancient history is not an exact science and that the Ancient Model offers enough evidence to be "competitively plausible"—the highest level of certainty that any theory of ancient history can achieve.[48]

Nationalism

In *Black Athena* we catch glimpses of the impact of nationalistic thinking on the paradigm shift. In England, Bernal argues, there developed a strong philo-Semitic current. Accordingly, the English not only admired the Phoenicians, they saw lines of correspondence between themselves and this Semitic group. The French, it is alleged, tended to equate the Phoenicians with the English and thus manifested a dislike for them and hence inclined toward the Extreme Aryan Model. In the German-speaking world, as we have seen, it was assumed that a special relation existed between them and the ancient Greeks. Accordingly, they were not well disposed toward the Ancient Model.[49]

Childhood

Elsewhere, Bernal makes passing mention of a romantically and progressively inspired obsession with childhood. As Eric Hobsbawm remarks, "Youth—especially intellectual or student youth"—was the "natural habitat" of Romantic thought. The Greeks were seen as the childhood of Europe, and for these reasons held in much greater esteem than the "strangely dead" Egyptians.[50]

Other Variables

Bernal occasionally cites the INDUSTRIAL and FRENCH REVOLUTIONS as variables, but he does not elaborate upon this observation. CLIMACTIC DETERMINISM and NORTHERNISM are also external variables. Every now and then Bernal alleges that Romantics (German-speaking ones in particular) viewed cooler northern climates as more conducive to intellectual activity. The invading Aryan Hellenes were seen as having bestowed upon the Pre-Hellenes the fruits of their northern intellect.[51]

Throughout the Controversy scholars have suggested that Bernal ignored other factors which were relevant to the paradigm shift. In the *Journal of Women's History* Gerda Lerner charges that gender was one of these overlooked variables: "Bernal's volumes reflect a world and a discourse in which women do not exist. Invisible, excluded, and abolished, women are so marginal to the debate that the author literally never once refers to them."[52]

Lerner's accusation strikes me as both melodramatic and inaccurate. Bernal cites and discusses the work of women scholars throughout the two volumes. He also makes very brief mention of an oft-encountered association in nineteenth-century thought: Indo-Europeans were construed as masculine, white, active, and superior, while Semites were viewed as feminine, black, passive, and inferior. The real problem with Bernal's gender analysis, as Madeline Zilfi points out, is that he did not pursue these interesting lines of inquiry: "The equation of foreign with female is one of the most tenacious and pervasive themes in historical polemic from antiquity to Gobineau and beyond. Bernal passes over, with barely a comment, the equation of female as foreign and feminization as degradation, although it recurs in the works he cites."[53] I agree with Zilfi's argument, as well as her more reasonable comment that although such an investigation would have been of great interest, "Bernal cannot be expected to have pursued every line of inquiry." By the mid 1990s, it should be noted, the author forcefully incorporated this insight into his thesis.[54]

Further, I concur with Zilfi's charge that Bernal neglected to investigate the relation between the paradigm shift and "inveterate European anti-Muslim hostility." The regions once occupied by ancient Phoenicians and Egyptians were now inhabited, predominantly, by Muslims. The latter had been locked in a world-historical conflict with Christianity which stretched back, at least, to the battle of Tours and Poitiers in 732 C.E. Given the long history of anti-Islamic polemic in Western thought it would have been interesting to examine what happened to the Ancient Model in the great Islamic caliphates from the seventh century through the Ottoman Empire. Bernal's lack of attention to Islam, incidentally, leaves him, embarrassingly enough, vulnerable to the charge of Eurocentrism.[55]

Conclusion

I hope the preceding discussion forever inters the odd notion, cherished by journalists, culture warriors, and even a few serious scholars, that *Black Athena* explains the paradigm shift in terms of "racism and anti-Semitism." As we have seen, Bernal posits no fewer than fourteen variables (there may be more) in explaining the differing destinies of the Ancient and

Aryan Models. As the Controversy progressed, however, Bernal, somewhat oportunistically, seemed to abandon or play down some of his variables (e.g., anti-Semitism; see Chapter 9 below) and emphasize others (e.g., racism, gender). The original argument, anyhow, is far, far more nuanced than standard culture-war fare. The effort to introduce this type of multicausal complexity into an analysis of intellectual production is a welcome change from the rather simplistic race/class/gender approaches embraced by some less thoughtful scholars.

Be that as it may, discussions of Bernal's work—even among his most perceptive critics—invariably offered abridged versions of his hypothesis. Nearly all who summarized *Black Athena*'s contents spoke in terms of one, two, at most five, external factors. Bernal himself, inexplicably, vacillates in terms of the number and types of variables he describes when he outlines his thesis. Much of this has to do with the fact that Bernal tries to explain the fall of the Ancient Model in terms of one set of variables and the rise of the Aryan Model in terms of another. (Compare, for example, our two epigraphs.) As we shall see in the following chapter, this approach makes little sense; hence it is not surprising that the author cannot implement it with any consistency or coherence. All of these considerations are compatible with my belief that the author has not fully thought out the implications of his sociology of knowledge.[56]

I will argue that the unabridged version of the hypothesis, in all of its complexity, presents us with a variety of fruitful sociological dilemmas. Yet insofar as most scholars perceived *Black Athena* as a work about racism and anti-Semitism in the academy, it is of interest to see how they responded to this, the most titillating component of his thesis. Remarkably enough, this argument has met with general agreement. Even more surprisingly, *classicists* have usually accepted the claim that their intellectual ancestors were "racists and anti-Semites."

Edith Hall, whose overall assessment of *Black Athena* is not exceedingly positive, writes, "There is, moreover, little doubt that Bernal is correct in arguing that modern racial prejudice has been one of the reasons why cultural contact between ancient Hellenophone communities and ancient Semitic and black peoples has been and is still being played down." Glen Bowersock, of the Institute for Advanced Studies at Princeton University, remarks that "Bernal has shown us as no one has before the racist underpinnings of classics and *Altertumswissenschaft* in the West." Ann Michelini, who delivers a trenchant evaluation of Bernal's work, calls his accusation of racism and anti-Semitism in the academy "painfully persuasive." Observations of this nature could be repeated en masse.[57]

A vocal and heretical minority, however, has challenged the prevailing wisdom. In 1991 Michael Poliakoff cast a more critical eye on the manner in which Bernal's historiography was received: "The one constant in the scholarly response to *Black Athena* is the clear desire of the reviewers, including those who are critical of it, to admire the book. The typical reviewer reacts in shock, horror, or shame at the virulent racism and antisemitism Bernal documents, despite lingering questions about their *significance* in understanding antiquity and intellectual history."[58] The most tenacious development of this theme occurred in *Black Athena Revisited*. As noted in Chapter 3 above, contributors to this volume conducted rescue operations on the reputations of individual scholars Bernal casually and irresponsibly cast out to sea. Nevertheless, many of these authors had great difficulty in relegating his charges of racism and anti-Semitism to the realm of the utterly preposterous or the highly implausible. Guy MacLean Rogers, coeditor of *Black Athena Revisited*, concludes:

> Bernal's reconstruction of how some European scholars, in an atmosphere of racism and anti-Semitism (especially during the nineteenth century), attempted to root out the contributions of the ancient Egyptians and Phoenicians to early Greek civilization *seems to me to be beyond dispute*. Racism and anti-Semitism pervaded *some* lines of European historical inquiry about the ancient world. Some nineteenth-century scholars of antiquity did understand what we might today call cultural differences in terms of "race." But not all nineteenth-century scholars of the ancient world were racists and anti-Semites.[59]

Rogers, who is among the most aggressive critics of *Black Athena*, seems to yield quite a lot of ground. After all, the claim that racism, anti-Semitism, philhellenism, German nationalism—*anything but "the facts"*—pervaded historical inquiry is the fundamental theoretical insight of volume 1. Rogers admits that in *some* instances this was true. (Would he have even confronted this problematic had Bernal never published his ideas?) Other classicists, as noted above, admitted that in many instances this was true.

When we take into account the tremendous amount of condescension and abuse hurled at Bernal throughout the Controversy (not only in *Black Athena Revisited*), it seems that many scholars are making a fairly stunning concession. It is akin to ridiculing the core beliefs of Christianity, all while mentioning, in parentheses, that there is a good deal of truth in the claim that Jesus is our King, our Christ, our Lord, and our Savior. But not all is well with *Black Athena*'s sociology of knowledge. It is to this subject which I shall turn now.

5

The

Antinomies of

Martin Bernal

I mean scholarship has never been detached from the society in which its scholars lived. That's not to say that scholarship is the same as social convention, but there's always been a relationship between them. . . .

I see truth not as a place, but as a direction. You can be nearer or further away from it, even though you can't reach it. There are relatively good and bad histories. And the accusation I often get is, "Well, you're influenced by your society. How can you know that your work is going to be any more truthful or objective than anyone else's?" My response is I think my work is fitting the new archaeological data as it comes in better than the conventional wisdom.

—Martin Bernal, "On *Black Athena:*
An Interview with Michael Eric Dyson"

It is only in his brief discussions of Thomas Kuhn's oeuvre that Martin Bernal taps into the rich sociological tradition whose virtues he everywhere extols. Kuhn's studies in the history of science have had, undoubtedly, a large influence on *Black Athena*. Concepts such as *paradigm, paradigm shift, disciplinary matrix,* and *revolution* have all been borrowed from the Kuhnian lexicon. Bernal, we shall have opportunity to note, has even cast himself as a hero in a Kuhnian drama.[1]

The lack of sociological discussion during the Controversy has prevented many from noticing what I see as a relatively obvious point: *Black Athena* is based on epistemological assumptions which are entirely alien to Kuhn's discourse. Further, the lack of sociological scrutiny has resulted in the absence of any type of extended analysis or critique of Bernal's internal/external schema and his deterministic model of knowledge production. The examination of these neglected issues comprises my task in the present chapter.

Once completed, I will delineate some of the more positive aspects of Bernal's sociology of knowledge.

Internal Factors: The Peculiar Amalgam

Martin Bernal, as demonstrated in chapter four, attributes the downfall of the Ancient Model to "external" factors. Internal factors, conversely, are said to have been responsible for the rise of the Aryan Models.

What, then, are internal factors? Bernal indirectly equates them with "advances within the scholarly fields concerned," and "developments within scholarship itself." "Internalist developments," he writes in 1995, "are those that take place within a particular discipline." Unfortunately, this exhausts most of his theoretical attention to the subject. The only way to develop this analysis further is to assume that internal factors bear the opposite connotation of his somewhat more clearly defined external factors.[2] Using this approach, we might reconstruct his schema as follows:

EXTERNAL FACTORS	INTERNAL FACTORS
ideology	nonideological
social and political pressures	impervious to such pressures
overall atmosphere	unaffected by atmosphere
nonscholarly developments that account for fall of Ancient Model	scholarly developments that account for rise of Aryan Model

As far as I can tell, internal factors refer to scholarly discoveries and theories which were unaffected (or relatively unaffected) by external factors (i.e., the prevailing ideologies, events, etc., of the day).[3]

When Bernal says the Aryan Model came into being because of internal factors, he seems to suggest that authentic intellectual advances or discoveries, not the winds of the "atmosphere," steered scholars to this new theory. Among these advances, the most important, he claims, was the discovery of Indo-European. So the second premise of Bernalian sociology goes something like this: Intellectual work can be (relatively) unaffected by ideologies, the *Zeitgeist*, social and political pressures, and so on.[4]

In positing the category of internalist factors Bernal seems to subscribe—unintentionally, I think—to a conception of some type of objective scholarship. For, if the development of the Aryan Model is a scholarly (i.e., "internalist") development, then we must assume that it was somehow impervious to the many external atmospheric pressures discussed in Chapter 4 above. The author appears to presuppose that researchers are capable of producing knowledge about their world which is not determined by atmosphere. When Bernal speaks of internalist factors he seems to partition intellectual thought from the *Zeitgeist*. The scholarly realm is now, suddenly, autonomous.

There is clearly a contradiction here. Throughout *Black Athena* Bernal repeatedly, passionately, and convincingly argues that such a notion is a chimera. He professes a deep-felt conviction that scholarly knowledge is contingent upon external factors—that there is no such thing as academic research free of ideological tincture. In chapter 6 he declares, "I argue that the intellectual and academic developments have to be seen together with the social and political ones." In one passage (see below) the author contests "the image of the 'pure' and 'objective' scholar dealing with eternal verities." In the epigraph, it is noted that "scholarship has never been detached from society," and throughout *Black Athena* we see again and again how external factors determine scholarly work. Then, without explanation, he speaks of internal factors—scholarship unsullied by outside contaminating influences. My question is this: How could the Aryan Model, with its emphasis on blond northern Aryan invaders and white Pre-Hellenes, possibly *not* have been affected by nineteenth-century ideologies? Was this not the major point of Bernal's first volume?[5]

On strictly theoretical grounds there are many difficulties with the internal/external scheme as well. To begin with, *ideology* has proven itself to be one of the most stubbornly opaque terms in the sociologist's vocabulary. The concept, as many have shown, was ambiguous from its initial formulation in Marx and Engels's *German Ideology*. Further, it is not easy to establish an agreed-upon line of demarcation between ideology (no matter what the definition) and scholarly research. In order to understand this point, we might draw a parallel with well-known debates in Marxist thought.[6] Here is Michèle Barrett in *The Politics of Truth: From Marx to Foucault:*

> In recent years the base/superstructure metaphor, as an emblem of Marx's determinist position on ideology, has been criticised from a quite different point of view from the Hegelian tradition that Marx was rejecting. Since Marx's death the Marxist tradition has tended, particularly during the years of the Second International, to simplify the metaphor into one of straightforward "reflection" of economic relations of production in a superstructure conceived of as purely reactive. . . . A one-way model, which sees the economics of production simplistically as the domino at the beginning of a line of political, cultural, legal and intellectual pieces that will inevitably fall down when that first one is pushed, has been attributed to "Marxism" in general.[7]

As Barrett shows, this "one-way" or "domino" approach (i.e., economy determines intellectual thought) has increasingly yielded to a "bi-directional" conception. In other words, at least since the time of Gramsci researchers have been exploring not only how the base conditions the superstructure, but how superstructural elements influence the economic foundation of society.[8]

If we apply this "bi-directional" approach to *Black Athena*, we might claim that external versus internal is a false dichotomy. Ideology and scholarship—like base and superstructure—do not necessarily stand in a neat causal relation, with the former determining the latter. For these reasons—and this is my main point—they are not easily distinguishable from one another. This may be demonstrated by looking at the very nineteenth-century European intellectual scene discussed by Bernal. In reference to this period Edward Said observes, "Race theory, ideas about primitive origins and primitive classifications, modern decadence, the progress of civilization, the destiny of the white (or Aryan) races, the need for colonial territories—all these were elements in the peculiar amalgam of science, politics, and culture whose drift, almost without exception, was always to raise Europe or a European race to dominion over non-European portions of mankind." In *The History of Anti-Semitism*, Léon Poliakov points to the subtle nexus that existed between academic research and nonscholarly forms of intellectual production in the nineteenth century: "It is difficult to escape the impression that scholars allowed the discussion by the writers and polemicists to influence their thinking, and that an interchange imperceptibly took place between the prejudices of the populace and the specialists' laboratories."[9]

It is the existence of the "peculiar amalgam" and the "imperceptible interchange" which renders the internal/external scheme so inadequate. Said points to an *interface* between politics and culture. Poliakov calls attention to the *reciprocal influence* between academicians and polemicists. Bernal, at least when he is talking about internal factors, underestimates the degree to which ideology and scholarly work had mutually nourished and permeated one another. While the external/internal scheme posits a dichotomy between ideology and scholarship, the author needs to develop a model which accounts for their interpenetration.[10]

Thus I do not concur with Bernal's claim that internalist factors are primarily responsible for the rise of the Aryan Model. Surely, Aryanists had breathed the cultural air of their day; the so-called external developments must have influenced their scholarly undertakings as well. It seems fairly obvious that the tenets of the Aryan Model (e.g., "white" Pelasgians, "superior" invading Aryans, "superior" Indo-Europeans, etc.) are saturated with the race-thinking of the times. Conversely, if the Ancient Model fell it did so not only because of externalist factors. Men of science—who did not view themselves as racists, who employed what they regarded as the most exacting tools of scholarly inquiry, who were flush with a sense of their own objectivity—discarded or ignored this paradigm for what *they perceived to be* sound scientific reasons. As far as these scientists were concerned they were producing research, not racism. We should thus not be surprised to learn that in such an environment science was (what we would now label) racist and racialist, and that racism was elevated to the rank of science.[11]

The Variables Foul: The Case of Victor Bérard

In order to understand how much emphasis Bernal places on external factors—and thus how incongruous his appeal to internal factors actually is—we must look at his discussions of the French academician and journalist Victor Bérard (1864–1931). An examination of this issue permits us to observe the most extreme incarnation of his determinist model. In fact, the very extremity of the model forces the author to confront some of the problematic implications of his approach.

In the words of Cyrus Gordon, Victor Bérard was one of those "bold spirits" who "dared to maintain the Phoenician antecedents of Greek history." When seen through the optic of *Black Athena*'s categories, this means that Bérard was espousing the Ancient Model in a world governed by the Aryan paradigm. The dilemma which this raises for Bernal may be stated as follows: If racism, Romanticism, anti-Semitism, and so forth, had so pervaded the cultural air of nineteenth-century Europe, then how can one explain Bérard's unique immunity to their toxins?[12] The response that Bernal gives is so alarmingly determinist as to make Marxists seem like fluffy proponents of free will. I quote at length:

> I found it very moving to discover this articulate statement of the beliefs behind my own work written at the height of imperialism and the beginning of the Extreme Aryan Model. However, this fact itself appears to pose a challenge to my method of explaining these scholarly developments in externalist terms—that is, as being heavily influenced by outside social and political developments and the overall intellectual atmosphere. To overcome this challenge, I think it would be useful to look at three tiers of scholarship: the thoughts of individual scholars; their ability to teach and publish; and the general developments in scholarship. . . . *I believe that a German Bérard would have been impossible and an English one unlikely. . . . It was solely in France—with its post-1870 suspicion of German Aryanism—and among Republicans—with their hatred of Catholic Royalist anti-Semitism—that such thoughts could be thought.* One might even say, in a Romantic way, that Bérard's regional origin was important in that *there was a strong tradition of secular and socially radical individualism in both the French and Swiss Jura [where he grew up]. . . . Another important factor was that Bérard was not a "pure" academic: he had his outside, journalistic and political worlds to give him a wider perspective.*[13]

In this passage the author mentions the difficulties which the case of Bérard presented for his deterministic argument. This statement reflects what I see as Bernal's honest attempt to confront the shortcomings of his own hypothesis. Be that as it may, his reasoning is not convincing.

This passage provides two basic explanations for Bérard's dissent from the Aryan Models. First and foremost, Bérard's deviation from the type of intellectual position that a person of his day and age ought to have maintained (i.e., the Extreme and/or Broad Aryan Model) is explained by reference to his regional origin and nationality. It is because he grew up in Swiss Jura and lived in France, argues Bernal, that he managed to circumnavigate the hard-and-fast ideological currents of his day (i.e., German Aryanism).

This claim raises many questions. If region and nationality are so important, then how come so many French and Swiss contemporaries of Bérard steadfastly supported the Aryan Model? Bernal, it should be noted, is committing a methodological foul. He introduces a new variable (region) into his analysis when the old variables (racism, anti-Semitism, Romanticism) fail him—a process akin to a soccer player scoring a goal by virtue of a volleyball slap. For purposes of argument, let us accept that a scholar's region or nationality might differently determine his or her intellectual output. Yet even if we were to concede this point, it would create difficulties within the context of Bernal's overall hypothesis, for many of the other variables which he cites as reasons for the paradigm shift (e.g., imperialism, Eurocentrism, anti-Semitism, racism) simply explode national boundaries. Pointing to the nationality of a scholar does not effectively explain why that scholar managed to avoid the other, seemingly transnational, variables which hovered in the atmosphere. Does Bernal mean to suggest that the (Republican) French were any less beholden to imperialist, anti-Semitic, and Eurocentric thoughts and practices than their neighbors? Is nationality a metavariable, one that cancels out all others when explaining the production of knowledge?

Apparently, Bernal seems to thinks so. For in the same passage he proceeds to make one of the most radical claims of his entire work. He suggests that the thoughts which came to Bérard were unthinkable in Germany. This is determinism *pur et dur!* Human thought is wholly conditioned by one overarching independent variable, in this case nationality. This position presupposes a completely undifferentiated German society, one in which no single individual could think as would a French person—or a person from the French and Swiss Jura—located a few hundred miles away. (Unfortunately for Bernal, no less a German than Friedrich Nietzsche seems to ascribe to the Ancient Model on the pages of his raucous *We Classicists.*)

The reference to profession serves as Bernal's second explanation for Bérard's dissent. Yet the author never explains why it is that journalists should be less susceptible to ideological distortion than scholars. Is it true that French journalists of the period—and I remind the reader that Bérard's major work appeared at exactly the same time as the Dreyfus affair—were endowed with some capacity to overcome irrational prejudices?[14]

The problematic issue of Bérard was touched upon in the Controversy. In a response to John Ray, Bernal slightly modifies his original position:

[Ray's] first objection is to my view (as he sees it) of scholars as mere puppets of the prejudices of their times. This is of course a case of the crucial and insoluble debate between determinism and freewill. It is certainly true, on the one hand, that I emphasize the former, which I believe is useful as a corrective to the image of the "pure" and "objective" scholar dealing with eternal verities. On the other hand, *I had hoped that I had made it clear, particularly in my discussion of Victor Bérard* [passage cited above], *that I believe that the academic sphere is only indirectly*

controlled by the state and society and that there is considerable scope
for free and original thought. . . . If I did not believe this, it would be
impossible to explain the development of my own ideas and the response
to them—though the favourable tone of the latter has caused some difficulties for my sociology of knowledge.[15]

Once again, Bernal's willingness to call into question his own hypothesis is
laudable. Yet his response is again unpersuasive. For the autonomy of the
"academic sphere" is precisely what he denied in the earlier passage to which
he alludes. As we just saw, the Frenchman's exceptionalism is determined by
the fact that he enjoyed the "wider perspective" of a journalist as opposed to
the blinkered view of a scholar.

There is a further difficulty in Bernal's rejoinder, and it centers around
the notion of "free and original thought." Put simply, his conceptual scheme
does not permit for anything to be free and original in Bérard's thought, or anyone else's; the latter was differently determined—but determined nonetheless—by the variables of region, nationality, and profession. Bérard is not
construed as an agent, but a vessel. He does not stumble across the truth of
the Ancient Model as a result of some ineffable creative genius, but rather
because of the impact of a peculiar confluence of external factors.

Other commentators have called attention to the highly deterministic
aspects of Bernal's hypothesis. In a thoughtful submission Frank Turner
remarks: "[Bernal] ascribes these intellectual events [the paradigm shift] to causes
arising from the emergence of the idea of progress, the emergence of racial and
racist thought, the general phenomenon of Romanticism, and the rise of
scholarly professionalism. . . . Nineteenth-century classical scholarship appears
as a set of writings that simply rides the crest of these larger movements."[16]

Turner makes one further criticism of Bernal which bears repeating. He
charges that Bernal's "approach ignores . . . both the possibly autonomous character of the scholarly enterprise and the manner in which that enterprise is
actually part of the warp and woof of the larger epoch." As I read it, Turner
is calling attention to Bernal's tendency to relegate academic work to the sphere
of effect or "epiphenomenon" of external factors. Bernal did an excellent job
of showing how scholarship reflected, legitimated, and refined ideological agendas. What he failed to acknowledge, however, was the role which academic
research might have played in formulating these very agendas.[17]

Turner is actually proposing a reverse of Bernal's cause-and-effect model.
He is arguing that *scholarship* may determine the types of ideologies a society produces, and he seems to hint at the "bi-directional" approach mentioned
above. In a 1989 response to Turner, Bernal partly concedes this point, but
ultimately returns to his original argument: "I completely agree with Professor
Turner that the writing of history is a social phenomenon that affects the development of society. I do touch, for instance, on the aid which the Aryan
Model has given to imperialism. *Nevertheless, I believe that there are other*
forces which are more significant."[18]

Bernal's response to Turner indicates that he was willing to modify his extreme deterministic approach. By 1990 he would seem to make greater concessions: "My own vision is far more complicated and uncertain. I could describe it as believing that scholarship is semi-autonomous and only partially dependent on society, but I am convinced that there are fundamental links between the two and that *the predominant causal flow is from society to scholarship rather than the other way round.*"[19]

Finally, in 1992, Bernal would cede more ground: "I believe scholars are influenced both by their social and political environment, and by the material they study. So it's two forces working on them, and it's often difficult to tell which part of their conclusions comes from which force. Sometimes they double up, and sometimes they contradict each other. It's a complicated, fluid situation. I have no clear answer."[20] The argument in this last passage strikes me as Bernal's most convincing and sophisticated treatment of the problem. For the first time, he clearly articulates a model of knowledge production which integrates two analytical levels (the political environment, "the material they study"), as opposed to privileging one over the other.[21]

But the damage has already been done. Bernal's sociology of knowledge is undisciplined in the extreme. As we have just seen, when cornered by Bérard's position, regional origin suddenly assumes the status of an independent variable. Elsewhere, when trying to explain why Salomon Reinach—a French Jew—adhered passionately to the Extreme Aryan Model, Bernal improvises a new argument. Reinach's desire to assimilate is now seen as the factor which accounts for his devotion to this anti-Semitic model. When trying to explain why the decipherment of the outsider Michael Ventris was accepted by the academic status quo, Bernal points to his "personal charm." When the old variables fail him, the author simply extemporizes new ones. Suffice it to say, this is not the type of theoretical rigor that a professional sociologist of knowledge would find acceptable.[22]

This leaves us with the question of Bernal's purported Marxism. Hopefully, the reader now understands why I have labeled his sociology of knowledge deterministic. His approach differs significantly, however, from the type of determinism associated with vulgar Marxism. According to the latter, all forms of human thought are ultimately conditioned by material productive forces. In Bernal's writing, however, ideologies are often privileged as the variables which most directly determine scholarly production. This is not to say that he ignores the economic antecedents of the external factors which he discusses. Bernal is not an idealist: there are some brief discussions in his work regarding material factors as they pertain to racism, imperialism, philhellenism, and Eurocentrism. As regards other variables, however, the author eschews any serious investigation of material factors. He never discusses the Romantics as representatives of a particular class. The concept of progress is not placed within the framework of capital's international expansion, even though there is considerable warrant for doing so. Nor does Bernal point to the economic underpinnings of European anti-Semitism.[23]

In short, his analysis bears little resemblance to the types of inquiry which an orthodox Marxist might undertake. This type of researcher emphasizes and then reemphasizes the manner in which material productive forces *in and of themselves* affect social thought. In *Black Athena,* by contrast, scholarship seems directly subservient to ideologies. In fact the latter seem to mediate between the determining economic base and the superstructural intellectual sphere. His model could be described as follows:

economic factors
(sometimes) condition
IDEOLOGY
which always conditions
scholarship

What, then, to make of Bernal's claim that he was a "loose Marxist"? It seems clear that the author is not working within any orthodox Marxist tradition. Bernal's intense concentration on ideology and his relative lack of emphasis on economic factors bears some resemblance to the work of the "Western Marxists." Associated with this approach are theorists such as Antonio Gramsci, Jean-Paul Sartre, Georg Lukács, Louis Althusser, Theodor Adorno, and Herbert Marcuse, among others. Perry Anderson, in his assessment of Western Marxism, notes that these thinkers "constituted an entirely new intellectual configuration within the development of historical materialism." The novelty of their thought, as Russell Jacoby points out, was that they "shifted the emphases of Marxism from political economy and the state to culture, philosophy and art." As such, their analysis tended to concentrate on superstructural elements, as opposed to the base.[24]

Yet Bernal's inability to posit agency within his scheme makes it difficult to view him as a Western Marxist. In *Black Athena* scholars almost never appear to be free of overwhelmingly determining factors. Insofar as Bernal focuses mostly on ideology while relegating economic factors to a second tier of analytical prominence, he might be labeled a a "loose Western Marxist." Given the antinomies in his sociological schemata, even this label must be applied cautiously.

The Structure of Scientific Revolutions

We are now prepared to explore the question of Bernal's relation to the thought of the late Thomas Kuhn. *The Structure of Scientific Revolutions,* published in 1962, easily qualifies as one of the most influential academic works of the twentieth century. Even though this study concentrated almost exclusively on the hard sciences, many would agree with the opinion of one writer who suggested that Kuhn's method "is relevant to all fields of historical inquiry." Bernal himself shares this assessment. In volume 1 he notes that Kuhn's discussions of science have "heuristic utility for studying revolutionary change in the humanities."[25]

Put in simple terms, *The Structure of Scientific Revolutions* analyzed the process of scientific research and scientific discovery. Kuhn argued that one may conceive of the history of mature science in terms of two alternating structural phases. These he labeled "normal science" and "scientific revolution." During normal science a community of researchers trained in a specific subdiscipline works within the framework of a "paradigm." Kuhn's definition of this term is by no means unequivocal. In a now canonical 1970 article, Margaret Masterman observed that he used the word *paradigm* in "not less than twenty-one different senses."[26]

For purposes of brevity, I will follow Douglas Eckberg and Lester Hill, who conclude that a paradigm is "a cognitive framework" which is shared by an "integrated community of practitioners." For Kuhn, "normal science" is practiced when a paradigm is uncontested, when all the members of the relevant scientific community take for granted its superiority to other approaches. As such, during periods of normal science researchers are busy solving the problems that the paradigm has set out and employing its methods for solving these problems.[27] What they are not doing, however, is exploring any new scientific terrain. Kuhn writes: "No part of the aim of normal science is to call forth new sorts of phenomena; *indeed those that will not fit the box are often not seen at all.* Nor do scientists normally aim to invent new theories, and they are often intolerant of those invented by others. Instead, normal-scientific research is directed to the articulation of those phenomena and theories that the paradigm already supplies."[28]

"Scientific revolutions" are initiated when someone challenges normal science by forwarding a new paradigm. As M. D. King observes, "In the history of science periods of normal development, according to Kuhn, are separated by comparatively brief 'revolutionary' upheavals—extraordinary episodes during which a scientific community loses confidence in the ability of its governing paradigms to generate research strategies that will solve all the legitimate problems before them."[29]

In *The Structure of Scientific Revolutions* it is noted that a certain type of individual precipitates such a revolution. The epigraph which adorns the very first page of *Black Athena* features the following quote from Kuhn: "Almost always the men who achieve these fundamental inventions of a new paradigm have either been very young or very new to the field whose paradigm they change." There is, as the reader may have noticed, a self-reflexive dimension to Bernal's use of Kuhn. *The Structure of Scientific Revolutions* supplies a narrative into which the author of *Black Athena* has inserted himself. Martin Bernal is very new to the fields of antiquity, and in this sense the Sinologist seems to be brimming with revolutionary potential. The Revised Ancient Model may be seen as the work of a Kuhnian insurgent—a visionary who challenges the stultifying orthodoxy of normal science under the regime of the Aryan paradigm.[30]

In a recent interview, Giovanna Borradori referred to Kuhn's famous text as "the Trojan Horse within the walls of positivism." For when Kuhn wrote, "we may . . . have to relinquish the notion, explicit or implicit, that changes of paradigm carry scientists and those who learn from them closer and closer to the truth," he seemed to be contesting a scientific article of faith—namely, that the history of scientific research is the same as the history of progress toward the truth.[31]

In traditional discussions of science, each revolution is seen as building upon the advances made by its predecessor. For Kuhn—although he later vehemently denied it—as one paradigm replaces another there is no necessary cumulative increase in knowledge, no mandatory inching toward an absolute truth. Proximity to the truth does not necessarily change in the aftermath of a scientific revolution; only the paradigm changes. As Hollinger observes, "The theory offers a thoroughly nonteleological view of change: no idea of progress is implied, nor one of decline." Bernal must certainly disagree with this approach. For we are told in the second volume that the Revised Ancient Model is a substantive improvement upon its predecessor. *Black Athena* is not a story of a simple paradigm shift, but of a better paradigm, *tout court*.[32]

Yet another difference between Bernal and Kuhn might actually be a case of the former misreading the latter. Bernal assumes that each discipline invariably has one dominant paradigm. As the following observation made by Herminio Martins demonstrates, this is not what Kuhn had in mind: "Paradigms pertain to fields like the study of heat, optics, mechanics, etc.; there are not and cannot be paradigms of physics or chemistry. In other words paradigms are not discipline-wide but sub-disciplinary."[33] When Kuhn says "paradigm," he is conceptualizing a cognitive framework which dominates a sub-discipline. When Bernal says "paradigm," however, he envisions a framework which dominates an entire discipline—in actuality, more than a discipline: his Aryan paradigm rules over classics, Egyptology, Semitic linguistics, Mediterranean archaeology, and so on.[34]

For Kuhn, normal science works because a community of scientists takes it as a given that the theories and methods of their paradigm are fundamentally correct. It is this tacit consensus, this refusal to question what they simply "know" to be true, which accounts for their inability to "see" facts which contradict their positions. If they are blind to certain counterarguments, if they are intolerant of the claims of outsiders, it is a consequence of their steadfast devotion to their paradigm.

Conversely, those scholars discussed in volume 1 of *Black Athena* were blinded to the Ancient Model by, among other things, their racial hatred, their sense of religious and ethnic superiority, and their Eurocentric arrogance. It is one thing to say that researchers make mistakes because they are locked into the logic of a paradigm. It is quite another to say that—consciously or unconsciously—the paradigm itself is created and upheld by racists, anti-Semites, Eurocentrists, and Romantics.

Kuhn, needless to say, does not incorporate these variables into his analysis. His scientists act in good faith. If they err, if they are intolerant of dissenting viewpoints, it is because their paradigm has led them astray.

Kuhn's scientists are never shown to be prejudiced in the sense discussed by Bernal. On the contrary, they are endowed with the virtues of rationality and communicativeness. In a little-noticed passage Kuhn observes that scientists are "reasonable men." As such, when a new paradigm emerges, some scientists—reasonable men and women that they are—may be persuaded by the new counterarguments it presents.[35]

It emerges from this that reasoned discourse is a hallmark of mature science. As Theodore Schatzki notes, "Kuhn portrays science as a bundle of activities, which are embedded in wider forms of sociohistorical continuity, in which rational argumentation takes place by reference to disparate values and concepts, and in which people are able to grasp, discuss, and dispute one another's viewpoints without thereby being converted." Insofar as "reasonable men" are not racists or anti-Semites, few of the scholars discussed by Bernal could be said to resemble Kuhn's scientists. As for rational argumentation, Bernal repeatedly charges that all dissenters from the Aryan Model—regardless of the validity of their claims—were greeted with apathy and/or hostility. *Black Athena*, as we shall see, contends that reasoned discourse is a very infrequent occurrence within the context of the university.[36]

Bernal's attentiveness to the effects of racism, anti-Semitism, and Romanticism underscores the most glaring contrast between these perspectives. *Black Athena* examines the impact which beliefs prevalent in society at large have on scholarly work (the so-called "external factors"). The author views a scholar and a university as a node which is intersected by ideological vectors emanating from nonacademic precincts of the social body. As we saw earlier the imperialist project, geopolitical events, the slave trade, and anti-Semitism are all intimately connected to the paradigm shift.

Sociologists have been quick to note that *The Structure of Scientific Revolutions* lacks any notion of a nexus between science and society. Alan Dawe observes that for Kuhn science is a "closed system" in that external influences are never shown to penetrate scientific research.[37] John Urry, writing in the *British Journal of Sociology*, remarks: "If Kuhn's contribution was really a 'sociology of knowledge,' that is, an explanation of the *genesis* of *knowledge*, it would require an analysis of the relations between science and society, between science and different parts and groups within society, and between different parts and groups within science."[38] But Kuhn does not ignore only the relation between scientists and society, he also neglects to examine the manner in which power penetrates scholarly research. In fact, the issue of power—a concept with a lengthy sociological genealogy—is completely absent in *The Structure of Scientific Revolutions*. As Steve Fuller has argued, "the view that science systematically reflects, or legitimates, specific class interests more generally represented in society" has "no place in Kuhn's account of science." This work never asks, as does *Black Athena*, if scholarly research might represent the interests of a particular class, social group, or constellation of political interests. Thomas Kuhn is agnostic on the question of power.[39]

I would note that questions of this nature have assumed a central—perhaps even hegemonic—place in contemporary academic discourse. The most influential exponent of such a view is Michel Foucault, who in one of his famous discussions of "power/knowledge" notes: "'Truth' is linked in a circular relation with systems of power which produce and sustain it, and to effects of power which it induces and which extends it."[40]

Sandra Harding, a feminist epistemologist, writes:

> The problem with Kuhn's criterion is that in sciences that are important to dominant groups in socially stratified societies, lack of controversy about fundamentals is not a reliable or even plausible indicator of the absence of social, economic and political values. . . . Even more distressing is the history of well-intentioned research by the most distinguished of scientists which was inadvertently highly constrained by the sexist, racist, imperialist and bourgeois ethos of its period.[41]

Such an accusation cannot be made of Bernal's work. The humanities faculty of the university in *Black Athena* is in no way depicted as a cloister. Indeed, it is virtually overrun by the ideological agendas of dominant social groups.[42]

Consequently, I find Bernal's use of Kuhn problematic. His sociology of knowledge is predicated on assumptions which are entirely incommensurable with those of *The Structure of Scientific Revolutions*. Regardless of its worth, Kuhn's is the epistemology of a bygone era. Bernal, on the other hand, embraces a conceptualization of knowledge production which is fully consonant with the current *Zeitgeist*.

Conclusion

Up until this point I have called attention to many of the contradictions and shortcomings of Bernal's approach. Yet to be discussed are some of the positive contributions of his sociology of knowledge. In order to explore one particular theoretical issue, I will ask readers to bracket momentarily whatever suspicions they might have, and assume that the author's hypothesis regarding the superiority of the Ancient Model and its unjust rejection due to external factors is correct.

In Chapter 4 above, I listed each of Bernal's external factors one by one. This atomized recitation, while organizationally efficient, obscures one of the more intriguing elements of his work. The author often identified numerous interrelations between his variables. Let us first look at a number of passages in which this occurs:

> Throughout the 18th and 19th centuries we find a *de facto* alliance of Hellenism and textual criticism with the defence of Christianity.

These paradigms of "race" and "progress" and their corollaries of "racial purity," and the notion that the only beneficial conquests were those of "master races" over subject ones, could not tolerate the Ancient Model.

Racism and "progress" could thus come together in the condemnation of Egyptian/African stagnation and praise of Greek/European dynamism and change.

Thus the growth of childhood went hand in hand with the growth of Romanticism and "progress."

By the middle of the 18th century, however, a number of Christian apologists were using the emerging paradigm of "progress", with its presupposition that "later is better", to promote the Greeks at the expense of the Egyptians. These strands of thought soon merged with two others that were becoming dominant at the same time: racism and Romanticism.[43]

In Bernal's sociology, ideologies, geopolitical strategies, aesthetic movements seem suddenly to "come together," to link up, to concatenate, as Foucault might say. Yet no matter what the particular combination of variables, these led scholars, intellectuals, and artists to precisely the same conclusion: "Black" Africa and "Jewish" Phoenicia played no significant part in the construction of "white" Greek culture. Thus, German as well as French nationalists, Catholic and Protestant academicians, philologists and archaeologists, proponents and opponents of Romanticism, Enlightenment thinkers and Romantics, detractors and defenders of the French Revolution, enthusiasts of progress and those enamored of childhood, Karl Marx and John Stuart Mill—all concur on this one point.

What emerges is a theoretical problem of no small import: How can we account for the fact that scholars in different sociological space and time, with different personal and intellectual agendas, and often beholden to completely antagonistic world views, all seem to share the same general opinion about Afroasiatic influence on ancient Greece? For there are, after all, real contradictions between racism and Christian doctrine, positivism and Romanticism, Eurocentrism and nationalism, Marx and Mill. Yet everywhere in *Black Athena* we find sudden, even unprecedented, linkages between these differing approaches and individuals. What explains this intellectual homogeneity among such a heterogenous cohort? This is what I refer to as the *Black Athena* question.

I will not, of course, be able to conduct anything more than a cursory examination of this issue. For now, I will approach the problem from one particular angle, invoking what Stephen Turner calls "social theories of practices." These types of theories share the assumption that human beings know things that they do not even know that they know; that they "possess" knowledge about the world which exists in some sort of cognitive substrate, beyond the realm of discourse. Yet even though there is no conscious or discursive awareness of its existence, this knowledge influences the way agents think and behave.[44]

Theories of this nature have a distinguished pedigree in social theory. One thinks of the Annales school and the notion of "mentalities." Michel Vovelle describes them as "mental realities which are unformulated . . . which are apparently 'meaningless' and . . . which lead an underground existence at the level of unconscious motivation." Thomas Kuhn, according to some commentators, worked with a notion of "metaparadigms," or what Eckberg and Hill called "unquestioned presuppositions." Michael Polanyi refers to the "tacit dimension." Pierre Bourdieu speaks of the *doxa*, or as Loïc Wacquant defines it "a realm of implicit and unstated beliefs" which govern actions without the agent even realizing it. Erwin Panofsky—an influence on Bourdieu—would speak of the "mental habit" or the unconscious "principle that regulates the act" of human cultural production.[45]

Approaches such as these—and I stress that they are not necessarily identical—might be raised as a possible answer to the *Black Athena* question. Bourdieu's notion of *doxa*, for example, refers to "unthought assumptions." Since they are not objects of conscious deliberation they reside in the "universe of the undiscussed," and are thus undebated. In light of Bernal's hypothesis, we might say that nineteenth-century Europeans retained certain unthought assumptions about their social world. These might include the desirability of cultural and/or biological separation between Europeans on the one side and Semites and Africans on the other. Or these could comprise notions of the absolute, eternal intellectual superiority of "Western" civilization.[46]

These common denominator doxic assumptions bound together disparate individuals, be they artists, writers, scientists, or antiquarians. As such, any encounter with issues pertaining to Afroasiatic civilizations automatically ran the doxic program. In other words, when researchers confronted those ancient Greek texts which praised the ancient Egyptians, the logic of the *doxa* impelled them to doubt the integrity of the Greek sources, to conveniently ignore some inconvenient fact, to unconsciously disregard problematic data, and so on. Similarly, a librettist at work on an Egyptian theme was constrained to depict his subjects in an degrading "Orientalist" light, as would an author depicting this or that aspect of Phoenician antiquity.[47]

Some empirical studies of this period suggest that such a theoretical explanation might not be so far-fetched. As Nancy Stepan and Sander Gilman remark in their examination of scientific racism: "In studying the history of scientific racism, we have been struck by the relative absence of critical challenges to its claims from within mainstream science. The absence is in itself an interesting problem in the sociology of scientific knowledge, since controversy and contention are often taken to be characteristic of science and the route by which empirical certainty is established."[48] This absence of a challenge, or heterodoxy, witnessed in nineteenth-century racial science is a good example of the power of doxic assumptions.

I also wonder if there is not a connection between this type of doxic assumption which obviates critique and the process of "unconscious finagling," described by Stephen Jay Gould in his study of craniometry and race-thinking. When trying to account for the inaccurate findings of Samuel George Morton, findings which seemed to point to the intellectual inferiority of African-Americans, Gould proffers the following reconstruction: "Morton, measuring by seed, picks up a threateningly large black skull, fills it lightly and gives it a few desultory shakes. Next, he takes a distressingly small Caucasian skull, shakes hard, and pushes mightily at the foramen magnum with his thumb. It is easily done, without conscious motivation: expectation is a powerful guide to action."[49] This illustration again underscores the manner in which unrecognized beliefs may shape social action.

These observations are a useful corrective to the learned, sometimes mortal, but somewhat smug critique of *Black Athena* advanced by the intellectual historians Suzanne Marchand and Anthony Grafton. They write, "Intellectual historians shouldn't say, as first year undergraduates do, that everyone in a given period thought or felt alike." Perhaps, but intellectual historians ought familiarize themselves with various forms of Marxism, the Annales school, and contemporary critical theory before drawing such disrespectful parallels. Thus when Marchand and Grafton accurately discover that, "K. O. Müller did not so much reject the Ancient Model as ignore it," or that classicists of the period worked with certain unquestioned assumptions, they fail to draw into their discussion a rather significant body of social theory.[50]

The obvious objection to this scheme is that it is as deterministic as Bernal's model. Am I not merely substituting *doxa* for a Marxist "base" or Bernal's ambiguous causal ideologies? While this is true to a certain degree, I would like to stress that one need not be a Marxist determinist to agree that what Bernal called "external factors" do indeed play a role in knowledge production. Further, doxic assumptions, unlike material factors in vulgar Marxist thought, are not eternal. At certain points in history some individuals succeed, somehow, in making doxic assumptions the object of scrutiny. Bennett Berger has shown that once this occurs the previously unstated, unproblematic assumptions suddenly become arguable. Berger describes this moment: "The genie is out of the bottle; Pandora's box is open; Humpty Dumpty falls off the wall; Bourdieu's 'doxa' is transformed into orthodoxy and heterodoxy." Those who rise to the defense of the newly exposed *doxa*, in Bourdieu's scheme, are referred to as an orthodoxy. Of course, it is a heretic who has made these assumptions manifest.[51]

Our final question becomes, How do we account for heretics, individuals who make *doxa* manifest? In terms of *Black Athena*, how do we explain a Bérard, or a Bernal for that matter? What are the social bases of heresy? What are the social conditions which bind together those who are capable of radical intellectual and artistic innovation? Kuhn, as we saw, suggested that this is a function of being young, or new to a paradigm. Berger argues that this type of innovation is correlated with individuals whose "social biographies . . . have packaged their identities in unusual ways." Thus, people who migrate a lot, float in different "Simmelian social circles," have parents who are extremely young or old are agents of doxic destruction.[52]

These explanations seem plausible to me, though I wish to emphasize that a structural prerequisite for heretical activity lies in being very much a part of the structure. This point will be discussed in the next chapter.

6

A "Total

Contestation" of the

Research University

"Beware the Nonspecialist"

Martin Bernal's indictment of the modern research university is the most heretical component of the case he presents in *Black Athena*. Oddly, this wailing siren of an argument has gone almost entirely unnoticed amid the rhetorical riot which has raged throughout the Controversy. Upon first glance

110

the critique of academe forwarded in *Black Athena* appears somewhat commonplace. The university well is poisoned, Bernal maintained, by disciplinary chauvinism, networks of patronage, hyperspecialization, and inveterate philistinism. To charge that things are abysmally wrong on campus is neither unusual nor unprecedented. Two seasoned veterans of the culture wars have recently observed, "Academy-bashing is now among the fastest-growing of major U.S. industries."[1]

Yet upon deeper scrutiny one discovers another dimension to Bernal's critique, and as far as I can tell it bears little resemblance to recent academy-bashing. For *Black Athena* may be read as—to borrow a line from Foucault—"a total contestation" of the Western research university. It is insinuated that the latter was flawed from its inception; that it is congenitally biased against certain groups and certain types of knowledge claims; that by dint of its very structure it is incapable of accommodating dissent—indeed, the university is portrayed as an institution whose primary function consists of silencing heterodox voices.

Permit me, then, to delineate an aspect of Bernal's hypothesis which he tends to neglect, understate, and even misunderstand: In his sociology of knowledge the university itself is as responsible for the paradigm shift as any external factor he has discussed. The academy for Bernal is a field, a relay station, which exerts a magnetic pull on air-bound external factors. Once consolidated within the heavy machinery of the academy, these ideological vectors are processed into more elevated cultural forms, and then retransmitted into the nonacademic world with infinitely more intellectual coherence and power. For example, a crude, widely dispersed, anti-Semitic sentiment "in the air" is transfigured by the academy into an attenuated, rationalized doctrine of the categorical, transhistorical inferiority of the Jewish people. The university—not racism or anti-Semitism or Romanticism or whatever—is the key analytical variable in *Black Athena*'s sociology of knowledge.

In what follows I will articulate Bernal's very intriguing, very undeveloped, and very disorganized critique of the Occidental university. By pursuing this line of analysis, I will have occasion to reconstruct and refurbish his typologies of "insiders" and "outsiders." In so doing, I will construct my own typology of the academic heretic.

Tainted Origins, Bad Intellectual and Institutional Forms: Göttingen

Black Athena cannot be read as a tale about the decline of the research university. Its author is in no way beholden to the idea of the "moral collapse" or "ruin" or "decomposition" of a once illustrious institution. Insofar as this institution is held to have been on the wrong track since it embarked upon its journey, it cannot be said to have lost its way.[2]

In the fourth chapter of volume 1, Bernal offers an overview of the history of the "Enlightenment" University of Göttingen between 1775 and 1830. It was from here that the "academic attack on the Ancient Model" was launched. Leaning heavily on the work of R. Steven Turner, the author describes this celebrated institution as "the embryo of *all* later, *modern, diversified* and *professional* universities." By "diversified" he refers not to the existence of an eighteenth-century multicultural campus, but to the emergence of a division of intellectual labor which we might refer to as disciplinarity. For it was during this period that the academy parceled the pursuit of knowledge into discrete disciplines.[3]

Bernal's use of the term *professional* also necessitates explanation. Whereas the professionalization of the university may strike some as a laudable goal, in *Black Athena* it is viewed as a process whose effects were patently disastrous. While Bernal is less than thorough in his treatment of this issue, the following may be said with relative certainty. The concept of professionalism refers to a sort of ethos which gripped members of the burgeoning Göttingen faculty around the turn of the eighteenth century. This ethos consisted of the belief that detachment was a prerequisite for objective scholarship. (Ostensibly, the belief in objective scholarship must also be seen as part of this ethos.) Professors in the humanities now viewed themselves as scientists—impartial, precise, and blindly obedient to the facts. Unlike other thinkers of the period, they concentrated on specific areas of inquiry, using the newfangled methods of their particular discipline. The process entailed a new hierarchization of the intellectual order. The claims of the scientific university specialist were endowed with a singular legitimacy. The work of popular writers was now relegated to a secondary status.[4]

Aside from the apotheosis of the professor, this ethos of professionalism, alleges Bernal, engendered specific "institutional forms" and a specific "intellectual framework." Among the former he lists the rise of the scholarly journal with its obscurantist prose (i.e., prose which could be deciphered only by the professional and thus foreclosed the participation of the nonspecialist), the development of specific academic departments capable of securing state funding, and the invention of the seminar as a tool for training classics teachers. Elsewhere, Bernal calls attention to the development of student-teacher networks, a point which I shall return to later.[5]

As for the intellectual framework, Bernal argues that one of the distinguishing features of Göttingen research was a Romantically inspired emphasis on ethnicity and race as master variables for scholarly analysis. Léon Poliakov refers to Göttingen in this period as "a veritable hotbed of anti-Jewish propaganda." One thinks of faculty members such as the renowned Semitist and anti-Semite, Johann David Michaelis (1717–1791), Christoph Meiners (1745–1810; later to be praised by Nazi historians), and the more complex Johann Friedrich Blumenbach (1752–1840), whom we will discuss below.[6]

Altertumswissenschaft

If it is true that Friedrich Nietzsche forwarded "the most radical critique of classical scholarship ever made from within the profession," then Martin Bernal must be one of the most acerbic external critics of this discipline. While Bernal never gets around to calling them "screech-owls," he does, like Nietzsche, accuse students of Greco-Roman antiquity of political conservatism, intellectual cowardice, and rank careerism. He would certainly agree with Nietzsche's remark, "The philological profession—to see this as a problem."[7]

According to the author, the most important intellectual development associated with Göttingen was the emergence of *Altertumswissenschaft* (i.e., the science of antiquity), also known as *Philologie*. As Rudolf Pfeiffer notes, this discipline, with its concentration on "all aspects of the ancient world including religion," was soon to become the core "of secondary and university humanistic education in Prussia." From there it was later transported to Britain and the United States, where it became known as "classics."[8]

There are innumerable links between Göttingen and the development of *Altertumswissenschaft*. Many of the discipline's founders and leading lights, such as Christian Gottlob Heyne, Friedrich August Wolf, Karl Otfried Müller and Ernst Curtius, were either students or faculty at this university. Further, nearly all of the "institutional forms" as well as the "intellectual framework" discussed above could be identified in the pioneer discipline situated on the pioneer campus. Ethnicity and race, for example, were major intellectual preoccupations for these early classicists. In Bernal's estimation, most of these scholars were racists, anti-Semites, Romantics, Eurocentrists, and philhellenists.[9]

There are class dimensions to the new "science" of classics as well. *Altertumswissenschaft* played an important role in ideologically nurturing the "leaders of the future"—that is, the children of the elite. In *The Greek Heritage in Victorian Britain*, Frank Turner observes:

> General familiarity with the classics was once one of the distinguishing and self-defining marks of the social and intellectual elite of Europe. It had originated in thoroughly aristocratic times and endured through the first century of the liberal democratic age. To no small extent knowledge of the classical world and acquaintance with the values communicated through the vehicle of classical education informed the mind and provided much of the intellectual confidence of the ruling political classes of Europe.[10]

Situated as such within the burgeoning university, classicists were poised to eradicate the Ancient Model. Bernal writes, "I maintain that it is to the work of the Classicists that we owe the construction of that cultural trajectory that has served to establish Greece as the sole birthplace of 'Western Civilization' and the site of a unique, almost miraculous, spiritual development that supposedly elevates 'Western Man' to humanity's pinnacle." Throughout *Black Athena* the author pillories various classicists he believes have plotted this trajectory. In many ways, his text serves as a sort of antagonistic companion to *Classical Scholarship: A Biographical Encyclopedia*—a volume in which far more flattering portraits of the same scholars are drawn.[11]

At this point, I wish to intervene and refurbish the author's hypothesis. The university, through its hegemonic classics departments, collated Bernal's various "external factors" (racism, anti-Semitism, burgeoning capitalism, etc.) and transformed them into a refined discourse, or series of statements, about the ancient Greeks, Egyptians, Phoenicians, and others. In turn, these statements gave shape and strength to the political initiatives of nineteenth-century European governments pertaining to Africans and Jews. Notice that in my reconstruction there is no privileging or primacy of "external factors" over "internal factors." Rather, there is reciprocal interaction, or feedback, between the analytical levels. Be that as it may, the university emerges in my scheme (and I think Bernal's as well) as a—perhaps *the*—crucial node in a network of interrelated, albeit potentially autonomous, institutions.

In my understanding, however, the university is internally and externally dissentient. Within its walls scholars disagree—it is, and always has been, a field of competition and conflict. In Bernal's reading, by contrast, the nineteenth-century academy is an oddly homogenous, tension-free entity when it comes to the Ancient and Aryan Models. Nearly all of its workers in the humanities advocated the Aryan Model, the same Aryan Model which informed the thinking and action of politicians, generals, and industrialists. This is what makes his hypothesis so peculiar: The entire thrust of *all* nineteenth-century fields (e.g., politics, philology, art) pushes toward the Aryan Model with inexorable force and without major resistance.

Any student of the intellectual history of the period would deem this state of affairs utterly preposterous. The internal and external tensions within and between European societies during this period are well known. In my previous chapter, I attempted to lead Bernal out of this quandary by positing the existence of doxic beliefs. In other words, while internal and external dissent was everywhere, there were certain issues (e.g., the inferiority of Jews and African civilizations) which everyone, unthinkingly, agreed upon. This, I believe, is the only way Bernal can defend his rather homogenous conception of nineteenth-century thought on Greek origins.

The University Today

Perhaps the reader has noticed the clever rhetorical stratagem which Bernal deploys in his discussion of Göttingen and *Altertumswissenschaft*. In casting this institution as the pathological patriarch of the Western academic apparatus, the author is able to frame his critique of the university in the most pervasive terms possible. By demonstrating that the genetic structure of the storied protouniversity was defective, he permits his indictment to extend indefinitely through time and space. *Black Athena*, I wish to claim, is not a tale about one bad institution of higher learning, but a portrait of a severely dysfunctional Western university culture, with the discipline of classics at its moral and intellectual center. Once again, this is an idea which Bernal insinuates rather than documents.

The first volume of Bernal's work is subtitled *The Fabrication of Ancient Greece, 1785–1985.* The fabrication to which the author alludes—that is, the repression of the Ancient Model—stretches from the Golden Age of Göttingen right up to the publication of *Black Athena.* The implication is clear: the research university—of yesterday, of today—is also to be held accountable for the paradigm shift. It is no coincidence that the professionalism, disciplinarity, and disdain for the layperson which Bernal identified in Göttingen he will identify again in contemporary academe.

One of the major problems with today's university, argues Bernal, lies in its disciplinary structure. In his view the student is taught more than just theories and methods when being trained in a discipline, for the student also learns—often vicariously—those theories and methods which are to be excluded. A tacit assumption of *Black Athena* is that within every discipline one paradigm or model invariably functions as an intellectual orthodoxy. We have seen this supposition at work in Bernal's claim that the entire field of classics was and is dominated by the Aryan paradigm. Why, in Bernal's view, does this monopoly exist? In order to frame an answer to this question we might envision a symbiotic relation between a scholar and his or her discipline. The latter, as we just saw, bequeaths to the academician a paradigmatic framework. The scholar, in return, is responsible for maintaining the integrity of the discipline. This consists of conducting research within its accepted parameters, publishing the results, conveying this knowledge to the next generation, and—most significantly for Bernal—defending the paradigm from dissenters.[12]

It is this obsessively defensive posture, this tendency of academicians to act as suspicious gatekeepers of their field rather than welcoming hosts of open intellectual inquiry, which so concerns and infuriates Bernal. Innovations in thought, he charges, are almost impossible under such conditions. And here we arrive at a major theme in Bernal's sociology of knowledge: The disciplinary structure of the university—with its ethic of exclusion of other perspectives and its ethic of self-replication—is an impediment to accurate research, creative intellectual work, and scholarly progress.[13]

Bernal proposes that a department of "ancient studies" would presumably rectify the problem of monadic, incestuous, and uncommunicative disciplines. His new discipline—though perhaps this is not the proper term—would be characterized by dialogue among the presently atomized discourses of antiquity (Egyptology, Mediterranean archaeology, Semitic studies, classics, etc.). Under such an arrangement, classics would no longer occupy what Bernal sees as its leading position in the hierarchy of antiquity studies.[14]

Insiders

When the author speaks of the types of historical knowledge which Western societies produce he concentrates on the interrelations between two mutually exclusive demographic groups. He refers to these as "insiders" and "outsiders." Stated somewhat generically, insiders are professional academicians. Yet it is their peculiar psychological disposition which is of greatest interest to Bernal. Insiders, the author alleges, are intellectually conservative. They would rather defend their paradigm, regardless of its deficiencies, than strike out on behalf of a new one. Thus, the most obvious symptom of the disease which afflicts insiders—"paradigmatic myopia" we might call it—is an inveterate hostility to innovation. Bernal draws a distinction between "sins of omission" and "sins of commission." The latter necessitate forwarding some sort of new hypothesis or interpretation. This activity, he argues, is frowned upon in the professional study of antiquity: "At present, academic sins of commission are punished ferociously, while there is a great tolerance towards those of omission which involve uncritical acceptance of the status quo."[15] In a discussion of the implications of his Thera heresy (see Chapter 2 above), Bernal remarks: "The extraordinary slowness to accept the new evidence demonstrates the way in which scholars tend to rally to the structures they have been taught, and upon which they have spun their hypotheses; they demand absolute proof from challengers without pausing to reconsider the bases of their own beliefs, which in this case were extremely flimsy."[16]

Implicit in the discussion of insiders is the notion of voluntary self-censorship. The insider is not seen as coerced into accepting a dominant paradigm. On the contrary, his or her adherence to an orthodoxy is consensual. These considerations remind me of a remark made by C. Wright Mills in a discussion of the dangers which confront intellectuals who practice in the university:

> Yet the deepest problem of freedom for teachers is not the occasional ousting of a professor, but a vague general fear—sometimes politely known as "discretion," "good taste," or "balanced judgment." It is a fear which leads to self-intimidation and finally becomes so habitual that the scholar is unaware of it. The real restraints are not so much external prohibitions as control of the insurgent by the agreements of academic gentlemen.[17]

To this point, we have seen that an insider is an academician who is tethered to a discipline's dominant paradigm. Timidity of thought is viewed as his or her defining psychological characteristic. The question arises as to how the university generates this culture of insiders. Bernal's response, as I understand it, hinges on the following units of analysis: (1) the insider's network, (2) graduate school, (3) university presses, and (4) funding. Starting with the overarching concept of network, let us examine the following quote from Bourdieu: "A 'recommendation' by Y of a pupil of X may perhaps be repaid by a book review in a weekly written by a member of X's 'ideological family,' after X has drawn their attention to Y's book, taking advantage of an editorial committee meeting, an electoral commission or an electoral support committee."[18] This passage is culled from Bourdieu's study of the French university system, *Homo Academicus.* The passage exemplifies what Bourdieu refers to as a *"circuit of continuous exchanges"* which characterize the field of modern higher education. In a more rudimentary form, this notion of "a viciously circular mechanism of obligations which breed obligations" appears in *Black Athena.* Another useful idea from Bourdieu's analysis concerns the question of social reproduction. In Bourdieu's sociology, the university field manifests a sort of active inertia; tremendous efforts are exerted by scholars in order to replicate their own methodologies, theories, and paradigms.[19]

In *Black Athena* graduate school is seen as the first arena in which the circuit is established and replication occurs. Toward the end of volume 1, Bernal points to the case of a doctoral student at the University of Pennsylvania whose prose seems to contort in an effort to avoid disputing the Aryan Model of his professor. In reviewing a particularly diplomatic passage from the student's thesis, Bernal comments that it "shows signs of the difficulties involved when a student comes to conclusions that run counter to the strongly held views of his professor." The implication, of course, is that graduate school is a locus of paradigmatic replication.[20]

In terms of replicating an insider culture, graduate school might be seen as serving numerous functions. First, it inculcates the paradigm. Second, it is a place where students learn, in an apprenticelike manner, what Lewis Coser called "the rules of the academic game." Third, it serves as a screening center for the elimination of "undesirables." The latter term, seen through Bernal's optic, refers to those capable of original and critical scholarship. When the process is completed the ex-student will be raised to the rank of "dear colleague." The network is extended. New circular avenues of exchange are paved. And the vaunted tradition of scholarly replication continues.[21]

Academic publishing houses appear as another decisive command post in Bernal's analysis of the insider's network. University presses, it is maintained, serve to constrict, not enlarge, the flow of intellectual alternatives available to the reading public. Insofar as manuscripts and articles are almost always evaluated by other academicians, the circuit of exchanges and reproduction is again present. The author writes, "Control of university presses, and major influence over the commercial ones, allows academics supporting the *status quo* to 'maintain standards'—as they would express it—or, in other words, to repress opposition to orthodoxy." Bernal apparently lived this experience. In the 1995 special issue of the journal *Vest* he summarizes the problems he had getting his manuscript published: "Thus, as in Britain *Black Athena* did not pass through the academic processes normally required in the USA. It was only because of my peculiarly good connections with scholars in other disciplines that I was able to bypass them. It was not that the system had failed to filter out heresy."[22]

Last, Bernal concentrates on funding within the university. In a response to Mary Lefkowitz's *Not Out of Africa,* Bernal replies to her charge that Afrocentric historians are poor historians by claiming that they are only historians who are poor:

That Afrocentrists should make so many mistakes is understandable. Theirs is a sense of being embattled in a hostile world and of possessing an absolute truth that makes for less concern about factual detail. More important, however, are the extraordinary material difficulties confronted in acquiring training in the requisite languages, in finding time and space to carry on research, money to buy books or access to libraries, let alone finding publishers who can provide academic checks and competent proofreaders. None of these handicaps applies to [Mary] Lefkowitz, a scholar of Latin and Greek. She has for many years been tenured at a prestigious college and has been the recipient of foundation grants.[23]

For now we may forward a provisional, reconstructed definition of Bernal's insiders: *They are an informally unified community of academic specialists who, through their activities in a self-replicating network of exchanges, uphold the sanctioned paradigm (or one of the major sanctioned paradigms) of their discipline.*

Heretics (Inside/Outsiders)

In the introduction to volume 1 Bernal notes, "Fundamental challenges to disciplines tend to come from outside." Unfortunately, when discussing "outsiders" Bernal tends to lump together two groups under one heading. As such, I will again need to renovate a Bernalian category. There are, in my opinion, two distinct types of outsiders discussed in *Black Athena:* heretics and laypersons.[24]

Heretics are academicians who risk professional life and limb by dissenting from a discipline's dominant paradigm. The occasional classicist who disagreed with the Aryan Model in the nineteenth and early twentieth century may be considered an excellent candidate for this designation. The relations between insiders and heretics, as the reader might have guessed, are less than cordial. The reasons behind this mutual antipathy might be conceptualized in terms of a religious metaphor. Let us think of insiders as persons who believe themselves to be the orthodox members, or the "official" variant, of a particular religion. As Coser pointed out in *The Functions of Social Conflict*, the religious heretic poses especial dangers to the reigning orthodoxy:

> By upholding the group's central values and goals, he threatens to split it into factions that will differ as to the means for implementing its goal. *Unlike the apostate, the heretic claims to uphold the group's values and interests, only proposing different means to this end or variant interpretations of the official creed. . . . The heretic proposes alternatives where the groups wants no alternative to exist. . . .* In this respect, the heretic calls forth all the more hostility in that he still has much in common with his former fellow-members in sharing their goals.[25]

To transpose this insight into the key of academic life we could say that the heretic jeopardizes the aforementioned integrity of the discipline. Ostensibly, she challenges the fundamental tenets of the preferred paradigm. If correct, the heretic is poised to stimulate what Thomas Kuhn calls "a crisis"—a state of "large-scale paradigm destruction." It is in this manner that the outsider proposes alternatives where the insiders want none to exist.[26]

We should recall that the capacity to plunge a paradigm into a state of crisis is not an option available to nonscholars. When a journalist, a politician, a religious figure, businessperson, or a meddlesome trustee publicly criticizes university scholarship, the response from the academy is, typically enough, to ridicule the plaintiff. After all, what do *they* know about what *we* do? What credentials do *they* have?[27]

Yet the heretic, as Coser's remarks illustrate, cannot be dismissed with such ease. This individual has much in common with the insiders. By dint of her adherence to the values of university culture (e.g., the possession of scholarly credentials, conducting and publishing research, writing in a scholarly idiom) hers is recognized as a legitimate voice of dissent. This is why I disagree with Bernal's reference to heretics (and himself) as "outsiders." Heretics resemble insiders in many significant ways, and therein lies their unique capacity for subversion. For these reasons it is best to refer to heretics as *inside/outsiders,* a term I have borrowed from the Afrocentrist writer Jacob Carruthers's critique of *Black Athena.*[28]

It was Georg Simmel's observation that "the persecution of heretics and dissenters springs from the instinct for the necessity of group unity." In academe, the "circuit of exchanges" is one of the primary mechanisms of this unity.[29] And for this reason, as Bourdieu has shown, the heretic is extremely threatening:

> The founders of a heretical scientific order break the exchange agreement that is accepted, at least tacitly, by candidates for the succession: recognizing no other principle of legitimation than the one they intend to impose, they refuse to enter the cycle of the *exchange of recognition* which ensures an orderly transmission of scientific authority between the holders and the pretenders.[30]

In light of these considerations we might describe the academic heretic as an institutionally legitimate voice who makes illegitimate claims (e.g., transforming *doxa* into heterodoxy and orthodoxy) which may imperil the solidity and consequent reproduction of the insider's network; or, an insider who makes claims heard only on the outside.

Black Athena occasionally examines cases of intrepid heretics who dared to challenge the Aryan Model. For Bernal, insiders deploy one of two basic responses to the heretic. First, they ignore the scholarship of the latter. If this fails to minimize the threat significantly, the defenders of the status quo then engage in coordinated seek-and-destroy missions. Their express goal, according to Bernal, is to ridicule the research of the dissenter and, if possible, to destroy his or her scholarly reputation in the process.[31]

Laypersons (Outside/Outsiders)

Unlike insiders and heretics (inside/outsiders), laypersons are not professional academicians and for this reason they cannot be heretics. They have not received any formal scholarly training. They have little or no knowledge of the very peculiar and exclusive language of scholarship. (As Bourdieu and Passeron have remarked: "Academic language is a dead language . . . and is no one's mother tongue.") Consequently, they have no access to those fora in which legitimate knowledge claims are made (e.g., professional journals, monographs, interviews with the news media, university classrooms, scholarly conferences). As Louis Menand noted in his discussion of academic freedom, for those who are not specialists, the professional and specialized university "constitutes not a freedom but an almost completely disabling restriction."[32]

One thing which laypersons sometimes have, however, is an intense— often intensely personal—interest in the subject which the insiders have arrogated to themselves as their exclusive intellectual domain. In very rare instances an individual layperson has overcome the aforementioned disadvantages and made a significant contribution to a particular scholarly field. This usually consists of a claim or discovery which challenges the reigning paradigm of the discipline. Bernal grinningly reminds us that two of the more significant breakthroughs in the study of Greek antiquity were made by an eccentric tycoon (Heinrich Schliemann, who excavated the sites of Troy and Mycenae) and an architect (Michael Ventris, who was instrumental in deciphering Linear B). Elsewhere he declares, "I . . . hope to puncture the myth of professionalism and the belief that knowledge is the monopoly of academic specialists."[33]

This having been said we are now prepared to identify in *Black Athena* a congeries of new and heretofore unrecognized outrages against the academy. There is an unwritten, albeit sacrosanct, rule of scholarship which prescribes the proper relation between a researcher and his or her audience. This law stipulates that—other than professional colleagues—the true scholar has no relation with an audience. Our inquiries, in theory, are not aimed at any particular constituency; we have no fan base outside of the university. The academician's alleged disinterest extends not only to his or her results, but to the social identity of those who consume the research.[34]

By now we have learned that wherever there is a traditional scholarly ethos, Martin Bernal is somewhere in the vicinity wielding power tools. In discussing the *New York Times*'s refusal to review his first volume, Bernal suggests that a negative evaluation would have resulted in "a barrage of angry letters from my Black supporters." Elsewhere, he makes reference to the "positive response" to *Black Athena* "from the Black and other non-European communities." In this passage Bernal is not referring to scholars, but to communities of laypersons.[35]

Yet the author does not only identify a specific audience as his own—he actively solicits one as well. Like most controversial scholarly works, *Black Athena* was discussed at university symposia, the pages of the *New York Review of Books*, the *New York Times* (belatedly), scholarly journals, and so on. But Bernal refused to sequester his text within the provincial confines of American intellectual culture. Accordingly, he lectured at community centers, made himself available to mass-circulation magazines, spoke on popular radio shows, and aired his views on television. This type of aggressive engagement with a lay audience is highly unusual—and often highly stigmatized—within university culture.[36]

Yet all of this is just a prelude to *Black Athena*'s greatest heresy, for Martin Bernal suggests that laypersons may sometimes be better at assessing evidence than insiders. "Professional opinion," he writes, "should be studied carefully and treated with respect." Yet to this unremarkable statement Bernal adds a rather spectacular qualifier: The views of scholars "should not always be taken as the last word."[37] In another hair-raising passage, he asserts:

> To a layperson, the idea of close connections between Homeric Greece, Ugarit and biblical Palestine seems perfectly plausible in view of their historical and geographical proximity. . . . For the professional, things were "not so simple," and laymen, who had no idea of the details of the situation contained in the scholarly literature, had no right to challenge the experts. Unfortunately, however, much as academics would like it to be so—because their status and livelihood depend on it—*the obvious is not always false!* Sometimes it is possible to say in retrospect that members of the lay public have known better than the professionals.[38]

How to enrage the academic establishment: Tell individuals who have devoted their entire lives to the pursuit of highly specialized knowledge within the university system that their conclusions are not authoritative; then tell them that it is precisely because they pursued highly specialized knowledge within the university system that their claims are not authoritative; suggest that those who have *not* devoted their lives to the pursuit of specialized knowledge should have the last word in assessing these claims; and anoint these laypersons as a sort of civilian review board, invested with the authority to examine scholarly incompetence and misconduct.

A certain strategic motive may be identified in this effort to forge a union of heretic and lay communities. Bernal has put his own sociology of knowledge to work. Insofar as he knew very well that insiders typically ignore heretics, the author launched a preemptive strike. He went right to the people—he spoke publicly and passionately to students and educated laypersons. He exerted pressure on the academic field, not by aligning himself with politicians, artists, or religious figures, but by soliciting the interest of community activists, radicalized undergraduates, left-leaning journalists, and so on. By making *Black Athena* a work that could not be ignored, Bernal effectively neutralized the acidic indifference of the insiders' network. Realizing that this text could not be relegated to the shelves of bibliographical oblivion, the insiders were forced to confront its substantive claims.[39]

This confrontation was fraught with unexpected dangers. Those who attacked the work found themselves exposed to decidedly unscholarly reactions: some were booed at conferences where they expressed opposition to *Black Athena;* others were denounced as racists in the campus newspaper or in letters to the editor; a few were accused of being obsequious defenders of the status quo. Many felt that the statement of any disagreement with Bernal's theories led to an automatic charge of being a racist. Bernal—by his own admission—effectively "outflanked" the insiders by bringing his case to a general reading public. Given the notoriety of *Black Athena,* I would suggest that this tactic has worked quite well. Whether this is an entirely salutary development in terms of American intellectual culture is an altogether separate issue.[40]

This aspiration to convert the layperson from passive observer to active participant in the process of knowledge production is another central and unnoticed theme of Martin Bernal's work. It must be stressed that the author is not the first scholar to suggest this transvaluation of the existing intellectual order. Once again, Bernal's thought evinces clear correspondences with the work of contemporary university radicals. Some theorists have undertaken to recast the traditional relation between the knowledge expert and the layperson. No less a manifesto than Jean-François Lyotard's *Postmodern Condition: A Report on Knowledge* ends with the plea that computer scientists "give the public free access to the memory and the data banks."[41] A similar distrust and discrediting of legitimate knowers may be seen in Michel Foucault's remark in an interview with Gilles Deleuze: "In the most recent upheaval [May 1968], the intellectual discovered that the masses no longer need him to gain knowledge: they *know* perfectly well, without illusion; they know far better than he and they are certainly capable of expressing themselves."[42] This beheading, so to speak, of the knowledge expert, the intellectual, the scholar, and so forth, can be identified in some feminist pedagogies as well. There, it is often the professor's classroom hegemony which is called into question. In *Engaging Feminism: Students Speak Up and Speak Out,* the editors write, "We believe that the next step in feminist reconstructions of the academy is to challenge the authority relations of faculty (the class of knowers) to students (the recipients of knowledge) by developing a student-based critique of teaching and learning."[43]

The Specialist Strikes Back

One would think that this description of the besotted origins of the research university would elicit some type of reaction from those who have participated in the Controversy. Conservatives have failed to capitalize on their chance to reprimand Bernal for casting aspersions on one of the West's most revered institutions. Progressives have yet to use this argument as a means of buttressing the claim that only a radical break with the inglorious traditions of the past will save the university; missed was an opportunity to call for a new curriculum, new disciplinary structures, and zero tolerance for biased pedagogy.

The section on Göttingen has received sustained scrutiny from only one commentator. In his essay "Eighteenth-Century Historiography in *Black Athena*," the extremely erudite historian of science Robert Palter devotes a few punishing pages to Bernal's controversial reconstruction. In reading this piece one is able to recognize, with unusual clarity, one of the central tensions of the *Black Athena* controversy: the conflict between the academic specialist and the sweeping generalist.[44]

One cannot but be impressed by Palter's vast knowledge of eighteenth- and nineteenth-century French, British, and German scholarly literature as well as his command of contemporary secondary sources. Its vituperative tone notwithstanding, it must be acknowledged that his long essay advances some excellent criticisms of *Black Athena*. But let there be no doubt as to Palter's objectives: he wishes not only to set the record straight, but to prove that Martin Bernal is an amateur scholar, a professional ideologue, and a mediocre source for radical ideas at that. Early on Palter writes:

> Those today who are seriously concerned with formulating a radical political critique of contemporary scholarship—and, in particular, of contemporary classical scholarship—might wish to think twice before associating themselves with the methods and claims of Bernal's work; for his lapses in the most rudimentary requirements of sound historical study—traditional, critical, *any* kind of historical study—should make one wary of his grandiose historiographical pronouncements.[45]

In order to show that Bernal's investigation is partial (in both senses of the word) Palter performs a series of rhetorical acrobatics with an unusually high degree of difficulty. He begins his essay by audaciously pointing to arguments which Bernal *could have* cited in order to bolster his thesis of widespread Egyptophilia in eighteenth-century European high culture. Had the author of *Black Athena* been sufficiently schooled in the relevant scholarly materials, he would have referred to the work of French admirers of Egypt such as Jean Jacques Rousseau or the Abbé Henri Grégoire. Yet before the reader receives the impression that Bernal was correct in his Egyptophilia thesis but perhaps not very thorough, Palter demonstrates that he was wrong in his thesis and not very thorough. There were, after all, eminent French Egyptophobes in the eighteenth century, such as Diderot and Voltaire—a state of affairs that undoubtedly weakens Bernal's argument.[46]

In turning to eighteenth-century Britain, Palter continues to give his opponent an academic working over. Whereas Bernal argued that a playwright named Edward Young wrote "a series of Egyptian plays," Palter concludes that he wrote only one (which was performed for nine nights). He taunts, "There may be evidence of pervasive Egyptophilia in British plays of the eighteenth century, but Bernal has not found it." And on and on it goes. For purposes of brevity I have cited just a few of many instances in which Palter identifies mistakes, misreadings, and oversimplifications in *Black Athena*.[47]

In order to understand Palter's treatment of Göttingen, we must first identify the basic hypothesis which undergirds his analysis. Unlike most participants in the Controversy, Palter does not seem to accept the charge that racism and anti-Semitism affected eighteenth- and nineteenth-century scholarship. "Many otherwise critical readers," he avers, "have accepted (without much question) the account in volume I of how ethnic and racial biases, especially during the nineteenth and twentieth centuries, have distorted scholarly accounts of the ancient world." The specialist card is again played as it is suggested that "the uncritical acceptance" of Bernal's thesis is attributable to the fact that "so few historians of Modern Europe" have read *Black Athena*.[48]

The degree to which Palter believes that racism and anti-Semitism affected scholarship is not clear. He does, however, advance a rather tantalizing theory of his own. In a discussion of Britain he notes: "I begin by suggesting that *if racist beliefs and practices were centrally important in eighteenth-century British and American society, so was the opposition to such beliefs and practices.* (Which is not to say that racism and antiracism were 'equally' strong or entrenched in those societies.)"[49] In applying this theory to Göttingen, Palter notes that "there were *significant antiracist and universalistic (antichauvinistic) elements in German culture as a whole, and in Göttingen higher education in particular.*"[50]

To confirm this hypothesis Palter demonstrates that J. F. Blumenbach was no garden-variety racist. Bernal, it is charged, "makes little effort to grapple with the complexities and tensions in Blumenbach's thought." For the latter was far less ethnocentric than his colleagues when tackling the question of the intellectual and moral capacities of persons of African descent. Elsewhere, it is noted that racists on the Göttingen faculty did not go unchallenged. Palter cites the case of Georg Forster who wrote a stinging critique, albeit anonymously, of Christoph Meiners's racist positions. Even though Forster was not a professor at Göttingen (though Heyne was his father-in-law), he was nevertheless on close terms with many members of the faculty. His diatribe against Meiners was enthusiastically embraced by other members of the local professorate, a fact which Palter believes proves the existence of antiracism at Göttingen.[51]

Yet there are a few flaws in this critique that even a nonspecialist in eighteenth-century European intellectual history could identify. In the passage cited above Palter spoke of "significant" opposition to racism at Göttingen. Yet to show that there were a handful of antiracists—by my count, one who is named explicitly—in and around the Göttingen faculty does not seem to constitute a "significant" amount. Nor does the fact that Forster wrote the critique of Meiners anonymously suggest the existence of an intellectual atmosphere in which such antiracist ideas could be expressed with impunity.[52]

In commenting on the proportion of racist to nonracist figures in Britain Palter writes, "I have no statistical evidence on whether, as Bernal would have it, 'most 18th-century English-speaking thinkers . . . were racist' . . . but so far as I can see, neither does he." There are two fundamental problems with this last claim. Statistically speaking, Palter fails to mention that Bernal's argument is far more substantive than his. The latter's examples of eighteenth- and early nineteenth-century racists overwhelmingly outnumber the antiracists of the former. Yet this is nowhere near so important as the question of the relative power of the ideas under consideration. *Black Athena* does not merely charge that there were many racists in Britain, France, Germany, and America in the eighteenth and early nineteenth century. It is as concerned with the social location of these ideas and their bearers in the knowledge-producing world. Over and over again, Bernal shows how scholars beholden to racist ideas were situated at the intellectual and political command posts of the societies in question, be it in the university, politics, or influential literary circles. A simple head count of prominent eighteenth-century racists versus nonracists—which, I repeat, does not seem to tally in Palter's favor—is nowhere near so relevant as a comparison of the breadth of such ideas as well as their connection to figures and institutions of real social power.[53]

This brings us to the question of the "complexities and tensions" in Blumenbach's thought which Bernal the nonspecialist missed. Palter goes to great lengths (he even includes an appendix devoted to the subject) to sketch a rather flattering portrait of Blumenbach. Yet to prove that the noted racial taxonomist was not much of a racist himself—Palter has convinced me of this—does not necessarily weaken *Black Athena*'s argument so much as it calls attention to its author's proclivity for irresponsible statements. Bernal (as Palter himself acknowledges) never contended that Blumenbach was a racist on par with other thinkers of the period, though he did dub him a Eurocentrist. (Palter, however, seems to have missed a rather pointed jab at Blumenbach by Bernal in *Black Athena* 1: 27–28) Bernal did claim, however, that Blumenbach's research was wholly predicated on the variables of race and ethnicity, a point which Palter's appendix conveniently verifies. What Bernal in his reconstruction of eighteenth-century intellectual history finds significant about this scholar's oeuvre is his obsession with issues of race and racial hierarchy. To plead that Blumenbach was no racist is to miss Bernal's point. What was for Blumenbach a scholarly preoccupation, a research agenda, eventually provided others—many others—with an intellectual foundation for racist thought and practice.[54]

Further, Palter inexplicably concentrates his analysis of eighteenth-century German intellectual history on racism and racism alone. We have had numerous occasions to observe, however, that Bernal's explanation of the paradigm shift is not monocausal. While Palter is busy defending a few members of the Göttingen faculty from charges of racism, he leaves Bernal's well-documented charges regarding philhellenic sentiment at Göttingen uncontested. Nor is the influence of Romantic ideology addressed. This brings us to Palter's most glaring and inexplicable omission. Somehow, his entire analysis of Göttingen omits any reference to anti-Semitism—not, I think, an irrelevant issue when dealing with the German-speaking university of the eighteenth and nineteenth centuries.[55]

Conclusion

In his masterfully crafted collection of essays entitled *In Theory: Classes, Nations, Literatures,* Aijaz Ahmad briefly discusses some of the scholarly reactions which greeted Edward Said's *Orientalism.* In summarizing Bernard Lewis's well-known riposte, Ahmad observes: "His attack was unseemly on many counts, but the substantive point which Lewis raised was one of competence. What authorized Said to speak of Arab history and Orientalist disciplines? What degrees did he have? Did he know such-and-such a medieval Arabic dictionary? Did he know the meaning of such-and-such a word in the whole range of Arabic lexicography over ten centuries? Etc."[56]

We have seen this all before. The charge of incompetence (not to mention the unseemly tone) stands as one of the recurring motifs in specialist discussions of Bernal's work. "He is the armchair archaeologist par excellence," declare Lefkowitz and Rogers. The very title of L. Pearce Williams's truncated article "Why I Stopped Reading *Black Athena*" conveys the frustration which this text often arouses among its academic audience.[57] Frank Turner advances a far less acrimonious and far more constructive review of Bernal's text. Yet, as with Palter, Williams, and dozens of others, when the issue of Bernal's scholarly method is addressed one detects a little sulfur in the air:

> In my view it is this consistent absence of particularistic analysis that mars and from the standpoint of intellectual history almost fatally flaws the credibility of Professor Bernal's argument as it is presented. Such analysis does require the study of long German volumes, but it is the only way to master the material and to assert the argument in a scholarly responsible manner. And if that be a declaration of faith in the practices of professional scholarship on my part, then let Professor Bernal make the most of it.[58]

As regards scholarship, the principal complaints levied against *Black Athena* might be summarized as follows: Bernal makes mistakes that no competent scholar in my field would make. Bernal oversimplifies a complex reality. Bernal is oblivious to nuances in the materials he examines. Bernal's work, unlike mine, is singularly motivated by a political agenda.

What is astonishing, and initially disconcerting, is the fact that Bernal often agrees, in part or in whole, with these opinions. (Edward Said, I would add, did not react comparably to Lewis's critique.)[59] I call the reader's attention to

Bernal's response to Turner—one of the most revealing passages in the Controversy:

> There is clearly a fundamental difference between us. It is the old difference between "lumpers" and "splitters." I am a congenital lumper: I like putting things together and I am crude. I am more concerned with over-all form than I am with specific content. Clearly, any good history needs both tendencies. I do not think one can usefully be either purely abstract or purely empirical. . . . The points on the scale from pure abstraction to sheer empiricism at which Professor Turner and I strike the balance are very different. I am quite rightly attacked for subordinating details to broad-ranging schemes. On the other hand, writers like Professor Turner can be accused of shapelessness. There are clearly pitfalls on either side.[60]

Note this: To Turner's charge of "an absence of particularistic analysis" Bernal pleads guilty. He refers to his own scholarship as "crude." Later, in the same breath, he observes, "I was skating on very thin ice over huge areas." And to round this all off he adds this unsolicited comment: "I would be very grate-ful for more criticisms to try to improve this situation." This conciliatory tone is by no means unprecedented. Throughout the Controversy Bernal repeat-edly acknowledged that his opponents had made valid, even "fascinating" criticisms of his work. In fact, Bernal's praise and "fascination" for his oppo-nent's views often increases in direct proportion to the brutality of their remarks.[61]

As for the partisan nature of *Black Athena*, Bernal accepts blame here as well. Insofar as he views *all* scholarly work as political he can take pride in his uncommon candor. It should be recalled that his work has an explicit politi-cal purpose: "to lessen European cultural arrogance." In 1994 he points out that he attacks the Aryan Model "not merely because it is heuristically fruitless but because it is politically and culturally pernicious." In an earlier exchange with Palter, Bernal declares, "I am convinced that greater benefits are to be gained by the author laying his (or her) cards on the table and alert-ing the reader to his political position." Bernal agrees with his detractors: his work is politically motivated.[62]

Yet this willingness to accept criticism is not entirely attributable to the modesty and open-mindedness of Martin Bernal. These concessions, I submit, are equally indicative of his radically different understanding of intellectual and academic responsibility. In the exchanges among Turner, Palter, and Bernal one is not just witnessing a disagreement over historical facts and inter-pretations, but a conflict over the ontological status of the scholar. Although no one has realized it, both Bernal and his academic adversaries are beholden to completely distinct, perhaps even irreconcilable, conceptions of what a scholar *is* and how he or she should behave. This is, I believe, a central and often unrecognized component of the American culture wars, as well.

For the specialists, *Black Athena* commits inexcusable crimes against the professional and moral code of the academy. For them, competence in one's particular area of research is the sine qua non of the scholarly enterprise. And for these reasons they feel obliged to parade Bernal's numerous errata down the boulevard of scholarly ignomiry. In their view, a true scholar works within the established parameters of a particular discipline. He is not permitted to go traipsing through every department on campus. Instead, he limits the scope of his inquiry to an acceptably modest domain. Who besides Martin Bernal (and certain historical sociologists) would have the temerity to engage four thousand years of recorded history?

The scholar, they respond to Bernal, has *no* cards to lay on the table. He has no "audience." And as for our scholarly ancestors—because they are *our* intellectual ancestors and because they are dead—they are to be treated with deference. If one was a slaveholder, another an *S.S.* officer, then this is unfortunate, but at the same time irrelevant to their often outstanding scholarly contributions. As such, one must refrain from pointing to the inconsequential moral imperfections of our intellectual predecessors.

Hopefully the reader accepts that these statements, although much exaggerated, are relatively plausible representations of a traditional, though increasingly contested, scholarly ethos. Using these observations as a yardstick, let us proceed to examine the counterontology advanced in *Black Athena*. Bernal is calling for not only a new paradigm, not only a new discipline to replace classics ("ancient studies") but a new type of scholar as well. The un-Göttingenish person whom he wishes to resurrect—or cast in his own image—is a generalist. S/he asks broad questions. S/he looks at the big picture. S/he engages in dialogue with laypersons—their opinions are important! As if possessed by postmodern spirits, s/he trespasses across innumerable areas of academic specialization in order to conduct a proper inquiry. S/he has "politics." S/he takes it as a given that the ideological position of any given scholar is a relevant—perhaps even decisive—and legitimate object of scholarly scrutiny. S/he relates history to "our" lives. I could well imagine Bernal retooling the following claim from Nietzsche for his own purposes: "I mean, we need history for life and action, not for the smug evasion of life and action."[63]

The errors? They are an inevitable and unfortunate consequence of the type of intellectual operation Bernal performs. This much the author willingly and graciously admits. But what he will never grant his specialist interlocutors is that such errors invalidate the scholarly integrity of the *Black Athena* project. On the contrary, he believes that his mistakes are relatively minor when compared to theirs. For Bernal, as we just noted, "there are pitfalls on either side." The specialists, he maintains, are responsible for producing fundamentally flawed *paradigms*, a sin far greater than any of his minor factual mistakes.

So when Bernal concedes this or that point, he is merely rendering unto the specialists what is theirs—namely, what he considers to be the small, relatively insignificant details. What is important to him is the integrity of the general scheme. These priorities may be detected in a remark Bernal made to the American Philological Association: "Although much of what I have written is clearly wrong and will be discarded, I am convinced that later models will come out closer to the views of the classical and Hellenistic Greeks and latter day attempts to revive them than to the quite extraordinary Aryan Model."[64]

It is in light of the preceding discussion that we might understand why the Controversy has featured very little in the way of constructive critique or dialogue. In reading through the responses one is entertained, one is enraged, but one is almost never left to feel that some sort of progress is being made. The participants—perhaps "belligerents" would be a better description—are speaking past one another. In the specialists' estimation the types of errors found in *Black Athena* are of such magnitude as to nullify the work altogether. What the specialists have yet to understand is that the knockout punch they think they are delivering to Bernal when they identify yet another howler is experienced by him as a glancing blow.

Bernal frequently responds to an irate critic by noting that they actually agree on many things. In responding to one of Palter's broadsides, Bernal somehow concludes, "Professor Palter may not be delighted to read this but . . . I think that we share much common ground." An incredulous and exasperated Palter answers by simply restating his critique. What Bernal, for his part, fails to grasp is how superficial his admissions of error and attempts at achieving consensus sound to women and men who have watched him cheerfully and consciously defile nearly every sacrament of the scholarly vocation.[65]

Part Three

Black Athena

and the

Culture Wars

I freely admit that, according to white writers, white teachers, white historians and white molders of public opinion, nothing ever happened in the world of any importance that could not or should not be labeled "white."

—W.E.B. Du Bois, "The Superior Race"

But isn't Egypt, other issues apart, quite simply a part of Africa? That, it seems, is a merely geographical irrelevance. The civilisation of Pharaonic Egypt, arising sometime around 3500 BC and continuing at least until the Roman dispossessions, has been explained to us as evolving either in more or less total isolation from Africa or as a product of West Asian stimulus. On this deeply held view, the land of Ancient Egypt appears to have detached itself from the delta of the Nile, some five and a half thousand years ago, and sailed off into the Mediterranean on a course veering broadly towards the coasts of Syria. And there it apparently remained, floating somewhere in the seas of the Levant, until Arab conquerors hauled it back to where it had once belonged.

—Basil Davidson, "The Ancient World and Africa: Whose Roots?"

7

The Academic

Elvis

The shadow of a mighty Negro past flits through the tale of Ethiopia the Shadowy and Egypt the Sphinx.

—W.E.B. Du Bois, *The Souls of Black Folk*

Needing a vision of Africa that was compatible with both integrationist ideals and the need for racial pride, black historians looked for aspects of the African background that were closely tied to western civilization but were distinctively black. They found such a heritage in the histories of the ancient civilizations of Egypt and Ethiopia. In those civilizations they also found powerful arguments against the belief in black inferiority that dominated white American thinking in the late nineteenth century.

—Dickson Bruce, Jr., "Ancient Africa and the Early Black American Historians, 1883–1915"

What Need Have We of These Sacrifices?

Some participants in the Controversy have occasionally sacrificed scholarly precision for rhetorical advantage. The subject of Martin Bernal's relation to Afrocentric thought seems to have elicited an unusually large number of such sacrifices. Let me begin by offering the reader a methodological rule of thumb: The more intensely a mainstream scholar disagrees with *Black Athena*'s substantive arguments, the more likely she or her is to label its author an Afrocentrist. In *Not Out of Africa*, Mary Lefkowitz draws this association without ever stating it explicitly. Throughout her text she casually inserts all of Bernal's claims under the rubric of "Afrocentrist mythology." Guy MacLean Rogers, Lefkowitz's coeditor in *Black Athena Revisited*, is more forthright. In a 1995 issue of *Arethusa* he makes passing reference to "Afrocentrist scholars such as Martin Bernal." Neither present any evidence which might lead readers to the conclusion that Bernal is not an Afrocentrist.[1]

Lefkowitz and Rogers were apparently unaware of a 1992 interview with Michael Eric Dyson in which Bernal made precisely this claim. Perhaps they had not read that particular issue of *Z Magazine*. But Lefkowitz, at least, could not have overlooked Bernal's response to a piece written by one Mary Lefkowitz in a February 1992 issue of the *New Republic*. There he demurred: "I am not an Afrocentrist. I have never been an Afrocentrist. I do not believe that all good things come from any one continent."[2]

Be that as it may, fairness compels me to articulate a second methodological rule of thumb: Martin Bernal's relation to Afrocentric thought is far more complex and far less unambiguous than his statements would indicate. There are, undoubtedly, substantive theoretical differences between Bernal and the Afrocentrists; differences which his most energetic detractors consistently neglect to delineate. As we shall see, however, Bernal's general theories and much of his supporting evidence bear affinities to Afrocentric thought. Moreover, Bernal is far from averse to some of the political goals of those associated with this internally heterogenous movement.

Insofar as *Black Athena*'s core hypotheses and Afrocentric theory are discrete, albeit overlapping, positions, we must engage the question of what influences, if any, each has had on the other. Some suggest that *Black Athena* has had a profound impact on Afrocentrism. Molly Myerowitz Levine writes: "Radical Afrocentrists, who constitute one of Bernal's most receptive audiences, misuse his arguments to buttress claims for the irredeemable unreliability of 'European' historiography, for the identification of the Egyptians as racially black, and for the location of Egypt as the sole source of Greek and thus Western civilization."[3] Sarah Morris remarks, "His championship of Egypt has now bolstered the claims of irrational Afrocentrism; his emphasis on nationalism in scholarship has been corroborated in the most extreme manner."[4]

This argument strikes me as problematic in the following bipartite respect. To begin with—and here I state one final rule of thumb—there is no unified Afrocentrist position on *Black Athena*. Not all Afrocentrists have warmly embraced Bernal's work. As I will demonstrate, some of the most spectacularly vituperative attacks on this text have been written by members of this cohort. Accordingly, they have not consistently used his research to bolster or buttress their own controversial claims.

But this brings us to another difficulty with the opinion that Afrocentrists have been influenced by *Black Athena*. The belief in the existence of a sophisticated black ancient Egyptian civilization, an ancient Egypt which imparted its higher civilization to jejune Greeks, had been a staple of African-American thought well before the official advent of Afrocentrism in the 1980s and the publication of Bernal's first volume in 1986. These theories have been articulated in African-American letters for at least 180 years by pamphleteers and politicians, professors and pastors, black nationalists and black integrationists alike. To anyone familiar with this rich tradition—and Afrocentrists know it intimately—Bernal's theories are nowhere near so innovative (and influential) as mainstream commentators allege.

In this chapter, I will familiarize the reader with some of the nineteenth-century thinkers who championed what I shall refer to as the "Diasporic Ancient Model." I will proceed to trace the evolution of this approach to its more systematic formulation in the twentieth-century writings of W.E.B. Du Bois and Cheikh Anta Diop, and from there to its recent reception by Afrocentrists. This will permit us to understand how *Black Athena's* theories resemble and differ from those of the latter. In so doing, we will position ourselves to understand better the extraordinarily complex question of Bernal's relation to Afrocentric thought—a question whose answer cannot be reduced to the type of facile affirmations and categorical denials discussed above.

The Vindicationist Tradition: The Diasporic Ancient Model

In *Black Folk Here and There: An Essay in History and Anthropology,* St. Clair Drake examined the "vindicationist" tradition within African-American thought. This approach pitted an ideologically diverse array of black thinkers against "apologists for slavery who attempted to justify the 'peculiar institution' with the argument that Negroes were an inferior animal-like breed of mankind unfit to be treated as equals by other people." In an effort both to defend and to "improve" all members of what was then referred to as the "Negro race," nineteenth-century vindicationists often called attention to the glorious achievements of ancient—as opposed to modern—Africa.[5]

There are three general claims regarding ancient Egypt and Ethiopia which sporadically surfaced in the speeches, sermons, and scholarship of the vindicationists. The first was that the inhabitants of Egypt and Ethiopia were black. Second, it was maintained that both civilizations had attained an elevated, if not unequaled, degree of cultural sophistication. Last, Greece was cast as a tributary of these older African cultures.

Many early nineteenth-century vindicationists made ancient Ethiopia, as opposed to ancient Egypt, the primary object of their scrutiny.[6] Drake reports:

> By the middle of the nineteenth century, most literate black leaders in the United States were aware that the ancient Greeks and Romans had made favorable remarks about Ethiopians, since abolitionists, Black and White, used quotations from the *Iliad* and the *Odyssey,* from Herodotus, Dioscorus, and Strabo to defend black people when involved in polemics about their inborn capabilities. . . . Most who knew this knew that *ancient* Ethiopia was in the Nile Valley. They were also, no doubt, familiar with a statement by Herodotus that, in some translations, described Egyptians as having black skin and kinky hair.[7]

It was only after emancipation, argues Drake, that Egypt replaces Ethiopia as the central concern of the vindicationists.[8]

Historian Wilson Moses has traced one of the first examples of this esteem for ancient Africa in the United States to an editorial in an 1827 issue of *Freedom's Journal.* Two years later, similar sentiments are expressed in the writings of David Walker, one of the most important figures in the early history of black nationalism. In "Walker's Appeal," the fiery orator declares, "I would only mention that the Egyptians, were Africans or coloured people, such as we are—some of them yellow and others dark—a mixture of Ethiopians and the natives of Egypt."[9] Later, Walker adds: "When we take a retrospective view of the arts and sciences—the wise legislators—the Pyramids, and other magnificent buildings—the turning of the channel of the river Nile, by the sons of Africa or of Ham, among whom learning originated, and was carried thence into Greece, where it was improved upon and refined."[10]

In *A Text Book of the Origin and History, Etc., Etc., of the Colored People* (1841), James W. C. Pennington develops this theme: "Many . . . [will say] that we are not of Egypt; but I have shown from Herodotus that the Egyptians were black people, and from other facts that they are one with the Ethiopians in the great events of history."[11]

In 1854 Frederick Douglass would, with characteristic eloquence, engage this issue:

> It is not in my power, in a discourse of this sort, to adduce more than a very small part of the testimony in support of a near relationship between the present enslaved and degraded Negroes, and the ancient highly civilized and wonderfully endowed Egyptians. Sufficient has already been adduced, to show a marked similarity in regard to features, hair, color, and I doubt not that the philologist can find equal similarity in the structures of their languages. . . . It may safely be affirmed, that a strong affinity and a direct relationship may be claimed by the Negro race, to *that grandest of all the nations of antiquity, the builders of the pyramids.*[12]

Moving away from the antebellum period we find these propositions increasingly defended by means of scholarly disputation. Both Edward Wilmot Blyden et alia, in *The People of Africa* (1871), and Martin Delany, in *Principia of Ethnology: The Origin of Races and Color* (1879), issued polite but spirited challenges to prevailing opinion. Delany remarks, "And the fact is, that the Negro race comprised the whole native population and ruling people of the upper and lower region of the Nile—Ethiopia and Egypt—excepting those who came by foreign invasion."[13]

The minister, intellectual, and statesmen George Washington Williams pointed to an influential black high civilization in his massive *History of the Negro Race in America, 1619–1880* (1883): "Egypt borrowed her light from the venerable Negroes up the Nile [i.e., in Ethiopia]. Greece went to school to the Egyptians, and Rome turned to Greece for law and the science of warfare."[14] In developing his argument, Williams makes passing reference to Herodotus's discussion of blacks in the armies of Sesōstris, an argument well known to readers of *Black Athena.*[15]

It emerges from this brief, unoriginal, and incomplete survey that many of the general themes encountered in Bernal's work (and modern Afrocentrism) had already been stated in rudimentary form by the nineteenth-century vindicationists. Perhaps we might speak of a Diasporic Ancient Model. It shares with the Revised Ancient Model an extremely positive evaluation of Egyptian civilization. Similarly, this paradigm insinuates that the Egyptians significantly shaped the development of Greco-Roman culture. Adherents to this model drew on textual sources, Herodotus in particular, which were examined by Bernal more than a century later. Last, both models make analogous claims about the skin color of the ancient Egyptians. Bernal's Revised version, as we shall see, maintains that pharaohs of the First, Eleventh, Twelfth, and Eighteenth dynasties could "usefully" be called black.[16]

The Great Twentieth-Century Vindicationists: Du Bois and Diop

At the 1966 First World Festival of Negro Arts, W.E.B. Du Bois (1868–1963) and the Senegalese scholar Cheikh Anta Diop (1923–1986) were honored as the two writers "who had exerted the greatest influence on Negro thought in the twentieth century."[17] Both were similarly influential in cultivating and expanding the Diasporic Ancient Model.

For purposes of clarity I will refer to Diop as a "proto-Afrocentrist." That is, he produced the major body of his work well before this approach was officially christened in the 1980s by Molefi Kete Asante. The latter, regarded as the "founder of the Afrocentric philosophy," leaves little doubt as to the identity of his primary intellectual influence. "I am most keenly a Diopian," writes Asante—a tribute he would not extend to Du Bois.[18]

Diop, often referred to as "Pharaoh" by admirers, has played a leading role in establishing research paradigms for the present generation of Afrocentrists. Veneration of his work often takes unusual forms. A memorial volume in the *Journal of African Civilizations* features not one but two poems composed in his honor. Another contributor declares, "Posterity will undoubtedly place him in the company of Herodotus, Manetho, and Ibn Khaldun as an historian whose work not only changed the way we look at history but made history itself." In these quarters criticism of Diop's research is practically nonexistent. What little critique one finds is couched in the most cushioned prose.[19]

W.E.B. Du Bois has never achieved comparable standing within the Afrocentric pantheon. Asante avers that although Du Bois was a man of great brilliance, he was not an Afrocentrist. In another contribution, Asante makes this revealing comparison: "This is the age of Diop without whom the dignity of Africans would have continued to be defended, as Du Bois admirably did, by appeals to Eurocentric frames of reference." Although Du Bois has been accused of fealty to Eurocentric paradigms, his major themes pertaining to ancient Egypt are quite similar to those of the more appropriately Afrocentric Diop. As regards this issue, these scholars differ solely in the amount of attention they devoted to the subject. Throughout his lengthy career Du Bois addressed the question of ancient Africa sporadically. For Diop, by contrast, the concept of a black ancient Egypt was the theoretical omphalos of his scholarly research and political philosophy. In pursuing this line of inquiry Diop marshaled the findings of physical anthropology, comparative linguistics, Egyptology, and physics, among other disciplines. In so doing, he advanced what must be regarded as the most comprehensive and sustained exposition of the Diasporic Ancient Model.[20]

Interdisciplinarity notwithstanding, both scholars remained well within the theoretical parameters established by the nineteenth-century vindicationists. In *The World and Africa,* Du Bois would argue that Ethiopia was "the cradle of Egyptian civilization." He suggested that the Egyptians "regarded themselves as African" and "were an African people." Similarly, Diop endeavored to set Egypt both culturally and genetically within an exclusively African context. Ivan Van Sertima proffers this summary of his argument: "Egypt had been suckled at the breast of Ethiopia, which itself evolved from the complex interior womb of the African motherland." Egypt, then, is cast in the dual role of child (of earlier African civilizations, such as Ethiopia) and parent (of present ones). In an attempt to demonstrate the fundamental links between the past and the present, Diop argued that there existed substantial linguistic affinities between ancient Egyptian and various modern African languages.[21]

Both scholars would make analogous phenotypical assertions. Diop consistently maintained that ancient Egypt, from its earliest appearance in the historical record (and prior), was a black population. While allowing for occasional "crossbreeding" through infiltration, Diop would nevertheless posit the existence of a preponderantly black Egypt. In *The African Origin of Civilization* he would proclaim, "But what is certain is the preeminence of the Negro element from the beginning to the end of Egyptian history." In *The Negro,* Du Bois, for his part, would assert that "Egypt was herself always palpably Negroid":

> Of what race, then, were the Egyptians? They certainly were not white in any sense of the modern use of that word—neither in color nor physical measurement, in hair nor countenance, in language nor social customs. They stood in relationship nearest the Negro race in earliest times, and then gradually through the infiltration of Mediterranean and Semitic elements became what would be described in America as a light mulatto stock of Octoroons or Quadroons.[22]

As with many contemporary Afrocentrists, Diop defends the validity of race as a variable for scholarly analysis. Whereas many in today's academy have expurgated the concept and even the word *race* from publications and lectures, Diop and his followers show themselves to be quite attached to the term. In an interview with Charles Finch, Diop remarks: "The Europeans, all the Occidentals say there is no race. But they know very well what a white man is, they know very well what a yellow man is. But we don't know what a black man is."[23] Du Bois—who wrote during an earlier period in which this concept was far less problematic—was equally willing to embrace this notion.

As Wilson Moses observes: "Du Bois was fascinated by race which he conceived as a mystical cosmic force. He did not view the concept of race as a mere figment of depraved imagination, or as the fabrication of oppressor classes."[24]

The rudiments of the Diasporic Ancient Model are again evident as Du Bois remarks that Alexander and the Caesars sat at the feet of the Egyptians. Diop refers to the Egyptians as "the quasi-exclusive teacher of Greece in all periods on the road to civilization." The notion of Greeks *stealing* their cultural achievements from Egyptians surfaces in very distilled form in the work of Diop, but not, so far as I can tell, in the writings of Du Bois. It must be noted that the former did not originate this idea. Nineteenth-century writers, as we saw above, politely intimated this point. Mary Lefkowitz traces the first appearance of a more forthright and accusatory version to the writings of Marcus Garvey in the early twentieth century. The most thorough exploration of this theme occurs in George G. M. James's 1954 work, *The Stolen Legacy*, a text which Diop knew well.[25]

Both Diop and Du Bois advanced one idea which was absent in the work of the earlier vindicationists. We might refer to this as "the ideological critique." Du Bois would frequently contemplate the motivations behind the "degrading and discrediting [of] the Negroid peoples." In one instance he offered the following explanation: "It is especially significant that the science of Egyptology arose and flourished at the very time that the cotton kingdom reached its greatest power on the foundation of American Negro slavery." In the preface to his collection *The African Origin of Civilization: Myth or Reality*, Diop writes, "Our investigations have convinced us that the West has not been calm enough and objective enough to teach us our history correctly, without crude falsifications."[26]

Upon reading Diop, I think of K. Anthony Appiah's reference to his work, and Afrocentric scholarship in general, as "Europe Upside Down." For in the thought of the Senegalese polymath, ancient Egypt functions as a conspicuously symmetrical counternarrative to the Occidental tradition. Diop declares: "Egyptian antiquity is to African culture what Graeco-Roman antiquity is to Western culture. The building up of a corpus of African humanities should be based on this fact."[27] Ancient Egypt thus figures as a mirror image of the Aryanized Hellas: an (almost) pure black, pure African progenitor of a resplendent continental civilization.[28] In *The African Origin of Civilization*, Diop advances a conclusion which solders this point almost perfectly with his political commitment to Pan-Africanism: "The Ancient Egyptians were Negroes. The moral fruit of their civilization is to be counted among the assets of the Black World. Instead of presenting itself to history as an insolvent debtor, that Black world is the very initiator of the "western" civilization flaunted before our eyes today."[29] While Du Bois never advanced this counternarrative, he did share this particular aspect of Diop's political agenda. As Manning Marable has shown, Pan-Africanism (along with socialism) was one of Du Bois's "principal goals."[30]

A Very Serious Omission

It should be clear by now that much of the territory surveyed in *Black Athena* had been visited before. Regrettably, its author paid scant attention to the valuable resources provided by the vindicationists. As Margaret Washington observes in the *Journal of Women's History*:

> African and African-American scholarship is not part of Bernal's intellectual argument, although it is mentioned at the end. *Black Athena* rarely moves out of Europe, and this concentration creates an imbalance, dismissing a crucial dimension of analysis. Yet Bernal sees himself *"in the spectrum of black scholarship,"* rather than within *"academic orthodoxy."* I only wish he had explored the contributions and implications of that scholarship.[31]

Afrocentrists, the present caretakers of the vindicationist tradition, have come to a similar conclusion. "The European, Martin Bernal," writes Asante, has "advanced various aspects of Diop's historigraphy." Others have been less diplomatic. Manu Ampim suggests that Bernal "arrogantly overlooks" the research of black scholars who *"already anticipated every aspect* of Bernal's main thesis of the Ancient Model of civilization."[32]

Though Ampim somewhat overstates the case, his basic charge is not without merit. Examinations of massive Egyptian impact on Greek civilization are as old as the nineteenth century, as is the use of Herodotus to prove this contention. Asante's suggestion that Bernal was following in the footsteps of Diop is also warranted. Diop explored the issues of Egyptian colonization, volcanic eruptions, Crete's relation to Egypt, and the Kadmos narratives, albeit not in precisely the same manner as Bernal. The author of *Black Athena* invoked nearly all of the Classical and Hellenistic writers Diop had scrutinized decades before (Herodotus, Aristotle, Lucian, Apollodorus, Aeschylus, Strabo, Diodorus). Interestingly, the two men are using these sources for entirely different reasons. Diop tends to read them in order to find evidence of the blackness of the ancient Egyptians and their interrelations with Ethiopia. Bernal, on the other hand, cites these writers mainly to undergird his colonization hypothesis. (In fact, one need not be an Afrocentrist to maintain that Bernal works within a Diopian tradition. V. Y. Mudimbe observes that *Black Athena* "strongly accented Cheikh Anta Diop's hypothesis by diffusing the Senegalese scholar's 'black factor' into 'Afroasiatic roots' of classical Greco-Roman civilization.")[33]

Nor is Bernal's critique of the racist and Eurocentric tilt of academe without precedent. Du Bois and Diop repeatedly excoriated the scholarship of Egyptologists, physical anthropologists, and others. Du Bois preceded Bernal in identifying the rise of the American slave trade as inextricably bound to tectonic shifts in scholarly perceptions of the ancient world. Let it also be noted that Diop's entire corpus of publications may be read as an indictment of what Bernal called "Eurocentric arrogance."[34]

Bernal's brief discussion of Diop (three sentences) and Du Bois (a passing reference) and his complete disregard of the nineteenth- and twentieth-century vindicationists stands as one of *Black Athena*'s most disturbing shortcomings. Toward the end of his first volume Bernal reports that he became aware of these sources only after eight years of working on his manuscript. I have no reason to doubt that this is true, but in the name of lessening European arrogance, the author might have devoted more effort (in volume 2, for example) to studying the opinions of thinkers who were neither European nor white. Had he done so, he would have identified a formidable coalition of authentic intellectual precursors.[35]

Bernal has frankly acknowledged his error. In a response to Washington, he concedes that this was a "serious omission."[36]

An Afrocentrist without Portfolio?

While Bernal was quick to list his "outrages" against the classics establishment, he never discussed the comparable reactions his work elicited among Afrocentrists. His "serious omission" certainly upset many in "the Movement," but this was by no means the only point of contention.

The author of *Black Athena*—whose essential enemy is purity—argues that the ancient Egyptians were a *mixture* of different peoples. Bernal writes, "One of the reasons why the Egyptians were similar to African-Americans is precisely the mixture of caucasite with Central African types." While this statement may have done much to stimulate the interest of many black and white readers, it could hardly have done more to displease Afrocentrists. As Jacob Carruthers observes, "Bernal cannot simply admit that the ancient Egyptians were Black."[37]

The theory of a Hyksos invasion of the Aegean, the keystone of *Black Athena*, is also problematic. The Hyksos, as the reader will recall, were a mixed population who overran the Egyptian Delta and eventually washed ashore in the Aegean. Clyde Ahmad Winters, writing in the *Journal of Black Studies*, offers this appraisal: "Bernal's view of the Hyksos as the founders of Grecian civilization has nothing to do with the work of Afrocentric scholars."[38]

These surface disagreements underscore a more fundamental difference in the two approaches. As noted above, many Afrocentrists have little compunction about employing the concept of race as a variable for scholarly analysis. Théophile Obenga, one of Diop's most prominent disciples, is quoted as having stated that "the notion of race was recognized as valid by scientific research and that the study of races did not necessarily involve racialism." Bernal, advocating the current orthodoxy, notes, "I am very dubious of the utility of the concept of 'race' in general because it is impossible to achieve any anatomical precision on the subject." In many ways Bernal and some Afrocentrists are working from completely contrary premises: the very idea which one wishes to abolish from intellectual and political discourse is precisely that which the other endorses as an essential paradigm for scholarly research and social action.[39]

This brings us to what we might refer to as the "Mesopotamian outrages." The author of *Black Athena*—again walking in lockstep with the mainstream—contends that Mesopotamian culture developed prior to Egyptian civilization. Moreover, he argues that it was the former which "triggered" the development of the latter. From Diop onward, these two theories are the bane of the Afrocentrists. Van Sertima writes, "Nothing has annoyed me more than the almost religious insistence by some scholars that Mesopotamia profoundly affected Egypt in its formative stages."[40]

Bernal's understanding of the role of Semites in antiquity has also outraged some Afrocentrists. As we noted in chapter 2 above, Bernal posits a large Phoenician impact on Greece. (This is why the subtitle of *Black Athena* is *The Afroasiatic Roots of Classical Civilization*.) Tony Martin, in a very disturbing little book entitled *The Jewish Onslaught*, declares:

> Bernal, a Jew, was precipitously and prematurely adopted by many Afrocentrists, for his exposé of the European de-Africanization of Egypt. Ever anxious to place a white figure at the head of an African movement, *Newsweek* magazine and other major media sources, with much misguided help from Black folk, quickly crowned Bernal white king of the Afrocentrists. . . . If any of Bernal's Afrocentric followers had slowed down a bit in their speed reading of *Black Athena*, they would have noticed that he was as much or more concerned with a "Semitic" origin for Greek civilization as for African influence over Greece.[41]

In his article "The Problem of the Bernal-Davidson School," Manu Ampim concedes that the work of these two scholars has been important to the Movement. The remainder of his piece, however, chronicles the "the complicity of this School in the conceptual imprisonment and denigration of African people." Ampim goes on to accuse Bernal (and Basil Davidson) of "shameful treatment of Professor Diop."[42]

A few final contrasts. Unlike most Afrocentrist literature, *Black Athena* evinces little religious awe for ancient Egypt. Bernal certainly esteems this civilization, but he does not wish to adopt its moral and intellectual agenda as the basis for solving contemporary social problems. Bernal never speaks of a "stolen legacy." He uses more subdued terms, such as "borrowing" or "cultural diffusion," when describing the Greek debt to Egypt. Nor would he argue, as some Afrocentrists do, that the Phoenicians and/or the Pelasgians and/or the Greeks were black.[43]

It is in light of the preceding discussion that we may now understand why Winters concludes: "*Black Athena* is not the Afrocentric Bible on Black Egypt. We doubt that Diop would even agree with most of the thesis of this book."[44]

Complicating matters immeasurably is the fact that some prominent

Afrocentrists have cordially welcomed *Black Athena*. Asante, the master theorist of this school, devotes four pages of his *Kemet, Afrocentricity and Knowledge* to summarizing Bernal's argument. Significantly, he does not once refer to the text as "Eurocentric." Reverence for Diop notwithstanding, Afrocentrism is somewhat less monolithic than its critics—and some of its supporters—contend.[45]

Conclusion

To this point we have seen that neither Martin Bernal nor many Afrocentrists believe that Martin Bernal is an Afrocentrist. These disclaimers can be tracked down in any reasonably well-stocked college library, and this raises the question as to why Lefkowitz, Rogers, and the assembled punditry have persistently applied this label to the author of *Black Athena.*

In terms of swaying popular opinion, the coupling of Bernal with Afrocentrism is a rhetorical masterstroke. Throughout the 1990s the media have bombarded the American public with tragicomic images of Afrocentrist ice-people theorists, melanin researchers, and anti-Semites. Journalists have been far less inclined to report that not all Afrocentrists espouse these ideas. Asante, for example, has stressed that "racism is despicable." Elsewhere, he declares that Judaism and Christianity are not incommensurable with the Afrocentrist concept of *Njia* or "the Way." With my own ears, I have heard prominent figures in the Movement publicly denounce anti-Semitism. Be that as it may, the media portrayal, though greatly spectacularized, is not entirely contrived. As Tony Martin's writings or Leonard Jeffries's lectures amply demonstrate, there are indeed some proponents of the aforementioned positions among the ranks.[46]

Fully aware that Afrocentrist approval ratings are low within the academy, Lefkowitz and others ingeniously endeavored to blur the lines separating the radicals, the moderates, and Bernal. Lefkowitz, who has honed this strategy to perfection, goes a step further by affixing an apocalyptic dimension to her analysis. Throughout *Not Out of Africa,* the Holocaust and the fate of the former Yugoslavia are alluded to as coming attractions in a society whose universities grant screen space to Afrocentric ideas (i.e., Bernal's ideas). Following the path graveled by Arthur Schlesinger in *The Disuniting of America,* Lefkowitz asks: "What will happen some years from now, when students who have studied different versions of the past discover that their picture of events is totally incomparable with what their classmates have learned about their own ethnic histories? Will students of one ethnicity deny the existence of other 'ethnic truths,' with dire consequences akin to the ethnic conflicts in the former Yugoslavia?"[47]

This scenario is idealist in the extreme. It assumes that classroom lectures, not material inequality or historical factors or religious differences or a dozen other variables, may provide the necessary and sufficient preconditions for internecine strife. Lefkowitz also fails to take into consideration the possibility that minorities may advance "ethnic histories" precisely out of a desire to integrate with the dominant group. The nineteenth-century vindicationists, many of whom were impassioned integrationists, provide an excellent case in point. As Bruce observes:

> The early writers focused on ancient Africa because it resolved the problem of a dual identity in ways that an appreciation for modern Africa could not. Modern Africa was generally taken by black and white people alike as a primitive, backward continent. By contrast, the achievements of ancient Ethiopians and Egyptians were widely acknowledged and easily comprehended by Americans from antebellum times to the opening of the twentieth century. Even white Americans were fascinated and inspired by Egyptian civilization, drawn to it for public architecture and fully cognizant of its role in the creation of much that they took civilization to entail. *Thus if blacks could be shown to have been responsible for Egyptian greatness, they had done something that was prized by civilized people everywhere. Being black might give one a distinctive identity, but it was not incompatible with being "American" as well.*[48]

Unfortunately, these intriguing possibilities were rarely discussed in Lefkowitz's twin projects. Indeed, both works are characterized by a seeming aversion to what Max Weber once called "'inconvenient' facts." The major American precincts of intellectual opinion, for their part, were not about to explore intriguing possibilities or inconvenient facts either. From the *Village Voice* to *Newsweek* to the *New York Review of Books*, reviewers of *Not Out of Africa* and *Black Athena Revisited* spoke with astonishing, if not frightening, unanimity.[49] Even the minor precincts replicated the prevailing wisdom, as the following passage from the *Florida Times-Union* demonstrates:

> Classicist Mary Lefkowitz doesn't believe it and she makes it clear she's mad as hell and not going to take it anymore. She retaliates against Afrocentrism, initially targeting Martin Bernal, a Cornell sinologist, and his multivolume *Black Athena*. Bernal determined to take "European cultural arrogance" down a few pegs by reassigning the Greeks' achievements. Fine, except his research is loaded with errors and misstatements a sourcechecking freshman could spot.[50]

I say: More internships to place source-checking freshmen in the newsrooms of America!

But if critics of Bernal persistently label him an Afrocentrist—and I conclude that he is not—it must be conceded that he often gives them grounds for doing so. There are, as we noted, clear correspondences between theoretical aspects of *Black Athena* and positions maintained by the vindicationists and disciples of Diop. Bernal has shared platforms with high-profile Afrocentrists and expressed little or no criticism of their views. One of the first expositions of his hypothesis—published prior to his first volume—appeared in a special edition of the *Journal of African Civilizations,* a forum for Afrocentric writers.[51]

In his exchanges with Lefkowitz, the author has come to their defense by underscoring the institutional disadvantages which have historically confronted Afrocentrists who attempt to conduct scholarly research. In an interview with Walter Cohen, Bernal has stated, "In some ways I'm very pleased to provide ammunition for them." He refers to George G. M. James's *Stolen Legacy* as a "fascinating little book . . . [which] also makes a plausible case for Greek science and philosophy having borrowed massively from Egypt." Further, he has adopted a uniquely serene stance toward Afrocentric critics. Typically, Bernal responds to antagonistic classicists and Egyptologists with heat. To the best of my knowledge, he has never published a riposte to any of his Afrocentrist detractors.[52]

This brings us to the second mainstream critique of Bernal: the accusation that his work has bolstered or emboldened radical Afrocentrists. While I disagree, I must again acknowledge that there are some grounds for making this claim. By now it should be clear that *Black Athena* does not furnish Afrocentrists with many novel theoretical approaches pertaining to ancient Egypt or its denigration via modern racism. The vindicationists had said it all before. And in terms of the Movement's agenda, they had said it far better. If any Afrocentrists wanted to argue that the inhabitants of the Nile River Valley were black, or that European scholars were racist to the core, then they could have cited the work of Garvey, James, Diop, ben-Jochanan, or dozens of others. Bernal's far more nuanced and far less serviceable theories would be relegated to a footnote.

Thus, the substantive claims of *Black Athena* are, to Afrocentric ears, unremarkable. But that a white, Ivy League professor would make such claims is remarkable indeed—and not only to Afrocentrists. Bernal's text has accomplished what vindicationists and Afrocentrists could never achieve in a society where the "problem of the color-line" is etched miles into the ground. First, it has rescued the Diasporic Ancient Model from the oblivion to which it had been relegated by scholars of antiquity for nearly two centuries. Ostensibly, the extended play that *Black Athena* received in the popular media during the late 1980s was instrumental in bringing the previously peripheral claims of vindicationist and Afrocentric historians into the epicenter of American intellectual discourse.[53]

But *Black Athena* has not only helped disseminate Afrocentric themes, it has done much to legitimate them as well. With palpable bitterness, Afrocentrist Jacob Carruthers observes, "For at least 200 years, African champions of ancient Egypt have been asserting what Bernal (1987) concludes about Kemet; now that a European scholar has proclaimed it, the dialogue about the identity and significance of the Kemites has been reopened."[54] In this reading Martin Bernal figures as a sort of "Academic Elvis," watering down African-American traditions previously unknown to the mainstream, presenting them to a infinitely larger audience, and prospering handsomely for the replica he produced.[55]

Frank Snowden, an ardent critic of Bernal and Afrocentrism, remarks: "Bernal had demonstrated in the first volume of *Black Athena* that, *mirabile dictu,* at least one white man had finally adopted two major Afrocentric theses: (1) white racists had robbed blacks of an important part of their heritage by denying that Egypt was a black civilization; and (2) black scholars who disagree with Afrocentric views have been duped by white scholarship."[56]

If there is a tacit point of agreement between Carruthers and Snowden, then it is this: Whiteness is inextricably bound with what this society defines as legitimate scholarly work. For Snowden, Bernal's whiteness has endowed Afrocentric history with intellectual collateral which it does not deserve. Skeptical members of the establishment may now be told that one of their own has bought the Afrocentrist argument. For Carruthers, Bernal's whiteness is equally significant and equally distressing. That *only* a white man could render these themes noticeable to professional academicians illustrates one of Afrocentrism's most fundamental tenets. As Gerald Early observes, Afrocentrists believe that "society's dominant body of scholarship exhibits a decidedly 'white' or 'Eurocentric' bias in support of a 'white' or 'Eurocentric' political and social hegemony."[57]

I would note that Bernal himself has accepted this critique:

> Certainly, if a Black were to say what I am now putting in my books, their reception would be very different. They would be assumed to be one-sided and partisan, pushing a Black nationalist line, and therefore dismissed. . . Being not only white, male, middle-aged and middle class but also British in America has given me a tone of universality and authority that is completely spurious. But it's there! So I must thank my lucky stars, rather than any talent that I may possess for having got this far, even if this is as far as I go.[58]

These considerations permit us to deepen our conception of academic heresy. Assisting us in this endeavor is Afrocentrist Jacob Carruthers, who perceptively dubs Bernal "the inside outsider," the implication being that while Bernal advances a radical agenda, he does so from the established (and codetermined) status positions of being white, male, and a member of the academy in good standing. Heresy, as I have defined it in this study, is a function of being "inside" enough so as to assure that "outside" claims will come to the attention of other insiders.[59]

Whiteness—or being a member of any dominant group—does not necessarily entitle one to unopposed intellectual triumph. It does, however, go a long way in ensuring that one's claims will be acknowledged. It was precisely this acknowledgment which was denied to vindicationists for nearly two centuries.

8

Reconfiguring

the Ancient

Egyptians

Bernal's Strategic
Reading

Black Americans with an interest in this issue asked two perfectly logical questions that drew evasive answers from physical anthropologists,
wrapped up in technical jargon: "Why are people who look like us called
'white' or 'Hamite' if they live in Egypt but 'Negroes' if they live in this
country?" and "Why, if someone of that type turns up among the
Egyptian pharaohs is he classified 'white,' but if he lived in Mississippi
he'd be put in the back of the bus?"
        —St. Clair Drake, *Black Folk Here and There,* Vol. 1

Egyptians were Egyptians, the people of *Kmt* . . . neither black nor white
as races are conceived of today.
        —Kathryn Bard, "Ancient Egyptians and the Issue of Race"

As America prepares to turn the dark corner of the millennium, the question
of race occupies a privileged place in its national agenda. In a country with as
tormented a racial history as the United States, one might expect that this
subject would be relegated to the hinterland of intellectual inquiry. In reality,
the contemporary student of race encounters something that might be described
as a discursive cavalcade: the issues of race, race relations, and racism are discussed by commentators of every conceivable political, intellectual, and theoretical stripe, on an almost quotidian basis, in fora ranging from newspapers
to scholarly journals to the Internet to radio talk shows to television.

There is little doubt that Martin Bernal and his critics have all marched
in this peculiarly American procession. We should recall that only one mem-

ber of the holy analytical trinity of race, class, and gender was properly venerated in *Black Athena*. The author's analysis of gender, as we saw earlier, remained undeveloped. Class—forgotten Holy Spirit of American letters—was also ignored by Bernal. The subject of racism, however, stood as one of his most abiding preoccupations. Not surprisingly, nearly every single participant in the Controversy addressed this problematic in some way as well.[1]

The starting point of this analysis will be the identification of an apparent paradox. An aspect of this issue which Bernal had little to say about—the racial characteristics of the ancient Egyptians—became one of the most widely discussed and hotly contested components of his project. Conversely, the moral subtext of *Black Athena*—the demonstration of commonalities in the historical experiences of African-Americans and Jewish-Americans—was almost entirely ignored by both Bernal's supporters and his detractors. In the present chapter, devoted to an examination of the first half of this paradox, I will review the immense controversy which Bernal's pithy remarks on the Egyptian phenotype have stimulated.

In a 1992 review, Bruce Trigger remarked that although Bernal paid little attention to physical anthropology, the field is "a source of considerable importance for demonstrating movements of human populations." In what follows we will have an opportunity to examine responses to *Black Athena* written by practitioners of this discipline. The reader is warned that this inquiry will require us to survey some rather technical discussions about race—or *genetic affinities* to use the proper term—as rendered in the dialect of physical anthropology. The reader is also warned—and here there is cause for considerable concern—that the current author is not trained as a physical anthropologist. Among other things, this means that I am not qualified to assess the relative merits of arguments pertaining to melanin, craniofacial morphology, and monotypical variants.[2]

Emboldened by Bernal's approach, I will not let my lack of familiarity with this topic prevent me from discussing it at some length. Yet since I am more modest, or cowardly perhaps, no attempt will be made to advance any new hypotheses or to propose solutions to insoluble problems.

Useful Claims

From the cover of *Newsweek* magazine, which asked "Was Cleopatra Black?" to various articles printed in *Black Athena Revisited,* the question of the racial characteristics of the ancient Egyptians has loomed large in the Controversy. This state of affairs demonstrates the extraordinary degree to which *Black Athena* has become entangled with Afrocentrist claims. For while proponents of the latter discuss the Egyptian phenotype incessantly, Martin Bernal has had relatively little to say on this subject. Hundreds of pages and footnotes in *Black Athena* are devoted to external factors, chronological heresies, and invading Hyksos; only a few passages engage the problematic of applying racial categorizations to antiquity. As Bernal himself noted defensively in 1991, his work is only "peripherally concerned with this issue."[3]

The spectacularization of this claim may be attributed to a drawback in Bernal's presentation. What little he did say about the pigmentation of the Egyptians he said in the most ambiguous terms possible. Most of the author's views on this issue are adumbrated in one equivocal paragraph in the first volume:

> To what "race," then, did the Ancient Egyptians belong? I am very dubious of the utility of the concept "race" in general because it is impossible to achieve any anatomical precision on the subject. . . . Nevertheless I am convinced that, at least for the last 7,000 years, the population of Egypt has contained African, South-West Asian and Mediterranean types. It is also clear that the further south, or up the Nile, one goes, the blacker and more Negroid the population becomes, and that this has been the case for the same length of time. As I stated in the Introduction, I believe that Egyptian civilization was *fundamentally African* and that the African element was stronger in the Old and Middle Kingdoms, before the Hyksos invasion, than it later became. Furthermore, I am convinced that many of the most powerful Egyptian dynasties which were based in Upper Egypt—the 1st, 11th, 12th and 18th—*were made up of pharaohs whom one can usefully call black.*[4]

Oddly enough, Bernal would cite this same paragraph in 1989 as proof that, "in the text of my book, I make no claims that the Egyptians were black." If, however, many concluded that Bernal theorized that "Egypt was essentially African, and therefore black," then there were certainly grounds for doing so. The author does, after all, make reference to "a blacker and more Negroid" population in Upper (i.e., southern) Egypt. He makes explicit references to black Egyptians in numerous passages throughout his writings. Ostensibly, he also entitled his work *Black Athena*—but this is a point which we will come back to later.[5]

The phrase "pharaohs whom one can usefully call black" is a locution that is susceptible to a variety of misinterpretations. Bernal's remarks throughout the Controversy indicate that he subscribes to a belief in "social race," as opposed to "biological race." As such, he claims that even though the latter concept has little or no scientific validity, human beings nevertheless perceive the world in terms of socially constructed racial categories. In this manner, we manage to imbue superficial and highly flawed terms (*black* and *white*) with an unmerited facticity; we behave as if race actually exists, as if it correlates with moral and intellectual characteristics. It is in light of these considerations that we may understand the assumptions which undergird this remark. Bernal meant to say that by the criteria of the modern United States—where one is not white if one has even a particle of "African" blood—these pharaohs could legitimately be labeled "black."[6]

By employing the word "useful," however, this phrase can be (and was) read quite differently. To some commentators it seemed as if Bernal was suggesting that—regardless of the veracity of this claim—it is *politically* expedient to refer to pharaohs as black. In this interpretation, the expression of this sentiment is intended to function as a corrective to widespread racism. Bernal has, in fact, remarked that this particular statement and his project in general help "to counter the cultural debilitation to peoples of African descent brought about by implicit assumptions or explicit statements that there has never been a great 'African' culture which has contributed to world civilization as a whole and that 'Blacks' have always been servile."[7]

Another source of confusion centers around Bernal's reference to ancient Egypt's civilization as "fundamentally African." What is meant by this term? Is Egypt's Africanness a function of its being positioned on the continent of Africa? Is its Africanness based on the presumed fact that its inhabitants speak an Afroasiatic language? Is Africanness based on common genetic traits shared by all Africans? Does Bernal view Africanness as related to specific cultural practices? Or is Africanness some combination of all these variables?[8]

Bernal's only sustained treatment of any of these issues occurs in his reconstruction of Sesōstris's fabled visit to the Colchis. As the reader will recall, in the second volume of *Black Athena* it was theorized that an Egyptian monarch, Senswosret I, had invaded the Colchis in the early second millennium and stationed some soldiers there. Roughly 1500 years later Herodotus would claim to have seen their descendants, and he described them as dark-skinned (*melagchroes*) and woolly-haired (*oulotriches*). On the basis of this and other evidence Bernal suggests that Senswosret's Egyptian soldiers were black and hence similar claims could be made for the Egyptian population during the Twelfth Dynasty.[9]

The Response to Bernal: Frank Snowden

The most important evaluation of these views was advanced by the well-respected classicist Frank Snowden, Jr. His critique of *Black Athena* appears in a series of articles and responses published in 1989, 1993, and 1996. Even though the major assumptions of his first contribution were directly and forcefully challenged by the physical anthropologist S.O.Y. Keita in 1993, Snowden's position has evolved little in the intervening years. As I have suggested throughout this work, few scholars in the Controversy have interpreted the criticisms of their opponents as invitations to refine their positions or to stake out some common ground.[10]

Although Snowden's remarks about *Black Athena* are occasionally characterized by an acerbic tone, it must be stressed that he did not initiate this polemical engagement. In his first volume, Bernal referred to Snowden as an example of a scholar who has attempted to glean "what little credit the Aryan model allows to Blacks while accepting both of its prohibitions: the non-acceptance of a black component of Egyptian culture, and the denial of the Afroasiatic formative elements in Greek civilization." Bernal continues, "Most Blacks will not be able to accept the conformity to white scholarship of men and women like Professor Snowden." Here the author of *Black Athena* lapses, again, into a facile essentialism. There is, apparently, a proper black perspective, one which all black people should conform to and one which Professor Snowden has somehow failed to approximate.[11]

What makes Bernal's charge doubly inexcusable is that it is based on a rather superficial reading of Snowden's larger project. In two elegant and meticulously researched studies (*Blacks in Classical Antiquity: Ethiopians in the Greco-Roman Experience* and *Before Color Prejudice: The Ancient View of Blacks*) Snowden argued persuasively that "the onus of intense color prejudice cannot be placed upon the shoulders of the ancients." The Greek and Roman writers, he maintained, exhibited no prejudicial attitudes vis-à-vis darker-skinned peoples. With characteristic understatement Snowden would write, "Classical texts have often been misinterpreted because scholars have mistakenly attributed to antiquity racial attitudes and concepts which derive from certain modern views regarding the Negro." This does not strike me as an issue which has preoccupied the overwhelmingly white classics establishment. For Bernal to suggest that such an investigation constitutes conformity to white scholarship is simply preposterous.[12]

So if Frank Snowden enters the discursive arena in a somewhat irascible state, then it is certainly understandable. The main themes of his responses to Bernal (and his alleged Afrocentrist fellow travelers) may be summarized as follows: Snowden begins by charging the "Bernal-Afrocentrist" cohort with terminological inaccuracy. They are accused of using words such as *black*, *Egyptian*, *African*, and *Negro* "interchangeably as equivalents despite copious ancient evidence to the contrary." Further, they assume that "various color adjectives for dark pigmentation as used by Greeks and Romans are always the classical equivalents of Negroes or blacks in modern usage."[13]

In an effort to forward a more precise definition, Snowden undertakes to establish a basic principle of categorization: "Ethiopians whose skin was the blackest and whose hair was the woolliest or most tightly curled of all mankind *were the only people in classical texts who correspond roughly to the concept of blacks or Negroes as generally understood in modern usage.*" In other words, the physical characteristics of today's African-American or black person are approximated in antiquity solely by those the Greeks and Romans referred to as Ethiopians. Snowden writes, "The physical traits regularly associated with the classical word Ethiopian are in general the same characteristics included in modern anthropological classifications of Negroes: 'dark pigmentation, . . . a broad, low-bridged nose, thick everted lips and kinky or curly hair.'"[14]

The classical writers—and this is Snowden's major point—did not view the ancient Egyptians as belonging to the same physical or cultural categories as the Ethiopians. As such, the reference to extremely dark skin and curled hair describes only the latter, not the former. Snowden, for his part, construes the Egyptians as "a kind of intermediate population, an amalgam of white and Ethiopian."[15]

Drawing on evidence from Egyptian iconography, he infers that "blacks were not representative of the total population in Egypt." Snowden also observes that from the middle of the third millennium onward artists depicted Kushites (Nilotic peoples living to the south of the Egyptian border) with "tightly coiled hair and thick lips—characteristics clearly differing from those in their portrayal of Egyptians." Snowden's overall approach to the question of Egyptian phenotype may be summarized by his claim that it would be "inaccurate to describe ancient Egypt as either black or predominantly black."[16]

As noted above, the Colchians described by Herodotus were reported to have had dark skin and woolly hair. It is significant, Snowden contends, that Herodotus did not say that the Colchians had the "woolliest or the curliest [hair] of all mankind" or that they "were extremely black." For these distinctions were reserved solely for Ethiopians. This argument against Bernal may be parsed as follows: Herodotus's description of the Colchians does not employ the precise terms a Classical writer would use to refer to Ethiopians. Only Ethiopians are the equivalent of modern blacks. Ergo, neither the Colchians nor their purported Egyptian ancestors may be accurately seen as black.[17]

The basic source of the disagreement between Bernal and Snowden is not difficult to identify: the definitions of black which they use are wholly incommensurable. Snowden equates the term *black* or *Negro* exclusively with a particular type of skin pigmentation and hair. Bernal, conversely, has the infamous "one drop" rule in mind. In other words, *any* type of dark skin or African ancestry makes one in the modern United States a member of a constructed category (i.e., social race) known as black or African-American. In a rejoinder to Snowden, Bernal writes, "If . . . one used 'black' in the extremely broad sense in which it is used in the United States, most of the Egyptian population would have fitted into that category."[18]

Bernal, then, may be accused of a moralistic methodological relativism; today's definition of *black* is applied to the world of yesterday in order to strike down the racist belief in the cultural inferiority of African-Americans. Snowden, for his part, may be faulted for a sort of biological essentialism; *black* is defined not in cultural terms, but by reference to a rather narrowly defined inventory of physical characteristics. This latter approach, as we are about to see, is as problematic as the former.

The Response to Snowden: S.O.Y. Keita

In an equally spirited rejoinder, S.O.Y. Keita develops his argument by reading Snowden against Snowden. It has, after all, been one of Snowden's major contributions to prove that modern racial categories were simply nonexistent in antiquity. In assessing his rather rigid association of ancient Ethiopians with modern blacks, Keita asserts:

> There is a problem of language or logic here since the "ancient authors" did not have any race concepts, terms or *theory* synonymous with those

in "twentieth-century usage." Therefore searching for equivalents when the goals or theoretical underpinnings have not been the same is a logical error. It cannot be stated that the Graeco-Romans (or Egyptians) had no *race* concepts and then claim that their words or art depict "race." Their words and art only depict the ethno-nationalities which they knew, not "race," a more recent idea.[19]

Keita continues by suggesting that Snowden's understanding of what the so-called True Negro (i.e., the Ethiopian) looks like is predicated on outdated typologies of race, for recent research indicates that the question of phenotype, among other things, must be approached differently. We should not ask what race the Egyptians were but rather, "*with what external populations . . . of various periods and/or regions [do they] have the greatest biological affinities?*" Keita notes that the process of discovering genetic *affinities* is the real scientific challenge which confronts researchers, and on this issue "the classical texts are *silent.*"[20]

As noted above, Snowden views the Egyptian phenotype as attributable to a mixture of distinct black and white populations. For Keita, this is further evidence of Snowden's fealty to obsolete anthropological schemes. The latter, for example, never considers the possibility that the intermediate pigmentation of the Egyptian (i.e., possessing skin color between "black" and "white") could be explained in terms other than intermarriage between two distinct populations of Ethiopians and "Caucasians." In proposing a different explanation for the intermediate Egyptian phenotype Keita writes, "Nile Valley variation . . . *in the main* was probably due to the micro-differentiation from a common African (tropically adapted) ancestral population, and not the panmictic mixture of two or more distinct 'racial' groups."[21]

Put differently, Keita holds the position that Egyptians are the descendants of an indigenous African cohort. Their "intermediate" phenotype, then, is not a consequence of "crossbreeding" between distinct Ethiopian and white populations. There are, suggests Keita, a tremendous range of African pigmentations, and that of the Egyptians must be seen as representing one form which has developed through microevolution. In this conceptualization, Snowden's "True Negro," or Ethiopian, is construed as just "one variant in the range of real biological Africans." In terms of genetic relationships, Keita concludes that northern Nile Valley populations have "demonstrably greater biological affinity to populations from south of 'Egypt' than those from the Near East or Aegean." Keita's tendency to view Egyptian genetic affinities within a mostly African context is again evident in his assessment that Egyptians emerged from "a Saharo-Sudano-Nilotic (African)" base.[22]

Other Responses: Kathryn Bard and C. Loring Brace et al.

Two other contributions, that of the archaeologist Kathryn Bard and the physical anthropologist C. Loring Brace (and his research team), have discussed the phenotype of the ancient Egyptians in the context of Bernal's writings. These studies were originally published at roughly the same time (1993) as Keita's critique of Snowden. Accordingly, neither scholar could directly address the arguments we examined above. Of course, the articles of Bard and Brace were republished in *Black Athena Revisited* (1996). The readers of this volume—and American intellectual culture—would have been better served had the editors placed Keita's piece in this collection or asked Bard and Brace to address the issues raised in Keita's 1993 essays.

Bard and Brace share a few basic anthropological assumptions with Keita. All three scholars agree that race as we understand it today was not a relevant category for the Egyptians or other ancients. All express the belief, in unequivocal terms, that the concept of race is an invalid typological concept for the study of human genetic variation. Accordingly, each researcher searches for affinities or "biological relationships" as opposed to fixed racial essences.[23]

Unlike Keita, Bard argues that, from the perspective of material and physical remains, language, and culture, the Egyptians must be seen as "North African peoples" who are "*distinct from sub-Saharan Blacks.*" Beginning with an examination of Egyptian portraiture, she proposes that "the conventions of Egyptian art . . . do not represent humans as seen in perspective by the eye, but represent them in an analytical manner that transforms reality." Consequently, the "Black-painted skin" which appears in such work "could be symbolic of something of which we are unaware four thousand years later."[24]

While I am perfectly willing to accept that depictions of skin color in Egyptian portraiture and statuary referred to an entirely different reality, I would like to call attention to a possibility which has yet to be discussed. If black skin color in Egyptian artistic representation does not necessarily connote actual black subjects, can we conclude that the use of other colors to depict human pigmentation in Egyptian art is equally misleading? I have noticed that when researchers wish to prove that the Egyptians were not black they often point to portrayals of red and yellow artistic subjects as confirmation. Can we conclude from Bard's analysis that there is absolutely nothing to be learned from the examination of pigmentation in Egyptian statuary and portraiture?[25] And if this is indeed the case, how do we respond to those who use the same material as evidence against the extistence of black Egyptians?

Bard's rather sharp demarcation of Egyptian Africa from sub-Saharan Africa stands in direct opposition to Keita's view that Egyptians were descended from a "common African (tropically adapted) ancestral population." I would surmise that for Keita Bard's "North Africans" are construed as just another variant of an African phenotype. Moreover, Bard refers to the Egyptians as "Mediterranean peoples." Keita, however, argued that this term is unfounded in that "no one has demonstrated a Mediterranean 'cradle,' a single origin, a unique set of adaptive traits for 'Mediterranean,' or successfully explained how and when the 'Mediterranean Race' reached its far-flung proportions."[26]

C. Loring Brace's article, "Clines and Clusters versus 'Race': A Test in

Ancient Egypt and the Case of a Death on the Nile," is a complex and fascinating study of human genetic affinities. In order to comprehend Brace's argument—and I make no claims to have mastered all of its intricacies—we must draw a distinction between human traits which have adaptive significance and traits which are "adaptively insignificant." Skin color, for example, is an adaptively significant trait insofar as the production of melanin is an environmentally stimulated response to solar radiation. Following Darwin, Brace argues that selectively controlled traits (such as pigmentation) may be poor indexes of genetic relationships, for looking solely at similarities in skin color will not necessarily tell us much about the nature of biological relations between human populations. Indeed, individuals subjected to analogous environmental conditions in different parts of the world may develop similar phenotypes even though no pronounced genetic proximity exists between them.[27]

Brace argues that adapted traits, like skin color, are *clinally* distributed. This means that one finds this trait gradually differentiated in human subjects in accordance with gradual changes in the environment. Such an approach helps explain the oft-noted observation that the further south one goes up the Nile, the darker the pigmentation of its inhabitants becomes. Brace writes, "The quantity of melanin in the skin increases from the Delta southward up the Nile into the tropics, reaching a maximum at the equator." Throughout his essay Brace quotes the words of the anthropologist Frank B. Livingstone, "There are no races, there are only clines," as a means of showing the inherent uselessness of employing skin color to classify human populations. Brace writes, "Using a characterization of a single trait [i.e., skin color] that is under selective force control to generalize about any particular human population can only create confusion."[28]

A far better way to understand genetic affinities lies in the examination of nonadaptive traits. "Where traits have no adaptive significance," observes Brace, "neighbors will share traits with neighbors, and . . . they cluster together." In other words, populations that live within proximity, or "breeding distance," of one another are likely to share genes. The investigation of these nonadaptive characteristics, Brace points out, provides a far better gauge of the genetic relations between human populations, for these traits are not attributable to the pressures of selective forces and thus might indicate true biological links between populations.[29]

To this point we have seen that skin color is a bad way of assessing genetic relationships. Instead, we are advised to look at trivial nonadaptive features as a means of determining biological affinities. In his study Brace concentrates on nonadaptive aspects of human crania. Brace is well aware that this line of inquiry has a checkered past. As Stephen Jay Gould demonstrated in *The Mismeasure of Man*, "craniometry was the leading numerical science of biological determinism during the nineteenth century." Accordingly, Brace begins his article with an acknowledgment of the "theoretical poverty" of earlier studies of crania as well as its links to racial science.[30]

Having divested himself of the unsavory legacy of his disciplinary ancestors, the author proceeds to examine the relationships between different sample populations of crania which have been measured in terms of twenty-four variables (e.g., superior nasal bone width, bizygomatic breadth). Samples from Giza (Lower, or northern, Egypt) in the Late Dynastic period and Naqada (Upper, or southern, Egypt) in the Predynastic period are measured against samples representing the "eight major regionally identifiable clusters." These clusters are labeled "African, Amerind, Asian-Mainland, Australo-Melanesian, Eskimo-Siberian, European, Jōmon-Pacific and South Asian."[31]

The question then becomes: Which of the eight clusters do the two Egyptian samples most resemble? As with Bard's study, Brace's findings proffer evidence for the lack of genetic relations between Egypt and sub-Saharan Africa. He remarks: "Whatever else one can or cannot say about the Egyptians, it is clear that their craniofacial morphology has nothing whatsoever in common with Sub-Saharan Africans'. Our data, then, provide no support for the claim that there was 'a strong negroid' element in Predynastic Egypt."[32] Thus, in contrast with Keita's findings, Brace's research indicates that the Egyptians show greatest affinity with European populations. Although Brace does not seem to realize it, this finding actually supports one of Bernal's theories. Brace observes:

> That so many European Neolithic groups . . . tie more closely to the Late Dynastic Egyptians near the Mediterranean coast than they do with modern Europeans provides suggestive support for an eastern Mediterranean source for the people of the European Neolithic *at an even earlier time level than Bernal proposes* for the Egyptian-Phoenician colonization and influence on Greece early in the second millennium B.C.E.[33]

Brace seems to have misread Bernal. The latter posited Egyptian impact on the Aegean extending back as far as the seventh millennium B.C.E. If Brace's findings about the "eastern Mediterranean source for the people of the European Neolithic" are correct, then this would seem to provide an oblique boost for Bernal's theory of massive Egyptian linguistic and cultural influence on Aegean populations. On the other hand, Brace's findings might call into question the "fundamentally African" nature of the ancient Egyptians.[34]

All of these considerations about the genetic affinities of the Egyptians have had a bearing on the debate about the title of Bernal's work. In his 1989 response to Snowden, Bernal conceded: "I am now convinced that the title of my work should have been *African Athena. I have no doubt about Athena's African ancestry. My regret is based on the fact that 'black' is—to my mind—misunderstood to represent purely West African physical types."[35] Bernal goes on to note that the title *Black Athena* was one of a few possibilities which he had considered: "I must admit that I did originally suggest it as a possible title, *but on thinking it through I wanted to change it.* However, my publisher insisted on retaining it, arguing: 'Blacks no longer sell. Women no longer sell. But black women still sell!'"[36]

Keita's view of the Egyptians as descendants of Africans would seem to argue in favor of Bernal's amended title. If Bard and Brace are correct, then *Egyptian Athena* or *North African Athena* or perhaps *Egyptian, but Not Sub-Saharan, Athena* would be a more accurate name for this work. In any case, we can agree that the question of the Egyptians' genetic affinities has not been resolved.

Conclusion: Anachronism or Activism?

The attempt to extract racial and/or genetic data from the gracefully painted bodies and scattered skulls of ancient Egyptians is certainly a peculiar endeavor; poor Egyptians, forced to confess to an identity that they never even knew they had.

The Annales historian Lucien Febvre once declared that in the study of history anachronism is "the worst of all sins, the sin that cannot be forgiven."[37] The charge that Bernal's enterprise is sinfully anachronistic has been frequently made. Lawrence Tritle declares: "Bernal's intended assault on racism is laudable, but in the process he only succeeds in imposing nineteenth and twentieth century perceptions of race that have no place in what was and is the multiracial society of Egypt. Thus he distorts not only the texture of the past, but also subjects the ancient Egyptians to the indignity of racial stereotypes and attitudes spawned by the misguided modern age."[38] Mario Liverani maintains that Bernal's "historiography is old-fashioned and contradictory. He still attaches paramount importance to the concepts of 'race' and 'peoples.'" John Baines remarks that Bernal's arguments about "'blackness' . . . seem inappropriate to any society that does not have an overriding obsession with race."[39]

While these criticisms are, in many ways, valid, it seems to me that Bernal's approach is far more complex and far less naive than these remarks suggest. In a moment, I will point to some of the dangers inherent in *Black Athena*'s consciously politicized and highly moralized reading of the historical record. Prior to doing so, I would like to delineate some nuances of Bernal's argument which his critics seem to have overlooked.

To begin with, we must wonder if historians can ever avoid imposing the concepts of their day on the societies which they study. It was another major *Annales* historian, Marc Bloch, who observed, "In the last analysis, whether consciously or no, it is always by borrowing from our daily experiences and by shading them, where necessary, with new tints that we derive the elements which help us to restore the past." Tritle himself, it should be noted, refers to ancient Egypt as a "multiracial society"—an equally egregious imposition of modern nomenclature on the ancients. Keita, as we saw above, proposes that the Egyptians construed their world in terms of "ethno-nationalities." Of course, our understanding of "ethno-nationalities" is parasitic on the relatively recent idea (and formation) of the modern nation-state. It is highly unlikely that these terms, or Bard's reference to a "melting pot," were part of the Egyptians' cognitive framework. In short, it is simply inevitable that we will bring our conceptual vocabulary to bear on the Egyptians, if only for the obvious reason that we have no other conceptual vocabulary to use.[40]

In fairness to Tritle, perhaps he means to say that Bernal is imposing not only contemporary concepts but a present-day political ideology on to the past. Tritle is certainly correct, for as we have noted throughout this work, all scholarship is political as far as the author of *Black Athena* is concerned. But prior to indicting Bernal, I think it is important to situate his argument within its proper context. We must not forget that earlier researchers have imposed *their* political ideologies on ancient Egypt for decades—and they have not been so kind as to alert us to this state of affairs. As William Chester Jordan points out, there have been "excesses" on both sides. In a 1969 article Edith Sanders reviewed the awful odyssey of the "Hamitic hypothesis" in Western thought. The reader might take note of the manner in which Sanders's approach anticipates Bernal's critique of nineteenth-century academe:

> Perhaps because slavery was both still legal and profitable in the United States, and because it was deemed necessary and right to protect it, there arose an American school of anthropology which attempted to prove scientifically that the Egyptian was a Caucasian, far removed from the inferior Negro. . . . These theories attempted to include the Egyptians in the branch of the Caucasoid race, to explain their accomplishments on the basis of innate racial superiority, and to exclude the Negro from any possibility of achievement by restating his alleged inferiority and his position of "natural slave."[41]

In order to understand what Bernal is doing—and whether we approve of such an operation is an entirely different question—we must realize that he is having a conversation with the ghosts of Egyptology, classics, and physical anthropology. From Samuel George Morton's *Crania Aigyptica,* to the Dynastic Race Theory, to Charles Seligman's musings as to whether the Caucasian Hamites of Egypt had ever reached the "heart of Negroland," to all of the malefactors discussed in the first volume of *Black Athena,* the academic study of ancient Egypt has often shown itself to be predicated on patently racialist and racist assumptions.[42]

Bernal labels certain pharaohs black not because he would like to live in a world where all human accomplishments are classified under the mutually exclusive categories of white or black contributions to civilization, but because he wishes to challenge those explicit and implicit assumptions which suggest that all major contributions to civilization are made by whites. The author of *Black Athena,* then, imposes racial categories on the ancients in a highly conscious, one might even say strategic, manner. He is supremely aware of the "dubious utility" of the concept of race. Having read Davidson, Snowden, and Drake he is aware of the theory that this concept was conceived in the modern world, and that it is only there that it can be applied. In spite of this awareness, he still finds it useful to refer to some Egyptian rulers as black.[43]

One common response to this strategically racialized reading of the historical record may be summarized as follows: *Yes, I am well aware of past racist scholarship in my academic field. And I personally deplore racism. But why does Bernal have to bring this tortured, outdated discourse to the contemporary study of antiquity. Why does he have to dip our disciplinary biscuit into that old, rancid vinegar of racism and force us all to swallow?* There is little doubt that the types of racist scholarship discussed by Bernal are the relics of a bygone era. Few serious scholars currently subscribe to the types of overtly racist views discussed above. Indeed, throughout the Controversy the overwhelming majority of Bernal's critics have explicitly denounced racism.

This, I believe, is an excellent starting point. But to deplore racism is not necessarily the same as laying it to rest. Whether academicians like it or not, schoolchildren will need textbooks. These textbooks will need illustrations, and in these illustrations the Egyptians, the Greeks, the Romans, and others will have to look like something. The parents of these children—not to mention teachers, community activists, think-tankers, and politicians—are by no means uninterested in these representations, as Todd Gitlin has recently shown. This point is well captured by Sturt Manning, who points out that while scholars may haggle over all sorts of issues, "the ordinary public . . . would probably like to know if Bernal is right or wrong, not whether his is a valuable discourse set within the conflicting ideological dialectic of the present."[44]

Whether we deplore racism or not, we live in a society obsessed and haunted by race, a society where most think in terms of racial categories, and where, juristically at least, *race is real.* As the legal scholar Patricia Williams reminds us, "The simple matter of the color of one's skin so profoundly affects the way one is treated, so radically shapes what one is allowed to think and feel about this society, that the decision to generalize from such a division is valid." In a society where race and racism are real, the question of the skin color of the Egyptians—much to the chagrin of many, myself included—is a perfectly relevant question to engage. To bracket the issue, to say that the study of race is simply demeaning, is an approach fraught with risks. This stance provides no scholarly resistance to the racist beliefs of an earlier era and those of the present. Silence will most definitely not prevent these ideas from working their way into scholarly research and textbooks. I think of Hannah Arendt's remark in her 1945 article "The Seeds of a Fascist International": "It is a highly dubious achievement of Jewish counter-propaganda to have exposed anti-Semites as mere crackpots, and to have reduced anti-Semitism to the banal level of a prejudice not worth discussing."[45]

Bernal's "useful" claim, then, stimulates us to engage the racist legacy of our disciplinary ancestors. Ideally, the conscientious researcher might scrutinize his or her own preferred paradigm for any vestiges of such approaches. Further, it provokes many, quite literally, to reconfigure their conception of what the ancients may have looked like. Again, the prevailing conception of "white" Egyptians had been set in place by earlier generations of scholars. A reading of *Black Athena* provokes us to question this assumption.

But this effort to demonstrate the complexities and moral strengths of Bernal's thought should not obscure the fact that there are very real drawbacks in his approach. His rereading of the historical record is not so radical as it might originally appear. Whereas previous generations saw the Egyptians as white, Bernal turns the assumption on its head and refers to some of them as black. But inversion is not subversion. While the author succeeds in reversing the terms, he leaves the original paradigm of race perfectly intact. Instead of unequivocally debunking this concept—as did Bard, Brace, and Keita—Bernal inadvertently lets it breathe some final gasps.[46]

Another hazard of strategic readings is that they do not necessarily come with expiration dates. Once we have reversed the terms, once we make the anachronistic claim that Egyptians were black—simply as a means of combating the anachronistic claim that the Egyptians were white—chances are that we might get stuck there. Strategic readings will be read by individuals whose motivations might be far less honorable than those of their authors. The danger always exists that the effects of a political reading will linger indefinitely.

Yet the biggest problem such an endeavor presents is the kind of problem that most interests Bernal—namely, morality. In a recent essay entitled "Identity, Authority and Freedom: The Potentate and the Traveler," Edward Said has pointed to some of the dangers which strategic counternarratives present. In lamenting the nationalist doctrines that swept through Arab universities—and lingered there—in the aftermath of colonial rule, Said makes this eloquent plea:

> Do we say: now that we have won, that we have achieved equality and independence, let us elevate ourselves, our history, our cultural or ethnic identity above that of others, uncritically giving this identity of ours centrality and coercive dominance? Do we substitute for a Eurocentric norm an Afrocentric or Islamo- or Arabo-centric one? . . . In short, do we use the freedom we have fought for merely to replicate the mind-forged manacles that once enslaved us, and having put them on do we proceed to apply them to others less fortunate than ourselves?[47]

Finally, we must wonder about the integrity of the individual researcher who engages in strategic readings. If scholars enters their research projects with particular strategies in mind, it goes without saying that the imperatives of strategy will overcome the imperatives of balanced inquiry. This is perhaps one of the most recurring criticisms of *Black Athena*. As Minas Savvas writes,

"Research sometimes leads scholars to strange conclusions, but if the strange conclusions precede the research, as with *Black Athena,* then the results become more intriguing." Bernal is entirely vulnerable to this charge. The only response he can make is that all scholarly work is political. It is this claim which I wish to interrogate in my conclusion. For now, Said's words are again enlightening: "To make the practice of intellectual discourse dependent on conformity to a predetermined political ideology is to nullify intellect altogether."[48]

9

Contentious

Communities

"Blacks and Jews" and Black Athena

The troubled relationship between African-Americans and Jews survives in part through the pretense that relations were once better.
—Clayborne Carson, "The Politics of Relations between African-Americans and Jews"

Why, therefore, should anyone find surprising the perfectly natural fact that sometime allies reassess their ties and cut them?
—Jacob Neusner, "Blacks and Jews: New Views on an Old Relationship"

At first glance, the historical fortunes of blacks and Jews as recounted in *Black Athena* are conspicuously symmetrical. The Extreme Aryan Model banished both groups from Western civilization's garden of foundational myths. Complicit in this endeavor, the Occidental research university had, until recently, excluded persons of African and Jewish ancestry from its confines. And the senseless cruelty which their host societies have inflicted upon them, argues Bernal, flowed from the same poisoned ideological founts of race-thinking, Romanticism, Christian doctrine, and so on.

As we saw in the previous chapter, the author of *Black Athena* has little compunction about viewing the past through the moral and political optic of the present. Nor does he object to bringing a political agenda to bear on his scholarly work. Given the increasingly strained relations between African- and Jewish-Americans, one might surmise that Bernal intended for his historical narrative to provide grounds for symbolic reconciliation. "Since the late sixties," writes Cornel West, "black-Jewish relations have reached a nadir." An almost identical sentiment is expressed in the title of Nathan Glazer's 1984 article, "Jews and Blacks: What Happened to the Grand Alliance?"[1]

162

But if Bernal did indeed set out to broker some type of truce, to resurrect the storied grand alliance, he never made these intentions explicit. At no point in the Controversy did he say: *The events which have made blacks' and Jews' historical experiences so tragic were based upon almost identical ideological premises. As official "Others" of the West, you both share so much in common, most of it to be blamed on the pathological strains of European thought which germinated in the nineteenth century. I am convinced that an examination of these similarities could provide a healthy intellectual framework for reassessing the differences which separate you now.*

Bernal never said this. But the implicit presence of this theme in *Black Athena*, or some variant of it, strikes me as obvious. Oddly, almost no one else has identified the reconciliatory dimensions of this project. To the best of my knowledge, only one commentator has explicitly attributed similar political motives to the author. In an important, though inexplicably overlooked, interview with Bernal in *Social Text*, Walter Cohen submits:

> One of the extraordinary features of [Bernal's] work is its coding, even allegorizing, of contemporary issues in a way that seems reminiscent of far more censored societies. In a sense, the Egyptians and Phoenicians of *Black Athena* stand in for African-Americans and Jewish Americans. . . . Many liberal or radical African-Americans and Jewish Americans alike have been pained by the mutual hostility between these two groups in the last generation, following a period of self-conscious progressive alliance. Do you think *Black Athena* has an appeal in implicitly providing a historical or historiographical basis for the resumption of such an alliance in a shared sense of exclusion, now belatedly being corrected?[2]

Below I will have an opportunity to discuss Bernal's response to Cohen's question—a response as vague as it is provocative. Prior to doing so, it will be necessary to examine the other half of *Black Athena*'s allegorical equation. Earlier, we discussed the intellectual and moral merits of imposing the modern term *black* on the ancient Egyptians. In this, the penultimate chapter of this work, I would like to evaluate the author's bold coupling of ancient Phoenicians with modern Jews. This will require that we review his arguments pertaining to anti-Semitism and its relation to the divergent destinies of the Extreme Aryan, Broad Aryan, and Ancient Models.

From there, I will try to make sense of the wholly asymmetrical responses to Bernal's work in the black and Jewish communities of the United States. As we have seen, many African-American intellectuals and laypersons took note of *Black Athena*—their reactions ranging from censure to warm praise. The response in the American-Jewish community, however, was far less intense. Few Jewish-identified intellectual fora (e.g., *Reconstruction, Commentary, Tikkun, Midstream, Conservative Judaism, Journal of Jewish Sociology*) devoted much scrutiny to *Black Athena*. Moreover, some classicists, speaking specifically as Jews, responded to this work with palpable disdain.

The ambivalence and occasional hostility with which the American-Jewish intellectual community received *Black Athena* is a point of no small relevance to our inquiry. There are, I believe, a variety of explanations why Jews of various ideological stripes overlooked, or even strongly disagreed with, Bernal's roiling hypotheses. An investigation of this issue will better position us to address the question of *Black Athena*'s relevance to the study of contemporary black-Jewish relations.

A Forcible Conversion

In the final three chapters of his first volume Martin Bernal devotes his full attention to the question of anti-Semitism and its relation to the study of antiquity. One might rightfully ask what anti-Semitism has to do with either the Aryan or Ancient Models. After all, both paradigms concern themselves with the ancient Egyptians and Phoenicians, not the Israelites who are the ancestors of modern Jews.[3]

Bernal manages to factor anti-Semitism into his equation by making yet another of his spectacular—and hastily argued—conjectures. The author theorizes that in the nineteenth and early twentieth centuries, European scholars had come to conflate a pariah group living in their midst with a storied people who long ago disappeared from the historical record. On the first page of his eighth chapter Bernal confidently asserts, "The Phoenicians were correctly perceived to have been culturally very close to the Jews." Elsewhere he avers, "Consciously or unconsciously, all European thinkers saw the Phoenicians as the Jews of Antiquity—as clever 'Semitic' traders."[4]

Unfortunately, Bernal advances only one line of evidence as a verification of this hypothesis. The conceptual amalgamation of Phoenicians and Jews is seen as a consequence of groundbreaking philological discoveries made in the seventeenth and eighteenth centuries. It was then that scholars realized that Phoenician and its colonial dialect, Punic, were closely related to biblical Hebrew. Accordingly, both were classified as "Semitic" languages, a term derived from Shem, one of Noah's three sons, discussed in chapters 9 through 11 of the Book of Genesis. If I understand Bernal's argument, he wishes to claim that a linguistic correspondence between the ancient Phoenicians and Israelites suggested to scholars that there existed a blood relation between them as well. In an age in which language and race were eagerly confused—and through some sort of transitive property of racial science—the ancient Phoenicians were forcibly converted to Judaism.[5]

If Bernal is indeed correct, then his work provides a case study of how fealty to a paradigm can becloud scholarly vision. Convinced that language and race were inextricably bound, researchers somehow overlooked that the Phoenicians differed considerably from the Israelites. Even a cursory reading of the Old Testament—a text which would be highly familiar to any educated nineteenth-century European scholar—makes it clear that these groups had very little in common.

The authors of the Hebrew Bible (i.e., the Old Testament) exert tremendous efforts to demonstrate that Tyrians, Byblians, Sidonians, and Arvadians
(the biblical designations for the cities and their peoples which the Greeks
called Phoenicia) are religiously and politically distinct from the Children of
Israel. True, there are some early narratives which speak of friendly cooper-
ation between the Israelite king David, his son Solomon, and Hiram of Tyre.
But for the most part, the biblical prophets manifest a quasi-fanatical hatred
for their neighbors to the north. Much of this antipathy can be attributed to
the perception of differences between Phoenician religiosity and that of those
who authored and edited the corpus of texts which we refer to as the Hebrew
Bible.[6]

The Phoenicians worshiped the goddess Ashtoreth, not to mention a variety of Baals—a religious orientation which was simply intolerable to the
"Yahweh-alone party" who have left their imprimatur all over the sacred
Scriptures. In terms of religious praxis, the authors of the Hebrew Bible were
well aware of Phoenician child sacrifice, as were the Greek writers. In the estimation of one archaeologist excavating at Carthage, between 400 and 200 B.C.E.
very young children were sacrificed at the rate of "slightly fewer than one every
three days." This practice, and such others as funerary feasts, "ritual phle-
botomy," and sundry aspects of Baal worship, were the scourge of the biblical literati.[7]

In terms of political differences, the independent "Phoenician" cities of
Tyre, Sidon, Gebal, and Arvad formed alliances which were most definitely
not to the liking of various Israelite prophets. Perhaps this is the political context in which Ezekiel chastises the Sidonians:

> I am going to deal with you, O Sidon.
> I will gain glory in your midst;
> And they shall know that I am Lord,
> When I wreak punishment upon her
> And show Myself holy through her.
> I will let pestilence loose against her
> And bloodshed into her streets.
> And the slain shall fall in her midst
> When the sword comes upon her from all sides.
> And they shall know that I am the Lord.[8]

A further index of biblical hatred of the Phoenicians (and foreign women
as well) may be seen in the rather gratuitous descriptions of the Phoenician
princess Jezebel and her graphic murder at the hands of the reformer Jehu. In
short, it would require an advanced case of paradigmatic myopia for scholars to read the Hebrew Bible and come to the conclusion that modern Jews
can be easily equated with ancient Phoenicians.[9]

Although Bernal never mentions it, he is most likely the first researcher
to posit the coupling of Phoenicians and Jews in nineteenth-century social
thought. Much to the detriment of his theory, he has yet to identify any works

or passages in which scholars explicitly drew this association. In other words, he too seems to conflate blood and language. The assumption of a linguistic relation among Phoenician, Punic, and Hebrew made in the seventeenth and eighteenth centuries is simultaneously assumed to refer to an assumption of a biological relation between these groups. While this might be the case, Bernal has yet to document this association.

Semitic Race-Thinking

Black Athena's study of race-thinking as it pertained to Semites in general is far better documented. Bernal examines how Semitic-speaking peoples were understood within schematic hierarchies created by race-obsessed European scholars. As the reader might imagine, Semites faired rather poorly when measured against their Caucasian, Aryan, and European counterparts. The author surveys a wide selection of studies of the "Semitic race" and this fascinating and fairly detailed investigation constitutes one of the strengths of his intellectual history.

Bernal draws attention to a variety of different schemes which were advanced by nineteenth-century racialists. In some, Jews were seen as Caucasians. In others, world history was construed in terms of an epic conflict between Aryan and Semite, or Hellene and Hebrew. As the nineteenth century draws to a close, themes appear in the racial study of the Semites which anticipate forthcoming Nazi propaganda.[10]

The author's examination of modern European anti-Semitism is based on identifying two distinct frameworks through which Jews have been despised. He is interested in the transformation from a religious anti-Semitism to a racial anti-Semitism. He writes: "There has always been considerable overlap between religious hatred of the Jews and ethnic hostility to them. Nevertheless, it is equally true that there was a shift in emphasis during the 19th century from the traditional Christian *Judenhass* (hatred of the Jews) to a modern 'racial' anti-Semitism."[11]

This shift is examined in three countries. Things were at their worst in Germany. Bernal argues that here there was little difference between the two types of anti-Semitism. The author finds a more nuanced state of affairs in England, where he calls attention to this country's well-known philo-Semitic streak. England's Jews, Bernal reminds us, had played "an important role . . . in establishing Britain's financial and colonial supremacy in the late 17th and 18th centuries." Moreover, the English had often associated themselves with both the Phoenicians and the Jews. As for the former, Bernal remarks, "Many Victorians had a positive feeling towards the Phoenicians as sober cloth merchants who did a little bit of slaving on the side and spread civilization while making a tidy profit."[12]

The situation in France, as Bernal describes it, was even more complex. The Jews of that country were despised by Catholics and Royalists, but tolerated by liberal and progressive elements. The author devotes a section of his ninth chapter to discussing Gustave Flaubert's *Salammbô* and its notoriously "Orientalist" image of the ancient Phoenicians. He suggests that part of the French hatred for the Phoenicians was attributable to the aforementioned association between these Semites and their despised rival, *perfide Albion*, or England.[13]

The forcible conversion of the ancient Phoenicians to modern Judaism in particular, and the "Semitic race" in general, greatly altered nineteenth-century historical research. In a recent contribution, Bernal remarks, "The Phoenicians were then, as they had been at least since the Renaissance, chiefly associated with the Jews, with whom they shared a common language (Canaanite) and many religious and other customs." The study of the former now became inextricably bound with contemporary perceptions of the latter. The Ancient Model had spoken of massive Phoenician impact on ancient Greece.[14] In the nineteenth century, however, any notion of "Jewish" influence on Europe's foundational culture was unacceptable:

> The denial of Phoenician influence is clearly related to the strong anti-Semitism of the period, and in particular to its two climaxes or paroxysms—in the 1880s and 90s and the 1920s and 30s. The first of these followed the mass migration of East European Jews into Western Europe and crystallized around the Dreyfus Affair; the second came after the critical role of Jews in international Communism and the Russian Revolution and during the economic crises of the 1920s and 30s.[15]

It is within this ideological context that the Extreme Aryan Model was to arise. As the reader will recall, this model differs in one crucial respect from the Broad version: "The Broad, established by the 1840s, denied the tradition of Egyptian influence on Greece but for the most part accepted that of the Phoenicians. The Extreme denied even Phoenician influence."[16] Bernal's positing of an "Extreme" Model, with its rejection of both Egyptian *and* Phoenician impact, serves as the perfect vehicle for demonstrating metaphorical congruities between blacks and Jews. In an attempt to keep their "degenerate" blood and culture at a maximum distance from (Western) civilization, scholars endeavored to expatriate both groups from where they had been settled by the Ancient Model.

A "Happy Ending" and Bernal's Phoenician Problem

The two central events in twentieth-century Judaism—the Holocaust and the formation of the State of Israel—figure prominently in *Black Athena*'s analysis of the Extreme Aryan Model. In engaging these issues the author's prose becomes extremely purple, so to speak; he entitles his ninth chapter, with its examination of the rise of the Extreme Aryan Model, "The Final Solution of the Phoenician Problem, 1885–1945."

The end of the Second World War marks, for Bernal, the beginning of the end of anti-Semitic race-thinking. In a 1995 contribution he suggests that "the moral revulsion at the consequences of anti-Semitism, now made visible by the genocide of the Jews, stimulated a revision of conceptual frameworks in all disciplines." This ideological shift was accompanied by a lessening of restrictions on Jewish participation in the university. "From the late 1950s," writes Bernal " . . . Jewish students and academics became completely accepted in the leading universities."[17] It is on account of their progressive integration into American and European intellectual life that the author foresees a "happy ending" for scholarly approaches which seek to acknowledge the Phoenician contribution to Western civilization:

> The successful restoration of the Phoenicians' reputation required two preconditions, both of which have been fulfilled. *The first was the reincorporation of Jews into European life;* the second has been the great emphasis, within Jewish culture, on intellectual pursuits and the respect for academia. *The former has removed the conceptual barriers of anti-Semitism that made it impossible to recognize the Phoenician and Canaanite achievements;* the latter means that even the tiny number of Jewish scholars concerned with these issues can have a powerful effect on the academic *status quo.*[18]

Elsewhere Bernal asserts, "Increased Jewish self-confidence, though largely reflected in Zionism and religious revival, has had as an intellectual byproduct an attempt to restore the historical role of the Phoenicians."[19]

Yet the theory that postwar Jewish scholars in a less anti-Semitic university are busily restoring the Broad Aryan Model and the Phoenicians' honor is problematic to the core. In the previous section we examined Bernal's ingenious, though unproven, contention that nineteenth-century European researchers equated modern Jews with ancient Phoenicians. Less plausible is the argument that this assumption survived into the twentieth century—where it was embraced by *Jewish* academicians.[20]

It is one thing to claim that anti-Semites and race-thinkers in the nineteenth and early twentieth centuries adopted a they-all-look-the-same-to-me attitude in which Phoenicians and Jews were seen as interchangeable Semites, but what makes Bernal's analysis highly improbable is the assumption that Jews themselves would draw this association. How could Jewish readers of the Hebrew Bible overlook what archaeologist Patricia Bikai aptly refers to as its "religious anti-Phoenicianism"? Isaiah's gloomy pronouncement on Tyre or Ezekiel's broadsides aimed at the Sidonians make for some of the more remarkable imagery in a remarkable document. Bernal has forgotten that Jews do not share the same ideological convictions as nineteenth-century anti-Semites. It is David, Elijah, and Ruth who they revere, not Hiram, Jezebel, and Athaliah.[21]

The theory that Jews are natural "champions" of the Broad Aryan Model is further weakened when modern Middle Eastern geopolitics are taken into account. In *Black Athena* it is suggested that Israeli scholars have attempted to rescue the Phoenicians by arguing that the latter transmitted the alphabet to the Greeks at a far earlier point (and at a different place) than the Extreme Aryan Model alleges. But to borrow a term from Bernal, there are over-whelmingly powerful "external factors" which might impel many Israelis, not to mention all sorts of Zionists in the Diaspora, to challenge the Broad Aryan Model.[22]

The question we must pose to Bernal is this: Why might Zionists, at a period of heightening conflict between Israel and nearly all of its Arab neigh-bors (1948–1985) consciously or unconsciously feel any desire to celebrate some type of transhistorical, pan-Semitic unity with the Phoenicians? Insofar as the latter resided in regions of modern-day Lebanon, Syria, and Tunisia (where the PLO was headquartered for a period of time), might it not be more rea-sonable to assume that the ancient Phoenicians would be equated with Israel's Arab adversaries?[23]

At one point, the author seems to concede this point by enumerating the factors which made Cyrus Gordon and Michael Astour champions of the Phoenicians. Bernal writes, "Both men are self-consciously Jewish, but out-side the mainstreams of religion and Zionism." The implication here is that Zionists and religious Jews are not necessarily pro-Phoenician. As I have just intimated, this might be a plausible inference to draw, yet at no other point in his work does the author develop this theme. On the contrary, he every-where speaks of Jews as the benefactors of the Phoenicians and the Broad Aryan Model.[24]

Aside from these two rather iconoclastic scholars and a handful of oth-ers, Bernal does not identify a significant number of Jewish champions of the Phoenicians. I believe this is due to the simple fact that there are not that many Jewish scholars who are actually interested in this question. Most postwar Jewish Semitists have had absolutely nothing to say one way or the other about the Aryan or Ancient Models. Nor does evidence indicate that Jewish schol-ars are disproportionately represented in Phoenician studies. While there are not many resources available for approaching this type of issue, David Sperling's *Students of the Covenant: A History of Jewish Biblical Scholarship in North America* illuminates this problem somewhat. For among the dozens of postwar Jewish exegetes surveyed by Sperling and his cocontributor Baruch Levine, only a few can be said to demonstrate any sort of pronounced inter-est in the Phoenicians. Nor can it be said that Israeli scholars have welcomed *Black Athena* with open arms.[25]

Bernal's argument, then, is unpersuasive when measured by the standards of his own sociology of knowledge. He has not, in my opinion, identified any plausible "external factors" which might motivate Jewish scholars to promote the Phoenician cause actively. Further, he has yet to adduce any evidence which indicates that Jews evince a greater affinity for Phoenician research than any other religious, national, or ethnic group of scholars. And most important, he has neglected to call attention to the types of "inconvenient facts," which are essential to intellectually responsible scholarship of this nature. The author does not inform us that some of Gordon's most vehement critics were other

Jewish Semiticists. Here is H. L. Ginsberg in a 1963 issue of *Commentary*: "Professor Gordon's book [*Before the Bible*] is unfortunately impaired by its lack of scholarly sobriety." In fact, those familiar with Gordon and his heroic generation of Jewish Semiticists are widely aware of what is very cleverly called "the oral tradition"—or stories of personal and professional antagonism within this storied cohort. Needless to say, Bernal's sociology of knowledge cannot account for this state of affairs.[26]

Bernal's Jewish Problem

To this point I have reviewed and criticized Bernal's analysis of the interrelations among anti-Semitism, Judaism, and the Aryan Models. As a prelude to my discussion of black-Jewish relations, I will now turn my attention to the question of the reception of *Black Athena* in the American Jewish community.

One might expect that a widely discussed work which examines the interplay between anti-Semitism and scholarship would garner some attention in the Jewish lay community with its well-known proclivity for intellectual current affairs and its immense and heterogenous intelligentsia. This did not occur. As noted earlier, the outlets of Jewish-identified opinion all but ignored *Black Athena.* One might also surmise that such a text would become an object of discussion among Jewish academicians and scholars of Judaica. There is, of course, reason to believe that such individuals have participated in the Controversy, yet any attempt to identify "who is a Jew" runs into rather obvious methodological and moral problems. First, it is impossible to know with certainty, on the basis of a name, the group to which any person belongs. Second, and much more important, identity is a very problematic concept in these postmodern times. Suffice it to say that the ultimate decision as to who one is should be made by the person in question. Throughout the present study I have tried to refrain from speaking of any scholar's social identity unless he or she has explicitly made this information available.

That three classicists did precisely this has always struck me as peculiar. After all, while modern sociologists, scholars of gender, cultural theorists, anthropologists, and scores of others might routinely and enthusiastically tell us all about themselves in their publications, those who study Greco-Roman antiquity have been less than forthcoming in this regard. Against disciplinary convention, these classicists expressed their opposition to this text not only through historical and linguistic arguments, but in terms of their own personal experiences as members of this religious group. To a very minor extent, Molly Myerowitz Levine, who teaches at the historically black Howard University, made arguments of this nature. Levine, one of Bernal's most principled critics, charged that his study "reopens the nineteenth-century Pandora's box of racial hatred."[27]

More important, the classicist Paul Kristeller, writing in the *Journal of the History of Ideas,* challenges Bernal's contention that anti-Semitism was rampant in German higher education: "I can, on the basis of my own experience as a student in Germany, firmly assert that Bernal's statements on this matter are wrong, and merely reflect his own anti-German bias, justified when it concerns Nazi Germany, but not when applied to Germany before 1931 or even before 1933."[28] This hair-raisingly counterintuitive claim is followed by what must stand as one of the more dismissive attacks on *Black Athena*. Kristeller closes his article by stating, "Bernal's work is full of gross errors due to political prejudices and fashions and cannot be trusted in any of its assertions or statements unless it is confirmed by other, more reliable sources and authorities." But the most notable Jewish-identified critique of *Black Athena* was submitted by Mary Lefkowitz. In her many contributions to the Controversy—notably one made in a magazine associated with Jewish neoconservatism, the *New Republic*—she repeatedly equated Bernal's theories with Afrocentrism. In so doing, she also argued that such revisionist approaches to history were of a kind with Nazi propaganda.[29]

Prior to continuing, I will stress that the Jewish-American intellectual community is bewilderingly diverse. There is no homogenous Jewish position on anything—a truism reflected in countless jokes which Jews themselves are the first to recount. Yet while there are many different types of Judaism, I think that *Black Athena*, somehow, makes claims which are liable to alienate many of them. It goes without saying that this was absolutely not Bernal's original intention. By no stretch of the imagination is the author a "cultured despiser" of Judaism or an anti-Semite. On the contrary, the initial stimulus for this project was the author's desire to acquaint himself with the "scattered Jewish components" of his ancestry.[30]

In so doing, however, the author may have inadvertently pushed many of the buttons which elicit fears and misgivings within the guarded psyche of the American Jewish community. To begin with, Bernal's purported (and equivocal) relation to Afrocentrism could not have helped endear him to some Jewish readers. Rightly or wrongly Bernal has been associated with the latter; rightly or wrongly, Afrocentrists have been perceived as anti-Semites. Of a less ambiguous nature are Bernal's disparaging remarks on Zionism and the State of Israel. The author frequently criticizes the former and aligns the latter with the hegemonic Occident. He often speaks of "the building of Israel" as "a bastion of imperialism and 'Western Civilization.'" Such an approach is not likely to ingratiate the author to a large portion of Diasporic Jews. As a writer in *Commentary* notes, concern for "the welfare of the state of Israel" has become a fundamental constituent of identity for Jews around the world.[31]

Which brings us to Bernal's jeremiads served up to Jewish neoconservatives. As the reader will recall, Walter Cohen asked Bernal if *Black Athena* was an appeal to blacks and Jews to resume their old alliance. In a somewhat oblique response to this question Bernal answered that his project could be seen "as an appeal to right-wing Jews to return to the Jewish tradition of sympathizing with *all* the oppressed." In another contribution he would refer to "the tragedy of conservative Jews like Allan Bloom who champion the western 'heritage' while being denied a part of it by the reactionaries they admire." Once again, the author demonstrates his irritating penchant for assuming that members of certain groups must adhere to particular political positions.[32]

There are, however, substantive textual reasons which might explain some of the apathy and occasional hostility which Jewish-Americans expressed toward *Black Athena*. Throughout his text Bernal implies, though never explicitly states, that Jews are in some way part of the very problem which he describes. I cannot help but infer from his first volume that Jewish academicians have set up camp in the wrong ideological territory. They do, after all, espouse the Broad Aryan Model—a view which pointedly evicts ancient Egypt (i.e., Bernal's blacks) from the ground floor of western Civilization.

A related assumption of *Black Athena* is that Jews are, finally, insiders in the American academy. As we saw above, the author speaks of Jewish students and academics as "completely accepted in the leading Universities." Moreover, Bernal repeatedly asserts that many of the dominant figures in classics and Indo-European studies are now Jews. It will be noted below that there is in fact a disproportionately large Jewish presence in the American university. For now, however, we should recall that Bernal's entire project is fiercely critical of the university and the discipline of classics in particular. So when he suggests that academic forces are blocking the rise of the Revised Ancient Model, one cannot help but wonder if he is referring to all of those Jewish classicists.[33]

I hope the preceding discussion identifies some reasons which might account for the apathy and antagonism which greeted *Black Athena* in the Jewish community. No group, I surmise, enjoys being told that they have completely misread their own interests and betrayed their moral legacy. Let this not be taken as a claim that some Jews were not in favor of this work (though I cannot name them insofar as no one specifically said, "I am Jewish and I adore *Black Athena*"). Nor let this analysis be interpreted as claiming that Jewish scholars who criticized this work, including those mentioned at the beginning of this section, did so solely because they were Jews. I fully acknowledge the possibility that any academicians, be they Jewish, black, or otherwise, may have disagreed with the work simply because they were not persuaded by its arguments.[34]

Conclusion: Blacks and Jews—Asymmetries, Sociological Subtext

Theirs is the American interminority conflict with the longest bibliography and the most anthologies. It is a discussion with its own canon (works by Norman Podhoretz, James Baldwin, Harold Cruse), its own geographical signifiers (Ocean Hill–Brownsville, Crown Heights, Harlem), its own gendered division of labor (mostly men participate), and, as one commentator suggests, its own rituals of conflagration. It is a dialogue with its own central problematic as well. Nearly every contribution to the ongoing debate between blacks and

Jews, in some form or another, engages the same question: Are we similar or are we different? Somehow, *Black Athena* provides us with two completely contradictory answers to this query—and neither one is incorrect.[35]

As we have seen, a desire to rejuvenate the grand alliance—or, at least, to bring Jewish neoconservatives back to their senses—seems to have been one of Martin Bernal's animating political motivations. In order to realize this goal, the author invited his audience to discover blatant congruities between two distinct, albeit imbricated, narratives. *Black Athena* is a study of racism *and* racial anti-Semitism. The text examines the historical fortunes of blacks *and* Jews through an investigation of the historiographical treatment of ancient Egyptians and Phoenicians. Bernal gauges Western civilization's moral standing by its ability—or inability—to incorporate both groups into its foundational myth. Structured in this manner, *Black Athena* gently ushers its readers to the comforting conclusion that Jews and blacks have had meaningfully similar historical experiences.[36]

But somewhere along the way Bernal subverts his own moral allegory. For if the author wished to proclaim, "Blacks and Jews really have much in common!" then a countertheme in his work whispers, "But aren't they very different?" We might refer to this as *Black Athena*'s sociological mutiny. In spite of Bernal's desire to stimulate reconciliation, his analysis actually points to factors which explain why relations between these two groups are often so antagonistic.

When the author speaks of a "happy ending" for the Broad Aryan Model he might as well be talking about a "happy beginning" for American Judaism. Bernal's assumption that modern Jews are the benefactors of the ancient Phoenicians is, in the main, incorrect. Yet he is standing on firm sociological ground when he claims that in the postwar period Jews have established a formidable presence within the American academy.[37]

In 1971 Seymour Martin Lipset and Everett Carll Ladd, Jr., surveyed nearly every aspect of Jewish participation in the American university and concluded, "There is probably no country in which Jews have been able to do as well intellectually as in the United States."[38] Nearly a quarter of a century later Paul Ritterband would write: "Jews have become major figures in American academic and intellectual life. They are disproportionately employed in universities, and, more significantly, the more distinguished the institution, the higher the proportion of Jews. Jewish professors publish more articles and books, secure more grants; by every standard measure of success in academe, Jews have arrived."[39]

Of course, this academic prosperity is but an epiphenomenon of another major shift identified, accurately, by Bernal: the decline of anti-Semitism in the aftermath of the Second World War and a corresponding acceptance of Jews into the mainstream of American civilization. As Howard Sachar noted in his mammoth *History of the Jews in America*, by the 1960s anti-Semitism had "retreated to the fringes of American life." (Though Sachar went on to observe that the fringes were not to be taken lightly.)[40]

The lack of an obstacle-generating anti-Semitism in this country, has permitted Jews en masse to prosper as never before. In the words of one prominent Jewish editor, "America is the very first diaspora which is not exile."[41] Historian Henry Feingold offers some statistical support for this claim: "It is no secret that by the 1960s Jews had achieved a numerically disproportionate position in the technocratic, cultural, governmental, and managerial elites who administer and shape American society. They are the ethnic group with the nation's highest per capita income and the highest professionalization."[42]

In recent years, awareness of this unprecedented circumstance has led some Jewish-American commentators to wonder if anti-Semitism can still be considered relevant. A recent cover of *New York* magazine raised this very possibility: "As anti-Semitism fades and Jews assume ever-greater prominence throughout the Establishment, it's time for Jewish Americans to let go of the idea that they are outsiders."[43]

But could this magazine—any magazine—make a comparable statement about African-Americans? With the possible exception of Dinesh D'Souza and a few others, how many could claim that racism is now a nonissue, a slice of ugly Americana whose days have passed? This news would come as a surprise to the countless scholars, journalists, and artists who report that racism and its effects are alive and well. Cornel West undoubtedly pointed to a fact of supreme sociological significance when he observed that, for the first time ever, young black Americans have the highest suicide rate in the United States.[44] West asks:

> What has changed? What went wrong? The bitter irony of integration? The cumulative effects of a genocidal conspiracy? The virtual collapse of rising expectations after the optimistic sixties? None of us fully understands why the cultural structures that once sustained black life in America are no longer able to fend off the nihilistic threat. . . . The recent market-driven shattering of black civil society—black families, neighborhoods, schools, churches, mosques—leaves more and more black people vulnerable to daily lives endured with little sense of self and fragile existential moorings.[45]

These sentiments have been replicated in scholarly research ad nauseam. Andrew Hacker, in *Two Nations: Black and White, Separate, Hostile, Unequal,* cited census data which made his provocative title sound like an understatement. Analogously, Michael Eric Dyson, in *Reflecting Black,* could point to a battery of truly depressing and alarming statistics pertaining to young American black males.[46]

In light of these figures, it is not surprising that recent studies suggest that African-Americans are underrepresented on university faculties. The definitive source for such data, the *Journal of Blacks in Higher Education,* reports that in 1995 blacks comprised only 4.7 percent of full-time faculty in the United States. As Terry Leap has remarked, "Next to Hispanics, African Americans account for the smallest percentage of college and University faculty in the country." In the popular press, journalists often speak of a minuscule pool of qualified black doctoral candidates. Accordingly, administrators often complain—and the assertion is hotly contested—that the recruitment and retention of African-American faculty is extremely difficult.[47]

None of this means that all is gloom in African America. A variety of positive indicators must be mentioned: the steady growth of a substantial middle class; the rise of a superb intelligentsia which ranks among the most vibrant in the contemporary United States (and has dethroned the formerly leading Jewish intelligentsia); an upswing in black enrollment in higher education; tangible and hard-won gains in civil rights legislation and political representation. And Thomas Sowell is certainly correct in reminding us that among all of the different groups in this country, "none have had to come from so far back to join their fellow Americans."[48]

But this should not obscure the fact that a substantial portion of black America is in crisis. Aside from astonishingly high intermarriage rates, "crisis" is not a term that most Jewish-American leaders are presently wont to use in reference to their community. With the exception of political affiliation, one will find whopping sociological disparities between American blacks and Jews. For many contributors to the emerging genre of Blacks and Jews Literature these disparities are largely attributable to American racism. "The Jew is a white man," declared James Baldwin in his famous 1967 article entitled "Negroes Are Anti-Semitic Because They're Anti-White."[49] St. Clair Drake writes: "All similarities between the experiences of the Jewish people and the African people in North America pale into insignificance in the face of this fact of white racism; for it carries with it built-in privileges and access to opportunities for one denied to the other."[50]

This insight served as the analytical linchpin of Robert Weisbord and Arthur Stein's 1970 study *Bittersweet Encounter: The Afro-American and the American Jew.* This meticulously researched work could disabuse even the most optimistic member of the civil rights movement of the idea that African-Americans and Jewish-Americans share much in common. The authors begin their study by noting that "since the seventeenth century the historical experiences of the two groups in the United States have been significantly divergent." Confirmation of this finding is not difficult to identify. For example, historian Herbert Gutman's analysis of socioeconomic conditions in New York City at the turn of the century leads him to conclude, "One can say that Afro-Americans inhabited the same island as Jews and other immigrant groups, but lived in a different world."[51]

Many black and Jewish scholars have pointed out that these differences were manifest in the grand alliance (1910–1967) as well. David Levering Lewis, in his study of Jewish and black leadership organizations in the 1920s and 1930s, speaks of "a misperceived ethnic propinquity"—the erroneous and romanticized notion that both groups shared anything more than "an identical adversary—a species of white gentile." Nathan Glazer notes that even though both groups fought together in the 1940s and 1950s against discrimination, they did so for completely different reasons.[52]

Another important line of inquiry for the assessment of the grand alliance concentrates on the internal differences within each group. The African-American community is as bewilderingly diverse as the Jewish-American community. The same jokes are told. A noted Pan-Africanist once quipped that if blacks stood on the threshold of achieving full equality in the United States, they would argue as to whether to enter with the right foot or the left. The fractious nature of both groups—a similarity if there ever was one—is of relevance to placing the grand alliance within its proper context.[53]

As Clayborne Carson has demonstrated, those blacks and Jews who participated in civil rights activities were mostly radicals. In many ways their political and moral views were unrepresentative of the mainstream interests of their respective communities: "African-American and Jewish civil rights activists have often been distinguished from other members of their group because of their class and educational backgrounds or their assimilationist outlooks. Such activists are vulnerable to the charge that they have lost touch with their communities."[54]

My point is not to deny that there was a moment in history when some African- and Jewish-Americans jointly pursued noble goals. Rather, it is to demonstrate that any study of this alliance—as with any study of blacks and Jews in America—must recognize the differences both *between* and *within* these groups.

———

Black Athena's mutinous sociological theme tacitly confirms any hypothesis which stresses the asymmetrical experiences of blacks and Jews in the United States. One group espouses the Broad Aryan Model, the other a variant of the Ancient Model. One group has a surfeit of champions in the university. The other is still struggling to gain academic representation in proportion to its numbers. One group is less encumbered by the stereotypes which plagued it at the beginning of the century, while the other still confronts them on a quotidian basis. One group has been permitted en masse to assimilate into the mainstream; this invitation has been extended to far fewer members of the other. One group, Bernal implies, has embraced an academic ideology which discounts the accomplishments of the other. Perhaps this portrayal partly explains why laypersons in one group ignore *Black Athena*.

But does this mean that there are no points in common between blacks and Jews? Harold Cruse once asked, "How did two such divergent group types as Negroes and Jews come to be considered as allies in the first place?" *Black Athena* answers this question by pointing to substantial, if somewhat abstract, similarities between persons of African and Jewish ancestry. Yet all of the correspondences mentioned in the first paragraph of this chapter have one quality in common: they are not relevant to the recent African and Jewish experience in America.[55] This is a point which Julius Lester has made with abundant clarity: "While similarity of experience is important, a similarity of experience is not the same as *shared* experience. That is the crucial difference of which many blacks are keenly aware and many Jews are not. *Jews and blacks have parallel historical experiences in the broad context of Western civilization.* They do not share experiences common to both people in the same time and the same place."[56]

And herein lies a key to understanding the conflict between African- and Jewish-Americans. Any two groups which occupy such completely dissimilar sociological space, whose present group interests are so entirely different, whose historical experiences in one country are as incommensurable, are not likely to get along fabulously. That blacks and Jews have sometimes been able to work together, that they consistently vote for the same political candidates, that some members of each group still profess an almost spiritual admiration for the other—this is a far more challenging phenomenon for the sociologist to explain.[57]

Conclusion

We Scholars

Heresy in the University/Intellectual Responsibility/Passionate Ambivalence

The primary task of a useful teacher is to teach his students to recognize "inconvenient" facts—I mean facts that are inconvenient for their party opinions. And for every party opinion there are facts that are extremely inconvenient, for my own opinion no less than for others. I believe the teacher accomplishes more than a mere intellectual task if he compels his audience to accustom itself to the existence of such facts. I would be so immodest as even to apply the expression "moral achievement," though perhaps this may sound too grandiose for something that should go without saying.

—Max Weber, "Science as a Vocation"

To say scholarship is political is not *necessarily* to say it is consciously or deliberately partisan but merely to recognize that we produce knowledge from a particular position or perspective. This does not refute the need to try to be objective nor does it argue for relativism.

—Cheryl Johnson-Odim, "Comment:
The Debate over *Black Athena*"

Readers of the present study might feel empowered or enervated to learn that Martin Bernal intends to put a third and fourth volume of *Black Athena* into print. Prior to their appearance an edited volume of responses to *Black Athena Revisited*, entitled *Black Athena Writes Back*, is scheduled to appear shortly. Beyond that, his forthcoming research agenda has not been set. But Latinists take heed: in a 1993 interview he half-jokingly suggested that his future plans might include a "'march on Rome.'"[1]

Were the author not to publish another syllable, it is safe to say that his recent march through the fields of antiquity will be remembered by the locals for some time. Whether his ideas will perish or prosper in the coming decades is a question that I can answer only equivocally. They will, most likely, do a little bit of both. Yet the following caveat should accompany any attempt to evaluate this text: *Black Athena* is as much, if not more, a work of synthesis as it is an original contribution. Its theories are usually conscious borrowings from, or glosses upon, earlier research. To pass judgment on any one of its initiatives is, quite often, to render an opinion on a preexisting school of thought as well.

The author resuscitates the much-maligned Gordon-Astour approach of the 1950s and 1960s, taunting its detractors with cries of *Nous revoila!* Seemingly inadvertently, he has vindicated the African-American vindicationists. Conversely, he more than occasionally embraces orthodox positions, as when he subscribes to the major tenets of the Indo-European hypothesis. (I think of Bernal's wry riposte to a critic who made a similar point: "I do not see why I—or anyone—should be expected to be radical in every respect.") *Black Athena* is pastiche, a mix and match of theories and paradigms emanating from nearly every period and ideological quadrant of the academic grid. The heterogeneity of the text makes it exceedingly difficult to dismiss or champion it as a whole. That so many were willing to execute either operation strikes me as a failure of scholarly integrity.[2]

For these reasons, I shall refrain from rendering a final sweeping verdict. I will, however, insist on two points. First, all scholarly disciplines need a Bernal or two—though no more than that. Although they do not usually realize it, academic orthodoxies—I do believe they exist—are greatly enriched by creative, erudite, and widely read interlopers such as Bernal. To rephrase an old sociological idea: orthodoxies need heresies, invoke heresies, and are, in part, constituted by their confrontation with the heretical. (Please note that I champion heretics, not apostates. I do not share Bernal's enthusiasm for the participation of laypersons in scholarly research.) Second, the time has arrived for the creation of a disciplinary common market. Scholars in all of the presently atomized fields of antiquity must speak (and listen) to one another. I categorically endorse Bernal's plea for a new metadiscipline of "ancient studies" or Molly Myerowitz Levine's proposed department of "ancient Mediterranean studies."[3]

In what follows I would like briefly to appraise, as best as I can, the major historical and sociological initiatives of *Black Athena*. Most of this chapter, however, will concentrate on the lessons learned from the Controversy as they pertain to the status of dissent in the American university and the nature of professorial and intellectual responsibility.

The Historical Argument

Ancient historians have usually evinced little appreciation for the "craggy melody" of social theory. In biblical studies and classics, for example, those who use legitimate sociological methods comprise a tiny fraction of these disciplines' numerous practitioners. The greatest sociologist of antiquity died three quarters of a century ago. Max Weber—whose central problematic was the emergence and development of occidental bourgeois rational capitalism—has left us with *Ancient Judaism* and *The Agrarian Sociology of Ancient Civilizations.* As members of the Weber industry are quick to point out, these very serviceable texts have been mostly ignored by ancient historians. They may be somewhat "outdated," but they have yet to be "surpassed."[4]

*Black Athena'*s very simple sociology of knowledge—coupled with its massive popularity—has forced antiquarians to listen to a few bars of popular social science. His modular approach is a useful import. If I may speak from personal experience, sociologists love to frame their research in terms of competing models; ancient historians do not. One of the great intellectual contributions of Bernal's work, I believe, is his attempt to identify various assumptions which have oriented the work of those who ponder the ancient world. Having read through a considerable number of historical studies, he posited the existence of four basic metaparadigms which have informed the study of the distant past. Any researcher who has ever tried to extract these submerged common-denominator assumptions from the murky doxic depths can appreciate his efforts.

Ancient historians might be advised to approach Bernal's models as Weberian ideal types. As Stephen Kalberg has remarked, ideal types are "hypothesis-forming models." In no way do they aspire to "replicate" external reality. Instead, ideal-typical schema serve as "conversation starters"— ideas which orient a community of researchers around a particular problematic. At the very least, all can agree that Bernal has succeeded in starting a conversation. If we understand the Ancient Model not as an attempt to depict reality precisely as it was—as a few of Bernal's critics have—but as a general, and correctable, scheme which concentrates our research initiatives, we will permit ourselves to pose fecund questions. Most prominently: Did the Greeks really believe that they were intellectually indebted, colonized by, or related to Egyptians and Phoenicians? Bernal has convinced me, anyhow, that some incarnation of this belief was present in some precincts of Classical and Hellenistic thought. It appears only sporadically, vaguely, in the interstices of larger, more consciously articulated narratives, but nevertheless it is there. This is a significant discovery—or more accurately, rediscovery.[5]

Yet it is one thing to recognize that the Greeks believed in this Oriental influence, but entirely another to claim that they were always correct in doing so. For these reasons, I concur with the standard critique of *Black Athena*: The author does place far too much faith in the accuracy of ancient documents. If the project is to advance, it is incumbent upon him to develop some formal criteria which ascertain when we can and cannot trust a primary source. Conclusions of this nature usually emerge from extremely specialized work, a research mode which the author is often eager to disparage. As for his detractors, they too must gaze into the self-reflexive hand mirror; it is incumbent upon them to take his concerns regarding the "argument from silence," the demand for "positive proof," and the attitude of *Besserwissen* more seriously.

In a broad sense, there is much to recommend in the Revised Ancient Model. It is neither unwarranted nor unprecedented to suppose that there was interaction among the Aegean, the Levant, and North Africa in the Bronze Age. Nor is it implausible to assume that this interaction was generally initiated by the more advanced civilizations which Bernal calls "Afroasiatic." Again, this is a perfectly useful—and by Bernal's own admission, unoriginal—heuristic which serves to direct research and generate hypotheses.

As for many of the specific tenets of the Revised Ancient Model, I am somewhat less enthusiastic. First and foremost, there is the question of presentation. The author must restate his historical arguments in a more readable, systematic, and coherent manner. Until he does so, I regret to say, many of his theories will not and cannot be seriously engaged. A restatement of the basic arguments advanced in volume 2—rendered in the clear and concise prose which characterizes many of his article-length contributions—would be of great use. Further, Bernal must go beyond merely thanking scholars for their "fascinating" criticisms of his work. If he takes his critics seriously—and he should—he will proceed to abandon, or at least thoroughly rethink, a variety of highly problematic initiatives.

As for the arguments themselves, many of the criticisms in *Black Athena Revisited* strike me as justified. As Guy MacLean Rogers suggested, Bernal should factor Mesopotamian, Hurrian, and Hittite influence on the Aegean into his hypothesis. Further, in attempting to prove that there exists an Afroasiatic substrate of the Greek language, he must respond to the thoroughly legitimate challenge of scholars like Tritle, Jasanoff, and Nussbaum. As we saw in Chapter 2 above, they charged that *Black Athena* relied too heavily on loan words, personal names, and the like. Accordingly, the author needs to address issues of phonology and grammar more thoroughly.[6]

There are a few aspects of the Revised Ancient Model which I still do not understand. First, what exactly sent the Hurrian/Indo-Aryans (i.e., the nucleus of the Hyksos) so frantically in motion, southward, in the eighteenth century B.C.E.? Second, by what cultural mechanism did these Hyksos permit themselves continually to swallow aspects of other cultures? Third, why do the Hyksos keep moving so soon after they reach Egypt? Why would they not have been content to stay in this relatively accommodating region? Last, where and how do the Phoenicians fit into the Hyksos hypothesis? I do not believe that these drawbacks and ambiguities necessarily invalidate the Revised Ancient Model. They do, however, require that Bernal make the appropriate corrections and alterations to his hypothesis. As such, he will need to enter into a more concessionary dialogue with philologists and archaeologists who criticized his work, regardless of the sometimes homicidal tone of their contributions.

In closing this section, I would submit that Bernal's remarks on "competitive plausibility" comprise his most salient contribution to the study of ancient history. The author has mercilessly exposed and exploited the central vulnerability of the vocation: our humbling incapacity to be certain that our historical reconstructions are anything but competitively plausible. This state of affairs is well known to most historians. So much so, perhaps, that they rarely feel obliged to address the matter in their articles and monographs.[7]

Be that as it may, *Black Athena* successfully baited more than a few classicists and Egyptologists into publicly expressing some good, old-fashioned positivist dogma. These writers demonstrated a great degree of confidence in the utter impossibility of his ideas and the verisimilitude of their own. Insofar as Bernal's historical argument was based on the research of many other scholars, and insofar as some of his theories were accepted by some of his critics, I do not believe that the categorical denials of his claims were justified. Outside of references to the paranormal, I doubt whether categorical denials are permissible in the study of antiquity. The "etiquette of humility" discussed in Chapter 3 above is the appropriate rhetorical orientation for scholars who work in this area.

Ideally, researchers will be able to use Bernal's remarks on competitive plausibility as a starting point for a dialogue on the method and theory of historical research. The time has come for a community of scholars, across all of the many disciplines and subdisciplines clustered around the study of antiquity, to reconfront questions such as these: Where and how do we draw the line between possibility and probability in historical reconstruction? Can such a line even be drawn? How do we remain open to new and plausible theories (or old and plausible theories) without fragmenting and crowding our journals and conferences to the point of incomprehensibility? And for those interested in the paradoxical nature of the human intellectual endeavor, or Kafka's "Hunger Artist": Why do so many intelligent people devote their entire lives to the study of the ancient world when so little of it may be understood?

The Sociology of Knowledge and History of Ideas

For a variety of reasons—not all of them involving the pursuit of intellectual excellence—college administrators have recently embraced the idea of interdisciplinarity with especial verve. Whatever one might think of it otherwise, *Black Athena* is an exemplar of the interdisciplinary spirit of fin de siècle America. From anthropologists to scholars of rhetoric, classicists to historians of ideas, there was a little something in this work to interest or enrage everybody—except sociologists apparently.

It was this component of Bernal's critique which helped expose the third major fissure in the Controversy. We have already examined radicals versus liberals/conservatives and generalists versus specialists. To this I would add, ancient historians versus social theorists (or those making use of such perspectives). When cornered by persnickety antiquarians, Bernal brandished his cudgel: his "sociology of knowledge." The older generation of classicists and Egyptologists, unaccustomed to "hey, hey, ho, ho" chants, the vicissitudes of ideological critique, and self-reflexive sociology, typically responded with fight-or-flight behavior. At one extreme they ceded the point to a person who seemed to articulate every grievance of a teeming, angry, multicultural constituency. The converse reaction, the attempt to "fight" his sociology of knowledge, will be discussed below.[8]

"I have tried," declares Bernal, "to introduce the sociology of knowledge into Classics and Ancient History." That ancient historians were forced to confront this discipline was a salutary development. Of course, one wishes that the imported goods were of greater quality. Bernal's sociology was deeply flawed and insubstantial. His basic scheme was contradictory. He paid no attention to recent developments in the field. He relied too heavily on Kuhn's *Structure of Scientific Revolutions*, a work singularly ill-suited to buttress arguments concerning the relation of science to power, ideology to Occidental chauvinism. (I would submit that the work of Pierre Bourdieu, with its view of the academic field "as a *space of conflict and competition*," his acute understanding of how the workings of the "field" obstruct intellectual innovation, his calls for heterodoxy within social science, his view of various disciplinary boundaries as "harmful to scientific practice," would provide far better theoretical models and spiritual inspiration for *Black Athena*.)[9]

College administrators take note: Interdisciplinary projects are typically characterized by a consistent unevenness. Their authors are, inevitably, far more competent in one scholarly area than in the other. The essential dilemma of interdisciplinarity might be phrased something like this: How can a scholar speak two academic languages when it takes such immense effort and talent to master even one? Bernal the Sinologist may, somehow, be on his way to mastering the languages and bibliographies of antiquity. He will need to master the sociological language as well.

The author's outdated model of "internal" and "external" developments was not precise enough to deal with the complex data he had adduced. The problem is that external and internal factors are not discrete or mutually exclusive; they interpenetrate one another. Bernal needs to find a model which accounts for that "peculiar amalgam" of "ideology" and what we call scholarship. In all fairness to the author, many social theorists and intellectual historians are still looking for such a model.

Another difficulty lies in the author's reliance on highly simplistic, overly deterministic explanations of intellectual production. As one critic put it, Bernal's scholars appear as "puppets . . . pulled by the strings of political expediency, romantic fantasy, or racist bigotry." Many respondents in the Controversy, however, delineated the tensions, contradictions, and paradoxes present within the biographies of those Bernal summarily labeled as chauvinists. Far from behaving like puppets, these nineteenth-century writers often manifested an acute awareness of the difficulties and drawbacks of their own views. In other instances, they embraced positions which would seem anything but chauvinistic.[10]

That Johann Gottfried Herder, for example, once harbored what we would call racist sentiments seems clear. But Robert Norton's essay demonstrated a variety of intriguing, often perplexing, counterfacts which served to offer a far more complicated picture of the person in question. Bernal is correct in seeing Johann Friedrich Blumenbach as a major architect of race-thinking. Yet Robert Palter's article identified nuanced, self-questioning, and even counterethnocentrist impulses in his thought. Blumenbach, as Palter acknowledges, did in fact place Caucasians at the head of his hierarchy of racial families. Be that as it may, Palter rightly maintains that it is not a waste of time, or "hairsplitting," to delineate the subtleties of Blumenbach's thought. Palter remarks, "Intellectual distinctions are at the heart of intellectual history; without them, the discipline becomes a mere game in which one searches for heroic or villainous precursors."[11]

The lesson learned is somewhat banal: The process of intellectual and artistic production cannot be understood merely in terms of, or reduced to, an analysis of class coordinates, political beliefs, religious affiliations, chauvinism, and so on. At the risk of sounding nonscholarly, human beings are complex. At the risk of sounding elitist, artists and intellectuals are very complex. One wonders if social scientists will ever develop a theoretical apparatus that can account for the social bases of all this complexity. (Perhaps we should cut our losses and fire-sale the problem to writers of fiction.) Insofar as professional social theorists are routinely flummoxed by this question, I am again sympathetic to Bernal's ambitious "errors."[12]

Yet I have much less sympathy for Bernal's unsubstantiated and haphazard allegations of racism and anti-Semitism. We have seen that the author was rash in applying these labels to George Grote (as pointed out by Guy MacLean Rogers), Karl Otfried Müller (as pointed out by Josine Blok), J. G. Herder (as pointed out by Robert Norton), and Max Weber (as pointed out by me). I do not doubt that many of the figures discussed in *Black Athena* were actually racists and anti-Semites, but since it benefits absolutely no one to have charges of racism and anti-Semitism hurled about recklessly, we ought to exert extreme caution in attaching these designations to others, be they living or dead.

Nor am I sympathetic to the author's tendency to advocate completely contradictory positions. A certain opportunism characterizes *Black Athena*. Its author excoriates the "argument from silence," but occasionally employs it himself. He sometimes claims that scholarship retains a certain autonomy from politics, and elsewhere declares that all scholarship is political. He vehemently denies being an Afrocentrist, but is patently sympathetic to their cause. He commits the "variables foul" with regularity. He often ridicules scholarly experts and their conservative culture of specialization, but relies almost exclusively on their specialized studies. As early as 1991 he labeled his own sociology of knowledge "crude," yet he continues to use it to this day.

Most important, the scholars he derides as racists, anti-Semites, Eurocentrists, and so forth, are the same ones whose theories he uses to erect his Revised Ancient Model. Bernal would state, in the *last* paragraph of his first volume, that a theory's "conception in sin" does not necessarily invalidate the theory. In 1993 he declares, "The fact that Classics was conceived in racism and anti-Semitism doesn't falsify the Aryan Model." It is as if Bernal suddenly realized how profoundly indebted he actually was to all of those university chauvinists and to the structures of inquiry they had painstakingly erected. By my estimation *Black Athena* borrows from and berates racists, anti-Semites, positivists, and Eurocentrists in equal measure.[13]

Establishmentarian scholars have traditionally—albeit tacitly—concluded that when it comes to a scholar's questionable morality, good research is good research, *basta*. This is Bernal's response as well. The problem is that he never seriously confronts the moral and intellectual implications of this paradox—the fact that individuals beholden to the most offensive political and social convictions can produce research of high quality. Even the "bad" research—the research that Bernal finds faulty—is instrumental in helping him develop his intriguing hypothesis. Read through his notes and bibliography and you will find that his thought, as with religious orthodoxy, is constituted by its confrontation with its adversary. Be that as it may, he dwells incessantly on the unsavory biographies of these scholars, without any consideration as to the immense role that scholarly tradition has played in helping him write an important book.

This is not to say that Bernal's sociology of knowledge was without its useful attributes. The sheer density of the variables which he uses to explain the paradigm shift is an achievement in itself. I hope I have disabused readers of the curious notion that *Black Athena* is a work about "racism and anti-Semitism." Its thesis is anything but monocausal or bicausal. Those who genuflect to the analytical trinity of race, gender, and class might use Bernal's work as an example of how a researcher may go about factoring more than three variables into an explanation of any given social phenomenon.

As noted in Chapter 5 above, the author identifies more than a dozen factors which impacted upon scholarly production. Moreover, Bernal explores the intricate, and sometimes inexplicable, linkages between seemingly contradictory ideological impulses. The idea of concatenated external factors, sudden and unexpected associations between conflicting world views, is emblematic of a laudable attention to complexity. This gives rise to what I called the *Black Athena* Question—an inquiry as to the influence of unarticulated assumptions (metaparadigms, *doxa*, etc.) on intellectual and artistic production.

Heresy in Today's University: Class

In my sixth chapter I examined Bernal's analysis of the tainted genealogy of the research university. Since I am not familiar with the fields of eighteenth- and nineteenth-century intellectual history, I cannot discern whether this argument is valid.

It is much easier to evaluate his discussions of contemporary academe, for by his own admission many of his predictions were mistaken. Contrary to Bernal's expectations, *Black Athena* garnered a wide audience of specialists. He was invited to express his opinions at innumerable academic gatherings. His ideas were debated openly in scholarly fora. His text gained considerable support among the radical tier—a cohort whose sizable presence in the university cannot be interpreted as a mere ruse of conservative intellectual hegemony. The classics establishment, which Bernal gleefully enfiladed, by and large handled itself with grace. Though there were some unpleasant moments, these scholars engaged his work, attacked it, made a sincere effort to understand its core arguments. As far as intellectual work goes, one cannot ask for much more. (Surely, a writer finds derision more desirable than apathy.) In contemplating the implications of being invited to participate in the 1989 volume *Classics: A Discipline and Profession in Crisis?* he marvels at the "kindnesses" he has received from classicists and their "striking generosity" and "commitment to scholarship."[14]

The reception accorded *Black Athena* could well stand as one of the most convincing pieces of evidence suggesting that the university is fulfilling its promise, that it accommodates dissent judiciously, that it both cultivates and listens to heterodox voices. In retrospect, one might look at the Controversy and deduce that the contemporary American campus is indeed a place where heresy is institutionalized, as Barrington Moore, Jr., might say. But the success of the heterodox work *Black Athena* should not be confused with the health of heterodoxy in the university in general.[15]

To be an academic heretic is a peculiar privilege. I will begin by pointing to the ongoing adjunctification of higher education. It is estimated that up to 40 percent of the current academic teaching force is comprised of part-time professors. With the rise of vocationally based higher education (e.g., schools of business, communications, dentistry), the situation of instructors in the far less useful humanities and softer social sciences stands to get much worse. Martin Bernal, the tenured humanist, is the sociological opposite of the adjunct humanist. He is securely and permanently employed. As far as his research is concerned, he is subject only to his own whims. (Recall that the government department at Cornell was not pleased with his project, "but they couldn't do much about it.") Tenured and in good standing at a prestigious Ivy League university, the author was entitled, so to speak, to his heresy. That he is still around to tell his story, still employed, and still publishing is a state of affairs that should stand as Exhibit A in any coming defense of the institution of tenure—and all indications are that such defenses will become increasingly commonplace.[16]

The university certainly worked well for Martin Bernal, an inside/outsider as Jacob Carruthers—an Afrocentrist and hence an outsider—dubbed him. But I am not yet convinced that it would work quite so well for an Afrocentrist, or a part-time college instructor. Would a similarly heterodox text by an adjunct—whether a "young" Ph.D. or a graduate student—have received a comparable reception? Would the adjunct have found a publisher? But more to the point: How frequently could a project of such unorthodox dimensions even be conceived by a person orienting his or her actions and thoughts to the penetration of "the circuit of continuous exchanges"?

The reader will recall that I disagreed with the contention that intellectual production is entirely determined by external factors. I cannot and will not rule out the possibility of a part-time incarnation of Bernal—a twenty-nine-year-old contrarian from whose pen or software explodes a revolutionary blockbuster. Yet social factors, while not entirely determining, are by no means fictitious. The present crisis in higher education may not be enough to eviscerate all dissenters, but it certainly can make them exceedingly rare. It is precisely from these expatriates, however, that many American intellectuals of the twenty-first century will emanate. I think of Anthony Gidden's observation that "intellectuals may be radicalized . . . when normal routes to academic careers are blocked." An entire generation of scholars—trained, published, underemployed, adjuncted, unemployed—will one day also cry *Nous revoila!* The more talented among them will visit upon the university not the controlled, relatively constructive anger of the heretic, but the more apocalyptic wrath of the apostate.[17]

Heresy in Today's University: Race

But the question of dissent in the university need not be viewed only through the optic of class and professional status. In Chapter 8 I called attention to an assumption shared by two critics of *Black Athena* who otherwise held few opinions in common. That Martin Bernal was white, both seemed to agree, did much to endow his work with a certain legitimacy. Though I do not wish to endorse facile identity politics, I find this claim entirely plausible. Could an African-American scholar making a comparable argument have received the sort of response which greeted Martin Bernal?

Perhaps this case could be made a bit more concretely. St. Clair Drake's *Black Folk Here and There* appeared in print in 1986, the same year as the first volume of *Black Athena*. To a certain degree, it covered much of the same ground as the latter. It too touched upon the question of the Egyptian phenotype. It too talked about racism in the academy. It too was interdisciplinary. It too made good use of the relevant scholarly literature. It too had its moments of insightfulness peppered with instances of quirkiness. Yet the work of the well-respected anthropologist, a professor emeritus at Stanford University, has been consigned to the fate of most academic texts—that is, it has been read by very few laypersons and a few specialists. A second volume released in 1990, a year before Bernal's second installment, was equally neglected.

My argument is, in fact, starting to sound like identity politics. On the basis of one example, I seem to conclude, white heretics are engaged, black heretics are ignored. I reiterate a point made earlier. White skin privilege, or gender, or tenured status, or heterosexuality, or whatever does not necessarily ensure that a heretic's ideas will be feted as an epiphany. In today's university these factors operate more subtly. They do, however, play some role in granting a work an audience, and thus the possibility that its controversial claims will be discussed and responded to as well. As regards heresy, we cannot underestimate the importance of this advantage. Extrapolating from Weber's definition of the charismatic prophet, I would state that without an audience there is no heretic. Of course, unlike the bearer of charisma, the heretic's audience is made up not of "followers" or "disciples," but of hecklers—a negative audience, if you will.[18] Bernal himself has suggested that his social identity lent a certain legitimacy to his enterprise. Here he is discussing the reasons the Jewish scholars Cyrus Gordon and Michael Astour were dismissed while he, who is not perceived as Jewish, was not:

> The message was "Well, of course, they would push the Semitic component of Greek civilization, wouldn't they. They have a vested interest, they're Jewish." It was not their knowledge or intelligence that was questioned, but their judgment. It was their detachment and objectivity that were denied. . . . This raises a very interesting general issue: the belief that Jews, women, Blacks and other "minorities" were and are automatically supposed to be partial and partisan.[19]

The heretic, by my definition, simultaneously occupies inside and outside space. Bernal suggests, plausibly, that being white and male and non-Jewish stands as one of the most inside of identities in the research university. (Though, as we saw in Chapter 9, being Jewish in the academy is also an inside identity.) On the basis of the limited empirical evidence discussed above, I must agree that in the Controversy social race did play some part in *Black Athena*'s success. In a more formal sense I would note the following paradox: The more one resembles the members of a social group (in terms of the mutually codetermining variables of intellectual orientation, social identity, race, class, religious preferences, and ethnicity, and dozens of other variables), the more likely one is to be successful in undermining its core beliefs. Following Bourdieu, I would posit a sort of iron law of heresy: "The propensity to take risks—in all kinds of investments—is a function of objective security and the confidence which that encourages."[20]

To be an academic heretic, then, is a peculiar privilege; there are far worse destinies to which a dissenting intellect might be subjected. It is certainly less desirable to be completely ignored, to have no right to participate in a conversation, or to be coerced into silence. Martin Bernal, contrary to his occasional claims, is no outsider.[21]

Intellectual Responsibility: *lema sabachthani?*

I would like to begin this final section with a few clarifications of nomenclature. The terms *heretic, intellectual,* and *professor,* although sometimes imbricated, are certainly not identical. *Heretic* (in the academic sense) was defined in Chapter 5 above and will not figure prominently in the forthcoming discussion. Everybody knows what a *professor* is. This leaves us with the irritatingly multivalent *intellectual*. Lewis Coser writes, "Few modern terms are as imprecise as the term 'intellectual.'" A seemingly exasperated Daniel Bell laments, "The definitions of what they do, or are supposed to do, are so contradictory that one runs into difficulties at the very start in trying to circumscribe, let alone define, their activities."[22]

In light of these considerations, I will refrain from advancing any definition, other than to make the following remarks. Not all professors, obviously, are intellectuals. Nevertheless, a theme which has recurred in the sociological literature for decades is that the university is this country's central repository of artistic and intellectual talent, or as Edward Shils phrased it, "the scene and seedbed of the intellectual life in the United States." It was suggested earlier that economic factors are imperiling the seedbed, but this is not our present concern. For now, let us assume that any given professor, by virtue of his or her rigorous scholarly training, the structural position he or she occupies within the academic institution, and the prestige of the savant's uniform, has intellectual potential.[23]

In *The Last Intellectuals: American Culture in the Age of Academe* (1987), Russell Jacoby bemoaned the rise of the professor as specialist, and the fall of the public intellectual. Jacoby drew a sharp distinction between intellectual work and academic work. While reluctant to define the former, he suggested that a major component of a professor's intellectuality consists of his or her ability to engage with a nonacademic audience. The endeavor to solicit a public, and to speak to them about major social, political, and cultural issues in comprehensible prose, emerges as Jacoby's major criteria for genuine intellectual activity.[24]

Jacoby did not foresee the advent of the culture wars. Unexpectedly, in the early 1990s some scholars left the "lazy safety of specialization" and entered the crucible of public discourse. They crossed disciplinary lines and spoke to one another. They passed through the campus gate and spoke to nonacademics as well. Encouraged by academic presses, which were sometimes handsomely remunerated for such encouragement, these scholars abandoned their impenetrable, neologism-ridden prose and wrote in an idiom suited for the much sought after "cultivated layperson." Following Jacoby, I will refer to academics who have solicited this "general and educated audience" as "public intellectuals."[25]

Many who participated in the Controversy are candidates for this designation. Bernal, as we saw in Chapter 6, cunningly "outflanked" the specialists by going straight to the "people." Although his two volumes are not pleasures of text, it must be noted that he is a very effective and engaging public speaker. He displayed this talent in a variety of nonacademic settings ranging from radio talk shows to meetings with community groups to television interviews. Mary Lefkowitz also targeted a lay public in her *Not Out of*

Africa. Her text was written in a clear, accessible style, one that earned her extremely positive reviews. (Jacoby is certainly correct in noting that radicals would be wise to envy and emulate conservative—or liberal—writing and rhetoric.) Other scholars engaged Bernal's arguments on the pages of the *New York Times Book Review,* the *Times Literary Supplement,* the *New Criterion,* the *New York Review of Books,* and elsewhere. Some made themselves available to journalists, some appeared in documentaries, some debated Bernal at quasi-scholarly gatherings.[26]

Those public intellectuals who have participated in the *Black Athena* Controversy have replicated a discursive pattern often encountered in the culture wars. It was repeatedly charged that Martin Bernal grafted his political concerns onto the frail body of his scholarly research. Michael Poliakoff writes, "Bernal himself demonstrates how having an agenda can obstruct the pursuit of truth; and until he proves otherwise, there is every reason to regard his own writing with suspicion." Lawrence A. Tritle charges that "politics . . . has provided *Black Athena* with a receptive audience that finds Bernal's polemical style of writing history congenial." "*Black Athena* is pernicious," affirms David Gress, "because it serves a political purpose hostile to the culture of scholarship."[27]

Anyone familiar with the culture wars has encountered variants of this argument before. Those who attack radicals often make a proclamation about them which could be phrased as follows: We are scholars; they are political activists; or, as George Will put it, "political activists wearing academic gowns." This is sometimes accompanied by some sort of disclaimer: No one, of course, is perfectly objective, but around here we come pretty close.[28] Here is Mary Lefkowitz in *Black Athena Revisited*:

> In our view, classicists are historians who try to look at the past critically, without prejudice of any kind, so far as humanly possible. If classicists have indeed misinterpreted the facts about the Greeks' past, they certainly have not done so willingly. I know that I run the risk, in the aftermath of Foucault and poststructuralism, of seeming naive in my belief that some kind of objectivity is possible, but it is my view that classicists and ancient historians would have been only too delighted to discover the true answer, whatever it was, *if it were possible to know it.*[29]

What is perplexing about this passage, and other disclaimers of this genre, is the degree to which it assumes that contestations of objectivity, truth, and so on, are some sort of very recent, very misguided theoretical contagion of Gallic provenance. Yet any social theorist, whether conservative or radical, knows that this is not the case. When one blithely proclaims, "We're pretty objective around here," one reasons as if Marx and Engels had never written *The German Ideology,* as if Karl Mannheim's encounter with Marx and Weber never yielded the collection of essays *Ideology and Utopia,* as if the Western Marxists all perished, unpublished, in dungeons and death camps, and as if the Frankfurt School was nonexistent. In short, these writers seem almost willfully oblivious to a rich theoretical tradition which would make their simple affirmations of truth and objectivity very problematic in very many ways.

I think we are again witnessing one of those discursive fissures mentioned in my Introduction. An episetemological canyon does indeed seem to separate conservative culture warriors (and many ancient historians) from both social theorists and contemporary radicals. Starting with social theorists, I call attention to Bennett Berger's spirited defense of determinism, *An Essay on Culture: Symbolic Structure and Social Structure.* Among this text's many interesting features—including a discussion of the film *Rollerball*—Berger analyzes nine recent studies in the sociology of culture. He examines how the authors, including himself, perform their "ideological work"; how they finesse contradictions in their text; how they strategize their arguments to ensure professional advancement; how they reconcile personal convictions with potentially contradictory findings in their research; how they craftily preempt the forthcoming objections of their critics, and so on.[30]

Usually, Berger ends his discussion of each study with the locution, "Now, that's good ideological work," or, "reasonably effective ideological work," or "brilliant ideological work." Berger, while perhaps glib, is in no way sarcastic or condescending toward these writers. On the contrary, he greatly esteems most of the texts he discusses. (He even recommended three of them for publication.) "That ideological work is done in . . . research," he asserts, "does not necessarily (although it may, and occasionally does) indicate flaws or weaknesses in the work." For him, ideology is a constitutive, unavoidable aspect of the scholarly endeavor. We scholars all do ideological work. Proclaim this, or some variant of it, at the annual meeting of the American Sociological Association and you will procure little more than polite nods and blank stares.[31]

To a person who has read only scholarship on ancient history and/or conservative culture war literature, however, Berger's text, independent of its disquisition on *Rollerball*, verges on the surreal. For these writers, there is nothing "good" or "excellent" about "ideological work," because good scholarship has no ideology, *tout court.* That a well-respected sociologist—and no sloganeering radical at that—should have so little compunction as to refer to research (which he esteems) as "ideological" indicates the degree to which practitioners of this discipline have disposed of unreconstructed notions of objectivity and truth.

Bernal, who had a general sense, as opposed to a precise understanding, of the types of sophisticated arguments made by Berger, replicated the standard vulgar radical culture war response to the conservatives. He made explicit reference to his own political goals in writing *Black Athena.* He laid bare his opponents' ideological assumptions. He reminded them that objectivity was a ruse. He reasoned that since political positions were constitutive of all intellectual work, they should be freely acknowledged. I repeat a quote cited earlier: "I am convinced that greater benefits are to be gained by the author laying his (or her) cards on the table and alerting the reader to his political position." (Bernal never took the final radical step: to call his own preferred theory "ideological." The Aryan Model is "political" in *Black Athena*, but the Revised Ancient Model is simply closer to the truth.)[32]

The similarities to some radical positions are not difficult to discern. Armed to the teeth with the aforementioned traditions in social theory—which they have greatly enriched—the radicals rejoin: We are all, ostensibly, influenced by the political; there is no such thing as apolitical scholarship. To this they often add: "At least we have the temerity to acknowledge our positionality—that's the first step to honest intellectual work." Witness Stanley Fish lecturing the Right, and apparently the Left as well, on the question of the interrelation between politics and scholarship:

> Those who think they can *choose* politics are no less evading the fact of the political—the fact that point of view and perspectivity are irreducible features of consciousness and action—than those who think they can bracket politics. Politics can neither be avoided nor positively embraced; these impossible alternatives are superficially different ways of *grasping* the political, of holding it in one's hand, whereas properly understood, the political—the inescapability of partisan, angled seeing—is what always and already grasps us.[33]

The portrayal of the radical and conservative approaches mentioned above is admittedly generic. Nevertheless, it permits me to identify a recurring dialectic which surfaces in the writings of public intellectuals. Its poles may be described through two queries: How can a social-scientist, a historian, a literary critic, etc., claim that his or her conclusions are in any way true when it is so abundantly clear that these conclusions are inextricably bound with the social and political context in which he or she works and lives? And the converse: What kind of intellectual and moral world would we bring into being if we conceded that *absolutely nothing* in and of itself is either true, sacred, or beautiful? This is where we stand, still.

The present impasse has induced a state of widespread intellectual demoralization and paralysis among scholars. The concept of an anomic academy mentioned in my Introduction was a reference to a very acute sensation of standing in epistemological quicksand, of not knowing if anything one says is true, false, useless, hopelessly biased, or even worthy of being said. I do not think I exaggerate when I say that this is the fundamental intellectual quandary of our time.

My approach to this insoluble problem is a composite of basic insights in the sociology of knowledge (a major influence on contemporary radical thought) and conservative ideology. With the former, I accept that one's intellectual production is, to a very great degree, bound to the social. In *The Company of Critics: Social Criticism and Political Commitment in the Twentieth Century*, Michael Walzer (who is not a radical) rightly points out that "there is no realm of absolute intellectuality." In other words, no thinker can function as what Julien Benda once called "the mirror of the disinterested intelligence." I repeat: One does not have to be a Foucauldian, a postcolonial theorist, or a standpoint epistemologist to subscribe to this view.[34]

Conservatives, of course, rarely subscribe to this view. They have, however, correctly understood and honorably defended the ethical imperatives of scholarship. Making their description into a prescription, I would argue that the scholar is morally obliged to be ambivalent, morally obliged to try to minimize the influence of "external factors" on his or her work. The disciplined assassination of one's prejudices—that is the project and peculiar heroism of the scholar and the intellectual. Walzer referred to this as "critical distance," an idea certainly related to a notion of his teacher, Lewis Coser, that of "detached concern."[35]

It must immediately be pointed out that this conception of intellectual responsibility is quasi-utopian. Much in the way that ballet makes inhuman demands upon human limbs, and opera and Vocalese coerce voices into registers where most voices do not wish to go, critical distance requires that the intellect conduct operations it is almost genetically structured to resist. Weber's remarks in the epigraph are possibly the most profound expression of an ethic of critical distance ever recorded. The fact that Weber had a few failures of "critical distance" in his own illustrious career testifies to the immensity of the challenge. Surely Walzer was correct when he remarked that "critical distance is still measured in inches, and every inch is worried, agonized over, the subject of intense thought and afterthought."[36]

My admiration for those who have achieved their inches (Hannah Arendt in *Eichmann in Jerusalem* and Ralph Ellison in *Invisible Man* and *Going to the Territory*, come immediately to mind) leads me to disagree with Fish's remarks above. As with more than a few radical critics, he assumes that human beings are utterly helpless to resist the impact of the political on their social thought. As Thomas Haskell observes, for Fish scholars are "mere 'extensions' and 'reflections' coughed up by a soulless socio-cognitive machine that 'bespeaks' them and their possibilities." It is fealty to this assumption which explains the vulgar radical response to the vulgar conservatives. Since the political operates upon and dominates the self with inexorable force, then why not just go ahead and slap your cards right down on the table? What else could you or any other person possibly do?[37]

What is missing here is any notion of inner struggle, of inner tension, of self-questioning, of disciplining the self, or overcoming a not very clever, insightful, or interesting self. Hands off the self! In these approaches there is no possibility of intellectual transcendence: by this I mean, moments in a person's life when he or she somehow criticizes an idea, a concept, a person, an institution, an article of faith, a God held very dear—no matter how inimical this critique might be to objective interests and psychological well-being. *"lema sabachthani?"*—that is the formal credo of intellectual work.

I anticipate two objections to this scheme. First, that the fount of ideological distortion is opaque, that no amount of self-examination or self-discipline will yield insight as to the factors that affect our thought. In other words, we might not be able to understand the "external factors" which operate upon us because they are beyond the comprehension of situated agents. There is no way to refute this argument, and no serious student of sociology could deny its validity. Yet to accept such a claim is tantamount to arguing that scholarship is not necessary. In Bourdieu's famous formulation, for example, sociology endeavors "to uncover the most profoundly buried structures of the various social worlds which constitute the social universe, as well as the 'mechanisms' which tend to ensure their reproduction or their transformation." It is the responsibility of those who argue that we can never retrieve these "buried structures" to justify their continued presence in the university. So to this first objection I reply with Gramsci, "Pessimism of the intellect, optimism of the will."[38]

Second, it might be objected that to demand that professors establish distance from themselves is akin to depoliticizing them. Here my conception of public intellectuality emerges as a means of defending the status quo. Once again, it is impossible to rule out this perfectly valid objection. My only response is this: At this particular point in American history there is no shortage of advocates, think-tankers, partisan journalists, community activists, talk show hosts, public relations people, politicians, empowered undergraduates, and so on. These individuals are not about to establish critical distance from their religious, political, social, and economic interests. Nor should they.

I situate the public intellectual in structural opposition to members of these groups and their legitimate, democratic activities. I think of the following remark from Emile Durkheim on the responsibilities of "writers and scholars":

> Above all our action must be exerted through books, seminars, and popular education. Above all, we must be *advisors, educators.* It is our function to help our contemporaries know themselves in their ideas and in their feelings, far more than to govern them. And in this state of mental confusion in which we live, what is a more useful role to play? Moreover, we will perform it that much better for having thus limited our ambition. We will gain the confidence of the people all the more easily if we are attributed fewer selfish, hidden motives. The lecturer of today must not be suspected to be the candidate of tomorrow.[39]

The passage is, undoubtedly, not without its moments of elitism and condescension, yet I think it offers plausible ethical guidelines for intellectual activity. Durkheim does not encourage the scholar to enter the realm of the political lest he or she be suspected of being "the candidate of tomorrow." Compare this with recent calls for a politically engaged public intellectuality. Richard Rorty chides postmodernists for giving up "on the idea of democratic politics, of mobilizing moral outrage in defense of the weak." Another commentator argues that intellectual work "takes us into communities, into politics; into organizing, in short." Nothing could be further from my conception of the public intellectual. As noted earlier, many other elements of our society are willing and able to canvass, organize, and politicize. Moreover, critical distance and ambivalence are not easy to establish when one is defending the barricades.[40]

Of course, there are moments when fortifying the barricades is necessary for an intellectual, or for any person in defense of a democratic society. As Steven Lukes points out, such behavior was necessary for Durkheim "when the very ideals of the Republic were threatened." I agree. Durkheim should not have sat by, contemplating suicide rates in Schleswig, as Dreyfus languished. He did not. But how much less his students at the Sorbonne would have been willing to listen to him had he taken a predictably fixed partisan position on every single question he addressed. How little he would have been able to understand the gravity of that situation had he thrown himself, head-first, into every previous controversy of the day.[41]

In closing, a public intellectual/scholar establishes the trust of an audience, treats adversaries with consideration, writes in lucid prose, clarifies complex issues, apprises readers of "inconvenient facts," advocates unpopular opinions, questions and reveals his or her own motivations in doing so, and yes, ultimately, if possible, comes to a decision about the issue at hand. And, in exceptional moments, comes to the defense of the Republic, wherever that may be. That is my partial academic decalogue.

It was this conception of public intellectuality and scholarly work which guided the present inquiry. I do not believe that Bernal and his more vocal detractors obeyed each of these commandments, though one wonders if anyone actually could. It is for the reader to decide if the conception itself is valid and if I myself have adhered to its precepts.

Notes

Introduction

1. E. Hall, "When Is a Myth Not a Myth?" 333. This remark is taken from Hall's article in *Black Athena Revisited*. As with many contributions to that volume, the article was a reprint of a piece which was published elsewhere (1992). For purposes of clarity, I will refer to articles twice-published by citing the more accessible 1996 collection. Liverani, "Bathwater and the Baby," 421; Mudimbe, *Idea of Africa*, 104; Cohen, "Interview," 21. Johnson-Odim writes, "I, for one, do not believe ancient history will ever be the same after *Black Athena*" ("Debate over *Black Athena*," 88). Also see Burstein, "Review of *Black Athena 2*," 157; Poliakoff, "Roll Over Aristotle," 12. M. M. Levine would write in 1996 that *Black Athena* has "already begun to transform classical studies in America" ("Bernal and the Athenians," 2).

2. The contributors to *Black Athena Revisited* concentrated mostly on *Black Athena*. *Not Out of Africa* devoted some attention to Bernal's work, but the bulk of the analysis concentrated on various staples of the Afrocentrist canon. Counting the preface, there are twenty-one essays in *Black Athena Revisited*. The *Lingua Franca* piece was by Robert Boynton and entitled "The Bernaliad."

3. Kafka, *Letters to Milena*, p. 39; and see the accompanying *Newsweek* article by Begley et al., "Out of Egypt, Greece."

4. The first film, entitled *Black Athena*, was produced by Tariq Ali and Christopher Spence for the Bandung File. The second film, entitled *Who Was Cleopatra?* was produced by the Archaeological Institute of America. On *Black Athena* (the film), see the reviews by Georgakas, "*Black Athena*: Aryans, Semites, Egyptians and Hellenes"; P. Allen, "*Black Athena*"; and Haley, "Review of *Black Athena* (movie)." Temple University filmed the proceedings of their symposium, "Challenging Tradition: Cultural Interaction in Antiquity and Bernal's *Black Athena*." On the Internet debate, see Bernal, "The Afrocentric Interpretation of History: Bernal Replies to Lefkowitz," 93; the 1997 edition of Lefkowitz, *Not Out of Africa*, 233, n. 1; and the *Washington Post* editorial, "New Spaces, Old Debate."

5. G. Lerner, "Comment," 90.

6. Kafka, "Fratricide," 146.

7. See, for example, Ellison's essay, "The Novel as a Function of Democracy," in *Going to the Territory*, where he writes: "We are at once very, very unified, and at the same time diversified. On many, many levels we don't know who we are, and there are always moments of confrontation where we meet as absolute strangers" (317, 108). For Murray, see *Omni-Americans*, 22.

8. Bernal, "Image of Ancient Greece," 127 (emphasis added). See the almost identical quote in Bernal, "Greece: Aryan or Mediterranean?" 11. And see similar remarks in an Italian interview with Lo Monaco, "L'Occidente?"

9. See, for example *Newsweek's* cut-and-dry conclusion that Bernal argues that classicists were "racists and anti-Semites" (Begley et al., "Out of Egypt, Greece," 49). Bernal, "Image of Ancient Greece," 127. Elsewhere, Bernal writes that Greece is "quite rightly seen as the largest single source of European culture" ("Race, Class, and Gender," 987). Bernal's association of Jews with Phoenicians will be discussed, and contested, at length in chapter 9 below.

10. Though at least one significant avenue was not canvassed. As we shall see, *Black Athena* had little to say about gender issues. On the wide scope of Bernal's work, also see Verger, "Et si les Grecs étaient venus d'Afrique?" 17.

11. Cohen, "Interview," 6–7. For more on classics and the American Right, see M. Bernal, "Image of Ancient Greece," 127; and "Classics in Crisis," 73.

12. As Nisbet has pointed out, however, in earlier incarnations conservative thought was far less enamored of Enlightenment thinkers. (*Conservatism*, 2).

13. D'Souza, *Illiberal Education*, 116–117; and see below. In the *New Criterion*, see Gress, "Case against Bernal." The conservative disdain for Bernal also became apparent in the glowing reviews they bestowed upon Lefkowitz's twin projects. See Kagan's article in the *New Criterion*, "Stealing History"; and Palaima in *National Review*, "Corcyraeanization." The L. P. Williams quote can be found in "Why I Stopped Reading *Black Athena*," 39. Williams is a colleague of Bernal at Cornell, which has produced a disproportionately large number of the participants in the *Black Athena* Controversy. Let it be added that stalwart sponsors of conservative ideas, such as the Olin and Bradley foundations, funded Lefkowitz's *Not Out of Africa*. See Lefkowitz, *Not Out of Africa*, xvii, for a list of grants received. A Ford Foundation grant, however, went to *Black Athena Revisited* (xiv).

14. On Schlesinger and liberalism, see Nisbet, *Conservatism*, 101. Schlesinger's analysis of *Black Athena* in *Disuniting of America* (76) can be summarized thus: (1) portray Martin Bernal as an Afrocentrist, (2) cite the research of two or three of his most vociferous scholarly critics, (3) cite none of his scholarly supporters, (4) proceed to dismiss all of the claims of Bernal's thousand-page work, (5) make sure the entire operation exceeds no more than a few pages. The pieces in the *New York Review of Books* were Griffin, "Who Are These Coming to the Sacrifice?" and "Anxieties of Influence"; Vermeule, "World Turned Upside Down"; and a fourth piece in this same publication, by Lloyd-Jones, "Becoming Homer," reviewed Bernal's *Cadmean Letters*.

    Ray, in the *Times Literary Supplement*, "How Black Was Socrates?" Bernal, *Black Athena* 2: xxi, and "*Black Athena* and Her Reception," 23. In the same preface, Bernal notes that liberal intellectuals in the United States, as opposed to Britain, had reacted in an apathetic manner to his text (xvii). See also Bernal, "Responses to *Black Athena*," 72. Or perhaps we could cite an exchange between Bernal and Professor Robert Palter, one of his most insightful and vituperative critics. Responding to the former's insinuation that he was a conservative ideologue, the latter replied, "My political friends and foes all agree that my political convictions are left-tending (sort of like the *L*[ondon]*R*[eview of]*B*[ooks])" ("Whose Greece?"). Ray, whose earlier (1990) review of Bernal ("A Egyptian Perspective") was far more charitable, essentially eulogized *Black Athena* on the pages of the *Times Literary Supplement*, "How Black Was Socrates?"

15. If I err in this calculation, I err in favor of Bernal. It would not be unreasonable to assume that the ratio is 8:2. There were, however, exceptions to my rule, most prominently a rather negative review in the 1987 *Socialist Worker Review*: Hallas, "Absent Friends: Review of *Black Athena* 1."

16. Kimball, in Kurzweil et al., "Education beyond Politics," 351. Smelser, "Politics of Ambivalence," 41. In *Beyond the Culture Wars*, Graff observes that in terms of cultural conflict the liberal-pluralist and conservative solutions are "two sides of the same coin" (10). Also see Herf's remarks on the aforementioned gerrymandering: "How the Culture Wars Matter," 151, 158.

17. Patai and Koertge, *Professing Feminism*, 211. Howe answers his question in the negative ("Value of the Canon" 47); There are, in fact, many different theoretical suggestions as to where the split has occurred in American intellectual discourse. Gates has spoken of the conflicts between a "hard left" and a "liberal pluralist left" ("Good-bye, Columbus?" 205). P. J. Williams, *Alchemy of Race and Rights*, speaks

of a white Left and a black Left (153); Gutmann refers to essentialists and deconstructionists ("Introduction," 21). Hughes refers to the "politically and the patri-
otically correct" (*Culture of Complaint*, 87). Feher conceptualizes multiculturalists
and proponents of identity politics versus liberals ("Schisms of '67," 277, 283). Also
see Walzer's discussion of the types of liberalism ("Comment," 99); and Early,
"American Education and the Postmodernist Impulse" (221), on "metanarrative versus the idea of a series of pluralistic, differentiated, and antinomian social orders."
18. Glazer, *We Are All Multiculturalists Now*, 24.
19. Henry Giroux, "Insurgent Multiculturalism," 328; Asad, *Genealogies of Religion*,
303; Fish, "Boutique Multiculturalism."
20. Fraser, *Unruly Practices*, 2. Gitlin, *Twilight of Common Dreams*, 151, 152. On the
radical Left in the university, also see Jacoby, "Graying of the Intellectuals," 236,
and "Whither Western Civilization?" 307; Herf, "How the Culture Wars Matter,"
150; Shaw, "Pseudo-Reform in the Academy," 94; Jacoby, *Last Intellectuals*, 134.
21. Kimball, *Tenured Radicals*, xiii.
22. Inexplicably, the bibliography of *Black Athena Revisited* did not cite the work of
many European scholars who had reviewed *Black Athena*. Given the generally negative assessment of these writers, this would have bolstered the editors' arguments.
See the Bibliography of this volume for reviews of *Black Athena* in French,
German, and Italian, almost none of which were cited in *Black Athena Revisited*.
For reviews of Lefkowitz's two books, see Kagan, "Stealing History"; T. Carson,
"Greece Is the Word"; Palaima, "Corcyraeanization"; Griffin, "Anxieties of
Influence"; Elson, "Attacking Afrocentrism"; and Finn, "Cleopatra's Nose." As
Bernal and many others have noted, the editors refrained from including Bernal's
already published responses to the already published pieces in *Black Athena
Revisited*—a seeming violation of an unwritten academic code of ethics. See
Bernal, "Afrocentric Interpretation of History," 89; and Lefkowitz's response,
"Afrocentric Interpretation of Western History."; For less enthusiastic reviews of
these texts, see Berlinerblau, "*Black Athena* Redux: Review of *Not Out of Africa*
and *Black Athena Revisited*"; Meier, "Review of Lefkowitz's *Not Out of Africa*";
Loury, "Color Blinded"; Conyers, "Review of Mary Lefkowitz's, *Not Out of
Africa*"; Jeffrey, "Review of Lefkowitz's *Not Out of Africa*"; Cline, "Review of *Black
Athena Revisited*"; Roth, "Review of *Not Out of Africa* and *Black Athena
Revisited*"; Cudjoe, "Not a Racist Polemic." On the death of *Black Athena*, see
Ray, "How Black Was Socrates?" 3.
23. Basch, "Quels Ancêtres," 21; Yavitz, "She Wasn't Black" (in Hebrew); Griffin,
"Anxieties of Influence," 68.
24. Harding, *"Racial" Economy of Science*, 23–29, And *Whose Science? Whose
Knowledge?* 23. A contributor to *Feminist Theory and the Classics* comments,
"While I find that Bernal often errs toward another extreme in the details of his
analysis, I agree with the fundamental need to recognize the multiculturalism of
the ancient Mediterranean world" (Zweig, "Primal Mind," 172 n. 3). Though see
Rogers ("Multiculturalism," 435–439), who argues that *Black Athena* negates
the multicultural roots of Western civilization by focusing solely on its Afroasiatic
dimensions while ignoring the contributions made by other Near Eastern cultures.
25. Crouch, *All-American Skin Game*, 58; Taylor, "Politics of Recognition," 36;
Cohen, "Interview," 7.
26. Muhly notes that with the exception of radical feminists Bernal "speaks to practically every other revisionist faction in contemporary American education"
("Where the Greeks," 3). Also see Broadhead, "African Origins," 36. For discussions of Afrocentricity and education, see Schlesinger, *Disuniting of America*, 66–72;
Glazer, *We Are All Multiculturalists Now*, 55–77; Ortiz de Montellano,
"Multicultural Pseudoscience," and "Melanin, Afrocentricity, and Pseudoscience";
Sleeter and McLaren, "Introduction," 13.

27. Amin, *Eurocentrism*, 92.
28. A few differences between Bernal and Said may be stated as follows: In *Orientalism*, Said concentrates mostly on France and England. For Said, "Paris was the capital of the Orientalist world" (*Orientalism*, 51, 15, 19). In *Black Athena*, Bernal focuses heavily on Germany. Said traces the first Orientalist impulses to the writings of Aeschylus (57), an idea criticized sharply by Ahmad (*In Theory*, 183). For Bernal, by contrast, the ancient Greeks were free of such tainted interpretations of their history. It is only in the Enlightenment that Bernal's "Orientalism" begins. Said sees Orientalism as nurtured by "secularizing elements in eighteenth-century European culture" (120). Bernal, on the other hand, sees the influence of Christianity as a major variable in his analysis of the paradigm shift. Bernal argues that he differed from Said insofar as the latter viewed classics as "a model of detached objective scholarship" ("Black Athena," 66; and see Bernal, "Greece: Aryan or Mediterranean?" 3). Elsewhere, Bernal alleges that Said sees Orientalism as "a self-contained system which is entirely ideological and has relatively little to do with what's 'out there'" (Dyson, "On *Black Athena*," 58). In *Culture and Imperialism*, Said writes, "As Bernal has described it, a coherent classical philology developed during the nineteenth century that purged Attic Greece of its Semitic-African roots" (110; see also 15, 118, 312). Amin, *Eurocentrism*, 92; Ahmad, *In Theory*, 163; Inden, *Imagining India*. See Muhly, "*Black Athena* versus Traditional Scholarship," 105–106, for a comparison of these writers. Also see Anderson, "Myth of Hellenism." For a critical overview, see Prakash, "*Orientalism* Now." It would be not entirely accurate, however, to place Ahmad within the postcolonial cohort. Bond and Gilliam observe that *Black Athena* is "especially pertinent for unravelling dominant paradigmatic images and analysing the interests that created them. It demonstrates the use of talismanic—or magic—knowledge to distance the colonizer from the colonized, and to 'adjust' scholarship to a ruling class's interest during a particular era." ("Introduction," 8). Also see Bernal, "British Utilitarians," for more similarities to the post-colonial school.
29. Federici, "Introduction," xiii. In his review essay, "Another Blow to Eurocentrism," anthropologist Patterson lauds the timeliness of a book published in an age where "highly visible politicians and hack academics tout the uniqueness of the West and redefine what it encompasses" (42). Also see Harding, *"Racial" Economy*, 26. Bernal's work has been cited in literary journals; see for example, Blaut, "Debates," and his slipshod analysis of Weber's politics in *Antipode*; Andrea, "Early Modern Women,' in *Ariel*; Mehlman, "Core of the Core," in *Comparative Literature*; Lant in *October*, "Curse of the Pharaoh," (108 n. 66); and Dussel in *boundary 2*, "Eurocentrism and Modernity" (68). Outside of literary journals see the critical race theorist Delgado in the *Yale Law Journal*, "Rodrigo's Chronicle" (1371).
30. M. M. Levine, "Anti-Black and Anti-Semitic?" 32; Malamud, "Book Review," 318; Rabinowitz, "Introduction," 5; Haley, "Black Feminist Thought," 37.
31. Early, however, argues that Afrocentrism is an offshoot of the postmodern academy, along with black nationalism and group therapy ("Anatomy of Afrocentrism," 13). Moses argues that the views of Afrocentrists will most likely not be accepted by "establishmentarian black scholars, who constitute the faculties of the elite universities" ("In Fairness," 21). Some have charged that Afrocentrism is nationalistic, essentialist, and reactionary—a sort of reverse Eurocentrism. See Appiah, "Europe Upside Down"; McCarthy, "Contradictions of Existence," 328, 330; P. J. Williams, *Rooster's Egg*, 55; and more generally, see my discussion in Chapter 7.
32. D'Souza, *Illiberal Education*, 116; also see D'Souza's far more subdued treatment of Bernal, now cited as an authority, in *End of Racism*, 40, 43, 567 n. 76. For another culture war association between Bernal and the Afrocentrists, see Hughes's far more thoughtful *Culture of Complaint*, 135.

33. *Black Athena* was accorded the American Book Award in 1990. Much of the information in this section is gathered from private communications with the author and from his curriculum vitae, which he was kind enough to provide. Bernal dedicated his *Cadmean Letters* to his grandfather. For an extremely well documented psychosocial reading of Bernal's career and his authorship of *Black Athena,* see van Binsbergen, "*Black Athena* Ten Years After," 38–44.

34. Bernal's final rank was senior aircraftsman. He received the academic post at Cornell in 1972, hired at the rank of associate professor in the Department of Government.

35. For Bernal's own autobiographical remarks, see *Black Athena* 1: xii; "What Is It about the Vietnamese?" 26; "Mao's China"; "Down There on a Visit"; "Mao for All Seasons"; "North Vietnam and China"; "Travelling Light"; "Popularity of Chinese Patriotism." In an interview with Alessandra Baldini, Bernal looks back at his earlier career: "Io volevo dare una mano al movimento contro la repressione americana in Indocina" ("Classici d'Egitto," 117).

36. For some reviews of *Chinese Socialism,* see Jenner, "Visions of Great Togetherness"; Spence, "Chinese Dream Machine"; Gasster, "Review of *Chinese Socialism*"; and Rhoads, "Review of *Chinese Socialism.*"

37. Bernal, *Black Athena* 1: xii, xiii; Goldsmith, *Sage,* 17; Rogers, "Multiculturalism," 441. Leach writes, "Bernal's own 'Revised Ancient Model' is a product of his very unusual personal *Zeitgeist*" ("Aryan Warlords," 11).

38. N. Allen, "*Black Athena*: Interview with Bernal," 22.

39. The original was published by Free Association Books. The articles and reviews which preceded the publication of the first volume were Bernal, "Review of *Judaïsme et Christianisme,*" "Review of *Sign, Symbol, Script,*" "Black Athena Denied," and "Black Athena: The African and Levantine Roots of Greece." *Cadmean Letters* was published by Eisenbrauns. For a review, see Lloyd-Jones, "Becoming Homer." On Bernal as enfant terrible, see M. M. Levine, "Review Article: The Use and Abuse of *Black Athena,*" 446 n. 19.

40. For Bernal on his father, see *Black Athena* 2: xx; and Baldini, "Classici d'Egitto," 117. R. Young, "John Desmond Bernal," 47. John Desmond Bernal joined the Communist party of Great Britain in 1923 (Goldsmith, *Sage,* 31). On his wartime activities, see Goldsmith, *Sage,* 89–123, and on his support for Stalin and Lysenkoism, see 65, 182, 184, 206–207, 234; on Lysenkoism, see 193, 195, 196. For criticisms of the father in the Controversy, see, for example, Gress, "Case against Bernal." For some germane writings of John Desmond Bernal on science, see *Social Function of Science, Science in History,* vol. 4, *Science and Industry in the Nineteenth Century,* and *Marx and Science.*

41. R. Young, "John Desmond Bernal," 47. And on this big-picturism, see Goldsmith, *Sage,* 208, 213, 224.

42. Also to be noted is the fact that the father apparently despised the classics curriculum which he was subjected to (Goldsmith, *Sage,* 25). Further, both are popularizers who seek to write for wider audiences, though we could speculate as to intriguing tensions between father and son. Goonatilake ("The Son, the Father, and the Holy Ghosts," 1768), makes the point that "the son implicitly questions" his father's "Eurocentric view in describing the intellectual history of the world." Also see Egberts, "Consonants in Collision," 162–163. For more biographical information on Bernal, see van Binsbergen, "*Black Athena* Ten Years After," 42–44.

43. Durkheim, *Rules of Sociological Method,* 71.

44. George, *Crimes of Perception,* xi (emphasis added); Peters, *Heresy and Authority,* 15, 17.

45. Locke, *Letter concerning Toleration,* 23. See, for example, Leff, *Heresy in the Later Middle Ages,* 1; Berlinerblau, *The Vow,* 22–24.

46. P. L. Berger, *Heretical Imperative,* 28. Foucault, *History of Sexuality,* vol. 1, 93. On Foucault's use of this term, see James Miller, *Passion of Michel Foucault,* 108. Char, "Partage formel XXII," *Oeuvres complètes,* 160.

47. Bernal, *Black Athena* 1: 2 (emphasis in original).

48. Bourdieu and Wacquant, *Invitation to Reflexive Sociology,* 68, 37, 72; also see Bourdieu, *Homo Academicus,* 6; and "Vive la crise!" 784. Also see Calhoun, *Critical Social Theory,* 11, 35. On self-pleasuring, see Ahmad, *In Theory,* 7.

49. B. M. Berger, *Authors of Their Own Lives,* 152. The awesome scope of *Black Athena* and the difficulties it presents for evaluators has been remarked upon frequently: Baines, "Aims and Methods," 43; M. M. Levine, "Review Article: The Use and Abuse of *Black Athena,*" 445; Malamud, "Review of *Black Athena* 1," 320; Michelini, "Comment," 100; Cohen, "Interview," 10. I would submit that an entire faculty might be needed to get the job done. In order to engage all of the issues raised by *Black Athena,* it would necessitate nearly the entire humanities and social science faculty of a modern research university, not to mention a handful of professors in the hard sciences. The latter would be used in order to resolve the various controversies based on scientific methods of dating ancient artifacts (see below) and the budding acrimonious debate over the scientific and mathematical accomplishments of the Greeks versus those of the Egyptians. See Palter, "*Black Athena,* Afrocentrism, and the History of Science"; and Bernal, "Animadversions on the Origins of Western Science."

50. See Berlinerblau, "*Black Athena* Redux." As regards Gordon, I am happy to report that at a recent conference of the Society for Biblical Literature I delivered a paper entitled "Northwest Semites in the Aegean? Evaluating the Gordon-Astour-Bernal School." Dr. Gordon, who was in attendance along with many of his students, suggested that I was far too young and far too immature to discuss the types of issues presented in my paper.

51. Bernal himself calls attention to this aspect of his work in "Response to Jonathan Hall," 275. Also see Baines, "Aims and Methods," 28; and Coleman, "Did Egypt Shape the Glory That Was Greece?" 292.

Chapter 1. The Ancient Model

1. Bernal, "Race, Class, and Gender," 987. By the second volume Bernal would permit the equation between model and paradigm (*Black Athena* 2: 11). For the original statement of this position, see *Black Athena* 1: 1, 3. Also see Bernal, "First by Land," 3; and "Black Athena Denied," 3. For one of the few endorsements of Bernal's modular approach, see Green, "*Black Athena* and Classical Historiography," 56.

2. *Black Athena* 1: 1.

3. Bernal reconstructs the Ancient Model partly on the basis of the "Parian Marble," whose chronology of events is assumed to have begun somewhere around 1580 B.C.E. The assumption of oriental greatness refers mostly to the Egyptians.

4. *Black Athena* 1: 79, 81, 82 (emphasis added). Here Bernal bases himself on Herodotus's *Histories* 8.44, a somewhat veiled reference in Aesychlus's *Suppliants* (911–914) to the fact that the Pelasgians are of Greek soil, and a lost fragment of Euripides quoted in Strabon, 5.2.4. Also see Bernal, "Black Athena Denied," 6.

5. And to a lesser extent Bernal speaks of Aigyptos (associated with Egypt). Bernal also mentions Pelops as a major colonizer (*Black Athena* 1: 84) but the latter seems to fall out of *Black Athena*'s narrative. Aeschylus, *Suppliants* 332. Also see Isokrates, *Helen* 68. See Lefkowitz's objections to Bernal's analysis of these myths in "Ancient History, Modern Myths," 15.

6. *Black Athena* 2: 357; also see *Black Athena* 1: 109. In Bernal's view, according to the fourth-century writer Hekataios of Abdera, the Danaans were none other than those who had been forcibly expelled by a renascent Egypt. For Hekataios of

Abdera, see Diodorus 40.3.2, and *Black Athena* 2: 502. And for the views of Hekataios of Miletos, Bernal refers to a fragment in Jacoby, *Fragmente der Griechischen Historiker, 1a,* 1. And see Bernal's discussion of Aeschylus's punning in *The Suppliants* (*Black Athena* 1: 97). But see Michelini, "Comment," 102, who ripostes that no Greek writer, with the exception of Josephus, actually mentions the word *Hyksos.*

 7. Kirk, *Nature of Greek Myths,* 156. Also see *Black Athena* 1: 85.
 8. Euripides, *Phoenician Women,* 1.
 9. Ibid., 638. A similar Phoenician settlement is posited for the island of Thera. See Bernal *Black Athena* 2: 289, basing himself on Herodotus *Histories* 4.147.
10. *Black Athena* 1: 107; also see Bernal, "Black Athena Denied," 7. Plato, *Timaeus* 21e; also see Diodoros 5.57.5. Isokrates, *Helen* 68.
11. *Black Athena* 1: 108, 106, 107, 111, 116, 118, 103, 114–120, 103; Aristotle, *Metaphysics* 981b.20. On Isokrates's respect for Egypt, see *Busiris* 16–30. Bernal also calls attention to Plato's references to Egypt's massive influence on Greek culture. Bernal reiterates Karl Marx's well-known suggestion that *The Republic* was based on an Egyptian model. On the greatness and antiquity of the Egyptians, the author points to Diodoros 1.9.5–6. Bernal also cites the very favorable reports which visiting Roman emperors made of Egypt (*Black Athena* 1: 117, 118). Also see Bernal, "Black Athena and Her Reception," 12.
12. Literally, "the gift of the river" (Herodotus 2.5).
13. Herodotus, *Histories* 6.52. Bernal cites this passage in *Black Athena* 1: 75, and "Black Athena Denied," 5.
14. Herodotus, *Histories* 5.60. Reflexes of this tradition are preserved in Diodorus 5.57.5. Also see *Black Athena* 1: 79, 393–394.
15. A similar, though not identical, account may be found in the writings of Manetho (ca. 300 B.C.E.), who reports that Sesōstris "in nine years . . . subdued the whole of Asia, and Europe as far as Thrace" (*History of Egypt,* 34; and *Black Athena* 2: 197). Diodoros (d. 21 B.C.E.) adds that "Sesoōsis" went as far as India (1.55.2); and see 1.53–58; *Black Athena* 2: 199. Though see Bernal's discussion of Apollonios Rhodios's oblique reference to Colchians (246–247, 256). Herodotus, *Histories* 2.104. On Herodotus and Sesōstris, see S. West, "Herodotus' Epigraphical Interests," 300–301.
16. *Black Athena* 1: 108; also see 7, 23, 28, 84, 85, 90, 100, 102, 103, 104.
17. Bernal, "Race, Class, and Gender," 988.
18. Baines, "Aims and Methods," 40; Vermeule, "World Turned Upside Down," 278. For similar accusations, see Tritle, "*Black Athena*: Vision or Dream of Greek Origins?" 305–306. Also see Poliakoff, "Roll Over Aristotle," 14; E. Hall, "Myths Missing That Black Magic," 15; Coleman, "Did Egypt Shape the Glory That Was Greece?" 286.
19. Mudimbe, *Idea of Africa,* 97. Lefkowitz, "Ancient History, Modern Myths," 17; Burstein, "Review of *Black Athena* 2," 160. Bernal's attempt to deny these charges in "Responses to *Black Athena*," 74, is not especially convincing. On the issue of Herodotus and the truth of his accounts, see Moles, "Truth and Untruth." Also see S. West, "Herodotus' Epigraphical Interests." Thus, while Bernal accepts Herodotus's account of Sesōstris in the Colchis, most would not. In his 1978 article in *Harvard Studies in Classical Philology,* Armayor asked, "Did Herodotus ever go to the Black Sea?" He answers in the negative (Armayor, "Did Herodotus Ever Go to the Black Sea?" 47, 59–62).
20. Green, "*Black Athena* and Classical Historiography," 59.
21. Poliakoff, "Roll Over Aristotle," 14. Mudimbe observes that Bernal's project would have benefited from a "a more careful *critique historique* of the texts consulted" (*Idea of Africa,* 98). Also see Blok, "Proof and Persuasion in *Black Athena*," 708. For Bernal's remarks on this issue, see *Black Athena* 1: 217–218, 221.

22. Much to my surprise, I have been unable to identify a succinct statement of what source criticism actually is. Finley seems to define it as a method for "dealing satisfactorily with derivative [as opposed to primary] authorities" (*Ancient History*, 8). Koch ("Source Criticism," 165) remarks that the term can be used in "a very general sense," and I surmise that this is what Poliakoff had in mind when making this statement. Also see Barton, "Source Criticism." In what follows I will use the phrase in an admittedly broad sense as a means of describing a wide variety of exegetical approaches to the text. Also see Marchand and Grafton, "Martin Bernal and His Critics," 24–25.

23. Finley, *Ancient History*, 8, 9; and *Use and Abuse of History*, 18; Veyne, *Did the Greeks Believe in Their Myths?* 5, 6–15. Moles, for example, observes, Herodotus's "work, so far from being a mere mirror of history, is a glorious mixture: partly history, partly literature, partly prose . . . embracing true things, false things, things of indeterminate status, great things and small things ("Truth and Untruth," 98). Also see Berlinerblau, *The Vow*, 13–45; Hopkins, "Rules of Evidence."

24. D. Levine, *Flight from Ambiguity*, 24.

25. For an excellent discussion of this point, see Marcus, *Jephthah and His Vow*.

26. Ricoeur, *Freud and Philosophy*.

27. Bernal, *Black Athena* 1: 112. P. Gordon, "On *Black Athena*, 72.

28. P. Gordon, "On *Black Athena*," 72 (emphasis added).

29. Bernal, "Race, Class, and Gender," 988; "On the Transmission of the Alphabet," 1; "First by Land," 4. In volume 2 he speaks of Greeks in the fourth century B.C.E. as "accepting the Ancient Model" (*Black Athena* 2: 126, 128). Bernal, *Cadmean Letters*, 6; *Black Athena* 1: 120, 75; "Greece: Aryan or Mediterranean?" 5. Also see "Image of Ancient Greece," 120; "Afrocentric Interpretation," 93. Only in the second volume (187) does the author display some reservations about the existence of the Ancient Model in Classical antiquity.

30. *Black Athena* 1: 3.

31. Bernal views Plutarch, writing in the second century A.D., as the first critic of the Ancient Model (*Black Athena* 1: 112), though he also recognizes the rhetorical dimensions of this accusation (113, 119). It should be stressed that Plutarch is not criticizing a belief called the Ancient Model, nor a school which adheres to this belief, but rather a few stray remarks made by Herodotus to the effect that Egypt greatly influenced Greek culture.

32. Manning, "Frames of Reference," 256. I would agree with Green's contention that "Greek attitudes toward their past were much more ambivalent and wide-ranging than Professor Bernal would allow. . . . There were a number of competing symbolic universes that supported a multitude of social realities" ("*Black Athena* and Classical Historiography," 58).

33. Tritle, "Vision or Dream?" 305–306.

34. Hobsbawm, *Age of Empire*, 26. Also see Momigliano (*Studies in Historiography*, 7) on the idealization of antiquity; and Lowenthal, *Past Is a Foreign Country*, 74–124. Quoted in DeJean, *Ancients against Moderns*, 46. Bernal discusses this debate as well (*Black Athena* 1: 177–178).

35. Appleby et al., *Telling the Truth about History*, 37.

36. This is not to say that Bernal completely discredits modern source-critical methods. As we saw above, he placed the writings of Isokrates and Plato within the xenophobic and pro-Hellenic context in which they were produced. This is certainly a type of source criticism. But there is nothing in *Black Athena* approaching the extended, detailed analysis and working over of the text which is the hallmark of professional academic history writing. There are instances where Bernal mistrusts the ancient sources or at least discusses their limitations; see *Black Athena* 2: 5, 127, 204, 297, 298, 302, 303, 324–325, 337, 404. On *Besserwissen*, see *Black*

Athena 2: 195, 200, 239, 309, and *Black Athena* 1: 306, 118; also see Bernal, *Cadmean Letters*, 57.

37. Bernal, "First by Land," 7; *Black Athena* 2: 9.
38. Bernal, "Greece: Aryan or Mediterranean?" 8; *Cadmean Letters*, 32. Also see Bernal's interview with Fabrizio Tonello, "Grecia riva del Nilo," 25.
39. Lowenthal, *Past Is a Foreign Country*, 217.
40. *Black Athena* 2: 9; *Black Athena* 1: 328; also see Bernal, "British Utilitarians," 122.
41. Momigliano, *Studies in Historiography*, 111.
42. Ray, "Egyptian Perspective," 79. As Tritle ("Vision or Dream?" 305) and Poliakoff ("Roll Over Aristotle," 14) observe, Bernal employs his own *Besserwissen* when it is necessary to disregard ancient sources which do not confirm his hypothesis.
43. Lefkowitz, *Not Out of Africa*, 54.
44. Ibid., 89, 55, 60, 68, 64, 86, 58. On the high regard of the Greeks for the Egyptians, see 75, 84, 85. For similar arguments, see Coleman, "Did Egypt Shape the Glory That Was Greece?" 286–287. Also see Lefkowitz and Rogers, "Preface," xi, where it is noted that "ancient notions of Egyptian origins were based on surmise and mis-information."
45. Lefkowitz, *Not Out of Africa*, 66–67.
46. Ibid., 89; also see 86, 88. For a somewhat less critical assessment of Herodotus and other Greek historians, see Momigliano, *Classical Foundations*, 8, 9, 29, 30, 39, and *Studies in Ancient Historiography*, 141.
47. See Berlinerblau, *The Vow*; "The 'Popular Religion' Paradigm"; "Some Sociological Observations"; "Preliminary Observations"; Lefkowitz, *Not Out of Africa*, 61–62. For example, in *Black Athena Revisited*, Lefkowitz attempts to refute Bernal by calling attention to Herodotus's remark that Egyptian habits and customs were very different from those of the Greeks ("Ancient History," 15). Similarly Snowden ("Response" and "Bernal's 'Blacks' and the Afrocentrists") uses the words of Herodotus as a means of disproving Bernal's claims about the skin color of the Egyptians (see Chapter 8 below).

Chapter 2. The Revised Ancient Model

1. *Black Athena* 1: 8, 9.
2. *Black Athena* 2: 3 (emphasis added); also see xxii. And see Bernal, "Race, Class, and Gender," 989. These sentiments differ from the approach which Bernal said he would adopt in two separate 1990 contributions (*Cadmean Letters*, 1, and "Response to Sturt Manning," 281. Thus 1991 apparently marks a sort of turning point in Bernal's thought on competitive plausibility.
3. Reiss, "Review of *Black Athena* 2," 430; M. M. Levine, "Challenge of *Black Athena*," 10; Malamud, "Review of *Black Athena* 1," 319.
4. Most notably, by the second volume Bernal would reassess his theories regarding the extent of Afroasiatic influence in the Aegean. He would argue with greater enthusiasm that this influence occurred well before the second-millennium invasion of the Hyksos (*Black Athena* 2: 123, contra *Black Athena* 1: 18, 20, 22). On this point he seemed to be responding to the 1989 critique of Gary Rendsburg, who argued that Bernal focused too narrowly on the second as opposed to the third millennium ("*Black Athena*: An Etymological Response," 69). Elsewhere, and somewhat in con-tradiction to the latter emendation, Bernal would note that he overestimated "the extent of Near Eastern cultural penetration during the 'colonizations' and under-estimated the extent to which this took place" from the sixteenth to the fourteenth centuries (*Black Athena* 2: 362–363). Finally, in the second volume (xviii) Bernal would issue a sort of apology to the classics establishment. For another compar-ison of the volumes, see van Binsbergen, "*Black Athena* Ten Years After," 45.

5. Vermeule, "World Turned Upside Down," 273. Michelini, "Comment," 98.
6. Michelini, "Comment," 98.
7. Mills, *Sociological Imagination*, 25–49; Burstein, "Debate over *Black Athena*," 16.
8. Bernal, "*Black Athena* and the APA," 18–19; also see "Black Athena Denied," 54; *Black Athena* 1 xiii–xiv. Also see Trigger, "Brown Athena," 121. In referring to a Gordon-Astour-Bernal school I am abundantly aware that I am homogenizing a heterogenous reality. There were—and are—many other exponents of these views. The three individuals are not in accord on all issues. Their own positions have evolved throughout the decades. Be that as it may, I do think their claims overlap with sufficient frequency and coherence to merit being referred to as a school of thought. A short and incomplete list of scholars and texts who influenced Gordon and Astour or were contemporary allies would include Bérard, *Les Phéniciens*; on the influence of Bérard, see Astour, "Greek Names," 195–96; J. P. Brown, "Kothar, Kinyras, and Kythereia"; "Literary Contexts"; "Sacrificial Cult"; R. Brown, *Semitic Influence in Hellenic Mythology*; Germain, *Genèse de l'Odyssée. Le fantastique et le sacré*; Güterbok, "Hittite Version"; Levin, *Semitic and Indo-European*; Starr, *History of the Ancient World*; and *Origins of Greek Civilization*; and Webster, *From Mycenae to Homer*. Also see Edmunds, "Greek and Near Eastern Mythology." In the third chapter of the first volume, Bernal mentions some earlier proponents of these views, such as the Abbé Barthélemy (171) and the Abbé Terrasson (179). Also see Walcot, *Hesiod and the Near East*, and his eventual critique of Bernal, "Review of *Black Athena* 2." And see Bernal on Walcot, *Black Athena* 1: 365.
9. The emphasis on the second millennium and earlier should be compared to scholars who make similar arguments for Near Eastern influence but concentrate on the first millennium. The most important exponent of this approach is Burkert, *Orientalizing Revolution*. For Bernal on Burkert, see "Responses on the Comments," 57. C. H. Gordon, *Ugarit and Minoan Crete*, 12, 25, 30, 151; "Northwest Semitic Texts," 286; also see "Homer and the Bible," 43, 46, 107; "Foreword," xi; "Cultural and Religious Life," 53. On cosmopolitanism, ethnic integration, and internationalism, see C. H. Gordon, "Cultural," 52, 64, 65; *Ugarit and Minoan Crete*, 12; "Northwest Semitic Texts," 287; "Homer and the Bible," 47, 54. 56, 59. Astour, for his part, depicts eastern Cilicia in the second millennium as "a mixture of W[est]-S[emitic] and Hurrian elements living in close symbiosis and ethnic harmony and sharing the same civilization" (*Hellenosemitica*, 44, 111, also see 353). Bernal's Hyksos, as we shall see, are an amalgam of Indo-Aryan, Hurrian, Semitic, Egyptian, and Cretan elements. On cosmopolitanism, see Bernal in Goode, "Ancient Greece's Non-Greek Roots," 54. Similar themes in *Black Athena* will be discussed below.
10. See, for example, Astour's references to a "West Semitic ('Phoenician') armed penetration into the Aegean basin, including Greece," in the mid–second millennium. (*Hellenosemitica*, 109). C. H. Gordon writes, "From about 1800 to about 1400 B.C., Greece was dominated by Northwest Semites ('Phoenicians'), who linked it linguistically and culturally with the whole Semitic Levant" (*Ugarit and Minoan Crete*, 152), though Bernal has been justly criticized for not devoting more scrutiny to Mesopotamia in his defense of oriental influence, a point made by Lefkowitz ("Ancient History," 19), Baines ("Aims and Methods," 34), and in more general terms by Rogers ("Multiculturalism," 438–439). A similar accusation could not be made of Gordon or Astour.
11. *Black Athena* 2: 78; Astour, "Problem of Semitic," 292. Also see "Aegean Place-Names"; and *Hellenosemitica*, 355.
12. *Black Athena* 2: 147; for trading networks, see 69 and 521. Also see "First by Land," 15. C. H. Gordon would claim, "Even the biggest distances that the East Mediterranean sailor had to cross are tiny compared with those spanned in small craft by Pacific islanders" ("Homer and the Bible," 44). C. H. Gordon, "Mediterranean Factor," 19, 20, 27, 31; *Ugarit and Minoan Crete*, 17, 18; "Cultural and Religious

Life," 58. Also see Astour, "Greek Names,"; "Aegean Place-Names," 316; "Problem of Semitic," 291; and *Hellenosemitica*, 338, 348.

13. All of this complexity is made more complex by Bernal's suggestion that the Phoenicians also absorbed and promoted Egyptian culture in the Aegean (*Black Athena* 2: 245). On the East-to-West orientation, see *Black Athena* 1: 419. On the uneven nature of influence, see Bernal, "Black Athena—The Historical Construction," 25. Astour, for example, would write, "The ancestors of the Greek Danaans must have come to Greece from the Semitic East" (*Hellenosemitica*, 53, 69). Astour, "Greek Names," 194.

14. C. H. Gordon, *Common Background*, 216.

15. See, for example, Astour, *Hellenosemitica*, 69–70, 79.

16. Also see C. H. Gordon, "Canaanite Text from Brazil"; Cross, "Phoenician Inscription from Brazil"; C. H. Gordon, "Reply to Professor Cross"; Friedrich, "Die Unechtheit der Phönizischen Inschrift aus Parahyba"; Astour, *Hellenosemitica*, xii, xiv, 45, 46, 95, 334. Also see Astour, "Greek Names," 195; C. H. Gordon, *Ugarit and Minoan Crete*, 14. Writing in 1962 on the subject of Eteocretan, Gordon would refer to "the sneering onlookers, congenitally incapable of pioneer work, [who] are intellectual pygmies" ("Eteocretan," 211); also see "Homer and the Bible," 49; and "Language as a Means to an End." For reviews of *Hellenosemitica*, see Duke, "Review of *Hellenosemitica*"; McGregor, "Review of *Hellenosemitica*"; John Boardman, "An Orient Wave." See Bernal on the response to Gordon and Astour (*Black Athena 1:* 36). On the failure of the Gordon-Astour school, see Morris, "Daidalos and Kadmos," 39.

17. Renfrew, *Before Civilization*, 17, 30, 192, 211, 213–214; *Problems in European Prehistory*, 26, 265; *The Emergence of Civilisation*, 55. Also see Trigger, *History of Archaeological Thought*, 150–155; and "Brown Athena," 122–123. See Manning's remarks on "the Binford-Renfrew hegemony" in "Frames of Reference," 263. Crossland, "Linguistics and Archaeology in Aegean Prehistory," 6. Bernal, *Black Athena* 2: 14. See Burkert, *Orientalizing Revolution*, 7, where the existence of the isolationist hegemony is implied. For a discussion and critique of Renfrew's work and the social theory which informs it, see Shanks and Tilley, *Social Theory and Archaeology*, 31–37. Marchand and Grafton make the excellent observation that those on the outside or periphery of the academy advocate "diffusionism" while insiders opt for an "independent evolution" approach ("Martin Bernal and His Critics," 11, 27). On the retro nature of this diffusionist argument, see Verger, "Et si les Grecs," 17.

18. *Black Athena* 2: 66, also see 14; and *Black Athena* 1: 410, 407.

19. Though, as far as I can tell, Renfrew makes no specific reference to these scholars in his work. See Renfrew, "Problems in the General Correlation," 269; and *Archaeology and Language*, 3, 5.

20. Renfrew, *Before Civilization*, 192 (emphasis added) also see 119, 109.

21. For Bernal's views on the impact of Renfrew's politics on his scholarship, see "Responses to Critical Reviews," 128–129; and see Baines's challenge of this point, "Aims and Methods," 35. Also see *Black Athena* 2: 72, 67, 136, where Bernal refers to Renfrew's position as an "ideological construct." Also see Morris, "Greece and the Levant," 63.

22. *Black Athena* 2: 66 (emphasis added), 64–67, 69–77. Also see *Black Athena* 1: 16. Tritle, however, views Bernal as an extreme diffusionist ("Vision or Dream?" 310, 313, 320, 328 n. 5), as does Camporesi, who refers to Astour's and Gordon's theories as "*iperdiffusionistiche*" ("Review of *Atena nera 1*," 123). Yurco ("*Black Athena*: An Egyptological Review," 98) speaks of Bernal's "uncritical Egyptocentric diffusionism." On the political implications of diffusionism, see Baines, "Aims and Methods," 40–41; Shanks, "Greeks and Gifts," 56–57; M. M. Levine, "Review Article," 449; R. Young, "*Black Athena*," 279; Hall, "*Black Athena*," 249. Bernal,

as Trigger notes in "Brown Athena" (121), works in the tradition of such modified diffusionists as Oscar Montelius and Gordon Childe. Also see Trigger, *History of Archaeological Thought*, 158–161, 170. Notice the tremendous similarity of Childe's synopsis of Montelius's work and the assumptions of Bernal (Childe, "Orient and Europe," 10). For Renfrew's assessment of Childe and Montelius, see *Problems in European Prehistory*, 8–9, 15, 265, and *Archaeology and Language* 15–16. For Astour's use of Childe, see *Hellenosemitica*, 325, 329.

23. In this instance the author is actually borrowing an idea from Renfrew. Indo-Hittite (held by Bernal to be an ancestor of the Indo-European and Anatolian language families) is not Greek, though in *Black Athena's* scheme it is genetically related to this language (*Black Athena* 1: 78, and see 82–83, 13, though there is a somewhat different view on 81). And see Bernal, "First by Land," 13–16, and *Black Athena* 2: 217–218. See Renfrew, "Problems in the General Correlation," 274. And see Finkelberg, "Anatolian Languages."

24. *Black Athena* 2: 76–77, 68, 63, 184. See Astour, "Greek Names," 195; "Second Millenium"; and "Problem of Semitic in Ancient Crete"; C. H. Gordon, *Ugarit and Minoan Crete*, 23, 29–30; "Eteocretan"; and "Northwest Semitic Texts," 288. Also see Verger, "Et si les Grecs," 2. For an endorsement of the Cretan dimensions of Bernal's hypothesis, see Best, "Ancient Toponyms of Mallia."

25. *Black Athena* 2: 70–71, 73–74, 77, 415. See Branigan, *Foundations of Palatial Crete*; Weinberg, "Relative Chronology." Bernal's analysis also includes an examination of similarities in iconography (*Black Athena* 2: 75, 76) and cultic symbols (*Black Athena* 2: 164–165).

26. *Black Athena* 2: 128, 129, 135. See Tritle's dissent, "Vision or Dream?" 321–322.

27. *Black Athena* 2: 143 (emphasis added). Bernal concludes that the toponyms came in with the hydraulic projects and that the builders were West Semites and Egyptians (144, 141).

28. For Bernal, the invasion occurred in 2500 B.C.E., for mainstream Aryanists 2300 B.C.E. (*Black Athena* 2: 150, 228). See note 9 in Chapter 3 below for more on this invasion.

29. Bernal, "Race, Class, and Gender," 989. But Bernal argues that chariot technology arrived with the Hyksos.

30. *Black Athena* 2: 235; also see 195, 203, 424. For examples of the view which Bernal contests, see Baines, "Aims and Methods," 33–34, 44. Tritle, "Vision or Dream?" 324. Bernal views his Sesôstris argument as "the greatest single outrage" of *Black Athena* 2 (524).

31. *Black Athena* 2: 235, 236, 203, 188, 195.

32. Ibid., 188–189, 195, 234–235. Bernal, however, is not in total agreement with the Ancient Model. He rejects Diodoros's claim that Sesôstris penetrated India and is unenthusiastic about placing him in Thrace and Scythia. (*Black Athena* 2: 201, 245). Also see Bernal, *Cadmean Letters*, 32.

33. See *Black Athena* 2: 225. According to his theory, the expensive objects found in the Tôd Treasure may have been (1) taxes owed by communities in these regions to their metal-starved Egyptian suzerains, (2) booty returned to Egypt by its soldiers, and/or (3) gifts offered by "tribute-bearing foreigners." No matter which possibility is correct, this evidence suggests to Bernal that the Egyptians were in some way enmeshed and influential in the affairs of the aforementioned regions.

34. In particular, Bernal concentrates on the destruction of Assyrian trading colonies in central Anatolia. Ancient writers (e.g, Herodotus, Manetho, Diodoros) claimed that this king conquered "all of Asia," an idiom for the region referred to as Anatolia (*Black Athena* 2: 223).

35. Ibid., 246–247.

36. Ibid., 189, 258, 271, 266, 249–250.

37. Ibid., 258; also see 227, 234–235. This point was entirely missed by Lefkowitz, who

writes, "It does not trouble [Bernal] that Herodotus fails to state that Sesostris' armies conquered or even penetrated mainland Greece" ("Ancient History," 19).

38. *Black Athena* 2: 78; also see *Black Athena* 1: 17–18.

39. *Black Athena* 2: 494 (emphasis added).

40. In fact, there are two challenges to accepted chronologies in *Black Athena* 2. See Bernal's redating of Egyptian chronologies for the fourth and third millennia (206–216). And see the critique by Yurco, "*Black Athena*: An Egyptological Response," 68–72. Tritle, "Vision or Dream?"; Trigger, "Brown Athena," 122; and Weinstein, "Review of *Black Athena* 2," 382. *Black Athena* 2: 274–319. On the Thera dating, see Yurco, "*Black Athena*: An Egyptological Response," 83–84. Against the redating, see Tritle "Vision or Dream?" 317.

41. *Black Athena* 2: 288.

42. Ibid., 336.

43. Pritchard, *Ancient Near Eastern Texts*, 232, 233, 230.

44. E. Meyer, *Geschichte des Altertums*, 315–323; *Black Athena* 2: 321. Also see Yurco, "*Black Athena*: An Egyptological Response," 88.

45. *Black Athena* 2: 406, 41.

46. Ibid., 323.

47. Ibid., 381.

48. Ibid., 406, 379, 377, 376, 380. His dating of the MM III has shifted somewhat since the publication of volume 1 (2: xxxiii). Similar Hyksos-inspired changes are identified in Cretan weaponry, as well as in artistic representations where horses and chariots are suddenly featured (2: 367–373).

49. Ibid., 381, 45.

50. Stubbings, "Rise of Mycenaean Civilization," 635.

51. *Black Athena* 2: 397, 393.

52. Ibid., 408.

53. Ibid., 406; also see 407, 494.

54. Ibid., 525–526. But Bernal also argues that he overerestimated the impact of the colonizations and underestimated the subsequent influence of the Egyptian Eighteenth Dynasty (1567–1320 B.C.E.) (362).

55. Also see *Black Athena* 2: 58–59, 501; and *Black Athena* 1: 16, 35, 77, 86–87, 393–399, 427–433.

56. Herodotus, *Histories* 5:58–59; *Black Athena* 2: 502; Bernal, *Cadmean Letters*, 4; *Black Athena* 1: 432. Bernal also focuses on myths which speak of Kadmos refounding the city of Thebes. Bernal equates the Kadmos myth of a second founding with the moment in time when Hyksos princes arrived in Greece (*Black Athena* 2: 17, 58–59, 129, 151, 497–504). There were contrasting traditions that Danaos was responsible for the transmission of the alphabet. Bernal's attempt to reconcile these two traditions can be found in volume 2 (502–504).

57. Bernal, *Cadmean Letters*, 53 (emphasis added). A second wave of transmission is assumed to have occurred at the time of Phoenician expansion between the eleventh and ninth centuries (54).

58. In positing this scheme, Bernal has deviated greatly from the Ancient Model. The latter places the Hyksos arrival in the Aegean (= the colonization) *after* the Hyksos (= Danaans in the Ancient Model) had been expelled from Egypt (*Black Athena* 2: 404). According to the Revised Ancient Model, on the other hand, this process began ca. 1730, at precisely the same time that other groups of Hyksos were first consolidating their power in Egypt (363). Be that as it may, the author accepts the Ancient Model's assumption that those Hyksos who were expelled from Egypt were the Exodus Israelites and that this process occurred in the sixteenth century. Bernal sees the Exodus narratives as "a folk memory of the expulsion of the Hyksos" (357–358, and see 293). Bernal suggests that the Thera eruption of 1628 B.C.E. and its ensuing effects had something to do with the inexplicable natural phe-

nomena (bodies of water parting, volcanoes, etc.) discussed in the Book of Exodus. To review, the Ancient Model maintains that the Hyksos arrived at mainland Greece in the sixteenth century after having been ousted from Egypt. The Revised Ancient Model claims that the Hyksos arrived in the eighteenth century B.C.E., just a few years after arriving in Egypt Also see *Black Athena* 1: 20.

59. It is interesting to note that the first comprehensive philological analysis of *Black Athena* was actually quite positive. Gary Rendsburg, a professor at Cornell and a former student of Cyrus Gordon, would conclude that the etymologies proposed by Bernal "stand up to the tests of linguistic analysis" (*"Black Athena*: An Etymological Response," 80). Vermeule, "World Turned Upside Down," 273; Weinstein, "Review of *Black Athena* 2," 382; Jasanoff and Nussbaum, "Word Games," 182–183, 202. Also see Josephson, "Comments on Martin Bernal's *Black Athena*"; Egberts, "Consonants in Collision," 162.

60. Tritle, "Vision or Dream?" 317.

61. Yurco, *"Black Athena*: An Egyptological Review," 79. Also see J. Hall, *"Black Athena*," 250. It should be noted that Bernal makes an occasional effort to prove his hypothesis on the grammatical level of analysis, as when he speculates about the similarities in the definite article and demonstratives in Semitic and in Greek (*Black Athena* 1: 55–56). More recently, Bernal tries in "Responses to *Black Athena*," 83. Also see Astour's discussion of Linear A and West Semitic (*Hellenosemitica*, 345).

62. Bernal, "First by Land," 16.

63. *Black Athena* 1: 51–53, 20–21; Jasanoff and Nussbaum, "Word Games," 193–194; Lefkowitz, *Not Out of Africa*, 65; and "Ancient History," 16; Ray, "Egyptian Perspective," 80. Also see Coleman, "Did Egypt Shape the Glory That Was Greece?" 300n. 20; Yurco, *"Black Athena*: An Egyptological Review," 78; Tritle, "Vision or Dream?" 321; Serglo Pernigotti in Baldini, "Classici d'Egitto," 117. For a recent, and scathing, critique of Bernal's "Athena" etymology, see Egberts, "Consonants in Collision." And see Bernal's rejoinder, "Response to Arno Egberts."

64. Yurco, *"Black Athena*: An Egyptological Review," 74. Also see Weinstein, "Review of *Black Athena* 2," 383.

65. O'Connor, "Egypt and Greece," 53. Tritle ("Vision or Dream?" 311) argues that the campaigns of Sesōstris "are best left to the realm of legend and ancient nationalistic propaganda" (312). Also see Burstein, "Debate over *Black Athena*," 11.

66. Michelini, "Comment," 99; Yurco, *"Black Athena*: An Egyptological Review," 86; Coleman, "Did Egypt Shape the Glory That Was Greece?" 282; Vermeule, "World Turned Upside Down," 277.

67. Weinstein, "Review of *Black Athena* 2," 382; Lefkowitz, *Not Out of Africa*, 22.

68. Lefkowitz, *Not Out of Africa*, 22; Rogers, "*Quo Vadis?*" 450; Vermeule, "World Turned Upside Down," 276; Coleman, "Did Egypt Shape the Glory That Was Greece?" 284; Baines, "Aims and Methods," 33; Yurco, *"Black Athena*: An Egyptological Review," 91. And on Greek influence in later periods, see Burstein, "Debate over *Black Athena*," 6. Bernal, it should be stressed, does occasionally posit West-to-East movement (*Black Athena* 2: 419, 435, 494).

69. E. Hall, "Myths Missing That Black Magic,' 15; Burstein, "Debate over *Black Athena*," 7, 8; Whitney, "Is the American Academy Racist?" 8. Also see Kelly, "Egyptians and Ethiopians," 77. Åström surveys Swedish scholarship and makes a similar point in "Comments on Martin Bernal's *Black Athena*". Coleman, "Did Egypt Shape the Glory That Was Greece?" 280, 292; Muhly, *"Black Athena* versus Traditional Scholarship," 99; Guiliana Lanata in Baldini, "Classici d'Egitto," 117; Savino, "Macché ariani, erano negri." Burkert (*Orientalizing Revolution*, 5) argues that Bronze Age contacts are "generally and freely accepted" while first-millennium contacts are denied. Also see Mondi, "Greek Mythic Thought," 142;

Branham, "Hellenomania," 57; Morris, "Greece and the Levant," 57. One could view Vermeule's 1964 *Greece in the Bronze Age* (58, 63, 67, 71, 92, 93, 99, 106, 107) as yet another example of a willingness to work within the types of frameworks advocated by Bernal. Of course, Vermeule would emerge as a trenchant critic of Bernal.

70. Yurco, "*Black Athena*: An Egyptological Review," 95, 89. Also see Michelini, "Comment," 99; Baines, "Aims and Methods," 32–33.

71. *Black Athena* 2: 465, 481, 494, 521.

72. Bernal, "*Black Athena* and the APA," 24. Also see "Response to Jonathan Hall," 275.

73. He writes that the Hyksos' "chief long-term cultural impact seems to have been in transmitting other civilizations—Semitic into Egypt and 'Minoan,' Levantine and Egyptian into Greece" (*Black Athena* 2: 403–404).

74. Pelasgian, as noted above, contained an Indo-Hittite component. To some minor degree this Indo-Hittite substratum must be factored into the equation, though I place this in lowercase letters in deference to Bernal's belief that Indo-Hittite Pelasgian "left little trace in Greek" (*Black Athena* 1: 2).

75. Let us not fail to mention that Hyksos Egyptian and Semitic most likely contain some residue of Hurrian and Indo-Aryan, and possibly some of the language spoken in Minoan Crete.

76. N. Allen, "*Black Athena*: An Interview with Bernal," 18.

77. M. M. Levine, "Challenge of *Black Athena* to Classics Today," 12. Accordingly, I do not agree with Marchand and Grafton's claim ("Martin Bernal and His Critics," 8) that Bernal speaks of roots while his critics speak of influences. Bernal, for his part, speaks of both Afroasiatic roots *and* influences on ancient Greece.

78. *Black Athena* 1: 2.

Chapter 3. The Aryan Models

1. Bernal notes that "the Ancient and Aryan Models are not necessarily mutually exclusive" (*Black Athena* 1: 330, also see 62, 402, 439, 442). Bernal, "First by Land," 12; Dyson, "On *Black Athena*," 59; Bernal, *Black Athena* 2: 263, also see 10. On the future victory of the Revised Ancient Model, see Bernal, *Black Athena* 1: 402, 437; and "*Black Athena* and the APA," 25.

2. Renfrew, *Archaeology and Language*, 9. Cited in Halbfass, *India and Europe*, 63.

3. On the use of these varying terms, see Poliakov, *Aryan Myth*, 193, also see 173; and Renfrew, *Archaeology and Language*, 11. As Olender notes, "Different scholars used the same terms interchangeably to refer to a people, a race, a nation, or a family of languages" (*Languages of Paradise*, 11).

4. Renfrew, *Archaeology and Language*, 12. See Bernal, *Black Athena* 1: 226; and *Cadmean Letters*, 2. For Renfrew's objections to standard tenets of the Indo-European hypothesis, see *Problems in European Prehistory*, 16, and *Archaeology and Language*, 86, 90, 104.

5. Bernal, *Black Athena* 1: 330, 333, 12, and *Black Athena* 2: 154. Also see Gimbutas, "Destruction of Aegean"; and Mallory, *In Search of the Indo-Europeans*, 66–71; Renfrew, *Archaeology and Language*, 14, 37–41, 97, where he rejects these homeland theories.

6. This 1879 quote from Edward Augustus Freeman was cited in Pollock, "Deep Orientalism?" 82. Olender, *Languages of Paradise*, 7.

7. Bernal, "Case for Massive Egyptian Influence," 82.

8. Regrettably, Bernal said nothing about the Ancient Model in the Islamic high cultures of the Middle Ages. Such an analysis would have lent, undoubtedly, greater depth to his argument about the historical longevity of the Ancient Model. See Jefford's summary of the proceedings of the Claremont Conference, where the belief

that a pronounced appreciation for Egypt and Semitic cultures existed during the Renaissance is contested (13). Bernal's theories on the Renaissance rank among the least discussed of his initiatives. There were initial challenges to the Ancient Model in the eighteenth century issued by Jacob Brucker and Samuel Musgrave (*Black Athena* 1: 197, 211).

9. Bernal, *Black Athena* 2: 150, 131, 228, 399; *Black Athena* 1: 334. In fact, Bernal also referred to the Aryan Model as the "Northern Model" ("Black Athena Denied," 3). See also Gimbutas, "Destruction of Aegean." For a discussion and contestation of this dating of the Indo-European arrival, see Wyatt, "Indo-Europeanization of Greece"; and Gimbutas, "Proto-Indo-European Culture"; and more generally, Mallory, *In Search of the Indo-Europeans.*

10. *Black Athena* 1: 224; Olender, *Languages of Paradise,* 12; *Black Athena* 2: 339. Also see Poliakov, *Aryan Myth,* 2; Renfrew, *Archaeology and Language,* 15; and Bernal, "Black Athena and Her Reception," 11.

11. Giannaris, "Rocking the Cradle," 31; Vermeule, *Greece in the Bronze Age,* 70.

12. *Black Athena* 1: 7; and Bernal, "Race, Class and Gender," 988. There is some confusion in Bernal's discussion of Pre-Hellenes and Pelasgians. As far as I can tell, the author claims that the former term was routinely equated to the latter in the nineteenth century. Problematically, in another contribution he argues that the belief in "Pre-Hellenes" emerged only in the 1920s (*Cadmean Letters,* 6, contra *Black Athena* 1: 34, 48, also see 368, 390–392). Finkelberg has traced the first appearance of a theory of a non-Indo-European Pre-Hellenic substratum to the writings of Paul Kretschmer in 1896 ("Anatolian Languages," 3).

13. On Curtius, see *Black Athena* 1: 333, 32–33; and Bernal, "Black Athena Denied," 37.

14. Dyson, "On *Black Athena,*" 58. Elsewhere Bernal remarks, "The non-Indo-European-speaking yet Caucasian and somehow European Pre-Hellenes acted as a filter purifying the African and Semitic influences on Greek culture" (*Black Athena* 2: 14, 67).

15. *Black Athena* 1: 2, 7, 48. Also see N. Allen, "*Black Athena*: An Interview with Bernal," 18; and Bernal, "On the Transmission," 2; and "Image of Ancient Greece," 124. Archaeological attestation, argues Bernal, would first arrive only with Schliemann's excavations in the 1870s ("First by Land," 9). Bernal, "Greece: Aryan or Mediterranean?" 5; and "*Black Athena* and Her Reception," 11.

16. *Black Athena* 1: 4, 308–316, 359; *Black Athena* 2: 177; Bernal, "Black Athena Denied," 31–35; Reinach, "Mirage Oriental," 700. Also see Bernal, "British Utilitarians," 120–121, 124; "Image of Ancient Greece," 123; "Greece: Aryan or Mediterranean?" 8; Unte, "Karl Otfried Müller"; Müller, *Introduction*; and Müller and Donaldson, *History of the Literature.*

17. *Black Athena* 2: 195, 200, 237, 239. Also see Appleby et al., *Telling the Truth about History,* 53–54.

18. *Black Athena* 2: 94, 109. Other terms, such as *Egyptomania* and *Barbarophilia,* were used by proponents of the Aryan paradigm in order to describe the Greeks' perception of their relation and indebtedness to Afroasiatic cultures (*Black Athena* 1: 309–310, 118). As Bernal notes, "The many ancient references to the Egyptian and Phoenician colonization and the later cultural borrowings could now be dismissed as 'late,' 'credulous,' or simply 'unreliable'" (218). Davidson, "Ancient World and Africa," 4. On the fall of the Ancient Model, see *Black Athena* 1: 253, 283, 289, xv; and Bernal, "Greece: Aryan or Mediterranean?" 5.

19. *Black Athena* 1: 118.

20. Ibid., xv. Also see Bernal, "Image of Ancient Greece," 124; and "Race, Class, and Gender," 988; Cohen, "Interview," 3. In *Black Athena* 1: (375–376) Bernal argues that while Herodotus is ignored, broad Aryanists tend to respect the testimony of Thucydides, who did not mention Egyptian or Phoenician colonization on mainland Greece, but referred to Phoenician colonizations on the Greek islands.

21. *Black Athena* 1: 1, 34–35, 37, 393–399, 427–433; *Black Athena* 2: 469; "Greece: Aryan or Mediterranean?" 9–10.
22. *Black Athena* 1: 1–2, 34, 398, 426, 442. The Extreme Aryan Model enjoyed its greatest popularity between 1938 and 1973. It is Bernal's opinion that this model has started to crumble in recent decades. For the foundational texts, see Beloch, "Phoeniker am aegaeischen Meer"; Reinach, "Mirage Oriental"; Carpenter, "Antiquity of the Greek Alphabet"; "Greek Alphabet Again"; and "Phoenicians in the West."
23. *Black Athena* 1: 7.
24. Renfrew, "Problems in the General Correlation," 270, 273; and *Problems in European Prehistory,* 23–24, 27, 39. Georgiev, "Arrival of the Greeks"; Bernal, "Black Athena Denied," 4.
25. *Black Athena* 2: 14, 15, 21, 66; *Black Athena* 1: 410, 407. Bernal summarizes the view of the isolationists as follows: "They argue that Proto-Indo-European was never anything but a congeries of dialects spoken over Anatolia and the Balkans, of which the Greek spoken in Greece was one."
26. *Black Athena* 1: 2.
27. Ibid., 33.
28. *Black Athena* 2: 363; *Black Athena* 1: 439, 331; Bernal, "Greece: Aryan or Mediterranean?" 10; "Response to Edith Hall," 210; and "Race, Class, and Gender," 989.
29. G. Rendsburg, "*Black Athena*: An Etymological Response," 78. See Bernal's remarks in N. Allen, "*Black Athena*: Interview with Bernal," 18. Bernal argues that "50 per cent of the Greek vocabulary and 80 per cent of proper names" as well as "90 per cent of toponyms, divine and mythological names" are not of Indo-European origin. See *Black Athena* 1: 47; and Bernal, "First by Land," 12; Dyson, "On *Black Athena,*" 58; Bernal, "Phoenician Politics," 255.
30. Bernal writes: "Putting the Indo-European, Semitic and Egyptian roots together, I now believed that—with further research—one could provide plausible explanations for 80–90 per cent of the Greek vocabulary" (*Black Athena* 1: xiv, 58). Also see Bernal, "Race, Class, and Gender, 989; Goode, "Ancient Greece's Non-Greek Roots," 54. In 1997 Bernal suddenly offered a new breakdown. Now 15 percent of Greek was seen as having Semitic origins and 20 percent as having Egyptian origins ("Responses to *Black Athena,*" 88–89).
31. On the critique of Bernal's credibility qua scholar, see, for example, F. Turner, "Martin Bernal's *Black Athena,*" 104; Norton, "Tyranny of Germany," 409; Marchand and Grafton, "Martin Bernal and His Critics," 3, 4, 6, 7.
32. *Black Athena* 1: 206; Bernal, "Race, Class, and Gender," 1003, 1004.
33. Norton, "Tyranny of Germany," 406, 408–410.
34. Ibid., 406, 407.
35. *Black Athena* 1: 324, 328–329, 336.
36. Rogers, "Multiculturalism," 434. Nor does Bernal prove Grote's racism in "British Utilitarians."
37. Blok, "Proof and Persuasion," 713, 720, 709, 716–717, 714. Bernal concedes the error ("Response to Josine Blok," 213, 214).
38. Bernal, "First by Land," 32. As Frank notes, most of the text was published as an encyclopedia article in 1909. After Weber's death, his wife, Marianne, reprinted the entry in addition to other related selections (Frank, "Translator's Introduction," in Weber, *Agrarian Sociology,* 29).
39. Mommsen, *Max Weber and German Politics,* 8, 326, 327; Weber, "Science as a Vocation," 134. On Ploetz, see Mosse's remarks, cited in Nelson, "Max Weber on Race and Society," 31.
40. Cited in Nelson, "Max Weber on Race and Society," 35.
41. Manasse, "Max Weber on Race."

42. McNeal, "Review of *Black Athena 1*," 54.
43. Muhly, "Where the Greeks Got Their Gifts," 3; Pounder, "Review Article: *Black Athena 2*," 461.
44. Berlinerblau, *The Vow*; "Preliminary Remarks"; 'Popular Religion' Paradigm"; and "Some Sociological Observations." Bernal, "Race, Class, and Gender," 989; and *Black Athena 2*: 65; Lowenthal, *Past Is a Foreign Country*, 215.
45. *Black Athena 1*: 8; Bernal, *Cadmean Letters*, 1.
46. *Black Athena 1*: 8, 314; *Black Athena 2*: 438; Bernal, "First by Land, 8; "Black Athena Denied," 35–36; "Greece: Aryan or Mediterranean?" 8, 10; "Image of Ancient Greece," 123; *Cadmean Letters*, 1, 56; "Response to Josine Blok," 210. For a friendly assessment of competitive plausibility, see Johnson-Odim, "Debate," 85.
47. *Black Athena 2*: 163, 240, 349, 427, 482; *Black Athena 1*: 310. For examples of Bernal's own—sometimes conscious—use of the argument from silence, see *Black Athena 2*: 152, 166, 213, 391, 460. Also see Michelini ("Comment," 95), who finds this aspect of Bernal's argument "very powerful." But see Coleman, "Did Egypt Shape the Glory That Was Greece?" 289; Blok, "Proof and Persuasion," 715.
48. Bernal, "Classics in Crisis," 73 (emphasis added). Also see *Black Athena 2*: 65; Bernal, "Response to Sturt Manning," 280; and Bernal's discussion with Sally Humphreys in Raaflaub, *Anfänge politischen Denkens*, 401–404.
49. See Chapter 2 above for a full discussion of Bernal's shift in perspective. M. M. Levine, "Review Article," 443; R. Young, *"Black Athena,"* 277; and see Bernal's confusing remarks on this issue in "Race, Class, and Gender," 989–990. Also see *Black Athena 2*: 3–4, 65, 187, 307.
50. Coleman, "Did Egypt Shape the Glory That Was Greece?" 292; Rogers, "Quo Vadis?" 452; Vermeule, "World Turned Upside Down," 275.
51. Manning, "Frames of Reference," 267.
52. Lefkowitz, "Ancient History," 15–16 (emphasis added). At other points, however, Lefkowitz shows herself to be more aware of the difficulty of achieving such proof (5). See her article, "Not Out of Africa," 30.
53. Lefkowitz, *Not Out of Africa*, 5, 7.
54. Ibid., 63–64. For a readable account of the type of massive changes which a new discovery may stimulate, see Craigie's discussion of the impact of Ugaritic studies on the interpretation of the Hebrew Bible in *Ugarit and the Old Testament*, 67–90.

Chapter 4. Atmospheric Determinism

1. To the best of my knowledge and after consulting the *Social Sciences Abstracts* and the Sociofile data base, there is only one sociological review of *Black Athena*. It is two pages long and appears in the *Michigan Sociological Review* (Whit, "Review of *Black Athena 1*"). For an interesting discussion of what Bernal's sociological analysis lacks, see van Binsbergen, *"Black Athena* Ten Years After," 38–40.
2. Calhoun, *Critical Social Theory*, xxii; Bourdieu, "Vive la crise!" 779; Coser, *Maurice Halbwachs: On Collective Memory*, 34; B. M. Berger, *Essay on Culture*, 127; Leff, *History and Social Theory*, 2.
3. Anderson, "Myth of Hellenism," 14.
4. On Bernal as conspiracy theorist, see Whitney, "Is the American Academy Racist?" 8. R. B. Lloyd, "Review of *Black Athena 1*," 1547; Tritle, "Vision or Dream?"309; Poliakoff, "Roll Over Aristotle," 12; Muhly, *"Black Athena,"* 101; Rogers, "Multiculturalism," 429, 438; Baines, "Aims and Methods," 39; Lefkowitz, "Ancient History," 13; and "Not Out of Africa," 30, 33.
   On Bernal as reinventing the wheel, see those who (rightly) accuse him of making claims very similar to the African-American "vindicationist" school (see

Chapter 7 below]: M. Washington, "Revitalizing"; and Asante, quoted in Coughlin, "In Multiculturalism Debate," A6. Carruthers ("Outside Academia," 462) writes, "For at least 200 years, African champions of ancient Egypt have been asserting what Bernal concludes about Kemet." De Melis, *"Black Athena,"* 24.

On Bernal as a racist, "feeding racism," or working with racist paradigms, see Ferguson, "Review of *Black Athena,* volume one," 374; Reiss, "Review of *Black Athena 2,*" 434; M. M. Levine, "Review Article," 450; G. Lerner, "Comment," 93; J. Hall, *"Black Athena,"* 251–252; Vermeule, "World Turned Upside Down," 278.

On Eurocentrism: Goonatilake, "The Son," 1769; Baines, "Aims and Methods," 45; M. Washington, "Revitalizing," 111; Georgakas, *"Black Athena,"* 56; Reiss, "Review of *Black Athena"* 2: 433. And see Bernal's response to the charge of racism, "Response" (*Arethusa*), 315; Currie, "Review of *Black Athena 1,*" 328; Gress, "Case against Bernal," 40; White, "Civilization Denied," 38. Also see Hallas, "Absent Friends," 29, for the accusation that Bernal uses a European bourgeois method. For more on Marxism, see van Binsbergen, *"Black Athena* Ten Years After," 59.

5. E. Hall, "Myths Missing That Black Magic," 15. The differences between Marx and Bernal are obvious and abundant. Bernal's work evinces a profound appreciation for the cultural contributions of African and Asiatic civilizations. Marx's oeuvre—though not necessarily all of the Marxisms which it engendered—has been justifiably accused of harboring an inveterate Eurocentric bias. For a brilliant discussion of this issue, see Ahmad's essay, "Marx on India: A Clarification" in *In Theory.* Marx's "On the Jewish Question" perpetuated many of the anti-Semitic stereotypes which are anathema to Bernal. Finally and definitively, we could point to the fact that Bernal explicitly inserts Marx's name within the expansive and dreaded Aryanist category. He writes, "Marx had a lifelong love for Greece and completely accepted the prevailing view that in every aspect of her civilization Greece was categorically different from and superior to all that had gone before" ("Phoenician Politics," 244). Also see *Black Athena* 1: 295; Baldini, "Classici d'Egitto," 117; *Black Athena* 2: xx. And see the disapproving review in *Socialist Worker Review* by Hallas. For Marx's own views on the Greeks, see Lekas, *Marx on Classical Antiquity.*

6. Bernal, *"Black Athena* and the APA," 27.

7. Wilczynski, "Determinism," 143. Or, to cite another textbook definition, such a theory maintains that "for everything that happens there are conditions, such that, given them, nothing else could have happened" (Bhaskar, "Determinism," 117). Also see Popper, *Open Society,* 81–82. R. Williams, *Marxism and Literature,* 83. In *Marx and the Marxists,* Hook offered a standard critique of Marxist determinism: "It is as if one were to argue that the 'ultimate' or 'decisive' cause of the death of a victim of a hit-and-run driver was not the drunkenness of the operator nor the speed of the vehicle which struck him down but capitalism because whiskey and automobiles are commodities" (60).

8. Eagleton, *Marxism and Literary Criticism,* 17.

9. As R. Williams shows, the portrait of "vulgar Marxism," while justified in some limited respects, is for the most part a "caricature" of Marx's original thought (*Marxism and Literature,* 83). For a discussion of the ambiguities in Marx's treatment of the subject, see Barrett, *Politics of Truth,* 3–47; Gramsci, *Prison Notebooks,* 407, 377, 336. Also see Giddens, *Capitalism and Modern Social Theory,* 42. For discussion of the merits of determinism, see B. M. Berger, *Essay on Culture;* Ahmad, *In Theory,* 6.

10. It is somewhat difficult to grasp what he has in mind when he sporadically claims that the downfall of the Ancient Model is attributable only to "externalist" factors. For Bernal's somewhat equivocal references to the external/internal dichotomy, see *Black Athena* 1: 2, 10, 231, 316, 441. Bernal's reference to "externalism" on 437 is not quite clear. Also see Bernal, "Race, Class, and Gender," 991. As for inter-

nalist factors, by 1995 he would seem to retreat and say that the Aryan Model "can be at least *partially* explained in internalist terms" ("Race, Class, and Gender," 991, emphasis mine). In this same piece (1008) he acknowledges that the Aryan Model was affected by external variables as well. Also see Bernal, "Greece: Aryan or Mediterranean?" 9.

11. *Black Athena* 1: 330, 441.

12. Bernal, "Case for Massive Egyptian Influence," 82; "Race, Class, and Gender," 990; *Black Athena* 1: 380, 316, 400; and see Bernal's "Response to Josine Blok" (213), where his new discussion of internal and external factors renders his analysis even more confusing.

13. Bernal, "*Black Athena* and the APA," 27 (emphasis added). Also see Bernal, "Image of Ancient Greece," 121; "Greece: Aryan or Mediterranean." 6; "Black Athena Denied," 54.

14. At other periods in time, entirely different world views flit about the atmosphere. Thus, in the aftermath of World War II, according to Bernal, there existed an "anti-racialist atmosphere" (*Black Athena* 2: 322). The new atmosphere precipitated a change in scholarly views: the Hyksos, who had previously been viewed as Aryans, were now construed as Semites. Elsewhere, an ethos is considered an external factor—Bernal refers to the "great emphasis, within Jewish culture, on intellectual pursuits and the respect for academia" (*Black Athena* 1: 400).

15. On the unpopularity of determinism in American thought, see B. M. Berger, *Essay on Culture,* 4, For the Bernal quote, see "British Utilitarians," 98.

16. Bernal, "*Black Athena* and the APA," 25.

17. Bernal, "Case for Massive Egyptian Influence," 82.

18. In fact, in one contribution Bernal seems to suggest that racism and anti-Semitism were the two most important factors in the paradigm shift ("Case for Massive Egyptian Influence," 82). Also see *Black Athena* 2: 522, 11–12, for the quote above. Elsewhere he speaks of four variables with race again occupying a prominent place ("Race, Class, and Gender," 995).

19. Snowden, *Before Color Prejudice,* 63. And see Bernal on Snowden and this issue, "Race, Class, and Gender," 998–999.

20. Davidson, *African Slave Trade,* 25; and "Ancient World and Africa"; Drake, "African Diaspora and Jewish Diaspora," 27. But Bernal seems to shift perspective in "Race, Class, and Gender" (997–1000), where he follows Drake in arguing that racial stereotypes may be identified in late antiquity; also see Bernal, "*Black Athena* and Her Reception," 17.

21. Arendt, *Origins of Totalitarianism,* 160, 183–184. Also see *Black Athena* 1: 201–202, 30.

22. *Black Athena* 1: 241 (emphasis in original).

23. Ibid., 437. This state of affairs also sets the stage for the projected second coming of the Ancient Model in the body of Bernal's Revised Ancient Model.

24. Poliakov, *History of Anti-Semitism,* 3: 142, 309; though see Langmuir, *History, Religion, and Antisemitism,* 340, for the argument that considerable ambiguity about the Jews as a race existed. Also see Rose, *Revolutionary Anti-Semitism,* 14. For Bernal on racial anti-Semitism, see *Black Athena* 1: 33, 338; "On the Transmission of the Alphabet," 2; "First by Land," 10; and "Review of *Judaïsme et Christianisme.*"

25. Archaeologist Patricia Maynor Bikai has argued that Bernal underestimated the role that "religious anti-Phoenicianism" played in the paradigm shift. Bikai points out that the Hebrew Bible is replete with the raw materials for the construction of such a stereotype: "Long after Phoenicia ceased to exist, it remained the western world's 'evil empire,' the home of Baal and Astarte, the birthplace of Jezebel, the prototype of the 'alien other'" ("*Black Athena* and the Phoenicians," 72). In her view, it was not only anti-Semitism, but the prejudices of Bible-reading Christians which contributed to the downfall of the Phoenicians and, by association, the Ancient Model.

Scholars did not dislike the Phoenicians only because they were "related" to the Jews, but precisely because they were the "heathen" Phoenicians of the Old Testament. On anti-Semitic assumptions in studies of antiquity, see Burkert, *Orientalizing Revolution*, 2, 3, 34.

26. *Black Athena* 1: 387, 398, 400, 415; *Black Athena* 2: 343.

27. As Bernal notes, this conception stood as one of the "cardinal beliefs of the 19th century" (*Black Athena* 1: 30); also see Bernal, "Black Athena Denied," 12. For the standard treatment, see Nisbet, *History of the Idea of Progress*.

28. Gramsci, *Prison Notebooks*, 357; Koselleck, *Critique and Crisis*, 5; Arendt *Origins of Totalitarianism*, 143; Trigger, *History of Archaeological Thought*, 59.

29. Asad, *Genealogies of Religion*, 19, 12.

30. Manuel, *Prophets of Paris*, 62; *Black Athena* 1: 7.

31. Bernal, *Black Athena* 1: 8. Also see Appleby et al., *Telling the Truth about History*, 61–62.

32. Bernal, *Black Athena* 1: 27, 199, 201, 245, 214; and "Race, Class, and Gender," 991. For a critique of Bernal's discussions of progress, see Blok, "Proof and Persuasion," 723.

33. Also see Kuklick, *Puritans in Babylon*, 38.

34. Amin observes, "Bernal shows that the nineteenth-century 'Hellenomania' was inspired by the racism of the Romantic movement, whose architects were moreover often the same people whom Said cites as the creators of Orientalism" (*Eurocentrism*, 92). Arendt, *Origins of Totalitarianism*, 165, 170; though see a seemingly contradictory view on 168. Langmuir, *History, Religion, and Antisemitism*, 320.

35. Bernal, "Response to Jonathan Hall," 275; *Black Athena* 1: 28, 209, 292; "Race, Class, and Gender," 1004; "Black Athena Denied," 14; and *Cadmean Letters*, 5. For the impact of Romanticism on the archaeology of the period, see Trigger, *History of Archaeological Thought*, 66; Burkert, *Orientalizing Revolution*, 2; Mudimbe, *Idea of Africa*, 100. And see Drake's discussion of George Fredrickson's idea of "romantic racialism" (*Black Folk*, 1: 59). Bernal, "Image of Ancient Greece," 121.

36. Bernal, "Response to Jonathan Hall," 275. Also see Cohen, "Interview," 2. There does seem to be a contradiction, however, insofar as the Pre-Hellenes and Aryans were not seen in Bernal's Aryan Models as speaking related languages.

37. On the relation of German Romantics to Sanskrit, see Pollock, "Deep Orientalism," 82; Bernal, *Black Athena* 1: 185, 229, 230, 253, 284, 289; "Image of Ancient Greece," 121; "Race, Class, and Gender," 992; "First by Land," 5; and "*Black Athena and the APA*," 29.

38. Bernal, *Black Athena* 1: 24, 190, 192; "First by Land," 5.

39. Bernal, *Black Athena* 1: 182, 194. *Black Athena* 2: 195, 234; "Black Athena Denied," 10. Such an association, I would add, would have been particularly damning within the ambit of eighteenth- and nineteenth-century European intellectual culture. As Thomas has shown in *Religion and the Decline of Magic*, by the seventeenth century "magic was ceasing to be intellectually acceptable" (663).

40. Bernal, "First by Land," 5; "Race, Class, and Gender," 994; *Black Athena* 1: 27. Also, due to the discovery of linguistic similarities between German and ancient Greek, many Protestant scholars became interested in demonstrating the importance of their "ancestors'" contribution over and against those of the magical Egyptians (*Black Athena* 1: 193, 214–215).

41. *Black Athena* 1: 73; Amin, *Eurocentrism*, vii, xii. For the link with the idea of progress, see Manuel, *Prophets of Paris*, 81; and *Black Athena* 1: 198; Bernal, "British Utilitarians," 111, 115. Readers might recognize similar Eurocentric impulses in American archaeology as identified by Kuklick, *Puritans in Babylon*, 47, 51.

42. Bernal, "On the Transmission of the Alphabet," 2; "*Black Athena* and the APA," 25; Baldini, "Classici d'Egitto," 113.
43. Tilly, *Coercion, Capital and European States*, 91; Hobsbawm, *Age of Empire*, 59; and *Age of Revolution*, 20. Compare Hobsbawm's statistics with those of Said, *Orientalism*, 41.
44. P. Allen, "Review of *Black Athena* (film)," 1024. Bernal, *Black Athena* 2: 235. Bernal's analysis features an interesting case of African counterimperialism. In 1821 C.E., Ibrahim, son of the intrepid Albanian-born ruler of Egypt, Mohamed Ali, shocked Europe by landing troops on mainland Greece. In the following decades he would repeatedly antagonize the Europeans. One effect of this invasion was to set off an avalanche of pro-Greek and anti-Egyptian sentiment across Europe. See Bernal, *Black Athena* 1: 247–248.
45. Bernal, "Image of Ancient Greece," 126. The bibliography devoted to Gramsciana is capacious and cannot be listed here. The core text would be Gramsci's *Selections from the Prison Notebooks*.
46. Bernal, *Black Athena* 1: 24, 214–215; "Image of Ancient Greece," 122; "Black Athena Denied," 14, 24; "Race, Class, and Gender," 1003–1004. Also see Shavit, *Athens in Jerusalem*, 23. For more on the intense relation felt by Germans with the Greeks, see Norton, "Tyranny of Germany over Greece?" 405. Jenkyns, "Bernal and the Nineteenth Century," 413. And see the standard work on this issue, Butler, *Tyranny of Greece over Germany*.
47. Bernal, *Black Athena* 1: 318, 211, 324, 397. Also see Finley, *Ancient History*, 10, 21; Bernal, "Race, Class, and Gender," 995; and "Greece: Aryan or Mediterranean?" 7; Giannaris, "Rocking the Cradle"; Marchand and Grafton, "Martin Bernal and His Critics," 14.
48. Bernal, *Black Athena* 1: 9, 374. Also see Bernal, "Black Athena Denied," 42. He also refers to classics and ancient history as "exceptionally positivist disciplines." Also see Michelini, "Comment," 96.
49. For Bernal's longest exposition on nationalism, both modern and ancient, see "Race, Class, and Gender," 996–1003. On the French attitude toward the Phoenicians in light of their holdings in North Africa and the Middle East, see *Black Athena* 1: 337–338, 214. Also see Chapter 9 below.
50. Hobsbawm, *Age of Revolution*, 307. Though eventually, according to Bernal, the Egyptians were seen as children also. Bernal, *Black Athena* 1: 265, 225, 208; "First by Land," 6; "Image of Ancient Greece," 121; "Race, Class, and Gender," 992; "Greece: Aryan or Mediterranean?" 7; Lo Monaco, "L'Occidente?"
51. Bernal, "*Black Athena* and the APA," 25; "First by Land," 8; "Greece: Aryan or Mediterranean?" 7; *Black Athena* and Her Reception, 17; Cohen, "Interview" 2; Bernal, "Image of Ancient Greece," 121; "Race, Class, and Gender," 992–993, 1005; "Black Athena Denied," 17; "British Utilitarians," 100.
52. Lerner, "Comment," 93; also see M. Washington, "Revitalizing," 106.
53. Zilfi, "Martin Bernal's *Black Athena*," 116. Also see Richlin, "Responses," 113. For Bernal's brief remarks on this issue, see *Black Athena* 1: 345, 354; "Black Athena Denied," 45; "Image of Ancient Greece," 119; "British Utilitarians," 111.
54. Bernal, "British Utilitarians," 117. See, in particular, Bernal, "Race, Class, and Gender," 996, 1002, 1005–1007, 1008. In his later writings, Bernal also evinced a concern for the predicament of women classicists ("*Black Athena* and the APA," 19; "Responses to *Black Athena*: General and Linguistic Issues," 68).
55. Zilfi, "Martin Bernal's *Black Athena*," 115.
56. As our epigraph indicates, even Martin Bernal tends to attenuate the capacious argument which he advances in volume 1. In fact, I would note that the author not only attenuates but vacillates when discussing his explanation for the paradigm shift. In different contributions he enumerates different reasons to explain the shift. Whereas in the epigraph he mentions Christianity, progress, racism, and

Romanticism, elsewhere he writes, "The Ancient Model fell . . . because . . . it was incompatible with the paradigms of race and progress of the early 19th century" (*Black Athena* 1: 316). In another contribution he notes that the Ancient Model "was overthrown at the turn of the nineteenth century, by the revival of Christianity after the French Revolution and the triumphs of the concept of progress and of Romanticism" ("First by Land," 5). Nearly all of those, be they scholars or journalists, who have discussed Bernal's answer to this question have greatly underestimated its thickness and complexity. In fact, these reductive readings are so commonplace that we need not cite them, since nearly all commentators have greatly simplified Bernal's analysis. For a notable exception, see R. Young, "*Black Athena.*"

57. E. Hall, "When Is a Myth Not a Myth?" 184; Bowersock, "Review of *Black Athena* 1," 491; Michelini, "Comment," 95. Others who share this opinion are numerous; I offer a partial list: Hansen, "Introduction," 2; M. M. Levine, "Anti-Black and Anti-Semitic?" 34; Malamud, "Review of *Black Athena* 1," 321; Morris, "Daidalos and Kadmos," 40; Robert Pounder, "History without Rules," 464; Mudimbe (with a caveat), *Idea of Africa*, 99; Coleman, "Did Egypt Shape the Glory That Was Greece?" 288. See Luciano Canfora in Baldini, "Classici d'Egitto," 117; Leach, "Aryan Warlords," 11. As Bernal himself noted, "The general response to my work has been that the historiography is fine and reasonable, the archaeology may well be right, but the linguistics is wrong or crazy" (N. Allen, "*Black Athena*: An Interview," 22); also see *Black Athena* 2: xvi, 2; Dyson, "On *Black Athena*," 57; Branham, "Hellenomania," 58.

58. Poliakoff, "Roll Over Aristotle," 18.

59. Rogers, "Multiculturalism," 431 (first emphasis added); Lefkowitz, "Ancient History," 5; also see eyewitness accounts from Kristeller, "Comment on *Black Athena*," and Gress, "Case against Bernal," 40.

Chapter 5. The Antinomies of Martin Bernal

1. Bernal was initially hesitant to apply the term *paradigm* to the Ancient and Aryan Models. By the publication of volume 2, however, this reluctance subsided. The author now used *paradigm* as well as Kuhn's improved term, *disciplinary matrix* (*Black Athena* 2: 11). For the original statement of this position, see *Black Athena* 1: 1, 3.

2. Bernal, "Case for Massive Egyptian Influence," 82; *Black Athena* 1: 330, 402; "Race, Class, and Gender," 990; *Black Athena* 2: 342. The discovery of Ugaritic civilization is also seen as an internal development (*Black Athena* 1: 414. If I understand him correctly, he is saying that Claude F. A. Schaeffer's initial excavation of the site of Ras Shamra in northern Syria in 1929, and the subsequent decipherment of the many tablets found there, was an event untouched by ideology. It gave researchers new knowledge about the Bronze Age Levant, and this new knowledge was not ideologically inspired. Of course, these texts had to be interpreted at some point, and one would expect that "external factors" played some role here. Bernal, "*Black Athena* and Her Reception," 14).

3. I say "relatively" in light of Bernal's formulation in *Black Athena* 1: 441. Blok describes Bernal's internal factors as "normal, legitimate, and indeed valuable features of a scientific discipline" ("Proof and Persuasion," 708).

4. The working out of the decipherment of ancient Egyptian and the archaeological discoveries of Heinrich Schliemann in the 1870s are also considered internalist developments, albeit ones that had less of an impact on the rise of the Aryan Model (*Black Athena* 1: 441, 318, 253; *Black Athena* 2: 12; Bernal, "Image of Ancient Greece," 124; "Greece: Aryan or Mediterranean?" 9). Conversely, Bernal claims that no internalist developments caused the fall of the Ancient Model in the 1820s and 1830s.

The author argues that internal developments such as "the decipherment of cuneiform" and archaeological discoveries in the Bronze Age Aegean took place in the 1850s, thus *after* the Ancient Model was abandoned ("Race, Class, and Gender," 990; "Image of Ancient Greece," 120; "Greece: Aryan or Mediterranean?" 5–6).

5. *Black Athena* 1: 281. For most of his text, external factors (e.g., atmosphere) seem to determine internal developments (e.g., scholarship). The former are the cause, the latter the effect. But then, without explanation, Bernal reverses field by speaking of paradigms which somehow arise independently of ideological pressures. What happened to the atmosphere? Where did the external factors go? *Black Athena* 2: 282 makes the curious, highly unsociological claim that scientists have the capacity to be more objective than humanists and historians. This claim was contested by Baines ("Aims and Methods," 36) and Tritle ("Vision or Dream," 308).

6. Bernal never defines the term *ideology,* and this is problematic insofar as it is susceptible to so many different interpretations. See, for example, Eagleton, *Ideology,* where sixteen distinct definitions of the term are identified (1–2). Also see Eagleton, *Marxism and Literary Criticism,* 1–19. On the difficulties in Marx and Engel's initial usage, see Abercrombie et al., *Dominant Ideology Thesis,* 1–29; and Barrett, *Politics of Truth,* 3–17.

7. Barrett, *Politics of Truth,* 44.

8. Ibid., 38. See Gramsci, *Prison Notebooks.*

9. Said, *Orientalism,* 232; Poliakov, *History of Anti-Semitism,* 3: 139, 125.

10. Also see Blok, "Proof and Persuasion," 723.

11. We should recall that what we call racism today was the science of an earlier period. See Hannah Arendt, *Origins of Totalitarianism,* 160; Stepan and Gilman, "Appropriating the Idioms of Science," 171, 173, 172. In 1995 Bernal finally acknowledged that the internal/external scheme was "crude." Be that as it may, he would continue to employ this approach. ("Race, Class, and Gender," 990). Also see Cohen, "Interview," 10; and Bernal, *Black Athena* 2: xviii, for his own critique of his sociology of knowledge.

12. C. H. Gordon, "Foreword," xi. As Astour points out, Bérard was perhaps the "only scholar" who opposed the trend of refusing to admit "any Semitic influence upon Greece" (*Hellenosemitica,* xiii).

13. *Black Athena* 1: 380–381 (emphasis added).

14. See Nietzsche, "We Classicists," 325, 360, 370, 387; *Black Athena* 2: 175.

15. Bernal, "Responses to Critical Reviews," 119 (emphasis added); also see *Black Athena* 1: 382.

16. Turner, "Martin Bernal's *Black Athena,*" 101.

17. Ibid., 98.

18. Bernal, "*Black Athena* and the APA," 27 (emphasis added).

19. Bernal, "Responses to Critical Reviews," 126 (emphasis added).

20. Dyson, "On *Black Athena,*" 58. In a 1995 interview Bernal would argue that while "knowledge is always socially embedded it is not necessarily socially determined" ("Responses on the Comments," 54). The formulation as it stands is not entirely clear to me.

21. I am curious as to what Bernal means by "the material they study." Is he saying that the actual body of evidence a scholar examines might influence his or her conclusions? Or is he saying, as I think he is, that a judicious researcher can somehow avoid political and social pressures and more or less grasp the truth of the text or artifact being studied? Needless to say, Bernal's position on this issue has changed over the years, and I expect that further developments will arise in volume 3.

22. *Black Athena* 1: 406, 370–373.

23. For a discussion of this, see Mosse, *Crisis of German Ideology,* 18–30.

24. Anderson, *Considerations on Western Marxism*, 25; consequently, a "cultural and ideological focus" abounds in their work (78). Jacoby, "Western Marxism," 523; also see Jacoby, *Dialectic of Defeat*, 6.

25. On the influence of this book see, for example, Gutting, "Preface," v; Fischer, *Historians' Fallacies*, 162. As Hollinger observes, Kuhn's "terms have been employed explicitly by historians of art, religion, political organization, social thought and American foreign policy" ("T. S. Kuhn's Theory of Science," 196). See Urry, however, who contests this view of Kuhn's versatility ("Thomas S. Kuhn," 465). Also see Fuller, "Being There," 241; Perry, "Comparative Analysis," 38. On Bernal and Kuhn, see *Black Athena* 1: 1; *Black Athena* 2: xix, 11, 12; "*Black Athena*: The African and Levantine Roots," 70.

26. Masterman, "Nature of a Paradigm," 61. Acknowledging the ambiguous nature of this term, Kuhn later opted for "disciplinary matrix" (*Structure of Scientific Revolutions*, 2nd ed., 182). Also see Kuhn, *Essential Tension*, 297, 319.

27. Eckberg and Hill, "Paradigm Concept and Sociology," 121. Kuhn writes in *Essential Tension*: "A paradigm is what the members of a scientific community, and they alone, share. Conversely, it is their possession of a common paradigm that constitutes a scientific community of a group of otherwise disparate men" (294).

28. Kuhn, *Structure of Scientific Revolutions*, 24 (emphasis added). And see Popper's challenge, "Normal Science," 52.

29. King, "Reason, Tradition," 111.

30. Kuhn, *Structure of Scientific Revolutions*, 90, 203. What Kuhn's theory does not explain, however, is why the classics establishment ultimately did give *Black Athena* its day in court. It is undeniable that the work in question was widely reviewed and publicly discussed by scholars of Greco-Roman antiquity. Yet in the passage noted above, Kuhn maintained that normal science cannot even "see" findings that do not fit into its paradigmatic box. How can this state of affairs be explained? In an odd twist, Bernal had a chance to pose this question to Kuhn himself. In the preface to volume 2, Bernal discusses the surprise he felt when he learned that Molly Myerowitz Levine had arranged for *Black Athena* to be discussed at the annual meeting of the American Philological Society:

    > After the meeting had been announced but before it took place, I happened to meet the historian and philosopher of science Thomas Kuhn. His reaction was that the meeting was being held far too soon and that disciplines did not usually respond so quickly to fundamental challenges. My first response was to say that we were all living in a "post-Kuhnian age" in which the possibility of fundamental or "paradigmatic" shifts was now seen in all disciplines. My second answer, at another level, was to point out that the classicists might dismember me to their satisfaction. Kuhn's reply to this was that what actually happened at the meeting "was totally uninteresting." What was important was the legitimacy given by the holding of the meeting. (*Black Athena* 2: xix)

    This makes for an interesting anecdote, but it leaves us in the dark as to why the allegedly monolithic classics establishment granted Bernal's "legitimacy" in the first place. J. Hall argues that there is nothing revolutionary about Bernal's work since he is beholden to "a nineteenth-century conception of culture change or formation brought about externally by invaders or colonizers." ("*Black Athena*," 248–249, 252).

31. Borradori, *American Philosopher*, 153; Kuhn, *Structure of Scientific Revolutions*, 170.

32. Hollinger, "T. S. Kuhn's Theory of Science," 200. Also see Lakatos, "Falsification," 93; Feyerabend, "Consolations for the Specialist," 202. Kuhn has protested the type of reading of his work made by Hollinger; see Kuhn, "Reflections on My Critics," 261, 265; and *Structure of Scientific Revolutions*, 206. As Fuller notes, Kuhn "is notorious for disavowing most of the consequences wrought by his text" ("Being There," 241). On Bernal and Kuhn, see R. Young, "*Black Athena*," 278.

222 Notes to Pages 103–107

33. Martins, "Kuhnian 'Revolution,'" 19. Also see Eckberg and Hill, "Paradigm Concept," 123; Kuhn, *Structure of Scientific Revolutions,* 179.

34. Baines ("Aims and Methods," 42) has rightly noted that "ancient Near Eastern Studies are not a 'science' or a discipline in the Kuhnian sense." I would note that Kuhn himself was criticized for thinking that one paradigm dominates a field at any given time. Popper has argued that in some cases in the history of science there could be found several coexisting theories within one field ("Normal Science," 54).

35. Kuhn, *Structure of Scientific Revolutions,* 158. Also see King, "Reason, Tradition," 113.

36. Schatzki, "Objectivity and Rationality," 141. On the fact that scientists are communicative, see Kuhn, *Structure of Scientific Revolutions,* 177, 198, 202. In light of these considerations we may understand another difference between Bernal and Kuhn. The latter has great faith in the specialist, who is seen as the sole legitimate practitioner and executor of scientific work. He writes: "The responsibility for applying shared scientific values must be left to the specialists' group. It may not even be extended to all scientists, much less to all educated laymen, much less to the mob" ("Reflections on My Critics," 263). Bernal maintains precisely the opposite in suggesting that "informed lay" opinion is essential to the study of antiquity (see Chapter 6 below). Throughout *Black Athena* 1 Bernal recounts the ambivalence and antagonism which confronted those heretics who advanced positions closer to the Ancient Model (Heeren, Bérard, Astour, Gordon, Brown, and Bernal) (*Black Athena* 1: 297, 381–382, 420–422, 416–419, 414).

37. Dawe, "Extended Review, *144.*

38. Urry, "Thomas S. Kuhn," 471. Urry writes about Kuhn's views of scientific change: "It is an account of such change which abstracts it from the social, economic and value concerns of the encompassing society" (467). Also see Dawe, "Extended Review," 144, though it is Gutting's view that Kuhn opened up possibilities within the sociology of knowledge ("Introduction," 9, 11). In all fairness, it must be noted that Kuhn sometimes hints at the type of "truly" sociological position discussed by these writers; see, for example, Kuhn, "Reflections on My Critics," 238, and "Logic of Discovery?" 22.

39. Fuller, "Being There," 257.

40. Rabinow, *Foucault Reader,* 74. For an application of this principle to the *Black Athena* debate, see Bond and Gilliam, "Introduction," 2.

41. Harding, *Whose Science?* 98.

42. Another difference might be stated this way: For Kuhn, as Martins notes ("Kuhnian 'Revolution,'" 47), paradigms are irreversible. He writes that "once a paradigm is replaced it is never restored." This seems to conflict with Bernal's notion of a return of the Ancient Model in the body of the Revised Ancient Model. As a final difference it might be added that Kuhn seems to subscribe to the Aryan paradigm (*Structure of Scientific Revolutions,* 168).

43. *Black Athena* 1: 27, 32, 190, 208, 27. For more examples of these linkages, see 189, 210, 316, 284, 305.

44. S. Turner, *Social Theory of Practices.* It should be noted that Turner criticizes the type of "practice"-centered approach to be discussed below. And see Bohman, "Do Practices Explain Anything?"

45. Vovelle, *Ideologies and Mentalities,* 8. For some other studies of the Annales school, see the first chapter of Chartier's *Cultural History;* and Hutton, "History of Mentalities." For the initial discussion of "metaphysical paradigms," see Masterman, "Nature of a Paradigm," 65–66; Eckberg and Hill, "Paradigm Concept," 118; Polanyi, *Tacit Dimension;* Wacquant, "Towards an Archaeology of Academe," 185; Panofsky, *Gothic Architecture and Scholasticism,* 21.

46. Bourdieu, "Specificity of the Scientific Field," 279; *Outline of a Theory of Practice,* 168; *Logic of Practice,* 66; and also see his remarks on "tacit agreement" in

"Philosophical Institution," 6. As Calhoun observes, in Bourdieu's formulation *doxai* are opinions or beliefs which comprise the "taken-for-granted background conditions of life" (*Critical Social Theory*, 56, 151). Bernal himself, it should be noted, also seems to work with a general idea of *doxa*—and is aware of its Hegelian affinites—as when he points out that "the owl of Minerva flies only at dusk—that is, traditional beliefs are articulated only when they are under challenge" (*Black Athena* 1: 188). Also see Bourdieu and Passeron, "Sociology and Philosophy," 162.

47. Notice that I am positing a societywide *doxa,* not one predicated on the position of the actor within the field. So to be explicit, let me note that my conception of *doxa,* unlike Bourdieu's I would imagine, covers the field and its agents in its entirety. Bourdieu, by contrast, seems to speak of a doxa of a dominant class (Bourdieu and Wacquant, *Invitation,* 73–74).

48. Stepan and Gilman, "Appropriating the Idioms of Science," 171. The writers go on to show that the major criticisms of these approaches came from those outside the mainstream—thus, in our terms, not heretics but apostates.

49. Gould, "American Polygeny," 109, 102.

50. Marchand and Grafton, "Martin Bernal and His Critics," 6, 15, 31.

51. Also see B. M. Berger, *Essay on Culture,* 34; Bourdieu, *Outline of a Theory of Practice,* 164.

52. B. M. Berger, *Essay on Culture,* 140.

Chapter 6. A "Total Contestation"

1. This remark (from Nelson and Bérubé, "Introduction," 1) inadvertently conceals the crucial fact that this industry has been growing for a long time. As Jacoby demonstrates in *Dogmatic Wisdom,* laying siege to the ivory tower is a veritable American tradition—one that greatly predates the current round of fulmination. Also see Wacquant, "Towards an Archaeology of Academe," 185; Graff, *Beyond the Culture Wars.* For another study which argues that debates about canons and assaults on the university are nothing new, see L. Levine, *Opening of the American Mind.*

2. To borrow a few choice phrases from contemporary critics of academe: Wilshire, *Moral Collapse;* Readings, "University without Culture?"; Bloom, *Closing of the American Mind,* 347.

3. Bernal, "First by Land," 7 (emphasis added); *Black Athena* 1: 215. On the great accomplishments of Göttingen, see Bruford, *Germany in the Eighteenth Century,* 245; Schindel, "C. G. Heyne." The university itself was founded in 1737. R. S. Turner ("University Reformers," 510, 525) examines these themes of professionalism at the university. Also see La Vopa, "Specialists against Specialization."

4. For more on the professionalization of the university, see Wilshire, *Moral Collapse,* 48. It should be recalled that Göttingen's success and capacity to professionalize rendered it unique among contemporary institutions. As Palter notes, the eighteenth century was not a great time for most German institutions of higher learning ("Eighteenth-Century Historiography, *386).* F. Turner argues that Bernal has overemphasized the impact of professionalism on nineteenth-century scholarship ("Martin Bernal's *Black Athena,*" 105). For other contributions on professionalism and the university in general, see Menand, "Limits of Academic Freedom"; and *Black Athena* 1: 215. Bernal may have oversimplified some of these matters. As La Vopa shows, the early specialists endeavored to forward a highly unspecialized "soaring vision." Further, it appears that nineteenth-century German-speaking classicists themselves grew disenchanted with the overly specialized nature of their discipline ("Specialists against Specialization," 39, 27). On specialization, also see R. S. Turner, "University Reformers," 525. On professionalization, see R. S. Turner, "Historicism, *Kritik,*" 461.

5. *Black Athena* 1: 220, 281, 284, 286; Bernal, *"Black Athena* and Her Reception," 16. On state funding, see Bruford, *Germany in the Eighteenth Century,* 246. On the seminar, see Pfeiffer, *History of Classical Scholarship,* 176; and R. S. Turner, "Historicism, *Kritik,"* 460, 464, 467 (for condescension toward the lay public). On all of these mechanisms as actually helping to reduce dissent and free inquiry, see Stepan and Gilman, "Appropriating the Idioms of Science," 174.

6. *Black Athena* 1: 215; Bernal, "Black Athena Denied," 16, 17. He also points to the development of "source criticism." For more on this, see Chapter 3 above; *Black Athena* 1: 217–218; Poliakov, *History of Anti-Semitism,* 3: 177. For a discussion of these figures, see Poliakov, *Aryan Myth,* 173–174; and *History of Anti-Semitism,* 3: 135–136. On Meiners, see Blok, "Proof and Persuasion," 709.

7. Arrowsmith, *Unmodern Observations,* 307; Nietzsche, "We Classicists," 372.

8. *Black Athena* 1: 223, and 220, 288, 320, 223; Pfeiffer, *History of Classical Scholarship,* 183. Also see Bernal, "Classics in Crisis," 68; "First by Land," 7; "Paradise Glossed," 674; "Black Athena Denied," 18, 25. Also see F. Turner, *Greek Heritage,* 3. On the connection between Göttingen and Great Britain, see Butterfield, *Man on His Past,* 39. On the revolt of twentieth-century American classicists against nineteenth-century Aryan models, see M. M. Levine, "Multiculturalism and the Classics," 216.

9. *Black Athena* 1: 221, 28. Wolf coined the term *Altertumswissenschaft* (Pfeiffer, *History of Classical Scholarship,* 173–177). Also to be mentioned are Franz Bopp, founder of comparative Indo-European linguistics; see Schlerath, "Franz Bopp," 7, 10. For Ernst Curtius, see Chambers, "Ernst Curtius"; On Müller, see Unte, "Karl Otfried Müller."

10. F. Turner, *Greek Heritage,* 4–5. Also see F. Turner, "Martin Bernal's *Black Athena,* 108. On these class aspects, also see Bernal, *"Black Athena* and the APA," 29; "Black Athena Denied," 28; Haley, "Black Feminist Thought and Classics," 23. For eighteenth-century Göttingen, see Bruford, *Germany in the Eighteenth Century,* 237.

11. Bernal, "Greece: Aryan or Mediterranean?" 4. Also see Bernal, "Classics in Crisis," 69.

12. On the constraining aspects of disciplinarity, see Redfield, "Classics and Anthropology," 10. Also see Damrosch, *We Scholars,* 24, 29.

13. On the debilitating effects of paradigms, see *Black Athena* 1: 138.

14. On the possibility of "a new combined discipline" which includes classics but does not privilege its theoretical and methodological prerogatives, see Bernal, "Classics in Crisis," 74. Bernal's hope for a field which integrates all of the traditional disciplines of antiquity is seconded by classicist M. M. Levine, "Multiculturalism and the Classics," 218, 220. Sprinkled throughout volumes 1 and 2 are references to classicists who ignored or demeaned the research of nonclassicists (Semitists, Latinists, Egyptologists) who "encroached" upon their field. The author points to the existence of an implicit university pecking order in which scholars of Greek antiquity were permitted to make all definitive judgments on the veracity of any given scholarship pertaining to the ancient Mediterranean (*Black Athena* 1: 266, 420). Bernal argues that after 1880 the field of Egyptology was relegated to a subordinate position vis-à-vis Indo-European studies (138, 225). Also see Bernal, *Cadmean Letters,* 15; Poliakov, *Aryan Myth,* 256.

15. *Black Athena* 2: 34, 208; *Black Athena* 1: 3. The classics establishment, for Bernal, is the exemplar of an insider's network. The requirement that the prospective student master languages is seen as "a very effective barrier to keep out strangers, who have not been properly taught the ways in which the members of the discipline think" ("Classics in Crisis," 68). I would like to qualify Bernal's use of the term *conservative.* When the author speaks of this characteristic as being manifest in scholars, he is not necessarily referring to their political positions. While

it is true that many of the founders of *Altertumswissenschaft* were conservatives in the strict political sense (e.g., maintaining a Burkean abhorrence of the French Revolution), this does not apply to all of those insiders lambasted on the pages of *Black Athena*. See, for example, *Black Athena* 1: 288, and *Black Athena* 2: xx.

16. *Black Athena* 2: 274, 288.
17. Mills, "Social Role of the Intellectual," 297. Also see remarks on Durkheim by Bourdieu and Passeron, "Sociology and Philosophy in France," 170.
18. Bourdieu, *Homo Academicus*, 86. Compare this to Jacoby, *Last Intellectuals*, 145.
19. Bourdieu, *Homo Academicus*, 97 (emphasis added), 56, 143.
20. *Black Athena* 1: 427.
21. Coser, *Men of Ideas*, 282. Or, in Jacoby's words, "Any young academic who frontally challenges the discipline will be shown the door" (*Last Intellectuals*, 158).
22. *Black Athena* 1: 423, 276. *Black Athena* itself, the author charges, was a victim of the type of censorship discussed in this passage; see *Black Athena* 2: xvii, and "*Black Athena* and Her Reception," 20–21. Compare this with Bourdieu's remarks on "the established scientific order" in "Specificity of the Scientific Field," 271.
23. Bernal, "Afrocentric Interpretation of History," 87. Also see *Black Athena* 1: 271.
24. *Black Athena* 1: 3.
25. Coser, *Functions of Social Conflict*, 70 (emphasis added).
26. Kuhn, *Structure of Scientific Revolutions*, 67.
27. See, for example, Jacoby's remarks on this issue in *Dogmatic Wisdom*, 185; and Haskell, "Justifying the Rights," 60.
28. Carruthers, "Outside Academia," 471.
29. Simmel, *Essays on Religion*, 114–115.
30. Bourdieu, "Specificity of the Scientific Field," 272.
31. Bernal, "*Black Athena* and the APA," 33. In a 1996 speech, Bernal refined this model and described the standard academic response to the heretic: "ignore, dismiss, attack and absorb" ("*Black Athena* and Her Reception"). On "ignore," see *Black Athena* 2: 235, 469; *Black Athena* 1: 273, 399, 414, 428. Also see Bernal on the reception of George Bass's work ("*Black Athena* and Her Reception," 20), and Bass himself on problems of this nature ("Responses").
32. Bourdieu and Passeron, "Introduction," 8; Menand, "Limits of Academic Freedom," 8.
33. As opposed to a contribution *within* the established paradigmatic framework, laypersons introduce new paradigms. As nonacademicians, they are unfamiliar with the tenets of the old paradigm (*Black Athena* 1: 5, 6, 405); Cohen, "Interview," 16.
34. The closest I have come to finding a written statement of this sentiment is in Kuhn's *Structure of Scientific Revolutions* (168). Bernal is certainly aware that this ethos is correlated with the rise of Classical philology in the eighteenth century, among members of the Göttingen faculty, a fact he learned from R. S. Turner, "Historicism, Kritic," 467.
35. *Black Athena* 2: xxi, xvii.
36. Let us not forget that this sort of engagement with a general public is fraught with professional dangers as well. As Jacoby noted in *Last Intellectuals* (136–137), scholars who do find an interested public are often rewarded by being denied tenure. Also see Jacoby, *Dogmatic Wisdom*, 160.
37. *Black Athena* 1: 6, 5.
38. Ibid., 417 (emphasis in original); also see 438.
39. In volume 1 Bernal notes that "it is only when he or she has a wider, public status that the academic heretic can have any hope of publishing their 'unsound' ideas" (381).
40. Cohen, "Interview," 9. Also see *Black Athena* 2: xviii; Coleman, "Did Egypt Shape the Glory That Was Greece?" 291; M. M. Levine, "Review Article," 451. And

for a discussion of the strategy involved, see *Black Athena* 1: 381; and Bernal, "Responses to *Black Athena*," 66.

41. Lyotard, *Postmodern Condition*, 67.
42. Foucault, "Intellectuals and Power," 207.
43. These feminist pedagogies and the postmodern epistemologies have, in many cases, influenced one another to a great extent. Wyer and O'Barr, *Engaging Feminism*, 9. The authors of the widely read *Women's Ways of Knowing: The Development of Self, Voice, and Mind* subscribe to a similar approach. They suggest a model of "the teacher as midwife," in which the pedagogue focuses on not his or her own unique insights and erudition, "but the student's knowledge" (Belenky et al., *Women's Ways of Knowing*, 218). For a critique of this text and this particular approach, see Patai and Koertge, *Professing Feminism*, 161–167. For Afrocentric versions, see Schiele, "Afrocentricity," 157; Kershaw, "Afrocentrism," 163.
44. See, for example, Vermeule's remarks in "World Turned Upside Down" (271) and Weinstein, "Review of *Black Athena* 2," 383. The only other critic who touches on the critique of the university, albeit briefly, is the Israeli scholar Yacov Shavit in "Anti-University Intellectuals" (in Hebrew).
45. Palter, "Eighteenth-Century Historiography," 350–351.
46. Ibid., 353–359.
47. Ibid., 359.
48. Ibid., 350.
49. Ibid., 367 (emphasis in original).
50. Ibid., 377 (emphasis in original).
51. Ibid., 378, 380–382. Palter also argues (382) that Bernal has misunderstood the reasons behind Heyne's eventual break with Forster. See *Black Athena* 1: 222, for the original argument.
52. In fact, according to Palter, another anonymous critique of Meiners's racist views appeared two years prior to Forster's, in May 1789 ("Eighteenth-Century Historiography," 380 and n.63). Palter does not ask if all this anonymity is suggestive of the relative power of Meiners, the power of racist ideology, or both.
53. Ibid., 371.
54. Ibid., 378. For Bernal's treatment of Blumenbach, see *Black Athena* 1: 219–221, 27–28. As Rose observes in *Revolutionary Antisemitism*, "Blumenbach and Darwin, for example, had a great impact on German racist antisemitism, but they themselves were not at all anti-Jewish in their opinions" (13–14). See Palter, "Hume and Prejudice," for a similar defense of a maligned thinker.
55. Georg Forster's anonymous critique of Meiners is truly remarkable. That such an impassioned and principled statement of cultural relativism could be made in this period is astonishing, and we owe a debt of gratitude to Professor Palter for bringing this obscure document to our attention in "Eighteenth-Century Historiography" (Forster even seems to approximate the Ancient Model on page 240). Yet it must be stressed that Forster refers to Jews only in passing (242) and makes no specific references to anti-Semitism in this article. The essay can be found in Fiedler, *Georg Forsters Werke*.
56. Ahmad, *In Theory*, 173. On the Said-Lewis debate, see Prakash, "*Orientalism* Now."
57. Lefkowitz and Rogers, "Preface," x; L. P. Williams, "Why I Stopped Reading *Black Athena*."
58. F. Turner, "Martin Bernal's *Black Athena*," 104.
59. See B. Lewis, "Question of Orientalism," and Said's response in "Orientalism: An Exchange."
60. Bernal, "*Black Athena* and the APA," 26.
61. Ibid., 27, 30, 20; Bernal, "Response to Jonathan Hall," 275; "Response" (*Journal of Women's History*), 120; "Response to Robert Palter," 445; "Response to Josine Blok," 209.

62. *Black Athena* 1: 73, also see xii; Bernal, "Response to Robert Palter," 451; "Image of Ancient Greece," 127; "Response to Jonathan Hall," 276, though this position is somewhat difficult to reconcile with Bernal's claim in volume 2 that "a scholar should try as far as possible to detach her or his historical interpretation from any ideological preferences" (359). Also see Bernal, "Afrocentric Interpretation," 94.

63. Nietzsche, "History in the Service," 87.

64. Bernal, *"Black Athena* and the APA," 25. By 1997, after having been rather battered by the critique of specialists, Bernal would now posit the importance of a symbiotic relation between specialist and generalist ("Response to Josine Blok," 217).

65. Bernal, "Response to Robert Palter," 445; Palter, "Professor Palter Comments." Bernal was responding to Palter's article, *"Black Athena,* Afrocentrism, and the History of Science."

Chapter 7. The Academic Elvis

1. Lefkowitz, *Not Out of Africa,* 156. In an earlier contribution Lefkowitz writes, "His intellectual standards are higher than most of his fellow Afrocentrists" ("Not Out of Africa," 35). Also see D'Souza, *Illiberal Education,* 116, 117; Rogers, "Freedom in the Making of Western Culture," 88. Snowden ("Bernal's 'Blacks,'" 115) refers to "the Bernal-Afrocentrist approach" (also see 118).

2. Bernal remarks, "And I have much more sympathy for Afrocentricity, though I'm not an Afrocentrist myself" (Dyson, "On *Black Athena,*" 56). Also see Cohen, "Interview," 7; Bernal, "Roots," 5; "Questioning the History," B4; and Baldini, "Classici d'Egitto," 117. Lefkowitz's article in which the charge was made was entitled "Not Out of Africa."

3. M. M. Levine, "Review Article," 453.

4. Morris, "Legacy of *Black Athena,*" 172, though Morris adds that Bernal's bolstering was "not anticipated by the author" (173). Also see Snowden, "Bernal's 'Blacks,'" 118; Brace et al., "Clines and Clusters," 156; Pounder, "History without Rules," 463; Bowersock, "Rescuing the Greeks," 6. An article in the *Chronicle of Higher Education* points out that this text "has been taken up eagerly by black scholars who teach and conduct research from an Afrocentric perspective" (Coughlin, "In Multiculturalism Debate," A5). And see Beidelman, "Promoting African Art," 10.

5. Drake, *Black Folk,* 1: xvii; also see 1, 2, 32. On the prevalence of the theme of "Negro improvement," see Moses, *Wings of Ethiopa,* 103. The lack of interest in modern Africa will be explained in Dickson Bruce's remarks below.

6. On "Ethiopianism," see Moses, *Golden Age,* 156–169; Moses, *Wings of Ethiopa,* 102–103; Bruce, "Ancient Africa," 687; Drake, *Black Folk,* 1: 32; Drake, "African Diaspora," 37.

7. Drake, *Black Folk,* 1: 131; also see Drake, "African Diaspora," 37.

8. Drake, *Black Folk,* 1: 130.

9. Moses observes that this was "the first black newspaper in the United States" ("In Fairness to Afrocentrism," 16). Carruthers ("Outside Academia," 459) has identified an even earlier defense of this position, albeit outside of the United States. Carruthers cites David Nicholls's study of Haitian independence movements in the early nineteenth century, *From Dessalines.* Nicholls writes that the Haitian baron de Vastey "replied to those enemies of the black race . . . [that] these propagandists had forgotten that Africa was the cradle of the sciences and of the arts. . . . Egypt was the first civilized country in the world" (44–45). Walker's speech appears in Stuckey, *Ideological Origins,* 47. Also see Drake, *Black Folk,* 1: 130.

10. Walker, cited in Stuckey, *Ideological Origins,* 58.

11. Pennington, *Text Book,* 48; also see 12, 21, 22.

12. Douglass, cited in Foner, *Life and Writings of Frederick Douglass,* 2: 301 (emphasis in original).

13. Blyden et al., *People of Africa*, 9; Delany, *Principia of Ethnology* 68.

14. G. W. Williams, *History of the Negro Race*, 22. For more on Williams, see Bruce, "Ancient Africa," 686. For another example of the vindicationist approach, see the writings of Alexander Crummell, *Destiny and Race*, 202.

15. G. W. Williams, *History of the Negro Race*, 15. Also see Drake, "African Diaspora," 20. We see the insights of the nineteenth-century writers consolidated and served up in appropriate pedagogical form in Johnson's 1911 *School History of the Negro Race in America*. Johnson opens his study by noting: "*The pyramids of Egypt*, the great temples on the Nile, were either built by Negroes or people closely related to them. *All the science and learning* of ancient Greece and Rome was, probably, once in the hands of the foreparents of the American slaves. They are, then, descendants of a race of people once the most powerful on earth, the race of the Pharaohs" (9; emphasis in original).

16. *Black Athena* 1: 242. For a discussion of this problematic surmise, see the next chapter. For a critique of both Bernal and Drake, see Shack, "Construction of Antiquity," 114, 116. Not all African-Americans in this period maintained this enthusiasm for Africa; See Drake, *Black Folk*, 1: 117–121. For comprehensive discussions of nineteenth-century African-Americans who engaged these issues, see Bruce, "Ancient Africa"; Hilliard, "Bringing Maat"; and Spady, "Afro-American Historical Society." The analysis forwarded here leans heavily on the bibliographical sources they cite.

17. Mercer Cook, in C. A. Diop, *African Origin of Civilization*, xi. See Mudimbe, *Idea of Africa*, 23–26, for a discussion of some of Diop's intellectual precursors.

18. Houessou-Adin, "Big Con," 185. Asante, *Kemet*, v; and "Ideological Significance," 9. For a similar identification, see Leonard Jeffries cited in Cottman, "Campus 'Radicals,'" 29; Winters, "Afrocentrism," 171.

19. See Finch, "Meeting the Pharaoh," 28. Finch notes that Diop "must be considered the 'Pharaoh' of Afro-centric or Kamitic studies." B. Diop ("L'Antiquité africaine," 143) cautions that Cheikh Anta Diop might have disapproved of this moniker. The poems can be found in the *Journal of African Civilizations* 8 (1986), and are reprinted in Van Sertima and Williams, *Great African Thinkers*. Another special issue devoted to Diop's work was published by the journal *Présence Africaine*, no. 149–150 (1989). Finch, "Further Conversations," 227. For other appreciative readings, see Ampim, "Problem," 197; J. D. Walker, "Misrepresentation of Diop's Views"; Hilliard, "Bringing Maat," 132, 139; and "Cultural Unity," 103; Clarke, "Cheikh Anta Diop"; Carew, "Conversations with Diop and Tsegaye," 26; Spady, "Dr. Cheikh Anta Diop"; Clarke, "Historical Legacy"; Asante, "More Thoughts," 11; Obenga, "Propos préliminaire"; D.Diop, "Réflexions"; Case and Case, "L'héritage égyptien." For gentle criticism, but criticism nonetheless, of Diop, see Okafor, "Diop and the African Origin of Civilization"; and J. D. Walker, "Misrepresentation." For less appreciative reviews of Diop's work, see Jewsiewicki and Mudimbe, "Africans' Memories"; Mauny, "Nations, nègres et culture"; Appiah, "Europe Upside Down"; Lefkowitz, *Not Out of Africa*, 16–24, 157–160; Snowden, "Bernal's 'Blacks,'" 116–119.

20. Asante, *Kemet*, 117; and *Afrocentricity*, 16. Though in *Afrocentricity* (1) Asante refers to Du Bois as a "great prophet." Diop's interdisciplinarity, incidentally, was to have a profound affect on Afrocentrism. In *Kemet, Afrocentricity and Knowledge*, Asante speaks of the "the integration of all methods advanced by human beings into the intellectual inquiry" (36). Lam, "Égypte ancienne," 209; Okafor, "Diop and the African Origin of Civilization," 264.

21. Du Bois, *World and Africa*, 117, 99. Later on he argues that the Egyptians were Negroids (106, 105). Van Sertima, "Introduction," 8; C. A. Diop, "Beginnings of Man," 335. Asante speaks of "the organic, Diopian unity of African thought, symbols, and ritual concepts to their classical origins" (*Kemet*, 56). Also see

Clarke, "Cheikh Anta Diop," 115; Van Sertima, "Editorial," 3, 4; C. A. Diop, "Origin of the Ancient Egyptians"; and *Civilization or Barbarism*, 214–216.

22. See C. A. Diop, *African Origin of Civilization*, 50, 129; *Civilization or Barbarism*, 17; "Origin of the Ancient Egyptians," 15–16. Also see Spady, "Dr. Cheikh Anta Diop," 307; Okafor, "Diop and the African Origin of Civilization," 257; Diop, *African Origin of Civilization*, 166; on his definition of "Negro," see 136. Sources of possible crossbreeding are postulated as the Hyksos (209) and "white-skinned people" in the thirteenth century (213; and see 239, 131). Du Bois, *The Negro*, 14, 17. Also see Moses, *Golden Age* (145) on Du Bois's beliefs regarding race in ancient Egypt.

23. See Diop's interview with Finch, "Further Conversations," 235–236. Also see C. A. Diop, *Civilization or Barbarism*, 2, 16, 17, 67; and Diop and Obenga's responses as reported in Mokhtar, *General History of Africa*, 51. Also see Ampim, "Problem," 194. See the next chapter for a discussion of the turn away from "race" in scholarly research.

24. Moses, *Golden Age*, 133, 25. Also see Stepan and Gilman, "Appropriating the Idioms," 182; Toll, "Pluralism and Moral Force," 96–97; Appiah, "Ancestral Voices," 89.

25. Du Bois, *World and Africa*, 126, 105; Diop, *Civilization or Barbarism*, 152. On the notion or intimation of stolen culture, see Diop's remarks in Finch, "Interview with Cheikh Anta Diop," 232, 233; S. Moore, "Interview with Cheikh Anta Diop," 239, 241; Lefkowitz, *Not Out of Africa*, 131–132. The most powerful statement of this view can be found in a text well known to Diop—*The Stolen Legacy*, by George G. M. James.

26. Du Bois, *World and Africa*, 99, 118. Diop, *African Origin of Civilization*, xiv. In chapters with titles like "Modern Falsification of History," Diop would criticize the writings of (usually francophone) Egyptologists and physical anthropologists. Also see 45, 64, and 133, where Diop exclaims, "It is an intellectual swindle." *Civilization or Barbarism*, 1, 3, 16; Finch, "Meeting the Pharaoh," 33; Asante, *Kemet*, 44, 60.

27. Appiah, "Europe Upside Down," 24. Adopting a similar view, C. Walker writes, "Ultimately, Afrocentrism is Eurocentrism in blackface" ("Distortions," 35). Also see Watts, "Identity and the Status," 358; Schlesinger, *Disuniting of America*, 124; Savino, "Di che colore è la pelle di Ulisse"; C. A. Diop, "Origin of the Ancient Egyptians," 31; and his interview with the Nile Valley Executive Committee, in Van Sertima and Williams, *Great African Thinkers*, 288. Also see C. A. Diop, *Civilization or Barbarism*, 214; Asante, "African American Studies." 26. Gray, *Conceptions of History*, 20.

28. Afrocentrists, however, vehemently contest the proposition that they are Eurocentrists in reverse. See Houessou-Adin, "Big Con"; Hoskins, "Eurocentrism vs. Afrocentrism"; Asante, "African American Studies," 22; and "Afrocentic Idea in Education," 171; Winbush, "Anxiety and Afrocentricity," 33.

29. C. A. Diop, *African Origin of Civilization*, xiv; also see "Origin of the Ancient Egyptians," 32; "Beginnings of Man," 349.

30. Marable, *W.E.B. Du Bois*, 99, also see 92.

31. M. Washington, "Revitalizing," 111; also see White, "Civilization Denied," 38; Harding, *"Racial" Economy of Science*, 27; Johnson-Odim, "Comment," 88; Beidelman, "Promoting African Art," 10.

32. Asante, *Kemet*, 117; Ampim, "Problem," 198. Also see Gray, *Conceptions of History*, 68, who argues that Bernal proffered a similarly incomplete treatment of Diop's work. And see Carruthers's remarks below.

33. As we saw above, Herodotus's observations on the Egyptians, Colchians, and Sesòstris were examined by the nineteenth-century vindicationists. They also figured in Diop's work; see, for example, *African Origin of Civilization*, 1; and "Origin of the Ancient Egyptians," 21. Among Afrocentrists a similar respect for

Herodotus is seen (Asante, *Kemet*, 121; Okafor, "Diop and the African Origin of Civlization," 258). Diop's examination of these issues is made throughout *Civilization or Barbarism*; see, for example, 83, 84, 151, 21, 71, 203; also see *African Origin of Civilization*, 110, though for Diop the Phoenicians are seen as having originally been black (108). As for the Hellenistic and Classical sources, see Diop, "Origin of the Ancient Egyptians," 21–27. Bernal, however, does not use these sources in an identical manner to Diop, and he makes use of many writers not studied by Diop (also see Lefkowitz, *Not Out of Africa*, 23). Mudimbe points to another difference: Bernal concentrates on "diffusionist patterns that originated from Egypt toward the north, the west, and the east," while Diop concentrates on "interactions between the south and the north" (*Idea of Africa*, 102, 24).

34. The vindicationists, however, concentrated on Egyptologists while Bernal primarily attacks the classics establishment.

35. Also see Mudimbe, *Idea of Africa*, 101. Davidson writes that Bernal leaves "one without the slightest indication of the fact that the study of African history and humanity, in many disciplines, has become the concern of manifold colleges and universities in all the continents, not least in Africa itself" ("Ancient World and Africa," 10). Bernal ignored an even more detailed study of the Greek sources, conducted by William Leo Hansberry, a professor of classics at Howard University. The reader of his elegant studies will find an analysis of Greek sources pertaining to Ethiopia far more comprehensive than that found in *Black Athena*. Hansberry's *Africa and Africans as Seen by Classical Writers* was edited by Joseph Harris. For more on Hansberry, see Spady, "Dr. Cheikh Anta Diop." While Hansberry's work is listed in Bernal's bibliography, it is never mentioned in the body of his text. The same could be said about Bernal's treatment of George Wells Parker's works, such as *The Children of the Sun* and "The African Origin of the Grecian Civilization." *Black Athena* 1: 401.

36. Bernal, "Response" (*Journal of Women's History*), 130.

37. Dyson, "On *Black Athena*," 60; Carruthers, "Outside Academia," 469. Hilliard, in "Bringing Maat," warmly receives Bernal's text but nevertheless delineates one of the major differences between *Black Athena*'s approach and Afrocentric history: "Bernal has done an excellent job of documenting what he called the fabrication of information about KMT [Egypt], not the assertion that KMT was a black nation, a position that he never takes" (131).

38. Winters, "Afrocentrism," 176.

39. See Obenga quoted in Mokhtar, *General History of Africa*, 2: 51. On the other hand, Asante has expressed his reservations about "race" (Asante, *Afrocentricity*, 94–98; and *Kemet*, 17). *Black Athena* 1: 241. See the next chapter for a full discussion of race and its demerits.

40. *Black Athena* 1: 12, 15, 14. On this issue, see Yurco, "*Black Athena*," 67–68; C. A. Diop, *African Origin of Civilization*, 100–128; Van Sertima, "Editorial," 14; Newton, "Updated Working Chronology," 409; Carruthers, "Outside Academia," 467, 471.

41. Martin, *Jewish Onslaught*, 57–58. On the controversy surrounding Martin and his work, see Rogers, "Racism and Antisemitism in the Classroom."

42. Ampim, "Problem," 194, 195.

43. For examples of these types of claims, see Verharen, "Afrocentrism and Acentrism," 67; Winters, "Afrocentrism," 176, 178; C. A. Diop, *African Origin of Civilization*, 108. Also see Brunson, "African Presence."

44. Winters, "Afrocentrism," 175.

45. Asante, *Kemet*, 100–104. Also see Hilliard, "Bringing Maat." On the monolithism of Afrocentric thought, see Winbush, "Anxiety and Afrocentricity"; Hall, "Beyond Afrocentrism." For an interesting analysis of Afrocentrism, see Early, "Anatomy of Afrocentrism," 12; Early et al., "Symposium," Bernal, "Afrocentric Interpretation of History," 86; Glazer, *We Are All Multiculturalists Now*, 30.

46. Many of these reports have centered around Leonard Jeffries of City College. See Gourevitch, "Jeffries Affair"; Magner, "Politicians Press Officials"; DeParle, "For Some Blacks"; Traub, *City on a Hill*; Pooley, "Doctor J"; G. Himmelfarb, "Academic Advocates"; Asante, *Afrocentricity*, 109, 113.

47. Lefkowitz, *Not Out of Africa*, 8. Also see Rogers, "Racism and Antisemitism in the Classroom."

48. Bruce, "Ancient Africa," 695.

49. Weber, "Science as a Vocation," 147. See Kagan, "Stealing History"; T. Carson, "Greece Is the Word"; Palaima, "Corcyraeanization"; Griffin, "Anxieties of Influence"; Elson, "Attacking Afrocentrism."

50. Hart, "Review of *Not Out of Africa*," F-4.

51. Bernal, "Black Athena: The African and Levantine Roots of Greece."

52. See Bernal, "Afrocentric Interpretation of History"; Cohen, "Interview," 7; *Black Athena* 1: 38. And see Bernal's qualifier in *"Black Athena* and the APA," 32.

53. Du Bois, *Souls of Black Folk*, 1. Whether Afrocentrists seek this sort of visibility, and through this particular vehicle no less, is a question which I will leave in abeyance.

54. Carruthers, "Outside Academia," 462.

55. This term, in fact, was coined by Bernal himself, who used it in public lectures as well as in a private communication with the author.

56. Snowden, "Bernal's 'Blacks,'" 116. Aune ("Review of *Black Athena*, Volumes 1 and 2," 120) points out that Bernal is "the first 'mainstream' white scholar to draw attention to the remarkable body of literature about the 'stolen legacy' of African/Egyptian culture."

57. Early, "Anatomy of Afrocentrism," 12.

58. Bernal, *"Black Athena* and the APA," 20.

59. Carruthers, "Outside Academia," 462–463.

Chapter 8. Reconfiguring the Ancient Egyptians

1. Or, what Appiah and Gates have called "the holy trinity of literary criticism" ("Editors' Introduction," 1). On the lack of discussion pertaining to class, see, for example, Glazer, *We Are All Multiculturalists Now*, 16.

2. Trigger, "Brown Athena," 122; and *History of Archaeological Thought*, 417.

3. See Begley et al., "Out of Egypt, Greece"; Bernal, *Black Athena* 2: xxi.

4. Bernal, *Black Athena* 1: 241–242 (emphasis added). Also see Dyson, "On *Black Athena*," 60. For Bernal's most recent statement on this issue, see "Responses to *Black Athena*," 78–80.

5. Bernal, *"Black Athena* and the APA," 30. And for a similar claim see "Response" (*Arethusa*), 316. For those who accused Bernal of positing a black Egypt, see Vermeule, "World Turned Upside Down," 273; Poliakoff, "Roll Over Aristotle," 23; Bard, "Ancient Egyptians," 104; Muhly, *"Black Athena* versus Traditional Scholarship," 100; Gress, "Case against Bernal," 39. In an interview with Dyson, Bernal notes that "blacks had considerable power" in Egypt ("On *Black Athena*, 56). Grottanelli, "La grande conguira degli storici bianchi," 45. The association of "black" with Egypt is often made by Bernal. He attributed the rise of the Aryan Model to the desire of European thinkers "to keep black Africans as far as possible from European civilization" (*Black Athena* 1: 30 [emphasis in original]; also see 384). It could be countered that Bernal is referring to the perceptions of some scholars that the Egyptians might be black, and he is thus making no final judgment as to their phenotype. I do not think this is the case, as indicated by the references cited below. Also see Bernal's remarks on the blackness of Twelfth Dynasty rulers and similar considerations based on an analysis of portraiture vis-à-vis Eighteenth Dynasty monarchs (*Black Athena* 1: 384). And in the second volume, see 181, 189, 249, 250, 259, 268, 271, 338, 444, 475.

6. See, for example, Bernal's remarks in the passage cited above; "Response to Jonathan Hall" (275–276); Dyson, "On *Black Athena*," 56, 57; *Black Athena* 1: 242. On the problematic concept of race, see Marshall, "Racial Classifications," 116, 117, 118, 125; Also see Zack, *Race and Mixed Race*; Montagu, *Concept of Race*. Of course, none of this explains why Bernal referred to only the First, Eleventh, Twelfth, and Eighteenth dynasties as black. For, using the "one drop" rule as a reference point, we would assume that most Egyptian rulers could receive this designation; we must wonder why other pharaohs of other dynasties could not be called black as well. If they were indeed emerging from a mixed population, then in all likelihood they too would be seen as black by American standards. Tritle ("Vision or Dream?" 308) has pointed out that Bernal uses the term pharaoh inaccurately, insofar as it is "a New Kingdom term, one inappropriate to earlier periods of Egyptian history."

7. See, for example, Griffin, "Who Are These Coming to the Sacrifice?" 27; Bernal, "Response" (*Arethusa*), 316. There are other unresolved issues raised by the passage quoted above. To say that rulers of a particular dynasty are "black" is to leave in abeyance the question of the population at large. It is certainly not unprecedented to find that the ruling class of a society will differ from the masses they rule in terms of language, culture, genetic affinities, and so on. As such, we are left with an image of "black" pharaohs ruling over a mixed population of "African, South-West Asian and Mediterranean types."

8. A brief sampling of views on Bernal's reflections on Africa: Keita observes that "his belief that ancient Egypt was fundamentally African is correct, but he seems reluctant to support this aggressively using cultural and biological data" (*"Black Athena"* 311, also see 300, 301); Brace et al. see this reference as "misleadingly simplistic," arguing that in the Classical world there were three distinct Africas ("Clines and Clusters," 156); Vermeule writes that Bernal "wants Egyptian culture to be an undifferentiated part of African culture" ("World Turned Upside Down," 274). Also see Rogers, "Quo Vadis?" 448–449; Griffin, "Who Are These Coming to the Sacrifice?" 27; Poliakoff, "Roll Over Aristotle,' 23; and Bernal's further remarks on this issue, "Response" (*Arethusa*), 317; "*Black Athena* and the APA," 30–32. Some clarity on this issue comes in a 1990 selection where Bernal remarks that: (1) Egypt is on the African continent, (2) Egyptians spoke an Afroasiatic language, and (3) Egypt, unlike the Maghreb, is "connected to East and Central Africa by the Nile" ("Responses to Critical Reviews of *Black Athena*," 133).

9. See Snowden, "Bernal's 'Blacks,' Herodotus," 83; Herodotus, *Histories* 2.104.

10. See, for example, Snowden's 1993 "Response" to Keita. Snowden does not seem to respond directly to Keita's challenges. On this trend in the culture wars in general, see Goodheart, "Reflections on the Culture Wars."

11. Bernal, *Black Athena* 1: 435, 436. For Afrocentric reactions, see Carruthers, "Outside Academia," 470.

12. Snowden, *Before Color Prejudice*, 108; also see 58, 59, 63, 70–71, 99); *Blacks in Antiquity*, 216–218; "Response," 327; *Blacks in Antiquity*, ix. On Bernal's treatment of Snowden, see Kelly ("Egyptians and Ethiopians" 80), who remarks, "Is this not an example of the racism that Bernal elsewhere so piously deplores: an outstanding black classicist is viewed as an Uncle Tom because his scholarly conclusions are somehow 'white'!"

13. Snowden, "Bernal's 'Blacks' and the Afrocentrists," 115, 116, 113, 127. In the account that follows I am drawing out the main themes of Snowden's three major articles pertaining to *Black Athena*.

14. Snowden, "Bernal's 'Blacks' and the Afrocentrists," (emphasis added), 114 also see 118; "Response," 320—though the Ethiopians of the classical texts do not refer to populations inhabiting modern-day Ethiopia (*Blacks in Antiquity*, vii, 8–14); "Bernal's 'Blacks,' Herodotus," 84; and ""Bernal's 'Blacks' and the Afrocentrists,"

114. For an earlier approach somewhat reminiscent of Snowden's coupling, see Beardsley, *Negro in Greek and Roman Civilization,* xii.

15. Snowden, "Bernal's 'Blacks,' Herodotus," 85; "Response," 320; "Bernal's 'Blacks' and the Afrocentrists," 114. On the Egyptians as an "intermediate population," see Snowden, "Bernal's 'Blacks,' Herodotus," 92, 91. Here he again notes that there were "mixed black-white elements in the population of Egypt and northwest Africa . . . attested by the classical sources." And see Snowden's rebuttal to Keita pertaining to this charge, "Response," 325. Somewhat confusingly, by his 1996 contribution Snowden begins to discuss Nubians far more extensively than in his previous two contributions and speaks of "a mixed Egyptian-Nubian element in the population of Egypt at least as early as the middle of the third millennium B.C.E., and interracial intermingling continued as black soldiers increasingly served in the Egyptian army, married Egyptian women, and sired racially mixed children" ("Bernal's 'Blacks' and the Afrocentrists," 115). Also see *Blacks in Antiquity,* 4, 8. As we shall see momentarily, this view would be harshly criticized by Keita.

16. Snowden, "Bernal's 'Blacks,' Herodotus," 92, 89, 91; "Bernal's 'Blacks' and the Afrocentrists," 115. Also see O'Connor, "Ancient Egypt."

17. Snowden, "Bernal's 'Blacks,' Herodotus," 86, 87, 88; *Blacks in Antiquity,* 6. In 1989 (*"Black Athena* and the APA," 30), Bernal would charge Snowden with terminological inaccuracy, noting that there were two distinct Ethiopias in the world view of the Classical writers. For an alternative explanation of the origins of the Colchians, see Yurco, "*Black Athena,*" 82–83. On the question of the blackness of the Colchians also see Armayor, "Did Herodotus Ever Go to the Black Sea?" 57–62.

18. "*Black Athena* and the APA," 31; also see Bernal, "Response" (*Arethusa*), 316.

19. Keita, "*Black Athena,*" 298, also see 295.

20. Ibid., 298–299, 297, 312, 301.

21. On Snowden's use of outdated paradigms, see ibid., 299. In a response to Keita, Snowden countered by noting that the Classical writers showed awareness of both hypotheses—that is, the belief that the intermediate phenotype was (a) a mixture between blacks and whites, or (b) the environment influenced physical characteristics (Snowden, "Response," 324–326). This, however, does not seem to answer Keita's charge that Snowden himself uses outdated theories. For another refutation of the notion of crossbreeding between black and white populations, see Brace et al., "Clines and Clusters," 147; Keita, "Response to Bernal and Snowden," 330. Many would agree with Keita in noting that black-white intermixture is not necessarily responsible for the Egyptian phenotype. See Brace et al., "Clines and Clusters," 153, 158; Davidson, "Ancient World and Africa," 11; MacGaffey, "Concepts of Race," 16; M. M. Levine, "Review Article," 456 n. 55.

22. In a response to Keita, Snowden engaged few of his substantive points. The latter repeatedly argues that the former "virtually ignores ancient sources and the information provided by Greek and Roman authors relating to the physical characteristics of African blacks ("Response," 319, 322). Suddenly, Snowden emerges as an idiosyncratic ancient on the order of Martin Bernal! Snowden proceeds to reiterate his arguments about Ethiopians, albeit without addressing Keita's charge that these views are based on outdated and disproven assumptions. Snowden does, however, cite a passage from his *Blacks in Antiquity* (14, 7–8, which Keita seemed unaware of) which suggests that his definition of the Negro in antiquity is far less narrow than Keita made it seem (324). See Keita, "Response to Bernal and Snowden," 330, 332, 333; "*Black Athena,*" 311; Johnson-Odim, "Comment," 87.

23. Bard, "Ancient Egyptians," 106, 108; Keita, "*Black Athena,*" 298; Brace et al., "Clines and Clusters," 162; Yurco, "Were the Ancient Egyptians Black or White?" 24, 29; Tritle, "Vision or Dream?" 312. On the uselessness of the concept of race, see Bard, "Ancient Egyptians," 104; Brace et al., "Clines and Clusters," 130, 139, 162;

Keita, *"Black Athena,"* 295, 297, 311. On the search for genetic affinity, see Brace et al. (on "morphological proximity"), "Clines and Clusters," 139, 162; Bard, "Ancient Egyptians," 105; Keita, *"Black Athena,"* 297.

24. Bard, "Ancient Egyptians," 111 (emphasis added); though Yurco in the same volume writes of the possibility of a sub-Saharan element (*"Black Athena,"* 66–67); Bard, "Ancient Egyptians," 106, 107, 109. For Keita, conversely, the Egyptian portraiture reveals them to be East African ("Response to Bernal and Snowden," 330).

25. See, for example, Snowden, "Bernal's 'Blacks,' Herodotus," 89. Also see O'Connor, "Ancient Egypt"; Tritle "Vision or Dream?" 312; Baines, "Was Civilization Made in Africa?" 13.

26. Bard, "Ancient Egyptians," 104. On the Mediterranean link, see Keita, *"Black Athena,"* 302, 308; MacGaffey, "Concepts of Race," 4. These doubts could be posed to Bernal, who also saw Mediterranean types in ancient Egypt *"Black Athena 1:* 242).

27. Brace et al., "Clines and Clusters," 132. According to Brace et al., other adaptive traits controlled by selective forces include "lower limb attenuation, nose form, and tooth and jaw size" (150; 154, 148).

28. See Livingstone, "On the Non-Existence of Human Races," 279; Brace et al., "Clines and Clusters," 150, 159, 153. This observation, as Snowden shows, was first made by Philostratus (Snowden, *Blacks in Antiquity,* 4). These considerations can be brought to bear on Snowden's insistence that Ethiopians were the "True Negroes." Brace views "the use of the term 'Ethiopian' to stand for all the heavily pigmented people in Africa—as was done in classical antiquity, and from the Bible to Kipling"—as confusing ("Clines and Clusters," 151), for by placing all of these darkly pigmented peoples under one rubric, we run the risk of assuming genetic relationships where there are only similar adaptive responses. Brace argues strongly that it is precisely for this reason that terms for race based on skin color are inaccurate (148, 150).

29. Brace et al., "Clines and Clusters," 159, 152.

30. Ibid., 150, 131; Gould, *Mismeasure of Man,* 25, 53.

31. Brace et al., "Clines and Clusters," 134, 133.

32. Ibid., 145.

33. Ibid., 140 (emphasis added), 153, 155.

34. See, for example, Bernal, *Black Athena 2:* 63–77.

35. Bernal, *"Black Athena and the APA,"* 31.

36. Ibid., 32 (emphasis added). Also see Bernal, "Response" (*Arethusa*), 316. Muhly, who apparently overlooked the section of this quote which I italicized, countered: "Bernal has been teaching a course on *Black Athena* at Cornell for some years now and he has always used that title in his course. Is it not then one that he himself favors, rather than one forced upon him by his publisher?" (*"Black Athena versus Traditional Scholarship,"* 105). Muhly's logic is picked up by Snowden, "Response," 321. For more on Bernal's title and its drawbacks, see Brace et al., "Clines and Clusters," 156; Kelly, "Egyptians and Ethiopians," 80; Gress, "Case against Bernal," 391; Michelini, "Comment," 97; R. Young, *"Black Athena,"* 281.

37. Febvre, *Problem of Unbelief,* 5.

38. Tritle, "Review of *Black Athena* 2," 88. This quote is taken from the 1992 version of the article, since it differs somewhat from Tritle's 1996 version in *Black Athena Revisited* (312). Also see Brace et al., "Clines and Clusters," 162.

39. Liverani, "Bathwater and the Baby," 425; Baines, "Aims and Methods," 32.

40. Bloch, *Historian's Craft,* 44; Keita, *"Black Athena,"* 298. Bard's conclusion that "the Egyptians were Egyptians" seems eminently prudent, but many historians will find this to be a singularly uninformative declaration. Bard describes ancient Egypt as "a melting pot"—a concept whose applicability to *our* society is of ques-

tionable validity ("Ancient Egyptians," 104). For a point similar to mine, see Michelini, "Comment," 96.

41. Sanders, "Hamitic Hypothesis," 527–528; Jordan, *"Black Athena,"* 30; Bard, "Ancient Egyptians," 105; Yurco, *"Black Athena,"* 65–68; Keita, *"Black Athena,"* 302–307; MacGaffey, "Concepts of Race," 3.

42. For a summary of Morton's work, see the equally racialist 1865 review of Nott and Gliddon, *Types of Mankind,* 210–245. For a review of the Dynastic Race Theory and its affinities with the Aryan Model, see Yurco, *"Black Athena*: An Egyptological Review," 62–68. For Seligman's remarks, see *Egypt and Negro Africa,* 3, 8, and, more generally, *Races of Africa.* It must be stressed that Bernal does relatively little with racism in Egyptological circles. His analysis of racism was concentrated on classics.

43. But see Bernal's remarks on the emergence of racism in "Race, Class, and Gender," 997–1000.

44. A point which can be verified by reading the first chapter of Gitlin's *Twilight of Common Dreams.* Manning, "Frames of Reference," 262.

45. P. J. Williams, *Alchemy of Race,* 256. Also see Stepan and Gilman, "Appropriating the Idioms," 171; Arendt, *Essays in Understanding,* 140.

46. For a similar critique, see J. Hall, *"Black Athena,"* 252; Bernal, "Response to Jonathan Hall," 277.

47. Said, "Identity, Authority," 223–224.

48. Savvas, "Review of *Black Athena* 1"; 469. Said, "Identity, Authority," 220.

Chapter 9. Contentious Communities

1. C. West, "On Black-Jewish Relations," 145; Glazer, "Jews and Blacks," 105.

2. Cohen, "Interview," 15. Also see Johnson-Odim, "Comment," 85.

3. Bernal's analysis of anti-Semitism oscillates among five interrelated themes (and dozens of scattered hypotheses). These include (1) a theory that nineteenth- and twentieth-century scholars drew an identification between ancient Phoenicians and modern Jews, (2) a survey of scholarly opinions pertaining to the "Semitic race" during this period, (3) a discussion of the shift from racial to religious anti-Semitism, (4) an analysis of this shift within three countries (England, France, Germany) prior to the Holocaust, and (5) a brief survey of Jewish scholarship in the United States (and to a lesser extent England) in the aftermath of the Second World War. Here I define *anti-Semitism* in its colloquial usage as prejudice toward Jews, not toward Semitic-speaking peoples in general.

4. As far as I can tell, the use of the phrase "pariah people" in relation to the Jews was probably first used by Max Weber in his *Ancient Judaism,* 3. The phrase is most often associated with the writings of Hannah Arendt; see Young-Bruehl, *Hannah Arendt,* 121–122; *Black Athena* 1: 337, 344, 352, 33. Also see Bernal, "Image of Ancient Greece," 123; "Race, Class, and Gender," 999–1000; *Cadmean Letters,* 7. Bernal also argues that a refusal to see the Hyksos as Semites was motivated by anti-Semitism (*Black Athena* 2: 321, 322, 338, 340, 341, 342–344, 358).

5. *Black Athena* 1: 344. Bernal points out that the first association was made as early as 1640 by Samuel Bochart (169). Bernal also argues (xiv, xv) that Astour had associated anti-Semitism with anti-Phoenicianism, but he gives no citation. I have not been able to find any explicit reference to this in Astour's writing. Also see Gesenius's 1813 grammar, where the relation between Phoenician and Hebrew is posited (*Gesenius' Hebrew Grammar* 2, 10, 132 n. 1). Also see Gen. 5:32. In more recent times, scholars have come to refer to Phoenician, Punic, Hebrew, Moabite, and Canaanite as members of the northwest Semitic language family (See, for example, Moscati et al., *Introduction to the Comparative Grammar of the Semitic Languages,* 6–13; contra *Gesenius',* 1 n. 2. On the confusion between linguistic rela-

tion and blood relation, see Bernal, "Race, Class, and Gender," 988; and "Paradise Glossed," 673.

6. Arvad is mentioned in Ezek. 27:8, 11; and Gen. 10:18. For Byblos, called Gebal, see Ezek. 27:9. For Sidon and Tyre, see for example, 2 Sam. 5:11–13; 1 Kings 5:15–26; 1 Chron. 14:1; 2 Chron. 2; 2 Chron. 4:11–18.

7. See for example 2 Kings 23:13 and the Jezebel narratives mentioned below. The "Yahweh-alone party" was a term coined by Morton Smith of Columbia University as a means of describing the group he saw as responsible for the authoritative writing and editing of the Hebrew Bible (*Palestinian Parties and Politics*). On Phoenician religiosity, see Peckham, "Phoenicia and the Religion of Israel," 80; Smith, "Note on Burning Babies"; Harden, *Phoenicians*, 95; Clifford, "Phoenician Religion," 58. Stager, ("Carthage," 158); though it should be recalled that we are still uncertain as to many aspects of Phoenician religion and society (Clifford, "Phoenician Religion," 56). On some of these practices, see Peckham, "Phoenicia and the Religion of Israel," 80, 90 n. 14. On funerary feasts, see Clifford, "Phoenician Religion," 58. For the original condemnatory texts, see Isa. 23; Ezek. 27; Ezek. 28:11–23; Hos. 9:11–14; Zech. 9:1–4.

8. Ezek. 28:22–23 (trans. Jewish Publication Society, *Tarakh,* 940). In Jer. 47:3–4 the Tyrians and Sidonians are cast as allies of the Philistines.

9. For the Jezebel narratives, see 1 Kings 16:31; 1 Kings 18–21; 2 Kings 9:30–36.

10. On Jews as Caucasians, Bernal points to the work of Blumenbach, George Eliot, and Christian Lassen (*Black Athena* 1: 340). On the Aryan versus Semite view, see Bernal's discussions of Jules Michelet, Matthew Arnold, Ernst Renan, and Christian Bunsen, among others (341, 342, 256–347). Also see Bernal, "Paradise Glossed," 671, 673; *Cadmean Letters,* 11.

11. Bernal, *Black Athena* 1: 338; "Greece: Aryan or Mediterranean?" 9.

12. *Black Athena* 1: 338, 339, 342, 337, 347, 350; though Bernal is quick to point to English anti-Semitism as well (350–352). Also see Bernal, "Image of Ancient Greece," 123. For the impact of British philo-Semitism on early Zionism, see Laqueur, (*History of Zionism,* 183–190). For an interesting discussion of philo-Semitism in general, see I. L. Horowitz, "Philo-Semitism and Anti-Semitism."

13. *Black Athena* 1: 339, 352–358. On Flaubert's Orientalism, see Said, *Orientalism,* 184–189.

14. Bernal, "Greece: Aryan or Mediterranean?" 9.

15. Bernal, *Black Athena* 1: 367; also see 370, 387, 393; *Cademan Letters,* 6. The Broad Aryan Model survived until 1925–1935 (Bernal, "Greece: Aryan or Mediterranean?" 9). Bernal places the origins of the Broad version variously to 1815–1830 and 1830–1840 (*Cadmean Letters,* 6; "Image of Ancient Greece," 124).

16. Bernal, "First by Land," 9.

17. Bernal, "Greece: Aryan or Mediterranean?" 9. For similar observations, see *Cadmean Letters,* 19; "Image of Ancient Greece," 124; though Bernal is aware that the decrease in anti-Semitism occurred only gradually (*Black Athena* 1: 402–403; *Black Athena* 2: 343). Although Bernal seems not to realize it, the terms of his analysis have subtly shifted. In his eighth and ninth chapters in volume 1, he examined anti-Semitism and scholarship in three European countries. Yet by the tenth chapter he has abandoned Germany and France in favor of the United States, and to a lesser degree England. As far as I can tell, Bernal's analysis of postwar developments is mostly geared to the United States. For some examples of anti-Semitism in the American university of yesterday, see Kuklick, *Puritans in Babylon,* 104, 171, 173; Oren, *Joining the Club;* Strum, "Louis Marshall and Anti-Semitism," Hook, "Anti-Semitism in the Academy."

18. Bernal, *Black Athena* 1: 400–401 (emphasis added). Elsewhere, and somewhat in contradiction to his hypothesis, Bernal notes that anti-Phoenicianism actually intensified up to the mid 1960s (408). Also see *"Black Athena* and the APA," 19. Yet

when discussing the work of the nonacademic Leon Pomerance—a character who seems to have walked out of a Philip Roth novel—Bernal does not seem to believe that university anti-Semitism has lessened in recent years, or at least by 1977 (*Black Athena* 2: 276–277).

19. Bernal, "First by Land," 11; "Image of Ancient Greece," 124.
20. See, for example, Bernal, "Greece: Aryan or Mediterranean?" 10; though in fairness to him, he argues here that the movement to restore the Phoenicians' honor is much smaller than the dimensions of Jewish presence in the research university.
21. Bikai, "*Black Athena* and the Phoenicians," 69. Athaliah is the daughter of Jezebel, mentioned in 2 Kings 11:1–20.
22. *Black Athena* 1: 428–431, 442; *Cadmean Letters*. Yet Bernal points to an Israeli scholar who specifically disagrees with his hypothesis (*Black Athena* 2: 469–473).
23. I have chosen 1985 as a terminal date because this is the parameter Bernal proposes in the title of his first volume. Biblical Arvad, mentioned in Ezek. 27:8, 11, is located in modern western Syria (Pritchard, *Harper Concise Atlas*, 57). I would mention, however, that the Phoenicians have been claimed as ancestors by Christian Lebanese groups. This point is made by Bernal ("Responses to Critical Reviews," 113), who adds that these groups have cooperated militarily with the Israelis. Also see Zilfi, "Comment," 117, on contemporary political ideologies in Lebanon.
24. *Black Athena* 1: 415–416; Bernal, "Image of Ancient Greece," 124; *Cadmean Letters*, 20, on Astour's anti-Zionism. On these two scholars, see Bernal, "*Black Athena* and the APA," 19, 20; and "Responses to Critical Reviews," 113. See above and "Image of Ancient Greece," 124, where he declares that "the Broad Aryanists—led largely by Jewish scholars—are now gaining ground and will almost certainly succeed by the end of the century."
25. Bernal does identify a tendency of Jewish Semiticists to argue that the alphabet was introduced by the Phoenicians into the Aegean at an earlier date than commonly thought (Bernal, *Cadmean Letters*, 20). See Sperling, *Students of the Covenant*, though, in fairness to Bernal, Sperling is looking at scholars of the Hebrew Bible, not those in the broader field of northwest Semitic (1). In the fourth chapter of this work, Baruch Levine surveys fourteen scholars who received their doctorate between 1942 and 1965. Only three are specifically mentioned as interested in Punic and Phoenician. No greater percentage is evidenced in the fifth chapter, where the work of those who received their doctorates between 1965 and 1980 is examined. As for Israeli scholars, see the reviews of Shavit, "Anti-University Intellectuals"; Yavitz, "She Wasn't Black"; and see Finkelberg, "Anatolian Languages." We also might insert into this category Molly Myerowitz Levine's many contributions to the Controversy insofar as she once divided her time between Howard and Bar-Ilan universities.
26. Ginsberg, "Hebrews and Hellenes," 334.
27. M. M. Levine, "Review Article," 450; and see "Challenge of *Black Athena*," 14.
28. Kristeller, "Comment on *Black Athena*," 126.
29. What a different perspective Kristeller has from that of the non-Jewish Max Weber. See my discussion of Weber in Chapter 3 above. Also see Coser, "Georg Simmel's Style of Work"; Kristeller, "Comment on *Black Athena*," 127. See chapter 7 above for a discussion of Lefkowitz's use of Holocaust associations (*Not Out of Africa* 52; "Ancient History," 22; "Ethnocentric History," 13).
30. *Black Athena* 1: xiii.
31. See Lefkowitz, "Ethnocentric History," 13. Also see Bernal's remarks on Afrocentrism and anti-Semitism (Dyson, "On *Black Athena*," 60). For Bernal on Zionism, see "Greece: Aryan or Mediterranean?" 10; "Black Athena Denied," 54; "Image of Ancient Greece," 124. On the importance of Israel to American Jews, see Meyer, "Anti-Semitism and Jewish Identity," 40.

32. Cohen, "Interview," 16. Also see Bernal, "Image of Ancient Greece," 127.
33. Bernal, *Black Athena* 1: 403; "*Black Athena* and the APA," 19; Cohen, "Interview," 14.
34. Though see Bernal's interview with Dyson, where he speaks admiringly of the Jewish tradition of sympathy for the oppressed ("On *Black Athena*," 59–60).
35. And its own magazine as well! A recent announcement on the Internet advertised the magazine *Commonquest*, "the magazine of black-Jewish relations." In terms of anthologies, see Berman, *Blacks and Jews*; J. Washington, *Jews in Black Perspectives*; Hentoff, *Black Anti-Semitism and Jewish Racism*. Also see Weisbord and Stein, *Bittersweet Encounter*; Kaufman, *Broken Alliance*; Lerner and West, *Jews and Blacks*. For nonanthologized articles, see Gourevitch, "The Crown Heights Riot"; Friedman, "An Old/New Libel"; Brooks, "Negro Militants, Jewish Liberals"; Raab, "Blacks and Jews Asunder?"; Neusner, "Blacks and Jews"; Plax, "Jews and Blacks in Dialogue"; Black, "Farrakhan and the Jews"; Baldwin et al., "Liberalism and the Negro"; Baldwin, "Blacks and Jews"; Toll, "Pluralism and Moral Force"; T. Jacoby, "The Bitter Legacies of Malcolm X"; Boyd, "Will Blacks and Jews Ever Come of Age?"; "The Rift between Blacks and Jews"; Weitz, "Black Hostility—Jewish Naivete"; and "Black-Jewish Irrationality"; Fiedler, "Negro and Jew"; Raab and Kahn, "Civic and Political," 222–224; and all of the articles cited below. C. Carson ("Politics of Relations," 132) speaks of the "ritualistic" nature of the debate, which usually begins with a controversial statement by a black person, followed by a public condemnation from Jewish leaders. Hooks ("Keeping a Legacy of Shared Struggle," 232) has pointed out the gendered dimensions of the debate. Vorspan ("Blacks and Jews") argues that the debate is mostly about matters occurring in New York.
36. But Bernal's analogy is not exact. Jews have never seen the Phoenicians as relatives in the manner that some African-Americans have embraced the ancient Egyptians. E. Hall notes that Bernal is "offering to Blacks and Jews European 'roots,' aboriginal and central places in the European cultural history" ("Myths Missing That Black Magic," 18).
37. As Lipset and Ladd note, the peak of "overt anti-Jewish prejudice within academe" was in the 1920s and 1930s ("Jewish Academics," 90). Also see Steinberg, *Academic Melting Pot*, and note 17 above.
38. Lipsett and Ladd, "Jewish Academics," 99. Notable in this article is the authors' prediction that "there is reason to anticipate a decline in the commitment of intellectual Jews to the new brand of ritualistic leftism" (128).
39. Ritterband, "Modern Times and Jewish Assimilation," 377–378. Also see Hertzberg, "Jewish Intelligentsia," 37; Sachar, *History of the Jews in America*, 754–755; Puddington, "Black Anti-Semitism and How It Grows," 23. In fact, one Jewish scholar points out that Jews are even overrepresented in African studies (Sklar, "Africa and the Middle East," 137).
40. Sachar, *History of the Jews in America*, 791.
41. The comment was reportedly made by Martin Peretz, editor of the *New Republic*, as quoted by Furman, "Surviving Success," 11.
42. Feingold, "From Equality to Liberty," 113. Glazer ("Anomalous Liberalism of American Jews," 133), refers to Jews as "the most prosperous of all religious groups" in the United States. Also see Muravchik, "Facing Up to Black Anti-Semitism," 30. Weisbord and Stein write, "For the Jew, life is sweeter in America than anywhere else in the world" (*Bittersweet Encounter*, xiv, 14). Vorspan, "Blacks and Jews," 205.
43. Weiss, "Letting Go."
44. See D'Souza, *End of Racism*.
45. C. West, *Race Matters*, 15.

46. Hacker, *Two Nations,* 225–236. Dyson, *Reflecting Black,* 90; also see Duster, "Social Implications of the 'New' Black Urban Underclass."
47. Cited in Slater, ("Sunshine Factor," 91); also see Hacker, *Two Nations,* 234–235; *Journal of Blacks in Higher Education,* "Black Scholars Hold a Pessimistic Outlook," 74, and "Graduation Rates of African-American College Students," 44–45. Fechter, "Black Scholar"; William Banks, "Afro-American Scholars in the University." On African-American women in the academy, see C. Johnson, "All I'm Askin'"; Guy-Sheftall, "Black Feminist Perspective"; Magner, "Debate in African Studies"; R. Wilson, "Hiring of Black Scholars Stalls." Also see discussions such as Staples, "Racial Ideology and Intellectual Racism." A different explanation for this state of affairs is offered by Thernstrom, "On the Scarcity of Black Professors." See the forum in *Journal of Blacks in Higher Education,* "Why the Shortage of Black Professors?" where the significance and accuracy of this data is debated (25–34). And see Slater, "Sunshine Factor," 92; Leap, "Tenure, Discrimination, and African-American Faculty," 103. Also see Watts, "Dilemmas of Black Intellectuals."
48. On positive educational statistics, see *Journal of Blacks in Higher Education,* "Black Enrollments in Higher Education," 66–67, and "Blacks in Higher Education," 43. Also see Boynton, "New Intellectuals"; Sowell, *Ethnic America,* 224.
49. Baldwin, "Negroes Are Anti-Semitic," 35; and "Blacks and Jews"; and the response to this by Lester, "Academic Freedom and the Black Intellectual." For other discussions of the whiteness of American Jews see C. West, "On Black-Jewish Relations," 146, 150; Lester, "Lives People Live," 172; hooks, "Keeping a Legacy of Shared Struggle," 230, 234; Baldwin, "Blacks and Jews," 9; Hentoff, "Introduction," ix; Cruse, "My Jewish Problem," 155, 156, 158, 178, 183; Weisbord and Stein, *Bittersweet Encounter,* xii. See, however, M. Lerner's remarks about Sephardic Judaism in Lerner and West, *Jews and Blacks,* 59, 67. On intermarriage rates, see Ritterband, "Modern Times and Jewish Assimilation," 383. On the similarity in political affiliation, see C. Carson, "Politics of Relations," 134; Toll, "Pluralism and Moral Force," 92.
50. Drake, "African Diaspora and Jewish Diaspora," 27.
51. Weisbord and Stein, *Bittersweet Encounter,* 1; Gutman, "Parallels in the Urban Experience," 101. For other discussions of the different experiences in America, see Lester, "Lives People Live," 167, 172; C. Carson, "Politics of Relations," 135. Wieseltier points out that the experience of racism has been far more intense in the United States than anti-Semitism ("Taking Yes for an Answer," 255–256'); Toll, "Pluralism and Moral Force," 88–89.
52. Lewis, "Shortcuts to the Mainstream," 84, 83. For a similar theory of the effects of a common enemy, see Neusner, "Blacks and Jews," 25; Glazer, "Jews and Blacks," 106. The dates 1910–1967 are suggested by C. West, "On Black-Jewish Relations." West speaks of a "better age" as opposed to a "golden age" (146, 145). Of course the 1950s and 1960s were the most intense period of the alliance (Cruse, "My Jewish Problem," 143; Vorspan, "Blacks and Jews," 208).
53. I am paraphrasing remarks made by Professor John Henrik Clarke in March 1996 at a forum in which he, Bernal, Lefkowitz, and Rogers spoke. On internal differences, see C. Carson, the "Politics of Relations," 143; Cruse, "My Jewish Problem," 179.
54. C. Carson, "Politics of Relations," 135–136; and "Blacks and Jews in the Civil Rights Movement," 116.
55. Cruse, "My Jewish Problem," 143.
56. Lester, "Jewish Racism," 168 (emphasis added). Also see C. Carson, "Politics of Relations," 135; Watts, "Identity and the Status of Afro-American Intellectuals," 361.
57. A similar point is made by Neusner, "Blacks and Jews," 25.

Conclusion

1. Cohen, "Interview," 5. The volume *Black Athena Writes Back* (Duke) is scheduled to be released in 1999. This massive volume consists, partly, of responses by Bernal to his critics in *Black Athena Revisited.* After the release of this text, we expect to see the third volume. For other discussions of future plans, see *Black Athena* 1: 10, 63–73; *Black Athena* 2: 527; and "Responses to *Black Athena*," 65.
2. Bernal, "Response to Sturt Manning," 280.
3. See Chapter 6, note 14, above.
4. Here referring to Weber's famous formulation in "Science as a Vocation" (138), though there are attempts within the Society for Biblical Literature to make use of sociological methods. For a convenient reference to the major issues involved in the sociological study of the Hebrew Bible, see Chalcraft, *Social-Scientific Old Testament Criticism.* The problems which afflict biblical sociology were discussed in my address entitled "The Sociology of Israelite Religion: Where Do We Stand? Where Do We Go?" For discussions of the minimal impact which *Ancient Judaism* has had on both biblical scholarship and sociology, see Fahey, "Max Weber's *Ancient Judaism*," 62; Talmon, "Emergence of Jewish Sectarianism," 588; Petersen, "Max Weber and the Sociological Study," 137; Holstein, "Max Weber and Biblical Scholarship," 160; Eisenstadt, "The Format of Jewish History," 54.
5. Kalberg, *Max Weber's Comparative-Historical Sociology,* 91, 85, 92; also see B. M. Berger, *Essay on Culture,* 69. For another good use of models by Bernal, see *Cadmean Letters,* 58–59.
6. Rogers, "Multiculturalism," 436–439.
7. Or perhaps this is the result of the fact that ancient historians are far less likely than social theorists to make their own assumptions the subject of rigorous scrutiny. As Hopkins notes, "Ancient historians do not, I think, take kindly to methodological discussions in the abstract" ("Rules of Evidence," 179).
8. Redfield ("Classics and Anthropology") makes a similar argument, about the gap between anthropology and classics.
9. Bernal, "Response to Jonathan Hall," 276. The academic field, like all fields, possesses a *"specific and irreducible"* logic of its own (Bourdieu and Wacquant, *Invitation,* 97). Bourdieu, *Homo Academicus,* 95. On the call for heresy, see Bourdieu, "Vive la crise!"
10. Ray, "Egyptian Perspective," 79.
11. Palter, "Eighteenth-Century Historiography," 379, and see Chapter 3 above for the complete discussion of these issues.
12. As B. M. Berger aptly phrases it, "The social sciences and humanities recurrently generate new theoretical vocabularies (structuralism, functionalism, deconstruction, semiotics . . .) to apply to old problems that, ever recalcitrant, almost predictably defeat the efforts of old theoretical vocabularies to solve them" (*Essay on Culture,* 10).
13. *Black Athena* 1: 442, and see his remarks on Benedetto (357). He repeated the same passage on the first page of his second volume (*Black Athena* 2: 1, also see 323, 359); Cohen, "Interview," 8; Bernal, *Cadmean Letters,* 36 n. 5.
14. Bernal, "Classics in Crisis," 67; also see *Black Athena* 2: xviii, xx; Cohen, "Interview," 10, 13.
15. B. Moore, *Reflections on the Causes of Human Misery,* 91.
16. See Leatherman, "Growing Use of Part-Time Professors" and "Leaders of Scholarly Groups." Also see Damrosch, *We Scholars,* 70; Jacoby, *Dogmatic Wisdom,* 39; Benjamin, "Faculty Response to the Fiscal Crisis"; Nelson and Bérubé, "Introduction," 16; Lauter, "'Politial Correctness,'" 79.

17. Giddens, *Social Theory and Modern Sociology*, 261.
18. Weber, *On Charisma and Institution Building*, 48.
19. Bernal, *"Black Athena* and the APA," 20; also see *Black Athena* 2: 466; contra Muhly, *"Black Athena,"* 86.
20. Bourdieu, *Homo Academicus*, 109. In fact, Bourdieu has made the important suggestion that within the academic field heresies and orthodoxies actually legitimate one another (112).
21. Contra van Binsbergen, who sees Bernal as only recently having become an insider (*"Black Athena* Ten Years After," 40).
22. Coser, *Men of Ideas*, vii. Bell, *Winding Passage*, 119. Also see B. M. Berger, "Sociology and the Intellectuals," 281.
23. Shils, *Constitution of Society*, 263; also see Damrosch, *We Scholars*, 3; Coser, *Men of Ideas*, 263, 280–281; Jacoby, "Graying of the Intellectuals," 236; and *Last Intellectuals* 8, 6, 7, 118–119. On the assumption that the intellectual work is not necessarily enriched in the academy, see Jacoby, "Graying of the Intellectuals" and *Last Intellectuals*; B. M. Berger, *Authors of Their Own Lives*, 158; Hofstadter, *Anti-Intellectualism in American Life*, 416, 427; C. West writes: "There is a fundamental difference between an academic and an intellectual. An academic usually engages in rather important yet still narrow scholarly work, whereas an intellectual is engaged in the public issues that affect large numbers of people in a critical manner" (hooks and West, *Baking Bread*, 29).
24. Also see Jacoby, "Graying of the Intellectuals," 237.
25. On Jacoby and the advent of a new (black) cadre of intellectuals, see Boynton, "New Intellectuals," though Jacoby wrote passionately about the culture wars in his 1994 *Dogmatic Wisdom*. Jacoby, *Last Intellectuals*, 5, 235. Mills, *Sociological Imagination*, 21.
26. Jacoby, *Dogmatic Wisdom*, xvi.
27. Poliakoff, "Roll Over Aristotle," 18; Tritle, "Vision or Dream?" 304; Gress, "Case against Bernal," 42.
28. Will, "Intellectual Segregation," 78. I also think of two critics of Bernal, writing in *Black Athena Revisited*: "As linguists, we have no professional interest in the politically charged issues that most exercise Bernal" (Jasanoff and Nussbaum, "Word Games," 178).
29. Lefkowitz, "Ancient History," 5.
30. B. M. Berger, *Essay on Culture*, 75–119.
31. Ibid., 78, 35, 75–119.
32. For the accusation that some radicals fail to take this final step, see Shaw, "Pseudo-Reform in the Academy," 98.
33. Fish, "Common Touch," 249. For other statements of the inevitability of the political, see Menand, "Limits of Academic Freedom," 16; Goldberg, "Introduction," 11–12; Giroux, "Insurgent Multiculturalism," 336–337.
34. Walzer, *Company of Critics*, 40; also see Calhoun, *Critical Social Theory*, 58; Benda, *Treason of the Intellectuals*, 67.
35. Coser, *Men of Ideas*, 360.
36. In the same essay ("Science as a Vocation"), Weber argued that it was the professor's "damned duty" to speak his or her mind in a political meeting (145), yet this same professor must never bring such views into the lecture hall. Weber declares, "The prophet and the demagogue do not belong on the academic platform" (146). In *Max Weber and German Politics*, Mommsen writes:

   > In an assembly in Heidelberg, he called this the national task of the younger generation. "You know," he said, "what it means to stand up to an invading enemy who can no longer be offered military resistance . . . to give everything for the future, and abandon your personal hopes. The lot of the living is only imprisonment

and summary trial. . . . The first Polish official that dares enter Danzig will be met by a bullet." *Weber directed his appeal above all to students.* (312, emphasis added) Walzer, *Company of Critics*, 226.

37. Haskell, "Justifying the Rights of Academic Freedom," 77.
38. Cited in Bourdieu and Wacquant, *Invitation*, 7; Gramsci, *Quaderni del carcere*, 28: 2332.
39. Durkheim, *Morality and Society*, 59. Also see Coser, *Men of Ideas*, 249.
40. Rorty, "Intellectuals in Politics," 489; Lauter, "'Politial Correctness,'" 86.
41. Steven Lukes, *Emile Durkheim*, 332.

Bibliography

Abercrombie, Nicholas, Stephen Hill, and Bryan S. Turner. *The Dominant Ideology Thesis.* London: George Allen and Unwin, 1980.

Aeschylus. *The Suppliants.* Translated by Philip Vellacott. London: Penguin Books, 1961.

Ahmad, Aijaz. *In Theory: Classes, Nations, Literatures.* New York: Verso, 1994.

Allen, Norm. "*Black Athena:* An Interview with Martin G. Bernal." *Free Inquiry* 10 (1990): 18–22.

Allen, Peter. "*Black Athena.*" *American Anthropologist* 94 (1992): 1024–1026.

Amin, Samir. *Eurocentrism.* Translated by A. Moore. New York: Monthly Review Press, 1989.

Ampim, Manu. "The Problem of the Bernal-Davidson School." In Van Sertima, *Egypt,* 191–204.

Anderson, Perry. *Considerations on Western Marxism.* London: Verso, 1979.

———. "The Myth of Hellenism: Review of *Black Athena* 1. *Guardian,* May 3, 1987, 14.

Andrea, Bernadette. "Review Article: Early Modern Women, 'Race,' and (Post) Colonial Writing." *Ariel: A Review of International English Literature* 27 (1996): 127–149.

Aneer, G. "Comments on Martin Bernal's *Black Athena.*" *Vest* 8 (1995): 38–42.

Appiah, K. Anthony. "African-American Philosophy?" *Philosophical Forum* 24 (1992–1993): 11–34.

———. "Ancestral Voices: With Responses." *Salmagundi* 104/105 (1994): 88–135.

———. "Europe Upside Down: Fallacies of the New Afrocentrism." *Times Literary Supplement,* February 12, 1993, 24–25.

Appiah, K. Anthony, and Henry L. Gates, Jr., eds. "Editors' Introduction: Multiplying Identities." In Appiah and Gates, *Identities,* 1–6.

———. *Identities.* Chicago: University of Chicago Press, 1995.

Appleby, Joyce, Lynn Hunt, and Margaret Jacob. *Telling the Truth about History.* New York: W. W. Norton, 1994.

Arendt, Hannah. *The Origins of Totalitarianism.* New York: Harcourt Brace, 1979.

———. "'What Remains? The Language Remains': A Conversation with Günter Gaus." In Kohn, *Essays in Understanding,* 1–23.

Aristotle. *Metaphysics.* Translated by R. Hope. Ann Arbor: University of Michigan Press, 1960.

Armayor, O. K. "Did Herodotus Ever Go to the Black Sea?" *Harvard Studies in Classical Philology* 82 (1978): 45–62.

Arrowsmith, William, ed. *Unmodern Observations: Friedrich Nietzsche.* New Haven: Yale University Press, 1990.

Asad, Talal. *Genealogies of Religion: Discipline and Reasons of Power in Christianity and Islam.* Baltimore: Johns Hopkins University Press, 1993.

Asante, Molefi Kete. "African American Studies: The Future of the Discipline." *Black Scholar* 22 (1992): 20–29.

———. "The Afrocentric Idea in Education." *Journal of Negro Education* 60 (1991): 170–180.

———. *Afrocentricity.* Trenton, N.J.: Africa World Press, 1992.

243

Asante, Molefi Kete. "The Ideological Significance of Afrocentricity in Intercultural Communication." *Journal of Black Studies* 14 (1983): 3–19.

——. *Kemet, Afrocentricity and Knowledge.* Trenton, N.J.: Africa World Press, 1990.

——. "More Thoughts on the Africanists' Agenda." *Issue: A Journal of Opinion* 23 (1995): 11–12.

Astour, Michael C. "Aegean Place-Names in an Egyptian Inscription." *American Journal of Archaeology* 70 (1966): 313–317.

——. "Greek Names in the Semitic World and Semitic Names in the Greek World." *Journal of Near Eastern Studies* 23 (1964): 193–201.

——. *Hellenosemitica: An Ethnic and Cultural Study in West Semitic Impact on Mycenaean Greece.* Leiden: E. J. Brill, 1965.

——. "The Problem of Semitic in Ancient Crete." *Journal of the American Oriental Society* 87 (1967): 290–295.

——. "Review Article: Some Recent Works on Ancient Syria and the Sea People." *Journal of the American Oriental Society* 92 (1972): 447–459.

——. "Second Millennium B.C. Cypriot and Cretan Onomastica Reconsidered." *Journal of the American Oriental Society* 84 (1964): 240–254.

Åström, Paul. "Comments on Martin Bernal's *Black Athena.*" *Vest* 8 (1995): 43–47.

Aune, James. "Review of *Black Athena,* Volumes 1 and 2." *Quarterly Journal of Speech* 79 (1993): 119–122.

Baines, John. "The Aims and Methods of *Black Athena.*" In Lefkowitz and Rogers, *Black Athena Revisited,* 27–48.

——. "Was Civilization Made in Africa?" *New York Times Books Review,* August 11, 1991, 12–13.

Baldini, Alessandra. "Classici d'Egitto: Intervista con Martin Bernal." *Panorama,* November 24, 1991, 112–117.

Baldwin, James. "Blacks and Jews." *Black Scholar* 19 (1988): 3–15.

——. "Negros Are Anti-Semitic Because They're Anti-White." In Berman, *Blacks and Jews,* 31–41.

Baldwin, James, Nathan Glazer, Sidney Hook, and Gunnar Myrdal. "Liberalism and the Negro: A Round-Table Discussion." *Commentary* 37 (1964): 25–42.

Bard, Kathryn A. "Ancient Egyptians and the Issue of Race." In Lefkowitz and Rogers, *Black Athena Revisited,* 103–111.

——. "Toward an Interpretation of the Role of Ideology in the Evolution of Complex Society in Egypt." *Journal of Anthropological Archaeology* 11 (1992): 1–24.

Barrett, Michèle. *The Politics of Truth: From Marx to Foucault.* Stanford: Stanford University Press, 1991.

Barringer, F. "Africa's Claim to Egypt's History Grows More Insistent." *New York Times,* February 4, 1990, E6.

Barton, John. "Source Criticism, Old Testament." In Freedman, *Anchor Bible Dictionary,* 6: 162–165.

Basch, Sophie. "Quels ancêtres pour les Grecs?" *Quinzaine Littéraire,* January 16–31, 1997, 21.

Bass, George. "A Bronze Age Shipwreck at Ulu Burun (Kas): 1984 Campaign." *American Journal of Archaeology* 90 (1986): 269–296.

——. "Responses." *Arethusa,* special issue (1989): 111–113.

Bass, George, Cemal Pulak, Dominique Collon, and James Weinstein. "The Bronze Age Shipwreck at Ulu Burun: 1986 Campaign." *American Journal of Archaeology* 93 (1989): 1–29.

Beardsley, Grace H. *The Negro in Greek and Roman Civilization: A Study of the Ethiopian Type.* New York: Russell and Russell, 1967.

Beidelman, T. O. "Promoting African Art: The Catalogue to the Exhibit of African Art at the Royal Academy of Arts, London." *Anthropos* 92 (1997): 3–20.

Begley, Sharon. "Out of Africa, a Missing Link." *Newsweek,* October 3, 1994, 56–57.

Begley, Sharon, Farai Chideya, and Larry Wilson. "Out of Egypt, Greece." *Newsweek,* September 23, 1991, 49–50.

Belenky, Mary Field, Blythe Clinchy, Nancy Goldberger, and Jill Tarule. *Women's Ways of Knowing: The Development of Self, Voice, and Mind.* New York: Basic Books, 1973.

Bell, Daniel. *The Winding Passage: Essays and Sociological Journeys, 1960–1980.* New York: Basic Books, 1980.

Beloch, Julius. "Die Phoeniker am aegaeischen Meer." *Rheinisches Museum* 49 (1894): 111–132.

Benda, Julien. *The Treason of the Intellectuals.* Translated by R. Aldington. New York: W. W. Norton, 1969.

Benjamin, Ernst. "A Faculty Response to the Fiscal Crisis: From Defense to Offense." In Nelson and Bérubé, *Higher Education under Fire,* 52–71.

Bérard, Victor. *Les Phéniciens et l'Odyssée.* 2 vols. Paris: Librairie Armand Colin, 1927.

———. *La Résurrection d'Homère: Au temps des héros.* Paris: Bernard Grasset, 1930.

Berger, Bennett M. *An Essay on Culture: Symbolic Structure and Social Structure.* Berkeley: University of California Press, 1995.

———. "Sociology and the Intellectuals: An Analysis of a Stereotype." *Antioch Review* 17 (1957): 275–290.

Berger, Bennett M., ed. *Authors of Their Own Lives: Intellectual Autobiographies by Twenty American Sociologists.* Berkeley: University of California Press, 1992.

Berger, Peter L. *The Heretical Imperative: Contemporary Possibilities of Religious Affirmation.* New York: Anchor, 1979.

Berlinerblau, Jacques. "Black Athena Redux: Review of Mary Lefkowitz's *Not Out of Africa* and *Black Athena Revisited,* ed. M. Lefkowitz and G. MacLean Rogers." *Nation,* October 28, 1996, 42–48.

———. "The Israelite Vow: Distress or Daily Life?" *Biblica* 72 (1991): 548–555.

———. "Northwest Semites in the Aegean? Evaluating the Gordon-Astour-Bernal School." Paper delivered at the annual meeting of the Society for Biblical Literature, San Francisco, November 22, 1997.

———. "The 'Popular Religion' Paradigm in Old Testament Research: A Sociological Critique." *Journal for the Study of the Old Testament* 60 (1993): 3–26.

———. "Preliminary Observations for the Sociological Study of Israelite 'Official Religion.'" In *Baruch Levine Anniversary Volume.* Winona Lake, Ind.: Eisenbrauns, 1999.

———. "Response to Lefkowitz and Rogers." *Nation* December 30, 1996, 2, 23.

———. "The Sociology of Israelite Religion: Where Do We Stand? Where Do We Go?" Paper delivered at the annual meeting of the Society of Biblical Literature. New Orleans, November 23, 1996.

———. "Some Sociological Observations on Moshe Greenberg's *Biblical Prose Prayer as a Window to the Popular Religion of Ancient Israel." Journal of Northwest Semitic Languages and Literatures* 21 (1995): 1–14.

———. *The Vow and the 'Popular Religious Groups' of Ancient Israel: A Philological and Sociological Inquiry.* Sheffield, Eng.: Sheffield Academic Press, 1996.

Berman, Paul. "The Other and the Almost the Same." In Berman, *Blacks and Jews,* 1–28.

Berman, Paul, ed. *Blacks and Jews: Alliances and Arguments.* New York: Delacorte, 1994.

Bernal, John D. *Marx and Science.* New York: International Publishers, 1952.

———. *Science and Industry in the Nineteenth Century.* Bloomington: Indiana University Press, 1970.

———. *Science in History.* Vol. 4, *The Social Sciences: Conclusion.* Cambridge: MIT Press, 1971.

———. *The Social Function of Science.* Cambridge: MIT Press, 1964.

Bernal, Martin. "The Afrocentric Interpretation of History: Bernal Replies to Lefkowitz." *Journal of Blacks in Higher Education* 11 (1996): 86–94.

———. "Animadversions on the Origins of Western Science." *Isis* 83 (1992): 596–607.

———. *Atena nera: Le radici afroasiatiche della civiltà classica.* Translated by L. Fontana. Parma: Pratiche, 1991.

———. *Atenea Negra: Las raíces afroasiáticas clásicas.* Vol. 1, *La invencion de la antigua Grecia, 1785–1985.* Translated by T. de Lozoya. Barcelona: Editorial Crítica, 1993.

———. "Basil Davidson: A Personal Appreciation." *Race and Class* 36 (1994): 101–103.

———. "Black Athena: The African and Levantine Roots of Greece." In Van Sertima, *African Presence,* 66–82.

———. *Black Athena: The Afroasiatic Roots of Classical Civilization.* Vol. 1, *The Fabrication of Ancient Greece, 1785–1985.* New Brunswick, N.J.: Rutgers University Press, 1987.

———. *Black Athena: The Afroasiatic Roots of Classical Civilization.* Vol. 2, *The Archaeological and Documentary Evidence.* New Brunswick, N.J.: Rutgers University Press, 1991.

———. "*Black Athena* and the APA." *Arethusa,* special issue (1989): 17–37.

———. "*Black Athena* and Her Reception." *Vest* 8 (1995): 11–24.

———. "*Black Athena*—The Historical Construction of Europe." *Vest* 8 (1995): 11–24.

———. "Black Athena Denied: The Tyranny of Germany over Greece and the Rejection of the Afroasiatic Roots of Europe, 1780–1980." *Comparative Criticism* 8 (1986): 3–69.

———. "The British Utilitarians, Imperialism and the Fall of the Ancient Model." *Culture and History* 3 (1988): 98–127.

———. "Burkert's Orientalizing Revolution: Review of Walter Burkert, *The Orientalizing Revolution.*" *Arion* 4 (1996): 136–147.

———. *Cadmean Letters: The Transmission of the Alphabet to the Aegean and Further West before 1400 B.C.* Winona Lake, Ind.: Eisenbrauns, 1990.

———. "The Case for Massive Egyptian Influence in the Aegean." *Archaeology* 53–55 (September/October 1992): 82, 86.

———. *Chinese Socialism to 1907.* Ithaca: Cornell University Press, 1975.

———. "Classics in Crisis: An Outsider's View In." In Culham and Edmunds, *Classics,* 69–74.

———. "Down There on a Visit." *New York Review of Books,* June 17, 1965, 16.

———. "First by Land, Then by Sea: Thoughts about the Social Formation of the Mediterranean and Greece." In Genovese and Hochberg, *Geographic Perspectives,* 3–33.

———. "Greece: Aryan or Mediterranean? Two Contending Historiographical Models." In Federici, *Enduring Western Civilization,* 3–11.

———. "The Image of Ancient Greece as a Tool for Colonialism and European Hegemony." In Bond and Gilliam, *Social Construction,* 119–128.

———. "A Mao for All Seasons." *New York Review of Books,* January 16, 1969, 5, 25–28.

———. "Mao's China." *New York Review of Books,* May 6, 1965, 8–10.

———. "North Vietnam and China: Reflections on a Visit." *New York Review of Books,* August 12, 1971, 16–20.

———. "On the Transmission of the Alphabet to the Aegean before 1400 B.C." *Bulletin of the American Schools of Oriental Research* 267 (1987): 1–19.

———. "Paradise Glossed: Review of Maurice Olender, *The Languages of Paradise: Race, Religion, and Philology in the Nineteenth Century.*" *Studies in History and Philosophy of Science* 24 (1993): 669–675.

———. "Phoenician Politics and Egyptian Justice in Ancient Greece." In Raaflaub, *Anfäge politischen Denkens,* 241–261.

———. "The Popularity of Chinese Patriotism." *New York Review of Books,* February 25, 1965, 3.

———. "Questioning the History of Western Civilization: Response to Mary Lefkowitz." *Chronicle of Higher Education*, May 27, 1992, B4.

———. "Race, Class, and Gender in the Formation of the Aryan Model of Greek Origins." *South Atlantic Quarterly Journal* 94 (1995): 987–1008.

———. "Response." *Arethusa* 26 (1993): 315–318.

———. "Response." *Journal of Women's History* 4 (1993): 119–135.

———. "Response to Edith Hall." *Arethusa* 24 (1991): 203–214.

———. "Response to Jonathan Hall, 'Black Athena: A Sheep in Wolf's Clothing?'" *Journal of Mediterranean Archaeology* 3 (1990): 275–279.

———. "Response to Josine Blok." *Talanta* 28–29 (1966–19997): 209–218.

———. "Response to Robert Palter." *History of Science* 32 (1994): 445–464.

———. "Response to Sturt Manning, 'Frames of Reference for the Past: Some Thoughts on Bernal, Truth and Reality.'" *Journal of Mediterranean Archaeology* 3 (1990): 280–282.

———. "Responses on the Comments." *Vest* 8 (1995): 53–58.

———. "Responses to *Black Athena*: General and Linguistic Issues." *Talanta* 28–29 (1996–1997): 65–98.

———. "Responses to Critical Reviews of *Black Athena: The Afroasiatic Roots of Classical Civilization. Volume One: The Fabrication of Ancient Greece, 1785–1985.*" *Journal of Mediterranean Archaeology* 3 (1990): 111–137.

———. "Review of *Freedom in the Making of Western Culture*, by Orlando Patterson." *American Journal of Sociology* 97 (1992): 1471–1473.

———. "Review of *Judaïsme et Christianisme*, by Ernest Renan, Texts Selected by A. de Benoist." *French Studies* 39 (1985): 92–93.

———. "Review of *The Origins of Writing*, ed. W. Senner." *Journal of the American Oriental Society* 111 (1991): 826–827.

———. "Review of Sarah P. Morris: *Daidalos and the Origins of Greek Art*." *Arethusa* 28 (1995): 113–135.

———. "Review of *Sign, Symbol, Script: An Exhibition on the Origins of Writing and the Alphabet*, ed. M. Carter and K. Schoville." *Journal of the American Oriental Society* 105 (1985): 736–737.

———. "Review of *The Topography of Thebes: From the Bronze Age to Modern Times*, by Sarantis Symeonoglou." *Journal of the American Oriental Society* 107 (1987): 557–558.

———. "Roots: Response to Mary Lefkowitz." *New Republic* March 9, 1992, 4–5.

———. *Schwarze Athene: Die afroasiatischen Wurzeln der griechischen Antike: Wie das klassische Griechenland 'erfunden' wurde.* Translated by J. Rehork. Munich: List Verlag, 1992.

———. "Socrates' Ancestry in Question: Response to Mary Lefkowitz." *Academic Questions* 7 (1994): 6–7.

———. "Traveling Light." *New York Review of Books*, August 9, 1973, 21–23.

———. "Unacceptable Face of the Ancient Greek." *Guardian* March 2, 1987, 19.

———. "What Is It about the Vietnamese?" *New York Review of Books*, October 5, 1972, 24–28.

———. "Whose Greece?" Review of *Not Out of Africa*, by M. Lefkowitz, and *Black Athena Revisited*, ed. M. Lefkowitz and G. M. Rogers. *London Review of Books*, December 12, 1996, 17–18.

Best, Jan. "The Ancient Toponyms of Mallia: A Post-Eurocentric Reading of Egyptianising Bronze Age Documents." *Talanta* 28–29 (1996–1997): 99–129.

Bettini, Maurizio. "Ma Atena non era nera." *Repubblica*, January 30, 1992, 34.

Bhaskar, R. "Determinism." In Bottomore et al., *Dictionary of Marxist Thought*, 117–118.

Bikai, Patricia Maynor. "*Black Athena* and the Phoenicians." *Journal of Mediterranean Archaeology* 3 (1990): 67–75.

Black, Edwin. "Farrakhan and the Jews." *Midstream* 22 (1986): 3–6.

Blaut, J. M. "Debates: The Theory of Cultural Racism." *Antipode* 24 (1992): 289–299.

Bloch, Mark. *The Historian's Craft.* Translated by P. Putnam. New York: Vintage, 1953.

Blok, Josine. "Proof and Persuasion in *Black Athena:* The Case of K. O. Müller." *Journal of the History of Ideas* 57 (1996): 705–724.

——. "Proof and Persuasion in *Black Athena* 1: The Case of K. O. Müller." *Talanta* 28–29 (1996–1997): 173–208.

Bloom, Allan. *The Closing of the American Mind.* New York: Touchstone, 1987.

Blyden, E. W., T. Lewis, and D. D. Dwight. *The People of Africa.* New York: Anson D. F. Randolph, 1871.

Boardman, John. "An Orient Wave: Review of *Hellenosemitica,* by Michael Astour." *Classical Review* 16 (1966): 86–88.

Bohman, James. "Do Practices Explain Anything? Turner's Critique of the Theory of Social Practices." *History and Theory* 36 (1997): 93–107.

Bollack, M., and H. Wismann, eds. *Philologie und Hermeneutik im 19. Jahrhundert.* Vol. 2. Göttingen: Vandenhoeck und Ruprecht, 1983.

Bond, George Clement, and Angela Gilliam. "Introduction." In Bond and Gilliam, *Social Construction,* 1–22.

Bond, George Clement, and Angela Gilliam, eds. *Social Construction of the Past: Representation as Power.* London: Routledge, 1994.

Borradori, Giovanna. *The American Philosopher: Conversations with Quine, Davidson, Putnam, Nozick, Danto, Rorty, Cavell, MacIntyre, and Kuhn.* Chicago: University of Chicago Press, 1994.

Bottomore, T., Laurence Harris, V. G. Kiernan, and Ralph Miliband, eds. *A Dictionary of Marxist Thought.* Cambridge: Harvard University Press, 1983.

Bouchard, Donald, ed. *Language, Counter-memory, Practice: Selected Essays and Interviews by Michel Foucault.* Ithaca: Cornell University Press, 1992.

Bourdieu, Pierre. *Homo Academicus.* Translated by P. Collier. Stanford: Stanford University Press, 1988.

——. *The Logic of Practice.* Translated by R. Nice. Stanford: Stanford University Press, 1990.

——. *Outline of a Theory of Practice.* Translated by R. Nice. Cambridge: Cambridge University Press, 1992.

——. "The Philosophical Institution." In Montefiore, *Philosophy in France,* 1–8.

——. "The Specificity of the Scientific Field." In Lemert, *French Sociology,* 257–292.

——. "Vive la crise! For Heterodoxy in Social Science." *Theory and Society* 17 (1988): 773–787.

Bourdieu, Pierre, and Jean-Claude Passeron. "Introduction: Language and Relationship to Language in the Teaching Situation." In Bourdieu, Passeron, and St. Martin, *Academic Discourse,* 1–34.

——. "Sociology and Philosophy in France since 1945: Death and Resurrection of a Philosophy without Subject." *Social Research* 34 (1967): 162–212.

Bourdieu, Pierre and Jean-Claude, Passeron, and M. de St. Martin, eds. *Academic Discourse: Linguistic Misunderstanding and Professiorial Power.* Cambridge, Eng.: Polity Press, 1994.

Bourdieu, Pierre, and L.J.D. Wacquant. *An Invitation to Reflexive Sociology.* Chicago: University of Chicago Press, 1992.

Bower, B. "Beware of Greeks Bearing Culture." *Science News* 140 (1991): 380.

Bowersock, Glen W. "Rescuing the Greeks: A Classicist Defends the Traditional Version of Greek Cultural Achievement." *New York Times Book Review,* February 25, 1996, 6–7.

——. "Review of *Black Athena* 1." *Journal of Interdisciplinary History* 19 (1989): 490–491.

Boyd, Herb. "Will Blacks and Jews Ever Come of Age?" *Crisis* (February/March 1995): 26–33.

Boynton, Robert S. "The Bernaliad: A Scholar-Warrior's Long Journey to Ithaca." *Lingua Franca* (November 1996): 43–50.

———. "The New Intellectuals." *Atlantic Monthly* March (1995): 53–70.

Brace, C. Loring, with David P. Tracer, Lucia Allen Yaroch, John Robb, Kari Brandt, and A. Russell Nelson. "Clines and Clusters versus 'Race': A Test in Ancient Egypt and the Case of a Death on the Nile." *Yearbook of Physical Anthropology* 36 (1993): 1–31.

———. "Clines and Clusters versus 'Race': A Test in Ancient Egypt and the Case of a Death on the Nile." In Lefkowitz and Rogers, *Black Athena Revisited,* 129–164.

Branham, Bracht. "Hellenomania." *Liverpool Classical Monthly* 14 (1989): 56–60.

Branigan, Keith. *The Foundations of Palatial Crete: A Survey of Crete in the Early Bronze Age.* New York: Praeger, 1970.

Breckenridge, Carol, and Peter van der Veer, eds. *Orientalism and the Postcolonial Predicament: Perspectives on South Asia.* Philadelphia: University of Pennsylvania Press, 1993.

Briggs, W., and W. Calder III, eds. *Classical Scholarship: A Biographical Encyclopedia.* New York: Garland, 1990.

Broadhead, Frank. "The African Origins of 'Western Civ.'" *Radical America* 21 (1987): 29–37.

Brooks, Tom. "Negro Militants, Jewish Liberals, and the Unions." *Commentary* 32 (1961): 209–216.

Brown, John Pairman. "Kothar, Kinyras, and Kythereia," *Journal of Semitic Studies* 10 (1965): 197–219.

———. "Literary Contexts of the Common Hebrew-Greek Vocabulary." *Journal of Semitic Studies* 13 (1968): 163–191.

———. "The Sacrificial Cult and Its Critique in Greek and Hebrew." *Journal of Semitic Studies* 24 (1979): 159–173.

———. "The Sacrificial Cult and Its Critique in Greek and Hebrew (II)." *Journal of Semitic Studies* 25 (1980): 1–21.

Brown, Robert. *Semitic Influence in Hellenic Mythology.* New York: Arno Press, 1977.

Bruce, Dickson, Jr. "Ancient Africa and the Early Black American Historians, 1883–1915." *American Quarterly* 36 (1984): 684–699.

Bruford, W. H. *Germany in the Eighteenth Century: The Social Background of the Literary Revival.* Cambridge: Cambridge University Press, 1965.

Brunson, J. "The African Presence in the Ancient Mediterranean Isles and Mainland Greece." In Van Sertima, *African Presence,* 35–65.

Burkert, Walter. *The Orientalizing Revolution: Near Eastern Influence on Greek Culture in the Early Archaic Age.* Translated by M. E. Pinder and W. Burkert. Cambridge: Harvard University Press, 1992.

Burstein, Stanley. "The Debate Over *Black Athena.*" *Scholia* 5 (1996): 3–16.

———. "Review of *Black Athena 2.*" *Classical Philology* 88 (1993): 157–162.

Butler, E. M. *The Tyranny of Greece over Germany: A Study of the Influence Exercised by Greek Art and Poetry over the Great German Writers of the Eighteenth, Nineteenth and Twentieth Centuries.* Boston: Beacon, 1958.

Butler, J., and J. Walter, eds. *Transforming the Curriculum: Ethnic Studies and Women's Studies.* Albany: State University of New York Press, 1991.

Butterfield, Herbert. *Man on His Past: The Study of the History of Historical Scholarship.* Cambridge: Cambridge University Press, 1969.

———. *The Origins of History.* New York: Basic Books, 1981.

Calhoun, Craig. *Critical Social Theory: Culture, History, and the Challenge of Difference.* Cambridge, Eng.: Blackwell, 1996.

Calhoun, Craig. "Putting the Sociologist in the Sociology of Culture: The Self-Reflexive Scholarship of Pierre Bourdieu and Raymond Williams." *Contemporary Sociology* 19 (1990): 500–504.

Camporesi, Cristian. "Review of *Atena nera 1.*" *Religioni e Società* 18 (1994): 123.

Cantarella, E. "Venere di cioccolata." *L'unite,* May 11, 1992.

Cardona, G., H. Hoenigswald, and A. Senn, eds. *Indo-European and the Indo-Europeans: Papers Presented at the Third Indo-European Conference at the University of Pennsylvania* Philadelphia: University of Pennsylvania Press, 1970.

Carew, Jan. "Conversations with Diop and Tsegaye: The Nile Valley Revisited." In Van Sertima and Williams, *Great African Thinkers,* 19–27.

Carpenter, Rhys. "The Antiquity of the Greek Alphabet." *American Journal of Archaeology* 37 (1933): 8–29.

——. "The Greek Alphabet Again." *American Journal of Archaeology* 42 (1938): 58–69.

————. "Phoenicians in the West." *American Journal of Archaeology* 62 (1958): 35–5.

Carruthers, Jacob. "Outside Academia: Bernal's Critique of Black Champions of Ancient Egypt." *Journal of Black Studies* 22 (1992): 459–476.

Carson, Clayborne. "Blacks and Jews in the Civil Rights Movement." In J. Washington, *Jews in Black Perspectives,* 113–131.

————. "The Politics of Relations between African-Americans and Jews." In Berman, *Blacks and Jews,* 131–143.

Carson, Tom. "Greece Is the Word: Afrocentrism and Its Discontents." *Village Voice,* April 16, 1996, 20.

Cartledge, P. "Out of Africa: Review of *Black Athena* Two." *New Statesman and Society,* August 16, 1991, 35–36.

Case, F. I., and M.I.A. Case. "L'héritage égyptien: Perspectives culturelles de l'oeuvre de Cheikh Anta Diop." *Présence Africaine* 149–150 (1989): 101–109.

Chalcraft, David, ed. *Social-Scientific Old Testament Criticism: A Sheffield Reader.* Sheffield, Eng.: Sheffield Academic Press, 1997.

Chambers, Mortimer. "Ernest Curtius." In Briggs and Calder, *Classical Scholarship,* 37–42.

Char, René. *Oeuvres complètes.* Paris: Gallimard, 1983.

Chartier, Roger. *Cultural History: Between Practices and Representations.* Translated by L. Cochrane. Ithaca: Cornell University Press, 1988.

Childe, V. Gordon. "The Orient and Europe." *American Journal of Archaeology* 43 (1939): 10–26.

Clarke, John Henrik. "Cheikh Anta Diop and the New Concept of African History." In Van Sertima and Williams, *Great African Thinkers,* 110–117.

————. "The Historical Legacy of Cheikh Anta Diop: His Contributions to a New Concept of African History." *Présence Africaine* 149–150 (1989): 110–119.

Clifford, Richard J. "Phoenician Religion." *Bulletin of the American Schools of Oriental Research* 279 (1990): 55–64.

Cline, Eric. "Amenhotep III and the Aegean: A Reassessment of Egypto-Aegean Relations in the Fourteenth Century B.C." *Orientalia* 56 (1987): 1–36.

————. "Review of *Black Athena Revisited,* ed. M. Lefkowitz and G. Rogers." *American Journal of Archaeology* 100 (1996): 781–782.

————. "An Unpublished Amenhotep III Faience Plaque from Mycenae." *Journal of the American Oriental Society* 110 (1990): 200–212.

Cocks, G., and K. Jarausch, eds. *German Professions, 1800–1950.* New York: Oxford University Press, 1990.

Cohen, Walter. "An Interview with Martin Bernal." *Social Text* 35 (1993): 1–24.

Coleman, John E. "Did Egypt Shape the Glory that was Greece?" In Lefkowitz and Rogers, *Black Athena Revisited,* 280–302.

————. "Did Egypt Shape the Glory That Was Greece? The Case Against Martin Bernal's *Black Athena.*" *Archaeology* 45 (1992): 48–52, 77–81.

Collins, R. O., ed. *Problems in African History.* Englewood Cliffs, N.J.: Prentice-Hall, 1968.

Conyers, James L., Jr. "Review of Mary Lefkowitz, *Not Out of Africa.*" *Journal of Black Studies* 27 (1996): 130–131.

Coser, Lewis. *The Functions of Social Conflict.* New York: Free Press, 1964.

———. "Georg Simmel's Style of Work: A Contribution to the Sociology of the Sociologist." *American Journal of Sociology* 63 (1958): 635–641.

———. *Men of Ideas: A Sociologist's View.* New York: Free Press, 1965.

Coser, Lewis, ed. *Maurice Halbwachs: On Collective Memory.* Chicago: University of Chicago Press, 1992.

Cottman, Michael. "The Campus 'Radicals.'" *Emerge* (February/March 1994): 26–31.

Coughlin, Ellen. "In Multiculturalism Debate, Scholarly Book on Ancient Greece Plays Controversial Part." *Chronicle of Higher Education,* July 31, 1991, A6.

———. "*Not Out of Africa:* Wellesley Classicist's Book Seeks to Refute Afrocentric Views about Egyptian Influence on Ancient Greece." *Chronicle of Higher Education,* February 16, 1996.

Craigie, Peter. *Ugarit and the Old Testament.* Grand Rapids, Mich.: William B. Eerdmans, 1983.

Cross, Frank Moore, Jr. "The Phoenician Inscription from Brazil: A Nineteenth-Century Forgery." *Orientalia* 37 (1968): 437–460.

Crossland, R. A. "Linguistics and Archaeology in Prehistory." In Crossland and Birchall, *Bronze Age Migrations,* 5–15.

Crossland, R. A., and A. Birchall. *Bronze Age Migrations in the Aegean: Archaeological and Linguistic Problems in Greek Prehistory.* London: Duckworth, 1973.

Crouch, S. *The All-American Skin Game; or, The Decoy of Race.* New York: Pantheon, 1995.

Crummell, Alexander. *Destiny and Race: Selected Writings, 1840–1898.* Edited by W. J. Moses. Amherst: University of Massachusetts Press, 1992.

Cruse, Harold. "My Jewish Problem and Theirs." In Hentoff, *Black Anti-Semitism,* 143–188.

Cudjoe, Selwyn. "Not a Racist Polemic . . ." *Boston Sunday Globe,* April 22, 1996.

Culham, P., and L. Edmunds, eds. *Classics: A Discipline and Profession in Crisis?* Lanham, Md.: University Press of America, 1989.

Currie, H. M. "Review of *Black Athena 1.*" *Theory, Culture, and Society* 6 (1989): 328.

Damrosch, David. *We Scholars: Changing the Culture of the University.* Cambridge: Harvard University Press, 1995.

Davidson, Basil. *The African Slave Trade.* Boston: Little, Brown, 1980.

———. "The Ancient World and Africa: Whose Roots?" *Race and Class* 29 (1987): 1–15.

———. *The Search for Africa: History, Culture, Politics.* New York: Random House, 1994.

Dawe, Alan. "Extended Review of *A Sociology of Sociology,* by R. W. Friedrichs." *Sociological Review* 19 (1971): 140–147.

de Benedetti, R. "Il Cielo Infinito d'Oriente che Illuminio il Partenone." *Avvenire,* April 3, 1993.

De Melis, Federico. "*Black Athena.*" *Manifesto,* December 8, 1991, 23–24.

DeJean, Joan. *Ancients against Moderns: Culture Wars and the Making of a Fin de Siècle.* Chicago: University of Chicago Press, 1997.

Delany, M. *The Principia of Ethnology: The Origin of Races and Color, with an Archaeological Compendium of Ethiopian and Egyptian Civilization, from Years of Careful Examination and Enquiry.* Philadelphia: Harper and Brother, 1879.

Delgado, Richard. "Review Essay: Rodrigo's Chronicle." *Yale Law Journal* 101 (1992): 1357–1383.

DeParle, Jason. "For Some Blacks, Social Ills Seem to Follow White Plans." *New York Times,* August 11, 1991, 4–5.

Diodorus of Sicily. *The Library of History*, vols. 1, 3, 12. Translated by C. H. Oldfather and F. R. Walton. Cambridge: Harvard University Press, 1933–1967.

Diogenes Laertius. *Lives of Eminent Philosophers*, vols. 1 and 2. Translated by R. D. Hicks. Cambridge: Harvard University Press, 1950, 1970.

Diop, Babacar. "L'Antiquitè africaine dans l'oeuvre de Cheikh Anta Diop." *Prèsence Africaine* 149–150 (1989): 143–149.

Diop, Cheikh Anta. *The African Origin of Civilization: Myth or Reality* Translated by M. Cook. Chicago: Lawrence Hill, 1974.

———. "Africa's Contribution to World Civilization: The Exact Sciences." In Van Sertima and Williams, *Great African Thinkers*, 74–88.

———. "The Beginnings of Man and Civilization." In Van Sertima and Williams, *Great African Thinkers*, 322–351.

———. *Civilization or Barbarism: An Authentic Anthropology.* Translated by Y. L. Meema Ngemi. Chicago: Lawrence Hill, 1991.

———. "Iron in the Ancient Egyptian Empire." In Van Sertima and Williams, *Great African Thinkers*, 64–73.

———. "Origin of the Ancient Egyptians." In Mokhtar, *General History of Africa*, 15–32.

———. "Two Interviews with Cheikh Anta Diop." In Van Sertima and Williams, *Great African Thinkers*, 284–303.

Diop, Dialo. "Réflexions sur la pensée politique de Cheikh Anta Diop." *Présence Africaine* 149–150 (1989): 150–160.

Dover, K. "Thucydides 'as History' and 'as Literature.'" *History and Theory* 22 (1983): 54–63.

———. "Simia." *Liverpool Classical Monthly* 18 (1993): 46.

Drake, St. Clair J. G. "African Diaspora and Jewish Diaspora: Convergence and Divergence." In J. Washington, *Jews in Black Perspectives*, 19–41.

———. *Black Folk Here and There*, Vol. 1. Los Angeles: University of California Press, 1987.

———. *Black Folk Here and There*, Vol. 2. Los Angeles: University of California Press, 1990.

D'Souza, Dinesh. *The End of Racism: Principles for a Multiracial Society.* New York: Free Press, 1995.

———. *Illiberal Education: The Politics of Race and Sex on Campus.* New York: Vintage, 1992.

Du Bois, W.E.B. *The Negro.* 1915. Reprint. New York: Oxford University Press, 1970.

———. *The Souls of Black Folk.* 1903. Reprint. New York: Viking Penguin, 1989.

———. "The Superior Race." In Lewis, *W.E.B. Du Bois*, 470–477.

———. *The World and Africa: An Inquiry into the Part Which Africa Has Played in World History.* New York: Viking 1947.

Duke, T. T. "Review of *Hellenosemitica*, by Michael Astour." *Classical Journal* 121 (1965): 131–136.

Durkheim, Emile. *On Morality and Society.* Edited by R. Bellah. Chicago: University of Chicago Press, 1973.

———. *The Rules of Sociological Method.* Translated by S. Solovay and J. Mueller. New York: Free Press, 1964.

Dussel, Enrique. "Eurocentrism and Modernity (Introduction to the Frankfurt Lectures)." *boundary* 2 20 (1993): 65–76.

Duster, Troy. "Social Implications of the 'New' Black Urban Underclass." *Black Scholar* 19 (1988): 2–9.

Dyson, Michael Eric. "On *Black Athena*: An Interview With Martin Bernal." *Z Magazine* 5 (1992): 56–60.

———. *Reflecting Black: African-American Cultural Criticism.* Minneapolis: University of Minnesota Press, 1993.

Eagleton, Terry. *Ideology: An Introduction.* New York: Verso, 1991.

———. *Marxism and Literary Criticism*. Berkeley: University of California Press, 1976.

Early, Gerald. "Afrocentrism: From Sensationalism to Measured Deliberation." *Journal of Blacks in Higher Education* 5 (1994): 86–87.

———. "American Education and the Postmodernist Impulse." *American Quarterly* 45 (1993): 220–229.

———. "The Anatomy of Afrocentrism." In J. Miller, *Alternatives*, 12–15.

Early, G., W. Moses, L. Wilson, and M. Lefkowitz. "Symposium: Historical Roots of Afrocentrism." *Academic Questions* 7 (1994): 44–54.

Eckberg, Douglas L., and Lester Hill, Jr. "The Paradigm Concept and Sociology: A Critical Review." In Gutting *Paradigms and Revolutions*, 117–136.

Edmunds, Lowell. "Greek and Near Eastern Mythology." In Edmunds, *Approaches to Greek Myth*, 141–142.

Edmunds, Lowell, ed. *Approaches to Greek Myth*. Baltimore: Johns Hopkins University Press, 1990.

Egberts, Arno. "Consonants in Collision: Neith and Athena Reconsidered." *Talanta* 28–29 (1996–1997): 149–163.

Ehrich, Robert, ed. *Relative Chronologies in Old World Archaeology*. Chicago: University of Chicago Press, 1954.

Eisenstadt, S. N. "The Format of Jewish History: Some Reflections on Weber's *Ancient Judaism*." *Modern Judaism* 1 (1981): 54–73.

Ellison, Ralph. *Going to the Territory*. New York: Vintage, 1987.

Elson, John. "Attacking Afrocentrism." *Time*, February 19, 1996, 66.

Euripides. *The Phoenician Women*. Translated by P. Burian and B. Swann. New York: Oxford University Press, 1981.

Fahey, Tony. "Max Weber's *Ancient Judaism*." *American Journal of Sociology* 88 (1982): 62–87.

Febvre, Lucien. *The Problem of Unbelief in the Sixteenth Century: The Religion of Rabelais*. Translated by B. Gottlieb. Cambridge: Harvard University Press, 1982.

Fechter, Alan. "The Black Scholar: An Endangered Species." *Review of Black Political Economy* 19 (1990): 49–59.

Federici, Silvia. "Introduction." In Federici, *Enduring Western Civilization*, ix–xvi.

Federici, Silvia, ed. *Enduring Western Civilization: The Construction of the Concept of Western Civilization and Its "Others."* Westport, Conn.: Praeger, 1995.

Feher, Michael. "The Schisms of '67: On Certain Restructurings of the American Left, from the Civil Rights Movement to the Multiculturalist Constellation." In Berman, *Blacks and Jews*, 263–285.

Feingold, Henry. "From Equality to Liberty: The Changing Political Culture of American Jews." In Seltzer and Cohen, *Americanization* 97–118.

Ferguson, J. "Review of *Black Athena*, Volume One." *Religious Studies Review* 14 (1988): 374.

Feyerabend, Paul. "Consolations for the Specialist." In Lakatos and Musgrave, *Criticism*, 197–230.

Fiedler, Horst. *Georg Forsters Werke: Sämtliche, Schriften, Tagebücher, Briefe, Elfter Band*. Berlin: Akademie-Verlag, 1977.

Finch, Charles. "Further Conversations with the Pharaoh." In Van Sertima and Williams, *Great African Thinkers*, 227–230.

———. "Interview with Cheikh Anta Diop." In Van Sertima and Williams, *Great African Thinkers*, 230–237.

———. "Meeting the Pharaoh: Conversations with Cheikh Anta Diop." In Van Sertima and Williams, *Great African Thinkers*, 28–34.

Finkelberg, Margalit. "Anatolian Languages and Indo-European Migrations to Greece." *Classical World* 91 (1997): 3–20.

Finley, M. I. *Ancient History: Evidence and Models*. New York: Viking, 1986.

———. *The Use and Abuse of History*. New York: Viking, 1975.

Finn, Chester, Jr. "Cleopatra's Nose: Review of *Not Out of Africa,* by Mary Lefkowitz." *Commentary* 101 (1996): 71–72.

Fischer, David. *Historians' Fallacies: Toward a Logic of Historical Thought.* New York: Harper and Row, 1970.

Fish, Stanley."Boutique Multiculturalism; or, Why Liberals Are Incapable of Thinking about Hate Speech." *Critical Inquiry* 23 (1996): 378–395.

———. "The Common Touch; or, One Size Fits All." In Gless and Smith, *Politics,* 241–266.

Fitchue, M. A. "Afrocentricity: Reconstructing Cultural Values." *Black Issues in Higher Education,* September 23, 1993, 38–39.

Foner, P. S. *The Life and Writings of Frederick Douglass.* Vol. 2, *Pre–Civil War Decade, 1850–1860.* New York: International Publishers, 1950.

Foster, H. "The Ethnicity of the Ancient Egyptians." *Journal of Black Studies* 5 (1974): 175–191.

Foucault, Michel. *The History of Sexuality.* Vol. 1, *An Introduction.* Translated by R. Hurley. New York: Vintage, 1980.

———. "Intellectuals and Power." In Bouchard, *Language, Counter-memory, Practice,* 205–217.

Fraser, Nancy. *Unruly Practices: Power, Discourse, and Gender in Contemporary Social Theory.* Minneapolis: University of Minnesota Press, 1989.

Freedman, D. N., ed. *The Anchor Bible Dictionary.* Vol. 6, *Si–Z. New York: Doubleday,* 1992.

Friedman, Saul. "An Old/New Libel: Jews in the Slave Trade." *Midstream* 37 (1991): 12–14.

Friedrich, Johannes. "Die Unechtheit der Phönizischen Inschrift aus Parahyba." *Orientalia* 37 (1968): 421–424.

Fuller, Steve. "Being There with Thomas Kuhn: A Parable for Postmodern Times." *History and Theory* 31 (1992): 241–275.

Furman, Andrew. "Surviving Success: Jewish-American Fiction after Alienation." *Response* 65 (1996): 10–21.

Gabriel, J. "*Black Athena*: Two Views." *Science as Culture* 6 (1989): 124–129.

Gardner, J. "The Debate on 'Black Athena.'" *Classical Review* 41 (1991): 166–167.

Gasster, Michael. "Review of Martin Bernal, *Chinese Socialism." Political Science Quarterly* 91 (1976): 563–564.

Gates, Henry Lewis, Jr. "Good-bye, Columbus? Notes on the Culture of Criticism." In Goldberg, *Multiculturalism,* 203–217.

Genovese, E., and L. Hochberg, eds. *Geograpphic Perspectives in History.* New York: Blackwell, 1989.

Georgakas, Dan. "*Black Athena*: Aryans, Semites, Egyptians and Hellenes." *Cineaste* 19 (1993): 55–56.

George, Leonard. *Crimes of Perception: An Encyclopedia of Heresies and Heretics.* New York: Paragon House, 1995.

Georgiev, V. I. "The Arrival of the Greeks in Greece: The Linguistic Evidence." In Crossland and Birchall, *Bronze Age Migrations,* 243–253.

Germain, Gabriel. *Homère et la mystique des nombres.* Paris: Presses Universitaires de France, 1954.

Gerth, H. H., and C. W. Mills, eds. *From Max Weber: Essays in Sociology.* New York: Oxford University Press, 1958.

Gesenius, Wilhelm. *Gesenius' Hebrew Grammar.* 1813. 2nd English edition. Oxford: Clarendon Press, 1985.

Giannaris, C. "Rocking the Cradle: Review of *Black Athena* 1." *New Statesman,* July 10, 1987, 31.

Giddens, Anthony. *Capitalism and Modern Social Theory: An Analysis of the Writings of Marx, Durkheim and Max Weber.* Cambridge: Cambridge University Press, 1992.

———. *Social Theory and Modern Sociology.* Stanford: Stanford University Press, 1987.

Gill, C., and T. P. Wiseman, eds. *Lies and Fiction in the Ancient World.* Austin: University of Texas Press, 1993.

Gimbutas, Marija. "The Destruction of Aegean and East Mediterranean Urban Civilization Around 2300 B.C." In Crossland and Birchall, *Bronze Age Migrations,* 129–139.

———. "Proto-Indo-European Culture: The Kurgan Culture during the Fifth, Fourth, and Third Millennia B.C." In Cardona et al., *Indo-European,* 155–198.

Ginsberg, H. L. "Hebrews and Hellenes: Review of Cyrus Gordon's *Before the Bible: The Common Background of Greek and Hebrew Civilizations.*" *Commentary* 36 (1963): 333–336.

Giroux, Henry. "Insurgent Multiculturalism and the Promise of Pedagogy." In Goldberg, *Multiculturalism,* 325–343.

Gitlin, Todd. *The Twilight of Common Dreams: Why America Is Wracked by Culture Wars.* New York: Metropolitan Books, 1995.

Glazer, Nathan. "The Anomalous Liberalism of American Jews." In Seltzer and Cohen, *Americanization,* 133–143.

———. "Jews and Blacks: What Happened to the Grand Alliance?" In J. Washington, *Jews in Black Perspectives,* 105–112.

———. *We Are All Multiculturalists Now.* Cambridge: Harvard University Press, 1997.

Gless, D., and B. H. Smith, eds. *The Politics of Liberal Education.* Durham: Duke University Press, 1992.

Goldberg, David Theo. "Introduction: Multicultural Conditions." In Goldberg, *Multiculturalism,* 1–41.

Goldberg, David Theo, ed. *Multiculturalism: A Critical Reader.* Cambridge, Eng.: Blackwell, 1994.

Goldsmith, M. *Sage: A Life of J. D. Bernal.* London: Hutchinson, 1980.

Goode, Stephen. "Ancient Greece's Non-Greek Roots." *Insight,* April 11, 1988, 54–55.

Goodheart, Eugene. "Reflections on the Culture Wars." *Daedalus* 126 (1997): 153–175.

Goonatilake, Susantha. "The Son, the Father, and the Holy Ghosts: Review of *Black Athena 1.*" *Economic and Political Weekly* August 5, 1989, 1768.

Gordon, Cyrus H. *Before Columbus: Links between the Old World and Ancient America.* New York: Crown, 1971.

———. "The Canaanite Text from Brazil." *Orientalia* 37 (1968): 425–436.

———. *The Common Background of Greek and Hebrew Civilizations.* New York: W. W. Norton, 1965.

———. "Cultural and Religious Life." In Mazar, *The World History of the Jewish People,* 52–65.

———. "Eteocretan." *Journal of Near Eastern Studies* 21 (1962): 211–214.

———. "Foreword." In Astour, *Hellenosemitica,* xi.

———. "Homer and the Bible: The Origin and Character of East Mediterranean Literature." *Hebrew Union College Annual* 26 (1955): 43–108.

———. "Language as a Means to an End." *Antiquity* 115 (1955): 147–149.

———. "The Mediterranean Factor in the Old Testament." *Supplement to Vetus Testamentum* 9 (1963): 19–31.

———. "Northwest Semitic Texts in Latin and Greek Letters." *Journal of the American Oriental Society* 88 (1968): 285–289.

———. "Reply to Professor Cross." *Orientalia* 37 (1968): 461–463.

———. "Review of *Ancient Near Eastern Texts (Relating to the Old Testament),* edited by J. B. Pritchard." *American Journal of Archaeology* 56 (1952): 93–94.

———. *Riddles in History.* New York: Crown, 1974.

———. *Ugarit and Minoan Crete: The Bearing of Their Texts on the Origins of Western Culture.* New York: W. W. Norton, 1966.

Gordon, Pamela. "On *Black Athena*: Ancient Critques of the 'Ancient Model' of Greek History." *Classical World* 87 (1993): 71–72.

Gottwald, N. *The Tribes of Yahweh: A Sociology of the Religion of Liberated Israel, 1250–1050 BCE.* Maryknoll, N.Y.: Orbis Books, 1985.

Gould, Stephan Jay. "American Polygeny and Craniometry before Darwin: Blacks and Indians as Separate, Inferior Species." In Harding, *"Racial" Economy,* 84–115.

———. *The Mismeasure of Man.* New York: W. W. Norton, 1981.

Gourevitch, Philip. "The Crown Heights Riot and Its Aftermath." *Commentary* 95 (1993): 29–34.

———. "The Jeffries Affair." *Commentary* 93 (1992): 34–38.

Graff, Gerald. *Beyond the Culture Wars: How Teaching the Conflicts Can Revitalize American Education.* New York: W. W. Norton, 1992.

Gramsci, Antonio. *Quaderni del carcere.* Volume terzo, quaderni 12–29. Edited by Valentino Gerratana. Torino: Giulio Einaudi, 1977.

———. *Selections from the Prison Notebooks of Antonio Gramsci.* Edited by Q. Hoare and G. Nowell Smith. New York: International Publishers, 1987.

Gray, Christopher. *Conceptions of History in the Works of Cheikh Anta Diop and Théophile Obenga.* London: Karnak House, 1989.

Green, Tamara. "*Black Athena* and Classical Historiography: Other Approaches, Other Views." *Arethusa,* special issue (1989): 55–65.

Gress, David. "The Case against Martin Bernal." *New Criterion* 8 (1989): 36–43.

Griffin, Jasper. "Anxieties of Influence." *New York Review of Books,* June 20, 1996, 67–73.

———. "Who Are These Coming to the Sacrifice? Review of *BA 1.*" *New York Review of Books,* June 15, 1989, 25–27.

Grottanelli, Cristiano. "Atene è ancora li." *Manifesto,* December 8, 1991, 26–27.

———. "La grande congiura degli storici bianchi." *Indice* June (1992): 45.

Guidorizzi, G. "Stranezze che danno la misura di una crisi di idee." *Giorno,* September 22, 1993, 19.

Gullekson, Justin. "Non c'è posto in facoltà per il bianco senza status." *Avvenire,* May 12, 1992.

Güterbok, Hans. G. "The Hittite Version of the Hurrian Kumarbi Myths: Oriental Forerunners of Hesiod." *American Journal of Archaeology* 52 (1948): 123–134.

Gutman, Herbert. "Parallels in Urban Experience." In J. Washington, *Jews in Black Perspectives,* 98–104.

Gutmann, Amy. "Introduction." In Gutmann, *Multiculturalism,* 3–24.

Gutmann, Amy ed. *Multiculturalism.* Princeton: Princeton University Press, 1994.

Gutting, Gary. "Introduction." In Gutting, *Paradigms and Revolutions,* 1–21.

———. "Preface." In Gutting, *Paradigms and Revolutions,* v.

Gutting, Gary, ed. *Paradigms and Revolutions: Applications and Appraisals of Thomas Kuhn's Philosophy of Science.* London: University of Notre Dame Press, 1980.

Guy-Sheftall, Beverly. "A Black Feminist Perspective on the Academy." In Butler and Walter, *Transforming the Curriculum,* 305–311.

Hacker, Andrew. "Jewish Racism, Black Anti-Semitism." In Berman, *Blacks and Jews,* 154–163.

———. *Two Nations: Black and White, Separate, Hostile, Unequal.* New York: Ballantine, 1992.

Halbfass, Wilhelm. *India and Europe: An Essay in Understanding.* Albany: State University of New York Press, 1988.

Haley, Shelley. "Black Feminist Thought and Classics: Re-membering, Re-claiming, Re-empowering." In Rabinowitz and Richlin, *Feminist Theory,* 23–43.

———. "Review of *Black Athena* (movie)." *Classical World* 87 (1994): 241–242.

Hall, Edith. "Myths Missing That Black Magic." *Times Higher Education Supplement* (London), September 13, 1991, 15, 18.

——. "When Is a Myth Not a Myth? Bernal's 'Ancient Model.'" *Arethusa* 25 (1992): 181–201.

——. "When Is a Myth Not a Myth?" Bernal's 'Ancient Model.'" In Lefkowitz and Rogers, *Black Athena Revisited*, 333–348.

Hall, Jonathan. "*Black Athena*: A Sheep in Wolf's Clothing?" *Journal of Mediterranean Archaeology* 3 (1990): 247–254.

Hall, Perry. "Beyond Afrocentrism: Alternatives for African American Studies." *Western Journal of Black Studies* 15 (1991): 207–211.

Hallas, Duncan. "Absent Friends: Review of *Black Athena 1*." *Socialist Worker Review* (July/August 1987): 29–30.

Hansen, Hardy. "Introduction." *Arethusa* 27 (1994): 1–6.

Harden, Donald. *The Phoenicians*. New York: Frederick Praeger, 1962.

Harding, Sandra. "Introduction." In Harding, *"Racial" Economy*," 1–29.

Harding, Sandra, ed. *The "Racial" Economy of Science: Toward a Democratic Future*. Bloomington: Indiana University Press, 1993.

——. *Whose Science? Whose Knowledge? Thinking from Women's Lives*. Ithaca: Cornell University Press, 1993.

Harris, Joseph E. ed. *Africa and Africans as Seen by Classical Writers: The William Leo Hansberry African History Notebook*, Vol. 2. Washington, D.C.: Howard University Press, 1977.

Hart, Lenore. "Review of *Not Out of Africa: How Afrocentrism Became an Excuse to Teach Myth as History*." *Florida Times-Union*, April 21, 1996, F4.

Haskell, Thomas. "Justifying the Rights of Academic Freedom in the Era of 'Power/Knowledge.'" In Menand, *Future of Academic Freedom*, 43–90.

Hentoff, Nat. "Introduction." In Hentoff, *Black Anti-Semitism*, ix–xvii.

Hentoff, Nat, ed. *Black Anti-Semitism and Jewish Racism*. New York: Richard Baron, 1969.

Herf, Jeffrey. "How the Culture Wars Matter: Liberal Historiography, German History, and the Jewish Catastrophe." In Nelson and Bérubé, *Higher Education under Fire*, 149–162.

Herodotus. *Histories*. Translated by A. de Sélincourt. London: Penguin, 1988.

Hertzberg, Arthur. "The Jewish Intelligentsia and Their Jewishness." *Midstream* 30 (1984): 35–39.

Hilliard, Asa, III. "Bringing Maat, Destroying Isfet: The African and African Diasporan Presence in the Study of Ancient KMT." In Van Sertima, *Egypt*, 127–147.

——. "The Cultural Unity of Black Africa: The Domains of Patriarchy and of Matriarchy in Classical Antiquity." In van Sertima and Williams, *Great African Thinkers*, 102–109.

Himmelfarb, Gertrude. "Academic Advocates." *Commentary* 100 (1995): 46–49.

Himmelfarb, M. "American Jews: Diehard Conservatives." *Commentary* 87 (1989): 44–49.

Hobsbawm, Eric J. *The Age of Empire, 1875–1914*. New York: Vintage, 1989.

——. *The Age of Revolution, 1789–1848." New York: New American Library, 1962.*

Hochkeppel, Willy Von. "Philosophie. Eine Kolumne: Afrikanisches Philosophieren?" *Merkur* 48 (1994): 335–341.

Hofstadter, R. *Anti-Intellectualism in American Life*. New York: Vintage, 1963.

Hollinger, David. "T. S. Kuhn's Theory of Science and Its Implications for History." In Gutting, *Paradigms and Revolutions*, 195–222.

Holstein, Jay A. "Max Weber and Biblical Scholarship." *Hebrew Union College Annual* 46 (1975): 159–179.

Hook, Sidney. "Anti-Semitism in the Academy: Some Pages of the Past." *Midstream* 25 (1979): 49–54.

Hook, Sidney. *Marx and the Marxists: The Ambiguous Legacy.* Princeton: Van Nostrand, 1955.

hooks, bell. "Keeping a Legacy of Shared Struggle." In Berman, *Blacks and Jews,* 229–238.

hooks, bell, and Cornel West. *Breaking Bread: Insurgent Black Intellectual Life.* Boston: South End Press, 1991.

Hopkins, Keith. "Rules of Evidence." *Journal of Roman Studies* 67 (1978): 178–186.

Horowitz, Irving Louis. "Philo-Semitism and Anti-Semitism: Jewish Conspiracies and Totalitarian Sentiments." *Midstream* 36 (1990): 17–22.

Horowitz, Irving Louis, ed. *Power, Politics and People: The Collected Essays of C. Wright Mills.* New York: Ballantine, 1963.

Horowitz, M. G. "The Scientific Dialectic of Ancient Greece and the Cultural Tradition of Indo-European Speakers." *Journal of Indo-European Studies* 24 (1996): 409–419.

Hoskins, Linus. "Eurocentrism vs. Afrocentrism: A Geopolitical Linkage Analysis." *Journal of Black Studies* 23 (1992): 247–257.

Houessou-Adin, Thomas. "The Big Con: Europe Upside Down." *Journal of Black Studies* 26 (1995): 185–200.

Howe, Irving. "The Value of the Canon." *New Republic,* February 18, 1991, 40–47.

Hughes, Robert. *Culture of Complaint: The Fraying of America.* New York: Warner Books, 1994.

Hutton, Patrick. "The History of Mentalities: The New Map of Cultural History." *History and Theory* 20 (1981): 237–259.

Iggers, G. G. *The German Conception of History: The National Tradition of Historical Thought from Herder to the Present.* Middletown, Conn.: Wesleyan University Press, 1983.

Ikuenobe, P. "The Parochial Universalist Conception of 'Philosophy' and 'African Philosophy.'" *Philosophy East and West* 47 (1997): 189–210.

Inden, Ronald. *Imagining India.* New York: Basil Blackwell, 1990.

Isokrates. *Busiris.* Translated by Larue Van Hook. Cambridge: Harvard University Press, 1961.

———. *Helen.* Translated by Larue Van Hook. Cambridge: Harvard University Press, 1961.

Jacoby, Felix. *Die Fragmente der Griechischen Historiker: Erster Teil, Genealogie und Mythographie.* Leiden: E. J. Brill, 1957.

Jacoby, Russell. *Dialectic of Defeat: Contours of Western Marxism.* Cambridge: Cambridge University Press, 1981.

———. *Dogmatic Wisdom: How the Culture Wars Divert Education and Distract America.* New York: Doubleday, 1994.

———. "Graying of the Intellectuals: Conservatives and Dissenters in the 50's and 80's." *Dissent* 30 (1983): 234–237.

———. *The Last Intellectuals: American Culture in the Age of Academe.* New York: Noonday Press, 1989.

———. "Western Marxism." In Bottomore et al., *Dictionary of Marxist Thought,* 523–526.

———. "Whither Western Civilization? Review of *Debating P.C.* (ed.) P. Berman." *Nation,* March 9, 1992, 307–309.

Jacoby, Tamar. "The Bitter Legacies of Malcolm X." *Commentary* 95 (1993): 27–31.

James, George G. M. *The Stolen Legacy.* 1954. Reprint. Newport News, Va.: African Publication Society, 1989.

Jasanoff, Jay H., and Alan Nussbaum. "Word Games: The Linguistic Evidence in *Black Athena.*" In Lefkowitz and Rogers, *Black Athena Revisited,* 177–205.

Jefford, Clayton. "Review of Martin Bernal's *Black Athena:* Politics and the Past." *Institute for Antiquity and Christianity* 15 (1988): 10–13.

Jeffrey, Jonathan. "Review of Lefkowitz's *Not Out of Africa.*" *Library Journal,* February 1, 1996, 87.

Jeffries, Leonard, Jr. "Civilization or Barbarism: The Legacy of Cheikh Anta Diop." In Van Sertima and Williams, *Great African Thinkers*, 146–160.

Jenkyns, Richard. "Bernal and the Nineteenth Century." In Lefkowitz and Rogers, *Black Athena Revisited*, 411–420.

Jenner, W.J.F. "Visions of Great Togetherness: Review of Martin Bernal's *Chinese Socialism to 1907.*" Times Literary Supplement, *February 11, 1977, 151.*

Jervis, M. "Black and White Classics?" *History Today* 41 (1991): 3–4.

Jewish Publication Society. *Tanakh: A New Translation of the Holy Scriptures According to the Traditional Hebrew Text.* Philadelphia: Jewish Publication Society, 1985.

Jewsiewicki, B., and V. Y. Mudimbe. "Africans' Memories and Contemporary History of Africa." *History and Theory* 32 (1993): 1–11.

Johnson, Chalis. "'All I'm Askin' Is a Little Respect': Black Women in the Academy." *Black Scholar* 24 (1993): 2–6.

Johnson, Edward A. *A School History of the Negro Race in America from 1619 to 1890 Combined with the History of the Negro Soldiers in the Spanish-American War, Also a Short Sketch of Liberia.* 1911. Reprint. New York: AMS Press, 1969.

Johnson-Odim, Cheryl. "Comment: The Debate over *Black Athena.*" *Journal of Women's History* 4 (1993): 84–89.

Jordan, William Chester. "*Black Athena.*" *American Visions* (April 1991): 30–31.

Josephson, Folke. "Comments on Martin Bernal's *Black Athena.*" *Vest* 8 (1995): 35–37.

Journal of Blacks in Higher Education. "Black Enrollments in Higher Education Reach All-Time Highs." *Journal of Blacks in Higher Education* 12 (1996): 66–68.

———. "Black Scholars Hold a Pessimistic Outlook for African-American Prospects in Higher Education." *Journal of Blacks in Higher Education* 11 (1996): 74–76.

———. "Blacks in Higher Education: Some Solid Reasons for Hope and Cheer." *Journal of Blacks in Higher Education* 3 (1994): 43.

———. "The Number of Black Doctorates Down Slightly in 1994." *Journal of Blacks in Higher Education* 10 (1995–1996): 49.

———. "Why the Shortage of Black Professors?" *Journal of Blacks in Higher Education* 1 (1993): 25–34.

Kafka, Franz. "A Fratricide." In *The Basic Kafka.* New York: Pocket Books, 1979.

———. *Letters to Milena.* Edited by W. Haas; translated by T. Stern and J. Stern. New York: Schocken, 1974.

Kagan, Donald. "Stealing History." *New Criterion* 14 (1996): 54–59.

Kalberg, Stephen. *Max Weber's Comparative-Historical Sociology.* Chicago: University of Chicago Press, 1994.

Katz, S., ed. *The Midstream Reader.* New York: Thomas Yoseloff, 1960.

Katzoff, R., ed. *Classical Studies in Honor of David Sohlberg.* Ramat Gan: Bar-Ilan University Press, 1996.

Kaufman, Jonathan. *Broken Alliance: The Turbulent Times between Blacks and Jews in America.* New York: Touchstone, 1995.

Keita, S.O.Y. "*Black Athena*: 'Race,' Bernal and Snowden." *Arethusa* 26 (1993): 295–314.

———. "Further Studies of Crania from Ancient Northern Africa: An Analysis of Crania from the First Dynasty Egyptian Tombs, Using Multiple Discriminant Functions." *American Journal of Physical Anthropology* 87 (1992): 245–254.

———. "Response to Bernal and Snowden." *Arethusa* 26 (1993): 329–334.

———. "Response to Robert Pounder." *American Historical Review* 97 (1992): 1355–1356.

———. "Studies of Ancient Crania from Northern Africa." *American Journal of Physical Anthropology* 85 (1990): 35–48.

Kelly, David. "Egyptians and Ethiopians: Color, Race, and Racism." *Classical Outlook* 68 (1991): 77–82.

Kershaw, Terry. "Afrocentrism and the Afrocentric Method." *Western Journal of Black Studies* 16 (1992): 160–168.

Kimball, Roger. *Tenured Radicals: How Politics Has Corrupted Our Higher Education.* New York: Harper and Row, 1990.

———. "An Update on the Cultural Wars." *New Criterion* 14 (March 1996): 8–13.

King, M. D. "Reason, Tradition, and the Progressiveness of Science." In Gutting, *Paradigms and Revolutions*, 97–116.

Kirk, G. S. *The Nature of Greek Myths.* London: Penguin, 1990.

Koch, Dietrich-Alex. "Source Criticism, New Testament." In Freedman, *Anchor Bible Dictionary*, 165–171.

Kohn, J., ed. *Essays in Understanding, 1930–1954: Hannah Arendt.* New York: Harcourt Brace, 1994.

Konstan, D. "Review of *BA 1*." *Research in African Literatures* 19 (1988): 551–554.

Koselleck, Reinhart. *Critique and Crisis: Enlightenment and the Pathogenesis of Modern Society.* Cambridge: MIT Press, 1988.

Kristeller, Paul. "Comment on *Black Athena*." *Journal of the History of Ideas* 56 (1995): 125–127.

Kuhn, Thomas. *The Structure of Scientific Revolutions.* 2nd ed. Chicago: University of Chicago Press, 1970.

———. *The Essential Tension: Selected Studies in Scientific Tradition and Change.* Chicago: University of Chicago Press, 1977.

———. "Logic of Discovery or Psychology of Research?" In Lakatos and Musgrave, *Criticism*, 1–24.

———. "Reflections on My Critics." In Lakatos and Musgrave, *Criticism*, 231–278.

Kuklick, Bruce. *Puritans in Babylon: The Ancient Near East and American Intellectual Life, 1880–1930.* Princeton: Princeton University Press, 1996.

Kurzweil, E., et al. "Education beyond Politics." *Partisan Review* 59 (1992): 343–419.

La Polla, F. "E anche l'Ellade era dei Neri." *Resto del Carlino*, May 10, 1992.

La Vopa, Anthony. "Specialists against Specialization: Hellenism as Professional Ideology in German Classical Studies." In Cocks and Jarausch, *German Professions*, 27–45.

Lakatos, Imre. "Falsification and the Methodology of Scientific Research Programmes." In Lakatos and Musgrave, *Criticism*, 91–196.

Lakatos, Imre, and Musgrave, A., eds. *Criticism and the Growth of Knowledge.* Cambridge: Cambridge University Press, 1995.

Lam, Aboubacry Moussa. "Égypte ancienne et Afrique noire chez Cheikh Anta Diop." *Présence Africaine* 149–150 (1989): 203–213.

Lambrou-Phillipson, C. *Hellenorientalia: The Near Eastern Presence in the Bronze Age Aegean, ca. 3000–1100 B.C.* Göteborg: Paul Åströms Förlag, 1990.

Langmuir, Gavin. *History, Religion, and Antisemitism.* London: I. B. Tauris, 1990.

Lant, Antonia. "The Curse of the Pharaoh; or, How Cinema Contracted Egyptomania." *October* 59 (1992): 87–112.

Laqueur, Walter. *A History of Zionism.* New York: Holt, 1972.

Lauter, Paul. "'Political Correctness' and the Attack on American Colleges." In Nelson and Bérubé, *Higher Education under Fire*, 73–90.

Leach, Edmund. "Aryan Warlords in their Chariots." *London Review of Books*, April 2, 1987, 11.

Leap, Terry. "Tenure, Discrimination, and African-American Faculty." *Journal of Blacks in Higher Education* 7 (1995): 103–105.

Leatherman, C. "Growing Use of Part-Time Professors Prompts Debate and Calls for Action." *Chronicle of Higher Education*, October 10, 1997, A14.

Leatherman, C. "Leaders of Scholarly Groups Outline Response to Growth in Use of Part-Time Faculty." *Chronicle of Higher Education,* December 5, 1997, A18.

Leff, Gordon. *Heresy in the Later Middle Ages. Vol. 1, The Relation of Heterodoxy to Dissent, c. 1250–1450.* New York: Manchester University Press, 1967.

———. *History and Social Theory.* Tuscaloosa: University of Alabama Press, 1969.

Lefkowitz, Mary R. "The Afrocentric Interpretation of Western History: Lefkowitz Replies to Bernal." *Journal of Blacks in Higher Education* 12 (1996): 88–91.

———. "Ancient History, Modern Myths." In Lefkowitz and Rogers, *Black Athena Revisited,* 3–23.

———. "Ethnocentric History from Aristobulus to Bernal." *Academic Questions* 6 (1993): 12–20.

———. "The Myth of a 'Stolen Legacy.'" *Society* 31 (1994): 27–33.

———. "Not Out of Africa." *New Republic,* February 10, 1992, 29–36.

———. *Not Out of Africa: How Afrocentrism Became an Excuse to Teach Myth as History.* New York: New Republic Books, 1997.

———. "The Origins of the 'Stolen Legacy.'" In J. Miller, *Alternatives,* 27–31.

———. "Point of View." *Chronicle of Higher Education,* May 6, 1992, A52.

Lefkowitz, Mary R., and Guy MacLean Rogers, eds. *Black Athena Revisited.* Chapel Hill: University of North Carolina Press, 1996.

———. "Preface." In Lefkowitz and Rogers, *Black Athena Revisited,* ix–xiv.

Lekas, Padelis. *Marx on Classical Antiquity: Problems of Historical Methodology.* New York: St. Martin's, 1988.

Lemert, C., ed. *French Sociology.* New York: Columbia University Press, 1981.

Lerner, Gerda. "Comment." *Journal of Women's History* 4 (1993): 90–94.

Lerner, Michael, and Cornel West. *Jews and Blacks: A Dialogue on Race, Religion, and Culture in America.* New York: Plume, 1996.

Lester, Julius. "Academic Freedom and the Black Intellectual." *Black Scholar* 19 (1988): 16–43.

———. "The Lives People Live." In Berman, *Blacks and Jews,* 164–177.

———. "A Response." In Hentoff, *Black Anti-Semitism,* 229–237.

Levin, Saul. *Semitic and Indo-European: The Principal Etymologies with Observations on Afro-Asiatic.* Philadelphia: John Benjamins, 1995.

Levine, Donald. *The Flight from Ambiguity: Essays in Social and Cultural Theory.* Chicago: University of Chicago Press, 1988.

Levine, Lawrence. *The Opening of the American Mind: Canons, Culture, and History.* Boston: Beacon Press, 1996.

Levine, Molly Myerowitz. "Anti-Black and Anti-Semitic? Have Classical Historians Suppressed the Black and Semitic Roots of Greek Civilization?" *Bible Review* 6 (1990): 32–41.

———. "Bernal and the Athenians in the Multicultural World of the Ancient Mediterranean." In Katzoff, *Classical Studies,* 1–56.

———. "The Challenge of *Black Athena* to Classics Today." *Arethusa* (Special Issue): 7–16.

———. "Multiculturalism and the Classics." *Arethusa* 25 (1992): 215–221.

———. "Review Article: The Use and Abuse of *Black Athena." American Historical Review* 97 (1992): 440–460.

Lewis, Bernard. "The Question of Orientalism." *New York Review of Books,* June 24, 1982, 49–56.

Lewis, Donald Levering. "Parallels and Divergences: Assimilationist Strategies of Afro-American and Jewish Elites from 1910 to the Early 1930s." *Journal of American History* 71 (1984): 543–564.

———. "Shortcuts to the Mainstream: Afro-American and Jewish Notables in the 1920s and 1930s." In J. Washington, *Jews in Black Perspectives,* 83–97.

Lewis, David Levering. *W.E.B. Du Bois: A Reader.* New York: Henry Holt, 1995.

Lindberg, B. "Comments on Martin Bernal's *Black Athena.*" *Vest* 8 (1995): 48–51.

Lipset, Seymour Martin, and Everett Carll Ladd, Jr. "Jewish Academics in the United States: Their Achievements, Culture, and Politics." *American Jewish Yearbook* 72 (1971): 89–128.

Liverani, Mario. "The Bathwater and the Baby." In Lefkowitz and Rogers, *Black Athena Revisited*, 421–427.

Livingstone, Frank B. "On the Non-Existence of Human Races." *Current Anthropology* 3 (1962): 279–281.

Lloyd, G.E.R. *Methods and Problems in Greek Science.* Cambridge: Cambridge University Press, 1991.

Lloyd, R. B. "Review of *Black Athena* 1." *Choice* (June 1988): 1547.

Lloyd-Jones, Hugh. "Becoming Homer: *Epic Singers and Oral Tradition,* by A. B. Lord; *Homer and the Origin of the Greek Alphabet,* by B. Powell; *Cadmean Letters,* by Martin Bernal." *New York Review of Books* March 5, 1992, 52–57.

Locke, John. *A Letter concerning Toleration.* Edited by J. Tully. Indianapolis: Hackett Publishing Company, 1983.

Lo Monaco, Adriano. "L'Occidente? È nato in Africa." *Avvenire,* May 16, 1992.

Loury, Glenn. "Color Blinded." *Arion* 4 (1997): 168–185.

Lowenthal, David. *The Past Is a Foreign Country.* Cambridge: Cambridge University Press, 1985.

Lukes, Steven. *Emile Durkheim, His Life and Work: A Historical and Critical Study.* Stanford: Stanford University Press, 1985.

Lyotard, Jean-François. *The Postmodern Condition: A Report on Knowledge.* Translated by G. Bennington and B. Massumi. Minneapolis: University of Minnesota Press, 1993.

McCarthy, Cameron. Contradictions of Existence: Identity and Essentialism." In Nelson and Bérubé, *Higher Education under Fire*, 326–335.

MacGaffey, Wyatt. "Concepts of Race in the Historiography of Northeast Africa." *Journal of African History* 7 (1966): 1–17.

McGregor, Malcolm. "Review of *Hellenosemitica* by Michael Astour." *American Historical Review* 71 (1966): 521–522.

McNeal, R. A. "Review Essays: *Black Athena* 1." *History and Theory* 31 (1992): 47–55.

Magner, Denise. "Debate in African Studies." *Chronicle of Higher Education,* November 10, 1995, A19.

———. "Politicians Press Officials at the City College of New York to Punish Black-Studies Chairman for Remarks on Jews." *Chronicle of Higher Education,* September 4, 1991, A19–A22.

Malamud, Martha A. "Book Review: *Black Athena* 1." *Criticism* 31 (1989): 317–322.

Mallory, J. P. *In Search of the Indo-Europeans: Language, Archaeology and Myth.* London: Thames and Hudson, 1996.

Manasse, Ernst Moritz. "Max Weber on Race." *Social Research* 14 (1947): 191–221.

Manetho. *The History of Egypt.* Translated by W. G. Waddell. Cambridge: Harvard University Press, 1980.

Manning, Sturt. "Frames of Reference for the Past: Some Thoughts on Bernal, Truth and Reality." *Journal of Mediterranean Archaeology* 3 (1990): 255–274.

Manuel, Frank. *The Prophets of Paris: Turgot, Condorcet, St. Simon, Fourier and Comte.* New York: Harper and Row, 1965.

Marable, Manning. *W.E.B. Du Bois: Black Radical Democrat.* Boston: Twayne, 1986.

Marchand, Suzanne, and Anthony Grafton. "Martin Bernal and His Critics," *Arion* 5 (1997): 1–35.

Marshall, Gloria. "Racial Classifications: Popular and Scientific." In Harding, *"Racial" Economy*, 116–127.

Marcus, David. *Jephthah and His Vow*. Lubbock: Texas Tech University Press, 1986.

Martel, E. "What's Wrong with the Portland Baseline Essays?" In Miller, *Alternatives*, 37–42.

Martin, Tony. *The Jewish Onslaught: Despatches from the Wellesley Battlefront*. Dover, Mass.: Majority Press, 1993.

Martins, Herminio. "The Kuhnian 'Revolution' and Its Implications for Sociology." In Nossiter et al., *Imagination*, 13–58.

Marx, Karl, and Friedrich Engels. *The German Ideology: Part 1*. 1932. Reprint. New York: International Publishers, 1991.

Massoni, S. "Il razzismo discreto della civiltà ellenica." *Avanti*, July 3, 1992, 22.

Masterman, Margaret. "The Nature of a Paradigm." In Lakatos and Musgrave, *Criticism*, 59–90.

Mauny, R. "Nations, nègres et culture—A Review." In Collins, *Problems*, 16–23.

Mazar, Benjamin, ed. *The World History of the Jewish People*. First Series, *Ancient Times*; Volume 3, *Judges*. New Brunswick: Rutgers University Press, 1971.

Mehlman, Jeffrey. "Core of Core: A Phantasmagoria in Translation." *Comparative Literature* 49 (1997): 1–23.

Meier, August. "Review of Lefkowitz's *Not Out of Africa: How Afrocentrism Became an Excuse to Teach Myth as History*." *Journal of American History* 83 (1996): 988.

Menand, Louis. "The Limits of Academic Freedom." In Menand, *Future of Academic Freedom*, 3–20.

Menand, L., ed. *The Future of Academic Freedom*. Chicago: University of Chicago Press, 1996.

Meyer, Eduard. *Geschichte des Altertums, Erster Band, Zweite Hälfte*. Stuttgart: J. G. Cotta'sche, 1926.

Meyer, Michael A. "Anti-Semitism and Jewish Identity." *Commentary* 88 (1989): 35–40.

Michelini, Ann N. "Comment." *Journal of Women's History* 4 (1993): 95–105.

Miller, James. *The Passion of Michel Foucault*. New York: Simon and Schuster, 1993.

Miller, John *Alternatives to Afrocentrism*. New York: Manhattan Institute, 1994.

Miller, P. D., P. Hanson, and S. D. McBride. *Ancient Israelite Religion: Essays in Honor of Frank Moore Cross*. Philadelphia: Fortress Press, 1987.

Mills, C. Wright. "The Social Role of the Intellectual." In I. L. Horowitz, *Power*, 292–304.

———. *The Sociological Imagination*. New York: Oxford University Press, 1959.

Mokhtar, Gamal el Din, *General History of Africa*. Vol. 2, *Ancient Civilizations of Africa*. Abridged edition. Berkeley Calif.: UNESCO, 1990.

Moles, J. L. "Truth and Untruth in Herodotus and Thucydides." In Gill and Wiseman, *Lies and Fiction*, 88–121.

Momigliano, Arnaldo. *The Classical Foundations of Modern Historiography*. Berkeley: University of California Press, 1990.

———. *Studies in Historiography*. New York: Harper, 1966.

Mommsen, Wolfgang. *Max Weber and German Politics, 1890–1920*. Translated by M. Steinberg. Chicago: University of Chicago Press, 1990.

Mondi, Robert. "Greek Mythic Thought in the Light of the Near East." In Edmunds, *Approaches to Greek Myth*, 142–198.

Montagu, Ashley, *The Concept of Race*. New York: Collier Books, 1964.

Montefiore, A., *Philosophy in France Today*. Cambridge: Cambridge University Press, 1983.

Moore, Barrington, Jr. *Reflections on the Causes of Human Misery and upon Certain Proposals to Eliminate Them*. Boston: Beacon Press, 1972.

Moore, Shawna. "Interview with Cheikh Anta Diop." In Van Sertima and Williams, *Great African Thinkers*, 238–248.

Morris, Sarah P. "Diadalos and Kadmos: Classicism and 'Orientalism.'" *Arethusa*, special issue (1989): 39–54.

———. "Greece and the Levant." *Journal of Mediterranean Archaeology* 3 (1990): 57–66.

———. "The Legacy of *Black Athena.*" In Lefkowitz and Rogers, *Black Athena Revisited*, 167–174.

Moscati, Sabatino, Anton Spitaler, Edward Ullendorff, and Wolfram von Soden. *An Introduction to the Comparative Grammar of the Semitic Languages, Phonology and Morphology*. Wiesbaden: Otto Harrassowitz, 1969.

Moscati, S. "Atene non cosi' nera." *Tuttolibri (La Stampa)* 941 (January 28, 1995): 6.

———. "Son diventati neri gli dei dell'olimpo." *Tuttolibri (La Stampa)* 796 (April 4, 1992): 6.

Moses, Wilson J. *The Golden Age of Black Nationalism, 1850–1925*. New York: Oxford University Press, 1988.

———. "In Fairness to Afrocentrism." In J. Miller, *Alternatives*, 16–22.

———. *The Wings of Ethiopia: Studies in African-American Life and Letters*. Ames: Iowa State University Press, 1990.

Mosse, George. *The Crisis of German Ideology: Intellectual Origins of the Third Reich*. New York: Grosset and Dunlap, 1964.

Mudimbe, V. Y. *The Idea of Africa*. Bloomington: Indiana University Press, 1994.

Muhly, James. "*Black Athena* versus Traditional Scholarship." *Journal of Mediterranean Archaeology* 3 (1990): 83–110.

———. "Homer and the Phoenicians: The Relations between Greece and the Near East in the Late Bronze and Early Iron Ages." *Berytus* 19 (1970): 19–64.

———. "Where the Greeks Got Their Gifts." *Washington Post*, Book World, July 21, 1991, 3–4.

Müller, Karl Otfried. *Introduction to a Scientific System of Mythology*. Translated by J. Leitch. London: Göttingen, 1844.

Müller, Karl Otfried. and John William Donaldson. *A History of the Literature of Ancient Greece*. 3 vol. London: Longmans, Green, 1858.

Muravchik, Joshua. "Facing Up to Anti-Semitism." *Commentary* 100 (December 1995): 26–30.

Murray, Albert. *The Omni-Americans: Some Alternatives to the Folklore of White Supremacy*. New York: Da Capo, 1970.

Natter, W., T. Schatzki, and J. P. Jones III, eds. *Objectivity and Its Other*. New York: Guilford Press, 1995.

Nelson, Benjamin. "Max Weber on Race and Society." *Social Research* 38 (1971): 30–41.

Nelson, Cary, and Michael Bérubé. *Higher Education under Fire: Politics, Economics, and the Crisis of the Humanities*. New York: Routledge, 1995.

———. "Introduction: A Report from the Front." In Nelson and Bérubé, *Higher Education under Fire*, 1–32.

Neusner, Jacob. "Blacks and Jews: New Views on an Old Relationship." *Midstream* 41 (1995): 25–28.

"New Spaces, Old Debates." (editorial). *Washington Post*, April 29, 1996.

Newton, Steven. "An Updated Working Chronology of Predynastic and Archaic Kemet. " *Journal of Black Studies* 23 (1993): 403–415.

Nicholls, David. *From Dessalines to Duvalier: Race, Colour and National Independence in Haiti*. London: Cambridge University Press, 1979.

Niemeyer, H. G., ed. *Phönizier im Westen: Die Beiträge des Internationalen Symposiums über 'Die phönizische Expansion im westlichen Mittelmeerraum' in Köln vom 24. bis 27. April 1979*. Mainz am Rhein: Philipp von Zabern, 1982.

Nietzsche, Friedrich. "History in the Service and Disservice of Life." In Arrowsmith, *Unmodern Observations,* 73–145.

———. "We Classicists." In Arrowsmith, *Unmodern Observations,* 305–387.

Nisbet, Robert. *Conservatism: Dream and Reality.* Minneapolis: University of Minnesota Press, 1986.

———. *History of the Idea of Progress.* New Brunswick, N.J.: Transaction, 1994.

Njeri, I. "Rocking the Cradle of Classical Civilization." *Los Angeles Times,* February 1, 1991, E1.

Norton, Robert E. "The Tyranny of Germany over Greece? Bernal, Herder, and the German Appropriation of Greece." In Lefkowitz and Rogers, *Black Athena Revisited,* 403–410.

Nossiter, T. J., A. H. Hanson, and S. Rokkan, eds. *Imagination and Precision in the Social Sciences.* New York: Humanities Press, 1972.

Nott, J. C., and G. R. Gliddon. *Types of Mankind; or, Ethnological Researches, Based upon the Ancient Monuments, Paintings, Sculptures, and Crania of Races, and upon Their Natural, Geographical, Philological and Biblical History.* 8th edition. Philadelphia: J. B. Lippincott, 1865.

Obenga, Théophile. "Propos préliminaire." *Présence Africaine* 149–150 (1989): 1–3.

O'Connor, David. "Ancient Egypt and Black Africa—Early Contacts." *Expedition* 14 (1971): 2–9.

———. "Egypt and Greece: The Bronze Age Evidence." In Lefkowitz and Rogers, *Black Athena Revisited,* 49–61.

Okafor, V. O. "Diop and the African Origin of Civilization: An Afrocentric Analysis." *Journal of Black Studies* 22 (1991): 252–268.

Olender, Maurice. *The Languages of Paradise: Race, Religion, and Philology in the Nineteenth Century.* Translated by A. Goldhammer. Cambridge: Harvard University Press, 1992.

Oren, Dan A. *Joining the Club: A History of Jews and Yale.* New Haven: Yale University Press, 1985.

Ortiz de Montellano, Bernard "Afrocentric Creationism." *Creation/Evolution* 29 (1991–1992): 1–8.

———. "Melanin, Afrocentricity, and Pseudoscience." *Yearbook of Physcial Anthropology* 36: (1993): 33–58.

———."Multicultural Pseudoscience: Spreading Scientific Illiteracy among Minorities—Part 1." *Skeptical Inquirer* 16 (1991): 46–50.

Palaima, Thomas G. "Corcyraeanization." *National Review,* March 25, 1996, 54–55.

Palter, Robert. "*Black Athena,* Afro-Centrism, and the History of Science." *History of Science* 31 (1993): 227–287.

———. "*Black Athena,* Afrocentrism, and the History of Science." In Lefkowitz and Rogers, *Black Athena Revisited,* 209–266.

———."Eighteenth-Century Historiography in *Black Athena.*" In Lefkowitz and Rogers, *Black Athena Revisited,* 349–402.

———. "Hume and Prejudice." *Hume Studies* 21 (1995): 3–23.

———."Professor Palter Comments." *History of Science* 32 (1994): 464–468.

———."Whose Greece?" *London Review of Books,* February 20, 1997.

Panofsky, Erwin. *Gothic Architecture and Scholasticism.* Cleveland: Meridian Books, 1968.

Parker, George Wells. "The African Origin of the Grecian Civilization." *Journal of Negro History* 2 (1917): 334–344.

———. *The Children of the Sun.* Baltimore: Black Classic Press, 1981.

Patai, Daphne, and Noretta Koertge. *Professing Feminism: Cautionary Tales from the Strange World of Women's Studies.* New York: Basic Books, 1994.

Patterson, Thomas C. "Another Blow to Erocentrism: Review of *BA 1.*" *Monthly Review* 40 (1988): 42–45.

Peckham, Brian. "Phoenicia and the Religion of Israel: The Epigraphic Evidence." In Miller et al., *Ancient Israelite Religion*, 79–99.

Pennington, James W. C. *A Text Book of the Origin and History, Etc., Etc., of the Colored People*. Detroit: Negro History Press, 1841.

Peradotto, J. "Editorial." *Arethusa*, special issue (1989): 5.

Perry, Nick. "A Comparative Analysis of 'Paradigm' Proliferation." *British Journal of Sociology* 28 (1977): 38–50.

Peters, Edward. *Heresy and Authority in Medieval Europe: Documents in Translation*. Philadelphia: University of Pennsylvania Press, 1980.

Petersen, David. "Max Weber and the Sociological Study of Ancient Israel." *Sociological Inquiry* 49 (1979): 117–149.

Pfeiffer, Rudolf. *History of Classical Scholarship from 1300 to 1850*. Oxford: Clarendon Press, 1976.

Plato. *Timaeus*. Translated by Benjamin Jowett. In Edith Hamilton and Huntington Cairns, eds., *The Collected Dialogues of Plato, Including the Letters*. Princeton: Princeton University Press, 1982.

Plax, Martin J. "Jews and Blacks in Dialogue." *Midstream* 28 (1982): 10–17.

Plutarch. *On Herodotus's Malice*. Translated by A. G. Gent. In *Plutarch's Miscellanies and Essays*. Boston: Little, Brown, 1989.

Podhoretz, N. "My Negro Problem—and Ours, with Postscript." In Berman, *Blacks and Jews*, 76–96.

Poe, R. *Black Spark, White Fire: Did African Explorers Civilize Ancient Europe?* Rocklin, Calif.: Prima, 1997.

Polanyi, Michael. *The Tacit Dimension*. Garden City, N.Y.: Doubleday, 1966.

Poliakoff, Michael. "Roll Over Aristotle: Martin Bernal and His Crtitics." *Academic Questions* 4 (1991): 12–28.

Poliakov, Léon. *The Aryan Myth: A History of Racist and Nationalist Ideas in Europe*. Translated by E. Howard. New York: Basic Books, 1974.

———. *The History of Anti-Semitism*. Vol. 3, *From Voltaire to Wagner*. Translated by M. Kochan. New York: Vanguard Press, 1975.

Pollock, Sheldon. "Deep Orientalism? Notes on Sanskrit and Power Beyond the Raj." In Breckenridge and Vanderveer, *Orientalism*, 76–133.

Pooley, Eric. "Doctor J." *New York Magazine*, September 2, 1991, 32–37.

Popper, Karl. "Normal Science and Its Dangers." In Lakatos and Musgrave, *Criticism*, 51–58.

———. *The Open Society and Its Enemies*. Vol. 2, *The High Tide of Prophecy: Hegel, Marx and the Aftermath*. New York: Harper and Row, 1963.

Portelli, Sandro. "Mitologie diverse, un'unica 'storia.'" *Manifesto*, December 8, 1991, 24–256.

Pounder, Robert L. "Review Article, *Black Athena* 2: History without Rules." *American Historical Review* 97 (1992): 461–464.

Prakash, Gyan. "*Orientalism* Now." *History and Theory* 34 (1995): 199–212.

Pritchard, James, ed. *Ancient Near Eastern Texts Relating to the Old Testament*. Princeton: Princeton University Press, 1969.

———. *The Harper Concise Atlas of the Bible*. New York: HarperCollins, 1991.

Puddington, Arch. "Black Anti-Semitism and How it Grows." *Commentary* 97 (1994): 19–24.

———. "Speaking of Race." *Commentary* 100 (1995): 21–25.

Raab, Earl. "The Black Revolution and the Jewish Question." In Hentoff, *Black Anti-Semitism*, 15–42.

———. "Blacks and Jews Asunder?" *Midstream* 25 (1979): 3–9.

Raab, Earl, and Douglas Kahn. "Civic and Political: Intergroup Relations." *American Jewish Year Book* 90 (1990): 207–227.

———. "Civic and Political: Intergroup Relations." *American Jewish Year Book* 91 (1991): 121–139.

Raaflaub, K., *Anfänge politischen Denkens in der Antike: Die nahöstlichen Kulturen und die Griechen.* Munich: R. Oldenbourg, 1993.

Rabinow, Paul, ed. *The Foucault Reader.* New York: Pantheon, 1984.

Rabinowitz, Nancy Sorkin. "Introduction." In Rabinowitz and Richlin, *Feminist Theory,* 1–20.

Rabinowitz, Nancy Sorkin, and A. Richlin, eds. *Feminist Theory and the Classics.* New York: Routledge, 1993.

Ray, John D. "An Egyptian Perspective." *Journal of Mediterranean Archaeology* 3 (1990): 77–81.

———. "How Black Was Socrates? The Roots of European Civilization and the Dangers of Afrocentrism." *Times Literary Supplement,* February 14, 1997, 3–4.

———. "Levant Ascendant: The Invasion Theory of the Origins of European Civilization—Review of *BA* 2 and C. A. Diop, *Civilisation or Barbarism.*" *Times Literary Supplement,* October 18, 1991, 3–4.

Readings, Bill. "The University without Culture?" *New Literary History* 26 (1995): 465–492.

Redfield, James. "Classics and Anthropology." *Arion* 1 (1991): 5–23.

Reinach, Salomon. "Le Mirage Oriental." *Anthropologie* 4(1893): 539–578.

Reiss, Timothy J. "*Black Athena:* An Etymological Response." *Arethusa,* special issue (1989):67–82.

———."Review of *BA* 1." *Canadian Review of Comparative Literature* 16 (1989): 325–330.

———. "Review of *Black Athena* 2." *Canadian Review of Comparative Literature* 19 (1992): 429–435.

Rendsburg, Gary. "*Black Athena:* An Etymological Response." *Arethusa,* special issue (1989): 67–82.

Renfrew, Colin. *Archaeology and Language: The Puzzle of Indo-European Origins.* New York: Cambridge University Press, 1988.

———. *Before Civilization: The Radiocarbon Revolution and Prehistoric Europe.* New York: Knopf, 1973.

———. *The Emergence of Civilisation: The Cyclades and the Aegean in the Third Millennium B.C.* London: Methuen, 1972.

———. *Problems in European Prehistory.* Cambridge: Cambridge University Press, 1979.

———. "Problems in the General Correlation of Archaeological and Linguistic Strata in Prehistoric Greece: The Model of Autochthonous Origin." In Crossland and Birchall, *Bronze Age Migrations,* 263–275.

Rhoads, Edward. "Review of *Chinese Socialism.*" *Journal of Asian and African Studies* 14 (1979): 319–320.

Richlin, Amy. "Responses." *Arethusa,* special issue, (1989): 113.

Ricoeur, Paul. *Freud and Philosophy: An Essay on Interpretation.* Translated by D. Savage. New Haven: Yale University Press, 1972.

"The Rift between Blacks and Jews." *Time,* February 28, 1994, 28–34.

Ritterband, Paul. "Modern Times and Jewish Assimilation." In Seltzer and Cohen, *Americanization,* 377–394.

Rogers, Guy MacLean. "Freedom in the Making of Western Culture." *Arethusa* 28 (1995): 87–97.

———. "Multiculturalism and the Foundations of Western Civilization." In Lefkowitz and Rogers, *Black Athena Revisited,* 428–443.

———. "Quo Vadis?" In Lefkowitz and Rogers, *Black Athena Revisited,* 447–453.

———. "Racism and Antisemitism in the Classroom." *Midstream* 40 (1994): 8–10.

Rorty, Richard. "Intellectuals in Politics: Too Far In? Too Far Out?" *Dissent* 38 (Fall 1991): 483–490.

Rose, Paul L. *Revolutionary Antisemitism in Germany from Kant to Wagner.* Princeton: Princeton University Press, 1990.

Rosenau, P. M. *Post-Modernism and the Social Sciences: Insights, Inroads, and Intrusions.* Princeton: Princeton University Press, 1992.

Rosenthal, G. S. "Unity in American Jewry: Fact or Fiction?" *Midstream* 39 (1993): 8–11.

Roth, A. M. "Review of *Not Out of Africa* and *Black Athena Revisited.*" *American Historical Review* 102 (1997): 493–495.

Sachar, Howard. *A History of the Jews in America.* New York: Knopf, 1992.

Said, Edward W. *Culture and Imperialism.* New York: Vintage, 1994.

———."Identity, Authority and Freedom: The Potentate and the Traveler." In Menand, *Future of Academic Freedom,* 214–228.

———. *Orientalism.* New York: Vintage Books, 1979.

———. "Orientalism: An Exchange." *New York Review of Books,* August 12, 1982, 44–46.

Ste. Croix, G.E.M. de. *The Class Struggle in the Ancient Greek World: From the Archaic Age to the Arab Conquests.* Ithaca: Cornell University Press, 1981.

Sanders, Edith. "The Hamitic Hypothesis: Its Origin and Functions in Time Perspective." *Journal of African History* 10 (1969): 521–532.

Sasser, M. W. "Messages of the Million-Man March." *Midstream* 41 (1995): 5–6.

Savino, Ezio. "Di che colore è la pelle di Ulisse." *Giornale,* November 8, 1992.

———. "Macché ariani, erano negri." *Giornale,* February 16, 1995.

Savvas, Minas. "Review of *Black Athena 1.*" *Classical World* 82 (1989): 469–470.

Schatzki, Theodore. "Objectivity and Rationality." In Natter et al., *Objectivity,* 137–160.

Schiele, Jerome. "Afrocentricity: Implications for Higher Education." *Journal of Black Studies* 25 (1994): 150–169.

Schindel, Ulrich. "C. G. Heyne." In Briggs and Calder, *Classical Scholarship,* 176–182.

Schlerath, Bernfried. "Franz Bopp." In Briggs and Calder, *Classical Scholarship,* 7–12.

Schlesinger, Arthur, Jr. *The Disuniting of America: Reflections on a Multicultural Society.* New York: W. W. Norton, 1993.

Schölzel, Arnold. "Besprechungen: Review of *Schwarze Atena.*" *Argument* 215 (1996): 437–439.

Seligman, C. G. *Egypt and Negro Africa: A Study in Divine Kingship.* London: George Routledge and Sons, 1934.

———. *Races of Africa.* 1930. 3rd edition. London: Oxford University Press, 1959.

Seltzer, R., and N. Cohen, eds. *The Americanization of the Jews.* New York: New York University Press, 1995.

Shack, William. "The Construction of Antiquity and the Egalitarian Principle: Social Constructions of the Past in the Present." In Bond and Gilliam, *Social Construction,* 113–118.

Shanks, Michael. "Greeks and Gifts: Review of *BA* 1 and 2." *History Today* 42 (1992): 56–57.

Shanks, M., and C. Tilley. *Social Theory and Archaeology.* Albuquerque: University of New Mexico Press, 1987.

Shavit, Yaacov. "Anti-University Intellectuals" (in Hebrew). *Politikah* (November 1989): 37–39.

———. *Athens in Jerusalem: Classical Antiquity and Hellenism in the Making of the Modern Secular Jew.* Translated by Chaya Naor and Niki Werner. London: Littman Library of Jewish Civilization, 1997.

Shaw, Peter. "Pseudo-reform in the Academy." *Partisan Review* 63 (1996): 94–104

Shils, Edward. *The Constitution of Society.* Chicago: University of Chicago Press, 1982.

Simmel, Georg. *Essays on Religion.* Edited and translated by H. Helle and L. Nieder. New Haven: Yale University Press, 1997.

Sklar, Richard. "Africa and the Middle East: What Blacks and Jews Owe to Each Other." In J. Washington, *Jews in Black Perspectives,* 132–147.

Slater, R. B. "The Sunshine Factor: Freedom of Information Act Reveals Black Faculty and Administrative Employment Statistics at Major U.S. Universities." *Journal of Blacks in Higher Education* 7 (1995): 91–96.

Sleeter, Christine, and Peter McLaren. "Introduction: Exploring Connections to Build a Critical Multiculturalism." In Sleeter and McLaren, *Multicultural Education,* 5–28.

Sleeter, Christine, and Peter McLaren, eds. *Multicultural Education, Critical Pedagogy, and the Politics of Difference.* Albany: State University of New York Press, 1995.

Smelser, Neil. "The Politics of Ambivalence: Diversity in the Research Universities." *Daedalus* 122 (1993): 37–53.

Smith, Morton. "A Note on Burning Babies." *Journal of the American Oriental Society* 95 (1975): 477–479.

———. *Palestinian Parties and Politics That Shaped the Old Testament.* London: SCM Press, 1987.

Smith, W. S. *Interconnections in the Ancient Near East: A Study of the Relationships between the Arts of Egypt, the Aegean and Western Asia.* New Haven: Yale University Press, 1965.

Snowden, Frank M., Jr., *Before Color Prejudice: The Ancient View of Blacks.* Cambridge: Harvard University Press, 1991.

———. "Bernal's 'Blacks' and the Afrocentrists." In Lefkowitz and Rogers, *Black Athena Revisited,* 112–128.

———. "Bernal's 'Blacks,' Herodotus, and Other Classical Evidence." *Arethusa,* special issue (1989): 83–95.

Blacks in Antiquity: Ethiopians in the Greco-Roman Experience. Cambridge: Harvard University Press, 1970.

———. "Response." *Arethusa* 26 (1993): 319–327.

Sowell, Thomas. *Ethnic America: A History.* New York: Basic Books, 1981.

Spady, James G. "The Afro-American Historical Society: The Nucleus of Black Bibliophiles (1897–1923)." *Negro History Bulletin* 37 (1974): 254–257.

———. "The Changing Perception of C. A. Diop and His Work: The Preeminence of a Scientific Spirit." In Van Sertima and Williams, *Great African Thinkers,* 89–101.

———. "Dr. Cheikh Anta Diop and the Background of Scholarship on Black Interest in Egyptology and Nile Valley Civilizations." *Présence Africaine* 149–150 (1989): 292–312.

Specter, M. "Was Nefertiti Black? Bitter Debate Erupts." *Washington Post,* February 26, 1990, A3.

Spence, Jonathan. "The Chinese Dream Machine: Review of *China and the Search for Happiness,* by Wolfgang Bauer; *Chinese Socialism to 1907,* by Martin Bernal; and *Chinese Shadows,* by Simon Leys." *New York Review of Books* 24 (1977): 15–16.

Sperling, David, *Students of the Covenant: A History of Jewish Biblical Scholarship in North America.* Atlanta: Scholars Press, 1992.

Stager, L. "Carthage: A View from the Tophet." in Niemeyer, *Phönizier im Westen,* 155–166.

Staples, Robert. "Racial Ideology and Intellectual Racism: Blacks in Academia." *Black Scholar* 15 (1985): 2–17.

Starr, Chester. *A History of the Ancient World.* 4th ed. New York: Oxford University Press, 1991.

———. *The Origins of Greek Civilization, 1100–650 B.C.* New York: Knopf, 1961.

Steinberg, Stephen. *The Academic Melting Pot: Catholics and Jews in American Higher Education.* New York: McGraw-Hall, 1974.

Stephan, Nancy, and Sander Gilman. "Appropriating the Idioms of Science: The Rejection of Scientific Racism." In Harding, *"Racial" Economy*, 170–200.

Stevens, P. "On 'First Word,' January 1993." *African Arts* 26 (1993): 1.

Stocking, G. W., Jr. "Ancient Egypt and the Modern Human Sciences." *Science as Culture* 6 (1989): 130–135.

Stone, L., ed. *The University in Society*. Vol. 2; *Europe, Scotland, and the United States from the Sixteenth to the Twentieth Century*. Princeton: Princeton University Press, 1974.

Strabon. *Géographie* Vol. 3. Translated by F. Lasserre. Paris: Les Belles Lettres, 1967.

Strouhal, E. "Evidence of the Early Penetration of Negroes into Prehistoric Egypt." *Journal of African History* 12 (1971): 1–9.

Strum, Harvey. "Louis Marshall and Anti-Semitism at Syracuse University." *American Jewish Archives* 33 (1983): 1–12.

Stubbings, Frank. "The Rise of Mycenaean Civilization." In *The Cambridge Ancient History* Vol. 2, pt. 1. Cambridge: Cambridge University Press, 1973.

Stuckey, Sterling. *The Ideological Origins of Black Nationalism*. Boston: Beacon Press, 1972.

Talmon, Shemaryahu. "The Emergence of Jewish Sectarianism in the Early Second Temple Period." In P. D. Miller, et al., *Ancient Israelite Religion*, 587–616.

Tate, G. "History: The Colorized Version—or, Everything You Learned in School Was Wrong." *Village Voice*, March 28, 1989, 48–50.

Taylor, Charles. "The Politics of Recognition." In Gutmann, *Multiculturalism*, 25–73.

Taylor, Timothy. "Review of *Black Athena 2*, by Martin Bernal." *Antiquity* 65 (1991): 981.

Thernstrom, Abigail. "On the Scarcity of Black Professors." *Commentary* 90 (1990): 22–26.

Thomas, Keith. *Religion and the Decline of Magic*. New York: Scribner, 1971.

Tilly, Charles. *Coercion, Capital and European States, AD 990–1992*. Cambridge: Blackwell, 1992.

Toll, William. "Pluralism and Moral Force in the Black-Jewish Dialogue." *American Jewish History* 77 (1987): 87–105.

Tonello, Fabrizio. "Grecia riva del Nilo." *Manifesto*, December 8, 1992, 25–26.

Traub, James. *City on a Hill: Testing the American Dream at City College*. Reading, Mass.: Addison-Wesley, 1994.

———. "Ghetto Blasters." *New Republic*, April 15, 1991, 21–22.

Trigger, Bruce. "Brown Athena: A Postprocessual Goddess?" *Current Anthropolgy* 33 (1992): 121–123.

———. *A History of Archaeological Thought*. Cambridge: Cambridge University Press, 1995.

Tritle, Lawrence A. "*Black Athena:* Vision or Dream of Greek Origins?" In Lefkowitz and Rogers, *Black Athena Revisited*, 303–330.

———. "Review of *Black Athena 2*." *Liverpool Classical Monthly* 17 (1992): 82–96.

Turner, Frank. *The Greek Heritage in Victorian Britain*. New Haven: Yale University Press, 1981.

———. "Martin Bernal's *Black Athena*: A Dissent." *Arethusa*, special issue (1989): 97–109.

Turner, R. Steven. "Historicism, *Kritic*, and the Prussian Professoriate, 1790–1840." In Bollack and Wismann, *Philologie und Hermeneutik*, 2: 450–489.

———. "University Reformers and Professional Scholarship in Germany, 1760–1806." In Stone, *University in Society*, 495–531.

Turner, Stephen. *The Social Theory of Practices: Tradition, Tacit Knowledge, and Presuppositions*. Chicago: University of Chicago Press, 1994.

Unte, Wolfhart. "Karl Otfried Müller." In Briggs and Calder, *Classical Scholarship*, 310–320.

Urry, John. "Thomas S. Kuhn as Sociologist of Knowledge." *British Journal of Sociology* 24 (1973): 462–473.

Vaio, J. "George Grote." In Briggs and Calder, *Classical Scholarship,* 119–126.

van Binsbergen, Wim. "*Black Athena* Ten Years After: Towards a Constructive Re-assessment." *Talanta* 28–29 (1996–1997): 11–64.

Van Sertima, Ivan. "African Origin of Ancient Egyptian Civilization." In Van Sertima, *Egypt,* 1–16.

———. "Editorial." In Van Sertima, *Egypt,* 1–16.

———. "Introduction: Death Shall Not Find Us Thinking That We Die." In Van Sertima and Williams, *Great African Thinkers,* 7–16.

Van Sertima, Ivan, ed. *African Presence in Early Europe.* New Brunswick, N.J.: Transaction, 1985.

———. *Egypt: Child of Africa.* New Brunswick, N.J.: Transaction, 1995.

Van Sertima, Ivan, and R. Rashidi, eds. *African Presence in Early Asia.* New Brunswick, N.J.: Transaction, 1988.

Van Sertima, Ivan, and L. Williams, eds. *Great African Thinkers,* Vol. 1, *Cheikh Anta Diop.* New Brunswick, N.J.: Transaction, 1989.

Vercelloni, V. "E io leggo la storia con gli occhiali di Bernal." *Giorno,* September 22, 1993, 19.

Verger, Stéphane. "Et si les Grecs étaient venus d'Afrique?" *Actes de la Recherche en Sciences Sociales* 91–92 (1992): 1–3, 17–18.

Verharen, Charles. "Afrocentrism and Acentrism: A Marriage of Science and Philosophy." *Journal of Black Studies* 26 (1995): 62–76.

Vermeule, Emily T. *Greece in the Bronze Age.* Chicago: University of Chicago Press, 1964.

———. "The World Turned Upside Down: Review of *BA 2.*" *New York Review of Books,* March 26, 1992, 40–43.

———. "The World Turned Upside Down." In Lefkowitz and Rogers, *Black Athena Revisited,* 269–279.

Veyne, Paul. *Did the Greeks Believe in Their Myths? An Essay on the Constitutive Imagination.* Translated by P. Wissing. Chicago: University of Chicago Press, 1988.

Vickers, Michael. "Review of *Black Athena 1,* by Martin Bernal." *Antiquity* 61 (1987): 480–481.

Vorspan, Albert. "Blacks and Jews." In Hentoff, *Black Anti-Semitism,* 191–226.

Vovelle, Michel. *Ideologies and Mentalities.* Translated by E. O'Flaherty. Chicago: University of Chicago Press, 1990.

Wacquant, Loïc. "Towards an Archaeology of Academe: A Critical Appreciation of Fritz Ringer's 'Fields of Knowledge,'" *Acta Sociologica* 38 (1995): 181–186.

Walcot, P. *Hesiod and the Near East.* Cardiff: University of Wales Press, 1966.

———. "Review of *BA 2.*" *Greece and Rome* 39 (1992): 78–79.

Walker, Clarence. "The Distortions of Afrocentric History." In J. Miller, *Alternatives,* 32–36.

Walker, J. D. "The Misrepresentation of Diop's Views." *Journal of Black Studies* 26 (1995): 77–85.

Walzer, Michael. "Comment." In Gutmann, *Mutliculturalism,* 99–103.

———. *The Company of Critics: Social Criticism and Political Commitment in the Twentieth Century.* New York: Basic Books, 1988.

Washington, Joseph. "Introduction." In Washington, *Jews in Black Perspectives,* 11–16.

Washington, Joseph ed. *Jews in Black Perspectives: A Dialogue.* Rutherford, N.J.: Fairleigh Dickinson University Press, 1984.

Washington, Margaret. "Revitalizing and Old Argument: Black Athena and Black History." *Journal of Women's History* 4 (1993): 106–113.

Watts, Jerry. "Dilemmas of Black Intellectuals." *Dissent* 36 (Fall 1989): 501–507.
———. "Identity and the Status of Afro-American Intellectuals." In Nelson and Bérubé, *Higher Education under Fire*, 353–361.
Weber, Max. *The Agrarian Sociology of Ancient Civilizations.* Translated by R. I. Frank. New York: Verso, 1988.
———. *Ancient Judaism.* 1917–1919. Translated by H. H. Gerth and D. Martindale. New York: Free Press, 1952.
———. *Max Weber on Charisma and Institution Building.* Edited with an introduction by S. N. Eisenstadt. Chicago: University of Chicago Press, 1968.
———. "Science as a Vocation." In Gerth and Mills, *From Max Weber*, 129–156.
Webster, T.B.L. *From Mycenae to Homer.* London: Methuen, 1964.
———. "Homer and the Mycenaean Tablets." *Antiquity* 113 (1955): 10–14.
Weinberg, Saul. "Relative Chronology of the Aegean in the Neolithic Period and the Early Bronze Age." In Ehrich, *Relative Chronologies*, 86–105.
Weinstein, James. "Review of *Black Athena 2.*" *American Journal of Archaeology* 97 (1993): 381–383.
Weisbord, G. Robert, and Arthur Stein. *Bittersweet Encounter: The Afro-American and the American Jew.* Westport, Conn.: Negro University Press, 1970.
Weiss, Philip. "Letting Go: A Personal Inquiry by Philip Weiss." *New York Magazine,* January 29, 1996, 25–33.
Weitz, Marvin. "Black Hostility—Jewish Naivete." *Midstream* 38 (1992): 11–13.
———. "Black-Jewish Irrationality—Crown Heights 1992." *Midstream* 38 (1992): 9–12.
West, Cornel. "On Black-Jewish Relations." In Berman, *Blacks and Jews,* 144–153.
———. *Prophetic Thought in Modern Times,* Vol. 1. Monroe, Maine: Common Courage Press, 1993.
———. *Race Matters.* Boston: Beacon Press, 1993.
West, Stephanie. "Herodotus' Epigraphical Interests." *Classical Quarterly* 35 (1985): 278–305.
Whit, William. "Review of *Black Athena 1.*" *Michigan Sociological Review* 8 (1994): 95–97.
White, E. Frances. "Civilization Denied: Questions on *Black Athena.*" *Radical America* 21 (1987): 38–40.
Whitney, Gleaves. "Is the American Academy Racist?" *University Bookman* 30 (1990): 4–15.
Wieseltier, Leon. "Taking Yes for an Answer." In Berman, *Blacks and Jews,* 254–257.
Wilczynski, J. *An Encyclopedic Dictionary of Marxism, Socialism and Communism.* Berlin: De Gruyter, 1981. S. V. "Determinism."
Will, George F. "Intellectual Segregation: Afrocentrism's Many Myths Constitute Condescension toward African-Americans." *Newsweek,* February 19, 1996, 78.
Williams, George Washington. *History of the Negro Race in America, 1619–1880.* New York: Arno Press, 1968.
Williams, L. Pearce. "Why I Stopped Reading *Black Athena.*" *Academic Questions* 7 (1994): 37–39.
Williams, Patricia J. *The Alchemy of Race and Rights.* Cambridge: Harvard University Press, 1991.
———. *The Rooster's Egg.* Cambridge: Harvard University Press, 1995.
Williams, Raymond. *Marxism and Literature.* Oxford: Oxford University Press, 1977.
Wills, Garry. "There's Nothing Conservative about the Classics Revival." *New York Times Magazine,* February 16, 1997, 38–42.
Wilshire, Bruce. *The Moral Collapse of the University: Professionalism, Purity, and Alienation.* Albany: State University of New York Press, 1990.
Wilson, L. "Africa and the Afrocentrists." In J. Miller, *Alternatives,* 23–26.
Wilson, Robin. "Hiring of Black Scholars Stalls at Some Major Universities." *Chronicle of Higher Education,* June 2, 1995, A16.

Winbush, Raymond. "Anxiety and Afrocentricity." *Black Issues in Higher Education,* May 5, 1994, 33–34.

Winters, Clyde Ahmad. "Afrocentrism: A Valid Frame of Reference." *Journal of Black Studies* 25 (1994): 170–190.

Wyatt, William, Jr. "The Indo-Europeanization of Greece." In Cardona et al., *Indo-European,* 89–112.

Wyer, Mary, and Jean O'Barr, eds. *Engaging Feminism: Students Speak Up and Speak Out.* Charlottesville: University Press of Virginia, 1992.

Yavitz, Tzvi. "She Wasn't Black". (Hebrew). *Ha-aretz,* weekly supplement, April 23, 1996, 165.

Young, P. A. "Was Nefertiti Black?" *Archaeology* 45 (1992): 2.

Young, Robert. "*Black Athena:* The Politics of Scholarship." *Science as Culture* 4 (1993): 274–281.

———. "John Desmond Bernal." In Bottomore, *Dictionary of Marxist Thought,* 47–48.

Young-Bruehl, Elisabeth. *Hannah Arendt: For Love of the World.* New Haven: Yale University Press, 1982.

Yurco, Frank J. "*Black Athena:* An Egyptological Review." In Lefkowitz and Rogers, *Black Athena Revisited,* 62–100.

———. "Frank Yurco Replies." *Biblical Archaeology Review* 16 (1990): 64–74.

———. "How to Teach Ancient History: A Multicultural Model." *American Educator* 18 (1994): 32, 36–37.

———. "Were the Ancient Egyptians Black or White?" *Biblical Archaeological Review* 15 (1989): 24–27, 29, 58.

Zack, Naomi. *Race and Mixed Race.* Philadelphia: Temple University Press, 1993.

Zani, Gian Leonildo. "Review of *Atena Nera.*" *Pedagogia e Vita* (November/December 1993).

Zilfi, Madeline C. "Comment: Martin Bernal's *Black Athena.*" *Journal of Women's History* 4 (1993): 114–117.

Zweig, Bella. "The Primal Mind: Using Native American Models for the Study of Women in Ancient Greece." In Rabinowitz and Richlin, *Feminist Theory,* 145–177.

Index

Abercrombie, Nicholas, 220n. 6
Academic Questions, 6
adjunct faculty, 186–187
Adorno, Theodor, 101
Aeschylus, 24, 27, 32, 62, 65, 140, 202nn. 4, 5, 203n. 6
African-American intellectuals, 163, 175
African Americans and Jewish Americans, 162–164, 172–177; on university faculties, 174–175
African slave trade, 83, 140
Afroasiatic civilizations and languages, 28, 42, 46, 49, 55, 58, 59
Afrocentrism, 2, 5, 74, 117, 134, 199n. 26, 200n. 31; and anti-Semitism, 143; and the concept of "race," 138, 141; and C. A. Diop, 137; and W.E.B. Du Bois, 137; media portrayal of, 143; on Mesopotamian and Egyptian history, 142; relation to university radicalism, 11; and responses to *Black Athena*, 11–12, 134, 140–143
Ahmad, Aijaz, 11, 126, 200n. 28, 202n. 48, 215nn. 5, 9
Aigyptos, 27
Alexander the Great, 28
Ali, Tariq, 197n. 4
Allen, Norm, 201n. 38, 212n. 15
Allen, Peter, 88, 197n. 4
alphabet, 29; transmission of, 25, 53–54, 66, 169
Altertumswissenschaft, 91, 113–114
Althusser, Louis, 101
Amenemhe II, 47, 48
American Philological Association, 129
American Sociological Association, 191
Amin, Samir, 10, 87, 217n. 34
Ampim, Manu, 140, 142, 228n. 19, 229n. 23

Anatolia, 24, 25, 45, 47, 48; destruction levels in early second millennium, 47
Ancient Model, 23, 24, 26, 180; assumptions of, 26–28; critique of, 29–34, 180; defined, 26–29; dissent from in antiquity, 32; and external factors, 80–82, 94
ancient studies, 115, 128, 179
ancients vs. moderns, 34–38
Anderson, Perry, 78, 101, 200n. 28
Andrea, Bernadette, 200n. 29
Annales school, 107, 108, 157
anti-Semitism: and Afrocentrism, 143; decline of in United States, 173–174; discussion of in Robert Palter's analysis, 125; George Henry Grote and, 69–70; Karl Otfried Müller and, 70; responses to *Black Athena*'s arguments about, 12; as responsible for paradigm shift, 4, 66, 82, 84, 90, 164–172; Max Weber and, 70–71. *See also* racism
Appiah, K. Anthony, 139, 228n. 19, 229n. 24, 231n. 1
Apollodorus, 140
apostate, 187
Appleby, Joyce, 34
Arendt, Hannah, 83, 86, 159, 193
Arethusa, 57, 133
Argos, 27
argument from silence, 72, 181, 184
Aristotle, 24, 26, 28, 140
Arkadia, 46
Armayor, O. K., 203n. 19, 233n. 7
Aryan (language group), 60
Aryan Model (i.e., Broad Aryan Model), 23, 114; influence on Revised Ancient Model, 46; and internal factors, 94–96
Aryan race, 63
Asad, Talal, 7, 85

275

about, 197n. 4; foreign language translations of, 3; future volumes of, 178; impact of, 1–3, 197n. 1; and laypersons, 120–122; modern literary journals and, 11; multiculturalism's influence on, 57; on race, class, and gender, 147–148; political purpose of, 87; reviews of, 19, 126–127, 145, 186; sales of, 3; and sociology of knowledge, 77–78, 180, 182–183, 184, 185; volume one, 11, 14, 23, 40, 44; volumes one and two compared, 40–41, 73, 141, 205n. 4; volume two, 14, 15, 40, 41, 44, 47, 73; wide appeal of, 3–5; wide disciplinary scope of, 41, 179, 202n. 49

Black Athena question, 106–109, 185

Black Athena Revisited (Lefkowitz and Rogers), 2, 54, 68, 92, 148, 154, 197nn. 1, 2, 198n. 13, 199n. 22; and response to radical supporters of Bernal, 8, 9; reviews of, 9, 144, 199n. 22

Black Athena Writes Back (forthcoming), 178

Black Folk Here and There (Drake), 135, 187–188

Black Sea, 29

Blaut, J. M., 200n. 29

Bloch, Ernst, 80

Bloch, Marc, 157

Blok, Josine, 70, 184, 203n. 21, 214n. 47, 217n. 32, 219n. 3, 224n. 6

Bloom, Allan, 5, 171, 223n. 2

Blumenbach, Johann Friedrich, 112, 124–125, 184

Blyden, Edward Wilmot, 136

Boardman, John, 207n. 16

Bohman, James, 222n. 44

Boiotia, 46

Bond, George Clement, 200n. 28, 222n. 40

Borradori, Giovanna, 102

Bourdieu, Pierre, 17, 75, 107, 108, 110, 116, 117, 119, 120, 183, 188, 194, 202n. 48, 223n. 46, 225nn. 17, 22, 240n.9

Bowersock, Glen, 91

Boyd, Herb, 238n. 35

Boynton, Robert, 197n. 2, 239n. 48, 241n. 25

Brace, C. Loring, 153–157, 160, 232n. 8

Bradley Foundation, 198n. 13

Branham, Bracht, 211n. 69, 219n. 57

Branigan, Keith, 46

Broad Aryan Model (i.e., Aryan Model), 23, 24, 84; critique of, 68–71; defined, 61–68; on Egyptian colonization, 66; on Phoenician colonization, 66; and postwar Jewish scholars, 167–170, 172, 176

Broadhead, Frank, 199n. 26

Brooks, Tom, 238n. 3

Brown, John Pairman, 42

Brown, Robert, 42

Bruce, Dickson, Jr., 133, 144, 228n. 14

Bruford, W. H., 223n. 3, 224nn. 5, 10

Brunson, J., 230n. 43

Burkert, Walter, 206n. 9, 207n. 17, 210n. 69, 216–217n. 25, 217 n. 35

Burstein, Stanley, 30, 41, 56, 197n. 1, 210nn. 65, 68

Busiris (Isokrates), 28, 203n. 11

Butler, E. M., 218n. 46

Cadmean Letters (M. G. Bernal), 14, 54, 201n. 39

Calhoun, Craig, 78, 200n. 48, 223n. 46, 241n. 34

Cambridge University, 13, 15, 44

Camporesi, Cristian, 207n. 22

Canaan, 27

Canfora, Luciano, 219n. 57

Carew, Jan, 228n. 19

Carpenter, Rhys, 24, 66

Carruthers, Jacob, 119, 141, 145, 146, 186, 215n. 5, 227n. 9, 232n. 11

Carson, Clayborne, 176, 238n. 35, 239nn. 49, 51, 53, 56

Carson, Tom, 199n. 22, 231n. 49

Carthage, 165

Case, F. I., 228n. 19

Case, M.I.A., 228n. 19

Caucasian (language group), 60

Caucasus mountains, 24, 29, 48, 61

Celtic (language group), 60

Chalcraft, David, 240n. 4

About the

Author

Jacques Berlinerblau is an assistant professor and the director of Hebrew and Judaic Studies at Hofstra University. He is the author of *The Vow and the "Popular Religious Groups" of Ancient Israel: A Philological and Sociological Inquiry.* He has also written a variety of articles pertaining to sociological approaches to the Hebrew Bible and the study of "Popular Religion." He lives in Brooklyn, New York.